Public Employee Pension Funds

Robert Tilove

PUBLIC EMPLOYEE
PENSION FUNDS ✦

A Twentieth Century Fund Report

Columbia University Press
New York and London   1976

Robert Tilove is a Senior Vice President of Martin E. Segal Company, consultants and actuaries on employee benefits.

LIBRARY OF CONGRESS CATALOGING IN PUBLICATION DATA

Tilove, Robert, 1914–
   Public employee pension funds.
   Includes bibliographical references and index.
   1. Civil service pensions—United States—States.
2. Local officials and employees—United States—
Pensions. I. Twentieth Century Fund. I. Title.
JK2474.T55   353.9'3'5   75-33733
ISBN 0-231-04015-6

To Martha B. Tilove

Foreword

Aware of the Twentieth Century Fund's tradition of undertaking analytical research on financial institutions, New York State Comptroller Arthur Levitt suggested five years ago that there was a need for investigation of public employee pensions systems. This volume is the result of Mr. Levitt's prescience, which was quickly acted upon by the staff and the Trustees of the Fund. The growth of public employee pensions systems, a relatively recent development, has not until now been the subject of thorough and independent scrutiny, although these systems had already had great economic impact on public finance and employment. Indeed, because the nation's pension systems are highly fragmented, there has been little in the way of comparative analysis. Thus, the notion of a full scale evaluation was immediately recognized as a significant and timely project.

To carry it out, the Fund chose Robert Tilove, a pension expert who had helped draft legislation and had written a number of reports on the subject. He has produced a detailed examination of the enormous expansion of the benefits, costs, and funding policies of pension plans as a consequence of the unionization and collective bargaining practices of state and local public workers. His work touches on almost every aspect of public pension funds—their investment policies, their administrative structures, the way in which they influence (and are influenced by) the legislative process, their benefits to their members, and their increasingly heavy costs to taxpayers.

After the study got under way, Congress passed the Pension Reform Act of 1974. But this legislation did not mean that the study was overtaken by events. The new law failed to address a number of issues that Mr. Tilove treats at length. It also raised new issues that can be assessed more fully in the context of the information and analysis that Mr. Tilove has provided. His work is valuable not only to all those who have some knowledge of the importance and cost of pension plans; it is especially useful to taxpayers, now and in the future, who must pay the growing costs of these plans.

The Trustees of the Fund join me in expressing our appreciation to Mr. Tilove for the time and effort he expended on his study. He has made a contribution to informed judgment on the growing debate about the scope and nature of a critical public problem.

M. J. Rossant
Director
The Twentieth Century Fund
July 1975

Preface

This volume was commissioned by the Twentieth Century Fund to identify and evaluate the major public policy questions affecting public employee retirement plans. In doing so, it does not take knowledge of the nature of these plans for granted—a good deal of the contents is devoted to describing what these plans are like and their similarities to, or differences from, the pension plans of private industry.

I have expressed opinions and made policy proposals. These are personal; they are not to be taken as attitudes of the Martin E. Segal Company, the consulting firm with which I am associated, nor of anyone other than myself. Indeed, I want to express my appreciation to my firm for that freedom to express personal views and for the time of leave and the many accommodations necessary for the development and writing of this book.

There are a great many people who deserve thanks for their cooperation in furnishing information, including the great majority of the administrators of the state and large-city retirement systems. Special acknowledgment is due to Arthur J. Levitt, Comptroller of the State of New York; Kenneth Altman, Actuary of the New York State Employees' Retirement System; Harold N. Langlitz, Executive Director of the New York State Teachers' Retirement Board; Al Alazraki, Actuary of the New York State Teachers' Retirement System; the late Jesse Feld, who was the Actuary of the New York City Retirement Systems; Jonathan Scmwarz, present Actuary of those systems; A. A. Weinberg, then actuary to the Illinois Pension Laws Commission; John Manning, then Chairman of the Massachusetts Retirement Law Commission; Joseph B. Carroll, Executive Secretary, Massachusetts Teachers' Retirement System; Elwyn E. Mariner, former executive head of the Massachusetts Federation of Taxpayers Association and author of an unpublished history of the Massachusetts systems; William E. Payne, then Executive Officer of the California Public Employees Retirement System; and Edward S. Gibala, Executive Director, State Universities Retirement System of Illinois. I would like to thank the following, associated with the Social Security Administration: Charles L. Trowbridge, then Chief Actuary, and Al Rettig, Actuary's Office; Irving J. Jacobs, Chief, Coverage Planning Branch; and Alvin M. David, then Assistant Commissioner.

For staff assistance, I am obligated to Sherman Lieberman for actuarial work and to Marion S. Kaplan and Joyce Barrow for plan analysis. The editorial work of Harry Gersh has made the text clearer and more readable than it would otherwise have been.

To several of my colleagues, I am indebted for valuable criticism—Robert D. Paul, Jack M. Elkin, and John P. Mackin.

I want to express appreciation to my wife for her understanding indulgence of the extent to which the writing of this book cut into our personal lives.

> **Robert Tilove**
> *April, 1975*

Contents

1. The Need for a Public Policy Framework   1

2. Benefit Levels   9

3. Pensions as Wage Replacement   51

4. Goals and Limits for Retirement Income   70

5. Social Security and the Need for Reform   88

6. The Merits of Social Security Coverage   96

7. Integrating with Social Security   122

8. Funding   131

9. Actuarial Assumptions   174

10. Portability of Pension Credits   192

11. Investment Policies and Procedures   203

12. Pension Plans for Policemen and Firemen   222

13. Several General Policy Questions   241

14. New York State   260

15. Massachusetts   313

16. Illinois   327

17. Summary of Conclusions   339

    Index   359

Public Employee Pension Funds

1 ❋ The Need for a Public Policy Framework

> The large number and variety of pension and retirement laws now on the statute book . . . are startling; their proper understanding by the beneficiaries or the public is possible only after exhaustive study.
>
> · · · ·
>
> The pension legislation has grown from the first person law of twenty-five years ago . . . to nearly 100 laws which are contradictory, unsystematized, and pregnant with unknown cost.
>
> · · · ·
>
> About 100 new bills have been introduced this year into the Legislature relative to pensions. No consideration of cost, no study of principle involved, enters into the minds of those who seek extension. If the solution is not furnished, new legislation will complicate the situation year by year, making future effort for sound economic legislation well-nigh hopeless.

Written in 1914 by a Massachusetts commission on pensions, these words are remarkably pertinent today. Pension legislation for public employees is still as confusing and frustrating a subject as it was then. Controversy in every part of the country over the past sixty years is liberally sprinkled with the phrases "unsound," "bankrupting," "inequitable," "complex," and "patchwork." The decades have brought significant changes, but development of consistent policy on the pensions of public employees has continued to be a difficult challenge.

The problems are compounded from innate complexity, an incessant pressure for change, the fact that pension laws are commitments for decades into the future, and the further fact that the cost, often obscure or hidden, can be deferred to another generation.

It is not at all unusual for a state legislature to deal with dozens of pension bills at every session. The legislator, governor, or other public official often has difficulty judging the merits and implications because there is no clear overall policy to serve as a guide. The editorial writer has the same problem when the issue attracts public attention, and the voters themselves are of course least able to understand the issues.

The purpose of this study is to deal with the major public policy issues of the employee retirement systems of state and local governments. Its intention is to provide a background of fact, analysis, and criteria to help those who cope with the issues to develop for themselves a framework of policy.

Why has legislation in this area been a perennial problem? One obvious reason is that each group of public employees is intensely interested in its own pensions and becomes a source of persistent pressure. The general public does not share that degree of interest. Pensions are one of the areas of government policy in which the concern of a particular group is intense but that of the general public diffuse.

Understanding public employee pensions often requires specialized, and frequently quite technical, knowledge. At first blush, the subject seems simple but it soon becomes complicated. To understand the implications, in terms of equity, precedent, and ultimate cost, of the many varied proposals requires specialized knowledge.

Changes that seem minor may have far-reaching effects. Amendments that appear to apply to only a few employees, with seemingly negligible cost consequences, can establish an irresistible precedent for extension to many others. A change that results in minor benefit payments for the near future may entail major cost in the long run.

Another difficulty is that some public employees are in effect "insiders" in a position to determine the decisions on their own pension plans. The most obvious case, of course, is legislators: they write their own plans. Of course, they are subject to restraint from watchdog taxpayer groups or investigative reporters or public wrath. But insiders nevertheless have a real advantage—changes that appear to be innocuous or sweetly reasonable may turn out to be extremely costly.

Legislators are only the most obvious example. Their staff members may be another. When legislators liberalize their retirement benefits, they may extend the same advantages to their staff employees, who, after all, draft the bills. Judges are another case in point—their pensions are far above average partly because other government officials find it difficult to turn them down.

The same phenomenon, somewhat attenuated, is repeated at other levels of government. The executive who negotiates for the government as employer, the administrator whose judgment counts in decision-making, the attorney who drafts the legislation, each may be influenced by what the benefit proposal may do for him.

The ability to defer pension costs is a fundamental factor. This presents an almost irresistible attraction for an elected official, who can always win friends by giving in the present, while deferring cost so that somebody else—another elected official or another generation of taxpayers—will have to face the inevitable cost.

Essentially there are two ways of giving now and paying later. One is to legislate additional benefits but not fund for them, a procedure that can be accomplished by a number of methods—from an open policy of "pay-as-you-go" financing to a variety of more covert techniques for burying or obscuring the ultimate cost. The second method is simply to obscure or gloss over the importance of a change, regardless of its ultimate impact.

Still another complication in policy formation is the growth of collective bargaining on pensions. In several states, pensions are items for negotiation, subject to ultimate disposition by the legislative process. That poses a potential conflict. Should a legislature "rubber stamp" the results of negotiations? Or should it seek to impose its own policy?

One effect of collective bargaining is to proliferate the number of plans. Bargaining is based on bargaining units. If a given retirement plan embraces several such units, there may be effective pressure for diversity to allow each unit expression for its particular interests and priorities. Bargaining tends to add force to accommodation to particular employee units.

The diversity may itself encourage further change. What one group gets another may want. The phenomenon of "me-too-ism" or "leapfrogging" is well known. This experience predates collective bargaining; negotiations have simply added another stimulus.

The permanence of pension decisions is a very important element.

These decisions are relatively immune from reversal. Whether by law or by the dictates of equity, the pension promised to a public employee is seldom, if ever, revoked. It is a promise sealed by the employee's years of service, essentially an agreement that the employee has every right to expect to be fulfilled. Consequently, if a change turns out to be a mistake, it is very difficult to correct.

The swings of public opinion are still another complicating element in developing and maintaining a coherent policy. Taxpayer resistance sometimes creates an immovable barrier that turns away the demands of public employees, no matter what their merits may be. Tax rates or tax schedules, budget limits, competing priorities for public services or expenditures, shortfalls in revenues—each of these has frequently acted as a constraint effectively tying the hands of even sympathetic office-holders. At other times, public opinion may be neutral or even generous. Changes in the state of the economy and in the public's mood and the timing of elections are of vast significance in determining pension policy at any one time.

Private enterprises can make decisions or reach agreements on pensions and then, to a considerable extent, reflect the costs in increased prices. A public official does not have that leeway. The "price" of the public pension may be subject to veto, either through disapproval of the tax increase or through electoral defeat. Public reaction is an element in pension policy.

The average voter is often prone to judge public pension policy in the light of his own situation. A rural electorate, with no pensions to look forward to, may be unsympathetic to the pension demands of its public servants. By and large, however, it is a fact that voters are generally willing to approve for public employees higher pensions than they themselves enjoy.

The public—and sometimes public officials too—can be overly harsh in their judgments about public employees. There is an expectation among many that those who work for the government should be paid less than those who work for private enterprise. They are sometimes expected in effect to subsidize public service by accepting lower wages than their counterparts in industry. Hospital workers are frequently in that position, and until they began to negotiate, school teachers were as well. In fact, it has been the conviction of public employees that they are underpaid. Often true, it has been advanced as justification for pensions better than those of private industry. They consider this a fair balance—more retirement security to make up for underpayment during employment.

Frequently, public employees can win in pension benefits what the public will not grant in wages. The voter can recognize a wage increase and react to it; he is in no position to make the same appraisal of a pension plan.

Perhaps the most extreme case involves legislators. In many states the voters refuse to approve reasonable compensation for legislators, partly because the public takes a dim view of elected officials when they are judged collectively, and partly because the voter imagines that a legislator works only on the few days he is present and voting in the legislature. To compensate, legislators have in many states resorted to voting pensions altogether out of proportion to their pay.

All of these elements have for decades made a perpetual boiling pot of the state and local retirement laws. It should not be supposed, however, that the situation is one of utter chaos. There is an important element of order.

Still, the need for well-informed and coherent policy is probably greater now than ever before. These plans have attained a scope and level far greater than ever before.

Almost 8.5 million state and local employees were covered by 2,304 pension systems in 1972. About 90 percent were within the 110 largest systems. There were 1,437 systems with less than 100 members—totaling less than 1 percent of all employees.

State-administered systems covered 82 percent of the employees; local systems, the rest. And a majority of employees—64 percent—were in general systems (not restricted to particular occupational groups); the other 36 percent were in pension systems that had an occupational basis. (See Table 1.1 for a breakdown of the systems.)

In the main, public employee pension systems are older than most private pension plans. While a few private pension plans may have been established earlier, many of the public plans were written into law—especially in the industrialized states—long before the vast upsurge of private industry pension in the 1940s and 1950s.

Public pension systems have gone through three stages of historical development:

Table 1.1 ◆ **Number And Membership Of State And Local Retirement Systems, By Type Of System, 1966–67**

Type of System	Systems		Membership [a]	
	Number	Percent	Number (000)	Percent
All systems	2,304	100.0	8,407	100.0
Level of government				
State administered	176	7.6	6,921	82.3
Locally administered	2,128	92.4	1,485	17.7
Membership size				
10,000 or more	110	4.8	7,554	89.9
5,000 to 9,999	47	2.0	309	3.7
100 to 4,999	710	30.8	505	6.0
Less than 100	1,437	62.4	39	0.5
Coverage class				
General coverage	592	25.7	5,019	59.7
State administered	58	2.5	4,087	48.6
State employees only	12	0.5	610	7.3
State and local employees	37	1.6	3,262	38.8
Local employees only	9	0.4	216	2.6
Locally administered	534	23.1	932	11.1
Limited coverage	1,712	74.3	3,388	40.3
School and/or teachers	65	2.8	2,875	34.2
State-administered	39	1.7	2,626	31.2
Locally administered	26	1.1	250	2.9
Police and/or firemen	1,511	65.6	312	3.7
State administered	36	1.6	102	1.2
Locally administered	1,475	23.0	210	2.5
Other limited coverage	136	5.9	201	2.4
State administered	43	1.9	107	1.3
Locally administered	93	4.0	94	1.1

Source: U.S. Census Bureau, *1972 Census of Governments, Topical Studies,* Vol. 6, No. 1, *Employee-Retirement Systems of State and Local Government* (Washington, D.C., December 1973). Totals may not agree with component figures because of rounding.
[a] Currently active employees only; retired and inactive members not included.

(1) Prior to the 1920s—although lasting much longer in some states—plans were very simple arrangements, established without any idea of the ultimate cost, financed without reference to actuarial findings, often on a pay-as-you-go basis.

(2) During the 1920s, actuarially funded systems were established (New York, Massachusetts, and New Jersey started a little earlier).

These plans generally required contributions from employees as well as employers.

(3) The post-World War II boom created an upheaval in public employee systems. Benefit levels were increased; formulas were changed to accommodate to the new salary levels; money-purchase plans, career-average plans, and separate annuities based on employee contributions were generally replaced by guarantees of total benefits related to final salary. Social Security was extended to public employees, with the effect of raising total benefits. In the 1960s, some states began adding automatic post-retirement adjustments to catch up with the cost of living.

Today, every state has established in its legislation one or more retirement systems for its own employees. Localities are also provided for by way of state legislation, with the exception of a few large cities that have home rule. The largest cities have their own systems, even when they are subject to state legislation; most often, in fact, their plans have predated the state systems.

The structural arrangements are quite different from one state to another. State pension systems may cover all public employees, state and local, or there may be separate provisions for the two broad categories. Frequently there are separate plans or systems for special occupational groups such as teachers, university employees, policemen, firemen, legislators, judges. But whatever the arrangement, it is usually the state that regulates pensions.

Some states require all local governments to cover their employees within the state system or within a state-administered system for local employees. In others, the state-administered system is optional. Still other states mandate uniform retirement benefits (the plan) for employees of local governments, but leave the administrative and funding organization (the system) up to the local government. Another variant is for the state to empower local governments to adopt provisions within specified limits.

A state may have a single plan of benefits for all public employees, except groups such as policemen and firemen, implemented through many separate systems (e.g., Massachusetts), or it may have one system with many different plans of benefits (e.g., New York State Employees' System, with respect to its coverage of local governments other than New York City).

Two contradictory trends have become evident: one toward consolidation of plans and systems and the other toward proliferation of plans. Consolidation generally takes the form of bringing localities and local systems within a state system. Proliferation comes in response to pressures from specific occupational groups for their own plans or systems. Police and firemen have been particularly successful in separating themselves from other public employees, sometimes as a means of underscoring the special nature of their benefits and sometimes as a way of bringing all police or firemen up to a uniform level.

Public employee pension systems add up to an enormous social and economic force. Almost 15 percent of all nonagricultural employees in the United States work for state and local governments. Counting federal employees the percentage increases to 18 percent—almost one out of every five employees in the nation. And the trend is up: total government employment was 13.7 percent of total nonagricultural employment in 1960 and 18.7 percent at the beginning of 1973. Federal employment stabilized—at least temporarily—in the late 1960s, but state and local employment has increased 20 percent during the last five years.

Total contributions to state and local pension plans in 1972 exceed $9 billion, and benefits paid were over $4 billion. The state and local governments pay about six cents of every tax dollar for their retirement plans, and in the future, as the full cost becomes apparent, they will almost certainly absorb more.

Clearly, the dimensions are large—and they are growing. The policy issues are bulky as well as difficult. It may be of particular significance that in its 1974 legislation to reform and regulate private pensions, Congress voted for a two-year study to determine whether and to what extent the same sort of regulations should be imposed on the retirement plans of state and local government. There is, in short, wide recognition of the need for a framework within which to assess public employee pension policy.

2 ❖ Benefit Levels

Because of the great disparity in benefit levels that exists among public-employee pension plans, it is extremely difficult to compare them with the pension plans of private industry. However, on the whole, public plans do have some identifiable differences from the average private plan. Naturally, certain plans, public or private, are more generous than others. To know only that a plan is public or private does not provide much information as to its generosity or general content.

Despite the obvious pitfalls involved, it is possible to describe a "typical" plan for employees of state and local government, identifying the major features and the general level of benefits. Starting with a generalized version, the range of diversity within existing plans can be discussed, making appropriate comparisons with those of private industry.

Certain major features have existed among public plans for the past decade; the typical plan described below reflects those characteristics. Of course, this plan is hypothetical, but it is as representative as possible within the limitations of such generalizations.[1]

The Typical Plan

The typical employee of state or local government, if he or she has had thirty years of service, can retire at age 60, on a pension of 50 percent (and sometimes slightly more) of his average pay for the last five years of service. The employee can also draw full Social Security benefits after age 65 or reduced benefits after age 62. Full Social Security benefits normally increase his total retirement income

---

[1] Plans for special groups such as policemen, firemen, judges, and legislators are considered in later chapters.

to 66 to 80 percent of his final average salary. As of January 1972, the typical plan contained the following provisions:

Normal retirement benefits. "Normal retirement benefits," as the term is used here, refers to those benefits payable on retirement for age—not disability—and without reduction on account of age.[2] An employee may retire on normal benefits at age 60 if he has completed at least ten years of service.

Benefit formula. For each year of employment, the benefit is 1.67 percent of the final average salary times the years of service. After thirty years of service, for example, this would equal 50 percent of the final average salary. In this plan the "final salary" is the average salary earned in the most highly paid five years of the last ten.

Compulsory retirement. The employee must retire by age 70.

Early retirement. The employee may retire, at his option, at 55 if he has been employed for at least ten years. His benefit is reduced from the normal benefit payable at age 60, so that it is actuarially equivalent.

Vesting. If the employee leaves after ten years of service and does not withdraw his contributions, he is entitled to a normal or early retirement pension when he reaches the appropriate age.

Disability. The employee is entitled to a disability pension if he becomes permanently and totally disabled after ten years of service but before normal retirement age. This is equivalent to the normal pension, with a minimum, in most cases, of 25 percent of his final earnings. If the disability was caused by a job-connected accident, there is no service requirement for this benefit.

Death benefit in active service. If an employee dies after completing at least ten years of service, the amount paid to the beneficiary is one year's salary. For less than ten years' service, six months' salary plus his contributions, with interest, are paid to the beneficiary.[3]

If death occurs after the employee becomes eligible to retire, his beneficiary will receive an annuity equal to the benefit under a 100 percent joint-and-survivor option. Under this option, the employee's

[2] Sometimes the normal retirement benefit is dependent on years of service, regardless of age.

[3] Death benefits are most difficult to typify. Many systems pay annuities to survivors; some return employee contributions plus a matching amount; some pay lump-sum amounts, generally varying with service; and some pay nothing more than a refund of the member's contributions, with interest.

pension is reduced in exchange for the guarantee that the same amount will continue to be paid in case of death, to the beneficiary.

Death benefit after retirement. A retiring employee has several options as to the form of pension payment. For example, he can accept a reduced benefit for himself in exchange for payments of one kind or another to a survivor, such as a lump-sum or a life annuity equal to 50 or 100 percent of the employee's monthly pension.

Post-retirement adjustments. The pension will be increased annually, up to 3 percent, in accordance with changes in the federal Consumer Price Index.

Employee contributions. The employee contributes 5 percent of his pay; if he terminates employment, he can get a refund with interest.

Social Security. The employee is covered by Social Security, with no adjustment of benefits from the retirement system on that account.

The diversity of plans from this central model will become clear from the information that follows and the corresponding tabular data.

Pension Plan Survey

A survey was made, as of January 1972, of 129 of the largest state and local retirement systems. Although these represented only 6 percent of all public systems, they covered 7,256,900 employees, or about 70 percent of all employees enrolled in state and local retirement plans. The survey included all 50 of the plans covering state employees, plus that of Puerto Rico. Teachers' pension plans were part of the study in the 19 systems that are exclusively for teachers and 15 (all but a few) of the city teacher systems. In addition, the 16 largest cities in the country were canvassed with respect to all of their plans, and information was requested of any system reporting 5,000 or more members to the U.S. Census Bureau in 1967. Altogether, city and county systems for general employees were included from 32 such jurisdictions.[4]

The survey dealt solely with benefits for current or future service,

---

[4] Information was supplied through booklets, texts of the laws, and in some cases questionnaire responses. Capsule descriptions of the major benefit and contribution provisions of the systems were prepared and sent to the system administrators for checking. Most were verified, corrected, or amplified. Where there was no response, provisions were checked from documents and the descriptions are believed to be accurate.

disregarding different accrual rates that are sometimes provided for service before the plan was established, before the particular employee entered the plan unit, or prior to amendment. That choice was made because it is the ultimate future of the public systems that is the focus of this study.

In systems that have different benefit formulas for employees who are covered by Social Security and those who are not covered, the survey includes the benefits in effect for those employees covered by Social Security, since they constitute the majority. In statewide systems that permit local option on Social Security, the survey includes the benefits in effect for the bulk of the membership.

Some systems offer members a choice of benefit plans; in this case, the plan chosen by most members is included in the survey. Omitted are special plans and systems, generally covering relatively small numbers of employees, such as judges, legislators, and safety officers, and "closed systems" to which new employees are not admitted.

Normal Retirement Age

The central focus of this chapter is the prevailing features of the public systems. At the same time, the text notes the major changes in the systems over the past ten to fifteen years and also makes comparison with pension plans in private industry. Some readers may find it convenient to concentrate on the first aspect and, at least for a first reading, omit or simply scan the comparisons. To facilitate that sort of reading, the portions which deal with the comparisons are set in italics.

If comparisons are to be made between systems, a definition of "normal retirement benefits" is necessary, one that can be applied to all systems, regardless of the nomenclature used in state and local legislation. The term is most commonly used to refer to the benefit payable upon nondisability retirement without reduction on account of age; this is, in effect, the highest benefit available to the employee, giving consideration to salary and years of service. Since it is the most common, this is the definition chosen for the survey. Unfortunately, however, this meaning is not universally accepted. For example, the California Public Employees' Retirement System refers to age 60 as the "normal" retirement age, because that is the age upon which all calculations are based. A California employee who is not covered by Social Security can retire at age 60 on a benefit of 2 percent of final average salary per year of service. However, the law also provides for an actuarial increase if retirement is postponed for up to three years; therefore, to fulfill the definition of a "normal benefit" as one not reduced on account of age, the California system benefit is standardized in this study—that is, counted or classified—with 63 as its normal retirement age. This makes the benefit formula for normal retirement 2.418 percent of salary per year of service for males and 2.400 for females (the benefit rates that result after actuarial increase), instead of the 2 percent cited in the statute for age 60.

A similar but more radical difference in definition exists in the Arizona state system. Its statute defines the benefit formula in terms of retirement at 65 (1.5 percent times years of service); however, the benefit is increased for every year retirement is postponed, up to five years. Standardizing this formula, 70 becomes the normal retirement age and the normal benefit formula is 2.25 percent per year of service.

The standard definition of an early-retirement benefit is a benefit reduced because of age. Some systems pay what they call "early-retirement" benefits for retirement after thirty-five years of service, whatever the employee's age, with the amount unchanged. By the definition used here, thirty-five years of service becomes an alternate definition for normal retirement, rather than a qualifying condition for the early-retirement benefit.[5]

By these standardized definitions, about 70 percent of the systems have a normal retirement age that is under 65. The most common single age is 60, and that is generally tied to a requirement of at least ten years of service.

Most systems have only one rule for the normal retirement bene-

---

[5] An occasional plan reduces benefits on an age and/or service basis, to the extent that a retiring employee falls short of *either* threshold for normal-retirement benefits. For example, the Ohio Public Employees' Retirement System pays a benefit that is reduced by 3 percent for each year before the normal retirement date, which is either age 65 or whenever thirty-five years of service would have been completed, whichever is sooner. Consequently, an employee of 60 who retires with thirty-four years of service suffers a reduction of only the one year less than thirty-five years of service, and not for the five years less than age 65. That, too, has been classified as "early retirement," even though the reduction is not entirely based on age.

fit, a single combination of age and service. In these plans, 65 is a more common age than 60. However, a more complete picture includes those with two or more alternate provisions: for example, under a given plan, an employee may qualify for normal benefits at either age 65 with ten years of service, or at age 60 with twenty years of service. The results of merging all the eligibility conditions are summarized in Tables 2.1–2.4. In order of frequency, the most common practices are as follows:

Age 60, generally with a requirement of ten years or more of service; often with a lower threshold.

Age 65, with no minimum service required.

Age 55, in most instances on the basis of at least twenty-five (more commonly thirty or more) years of service; in a few exceptional cases with very little required service.

Any age, if thirty or thirty-five years of service have been completed.

Table 2.1 ◆ **Eligibility For Normal Retirement Benefits: General Employees And Teachers, State And Local Systems**

| | | | | | Years of Service | | | | | |
Age	Total	No mini- mum	Less than 5	5–9	10–14	15–19	20–24	25–29	30–34	35 or more
Total	196	49	6	26	39	5	15	9	30	17
Any	28	—	—	—	—	—	2	—	12	14
50	4	—	1	—	—	—	1	1	—	1
55	27	4	1	1	2	—	1	5	11	2
56–59	2	—	—	—	1	—	—	—	1	—
60	63	14	—	11	17	4	11	2	4	—
61–64	8	—	—	3	2	—	—	1	2	—
65	60	30	3	10	16	1	—	—	—	—
Over 65	4	1	1	1	1	—	—	—	—	—

Note: Numbers do not equal totals of Tables 2.2, 2.3, and 2.4; systems covering both teachers and general employees are counted only once in this table.

There are some differences among provisions for state employees, large-city employees, and teachers. For *state employees,* age 65 is the most common practice; and 60 next. Age 55 is exceptional, but does occur (Table 2.2).

Table 2.2 ◆ **Eligibility For Normal Retirement Benefits: General Employees, State Systems**

Age	Total	No mini- mum	Less than 5	5–9	10–14	15–19	20–24	25–29	30–34	35 or more
Total	82	23	4	11	16	1	4	3	13	7
Any	12	—	—	—	—	—	—	—	5	7
50	1	—	1	—	—	—	—	—	—	—
55	9	1	—	—	—	—	—	3	4	—
56–59	2	—	1	—	1	—	—	—	1	—
60	23	5	—	4	7	1	4	—	2	—
61–64	2	—	—	1	—	—	—	—	1	—
65	30	16	2	4	8	—	—	—	—	—
Over 65	3	1	1	1	—	—	—	—	—	—

Note: Some systems have multiple eligibility requirements and therefore may be counted more than once.

For teachers and the employees of local government (mostly large cities, in this survey) age 60 is more common than age 65 (Tables 2.3 and 2.4).

Table 2.3 ◆ **Eligibility For Normal Retirement Benefits: General Employees, Local Systems**

Age	Total	No mini- mum	Less than 5	5–9	10–14	15–19	20–24	25–29	30–34	35 or more
Total	39	10	1	2	9	0	6	2	8	1
Any	3	—	—	—	—	—	1	—	2	—
50	2	—	—	—	—	—	1	1	—	—
55	9	2	—	—	1	—	1	—	4	1
56–59	—	—	—	—	—	—	—	—	—	—
60	13	2	—	2	4	—	3	1	1	—
61–64	1	—	—	—	—	—	—	—	1	—
65	11	6	1	—	4	—	—	—	—	—
Over 65	—	—	—	—	—	—	—	—	—	—

Table 2.4 ◆ *Eligibility For Normal Retirement Benefits: State And Local Plans Covering Teachers*

Age	Total	No minimum	Less than 5	5–9	10–14	15–19	20–24	25–29	30–34	35 or more
					Years of Service					
Total	109	24	3	18	19	5	6	5	17	12
Any	17	—	—	—	—	—	1	—	6	10
50	2	—	1	—	—	—	—	—	—	1
55	13	1	1	1	1	—	—	2	6	1
56–59	1	—	—	—	—	—	—	—	1	—
60	36	7	—	6	9	4	5	2	3	—
61–64	6	—	—	2	2	—	—	1	1	—
65	32	16	—	9	6	1	—	—	—	—
Over 65	2	—	1	—	1	—	—	—	—	—

Trends in Normal Retirement Ages

This breakdown is much the same as in effect in 1961—with one important exception.[6] *There has been a sizable increase in the number of plans providing normal benefits to long-service employees, those with thirty or thirty-five years of service, regardless of age:*

> 1961   — 4 percent
> 1965–66—13 percent
> 1972   —20 percent

Similarly, the number of plans offering normal benefits by age 55 or after twenty-five years of service has increased:

> 1961   —17 percent
> 1956–66—13 percent
> 1972   —26 percent

[6] The major changes over the preceding eleven years are identified here by reference to three surveys by the Social Security Administration. The first was a survey, as of January 1961, of 118 large state and local systems, the members of which were also covered by Social Security. (U.S. Social Security Administration, *A Survey of State and Local Government Retirement Systems Covering Workers Also Covered under the Federal Old-Age, Survivors, and Disability Insurance Program, 1961* [Washington, D.C., 1962E.) The second was a resurvey of the same group as of January 1965, this time covering 151 large systems with 3.1 million members. (Joseph Krislov, *State and Local Government Retirement Systems . . . 1965; A Survey of Systems Covering Employees Also Covered by the*

Normal Retirement Age in Industry

Among private plans, from about 1961 to 1969, the normal retirement age was predominantly 65. In 1969, almost 70 percent of the workers covered by private plans had to be 65 to retire on unreduced benefits.[7] *About 25 percent were in plans that provided for normal retirement at an age younger than 65; another 6 percent had no age requirements. Where the normal retirement age was lower than 65, it was, in most cases, 62 or 60.*

A strong trend among private plans, evident in the late 1960s, favored payment of full benefits before age 65. While in 1962 only 10 percent of the workers were in plans that paid unreduced benefits if retirement occurred before 65, seven years later, 25 percent were in such plans.[8]

The trend was stimulated in part after the 1961 amendment of the Social Security Act to make men eligible for early retirement at 62, with actuarially reduced benefits. Age 65 was often displaced in favor of age 62, in a few cases by age 60, and occasionally by an even lower age. In the steel industry, for example, unreduced benefits were made available under certain circumstances after thirty years of service, whatever the age, or at 55 with twenty-five years of service. In the automobile industry, among others, the term "normal retirement age" still referred to age 65, but employees could retire at 62 on unreduced benefits, and benefits for retirement before 62 were reduced from the age 62 benefit. These changes had the practical effect of making 62 the normal retirement age, except for determination of deferred pension amounts for those who terminated with vested rights before retirement.

Full benefits before age 65 are particularly evident among the larger private plans. Among 100 selected negotiated plans which the U.S. Bureau of Labor Statistics has kept under constant analysis, 40 percent in the late

Federal Old-Age, Survivors, Disability, and Health Insurance Programs, Research Report No. 15 [Washington, D.C., S.S.A., 1966].) And the third was a survey, as of January 1966, of 87 systems without parallel Social Security coverage, covering 1.4 million members. (Saul Waldman, *Retirement Systems for Employees of State and Local Governments . . . 1966: Findings of a Survey of Systems Whose Members Were Not Covered Under the O.A.S.D.H.I. Program, Report No. 23,* [Washington, D.C., S.S.A., 1968].)

[7] Harry E. Davis and Arnold Strasser, "Private Pension Plans, 1960–69—An Overview," *Monthly Labor Review,* July 1970, pp. 45 ff. This article was based on an analysis of 1,010 plans constituting a cross-section of all plans filed with the U.S. Department of Labor pursuant to the Welfare and Pension Plans Disclosure Act. A similar finding was made in an analysis, as of 1971, of all pension plans covering 1,000 or more workers in New York State. According to the study, 64 percent of the plans did not pay benefits before 65, except on a reduced basis. New York State Department of Labor, *Private Pension Plans in New York State* (New York, 1973).

[8] Harry E. Davis, "The Growth of Benefits in a Cohort of Pension Plans," *Monthly Labor Review,* May 1971, p. 48.

1960s permitted full benefits for retirement at an age younger than 65.[9]
*While these selected plans are not necessarily representative of all negotiated
private plans, they encompassed a wide variety and included a number of
pacesetters.*

*A similar picture emerges from the study by the Bankers Trust Company of
the pension plans of 201 companies in the period 1965–1970.*[10] *The normal
retirement age was 65, with very few exceptions, both among "pattern" plans
(those negotiated by a union and falling into a union-wide pattern) and
among "conventional" plans (the others). However, many of the plans had
been amended to provide the equivalent of normal benefits for retirement at
62. At his option, an employee could retire on a full pension at age 62 in
one-third of the plans surveyed.*

*In some cases, a higher benefit was paid before 65 than after, because of a
supplementary amount paid until age 65 to make up for the absence of full
Social Security benefits before then. However, payment of this benefit is
usually contingent on plant shutdown, involuntary severance, or the company's consent to termination of employment. These conditions distinguish
such benefits from normal retirement, which should properly be reserved for
pensions payable as a matter of right upon any termination.*

*In summary, while many of the pacesetters in private industry have in ef-
fect reduced the normal retirement age to 62 (and in some cases to a younger
age), the great majority of workers covered by private plans still have to wait
until 65 to receive full benefits.*

BENEFIT FORMULAS

"Final-pay" plans, which base the benefit on some fixed percentage of final average salary (per year of service), are generally more
liberal than other types—they reflect salary increases to the point of
retirement. The public-employee retirement plans are overwhelmingly "final-pay" plans. "Final average salary" has a range of mean-

---

[9] Harry E. Davis, "Negotiated Retirement Plans—a Decade of Benefit Improvements, *Monthly Labor Review, May* 1969, pp. 11 ff.

[10] Bankers Trust Company, *1970 Study of Industrial Retirement Plans* (New York,
1972). This study included plans covering 7.8 million workers. It involved both negotiated and non-negotiated plans, although it omitted negotiated multi-employer plans,
which represented about 25–30 percent of private-industry coverage. The companies
surveyed were larger than average and were therefore not entirely representative,
reflecting higher-than-average benefit levels.

ings from salary in a five-year period to salary in the final year of employment (Table 2.5). Final average salary is the sole basis for determining benefits in 75 percent of the systems surveyed.

Table 2.5 ◆ **Type Of Normal Retirement Formulas: General Employee And Teacher Systems**

| | Number of Systems, by Type | | | |
| | | General Employees | | |
Formula	*Total* [a]	*State*	*Local*	*Teachers*
Total	129	51	31	70
Percentage of final average salary	97	36	28	51
Percentage of career average salary	5	4	—	3
Money-purchase annuity plus percentage of final average salary	15	4	2	10
Money-purchase annuity plus percentage of final average salary with fixed minimum percentage overall	2	1	1	—
Money-purchase	4	3	—	2
Flat benefit per year of service	—	—	—	—
Choice of money-purchase or fixed benefit	1	1	—	—
Other	5	2	—	4

[a] These numbers do not represent totals of those appearing separately for state, local, and teacher systems; in this column a system covering teachers and general employees is counted only once.

The remaining plans are either based on "pension-plus-annuity" formulas or compute benefits on average career salary. The pension-plus-annuity plans fix the retirement allowance in two parts. The first part is a "money-purchase annuity" financed out of accumulated employee contributions, which are converted at retirement into whatever amount they will actuarially support (whatever the "money" will "purchase"). The pension part of the retirement allowance, calculated as a percentage of pay, almost invariably the final average salary, is financed by the employer.[11] The pension part is generally responsive to changes in salary levels to the point of retirement, but the money-purchase annuity is not and diminishes in significance with inflation.

Pension-plus-annuity formulas were very common among the public-employee systems until about twenty years ago, when they began to give way to final-pay formulas.

One stage in this transformation was to underpin the pension-plus-annuity amount with a guaranteed minimum related to final average salary. For example, a plan may have provided an employer-financed pension per year of service of 1 percent of final average salary plus an annuity based on member contributions, the rates of which were originally fixed on the theory that at a normal retirement age they would suffice to "purchase" an annuity equal to another 1 percent. However, when it became obvious, after inflation, that the annuity fell far short of the matching 1 percent, a guarantee was added that the combination would not be less per year than 2 percent of final average salary. This meant in effect that benefits for most employees would be determined by the guaranteed 2 percent rate. There is bound to be a point at which the guarantee effectively displaces the pension-plus-annuity formula, which then remains as a vestigial provision, with application only to exceptional cases of very long service or postponed retirement.[12]

Career-Average Salary

Only five of the plans are based on "career-average salary." These are formulas that accrue a benefit in terms of a percentage of *each year's* salary. "Past service"—employment before the plan was started—is generally calculated on the basis of salary paid about the time the plan began. Although this date or salary base may later be moved up by amendment as a one-time adjustment for the results of past inflation, such a plan remains essentially "career average" be-

---

[11] Use of the term "annuity" for the employee-financed part and "pension" as the employer-financed part is not universal. In Pennsylvania, for example, the employer-financed part is referred to as the "state annuity."

[12] If the formula for the guarantee was high enough in relation to the pension-plus-annuity formula, so that anything other than the guarantee was bound to be relatively rare, the plan was in fact classified in this survey as a final pay plan.

cause benefits for *future service* benefits are based on each year's salary, not final pay.

Two systems—the Wisconsin Retirement Fund and the Minnesota Teachers—provided alternative formulas: a money-purchase benefit or a fixed-formula benefit. A few plans add minor fixed-dollar amounts to the percentage-of-pay benefits.

Trend Toward Final-Average-Salary Basis

The decisive shift toward basing benefits on final average salary is obvious from the findings of successive surveys, as shown in Table 2.6.

Money-purchase plans have virtually disappeared—from 20 percent in 1961 to 3 percent in 1972.

Table 2.6 ◆ *Plans Based On Final Average Salary, 1961–72*

		Plans based on final average salary	
Survey	*Plans in survey*	*Number of plans*	*Percentage of total*
1961 Survey of Plans with Social Security Before Social Security was added	117	68	58
As of January 1, 1961 (after Social Security)	118	76	65
1965 and 1966 Surveys	214	182	85
1972 Survey	129	114	90

Industry Practice and Final Salary

Most industry pension plans are not based on terminal salary levels. In 1969, only 27 percent of the workers covered by private plans were in plans based on final average salary. Of the others, 52 percent of the employees were in plans that took no account of earnings; and that category included all but 8 percent of the negotiated multi-employer plans. The remaining 21 percent were in plans that computed benefits on career-average earnings. [13]

Final pay is more common than career average. The trend has certainly

[13] Davis and Strasser, "Private Pension Plans, 1960–1969," p. 50.

been strongly in that direction. The Bureau of Labor Statistics found that, in terms of workers covered, plans using terminal pay had increased by 1969 to 27 percent from 20 percent in 1962.

The fact that the public plans are overwhelmingly on a final-pay basis and that private industry is not represents a very significant difference. All else being equal, benefits based on final average pay produce a much higher level of payment than does a career-average formula. The benefits of a final average plan range from about 50 to over 100 percent higher than the benefits of an otherwise identical career-average plan, assuming 4 to 7 percent annual salary increases (see Table 2.7).

Table 2.7 ◆ Ratio Of Benefits: Final Average Salary To Career-Average Plans

	Assumed Rate of Annual Salary Increase			
Years of service	*4%*	*5%*	*6%*	*7%*
	Final average salary based on 5 years			
25	143%	154%	165%	176%
30	155	169	184	198
35	167	185	203	222
	Final average salary based on 3 years			
25	148	161	174	188
30	151	166	184	212
35	174	194	215	237

RATES OF BENEFIT ACCRUAL

Percentage-of-pay benefits can generally be quantified by their annual rate of benefit accrual—1.5 percent, 2.0 percent, etc. There is variety among the plans that complicates a simple array. One is the pension-plus-annuity arrangement, in which the annuity benefit is not a simple percentage of pay. A second is a "step-rate" formula involving two percentages, each applicable to a different part of the salary. For example, South Carolina provides a benefit of 1 percent of the first $4,800 of salary plus 1.5 percent of the excess (the portion over $4,800). A third involves longevity step-rates, a sequence of rates that escalates with length of service. For example, those Illinois state employees who have companion Social Security coverage have the following schedule:

Years of service	Percentage of final average salary per year
First 10	1.0
Second 10	1.1
Third 10	1.3
Thereafter	1.5

Whether the employees are also covered by Social Security is another fundamental difference that must be taken into account in identifying levels of benefit accrual.

SYSTEMS WITH SOCIAL SECURITY BASED ON FINAL AVERAGE SALARY

Most of the systems have companion Social Security and pay benefits based on final average salary, and the most common provision is to compute the pension on the basis of a single rate (Table 2.8).

Single-Rate Formulas

Single-rate plans vary from 1 percent (Missouri) to 2.5 percent (Allegheny County, Pennsylvania). There is a large cluster at 2 percent. However, the employee-median class (that is, the 50 percent mark determined by the number of employees covered) is the one from just above 1.67 percent to just below 2 percent of final average salary.

The large-city systems cluster at 2 percent formulas, higher than either state employees or most teachers.

The liberalization among plans of this type in just seven years, from 1965 to 1972, was remarkable. Simple accrual values lower than 1.5 percent of final average salary covered 40 percent of the employees in 1965, but by 1972 they were down to 10 percent. Plans that paid 2 percent or more per year increased from 10 percent of the coverage to 40 percent.

Step-rates

About a fifth of the employees are covered by step-rate formulas that differentiate the lower and upper amounts of final pay. Most of

Table 2.8 ◆ *Normal Benefit Formulas Based On Final Average Salary: Systems Covering Employees With Social Security (Employees In Thousands)*

Benefit Accrual Rate per Year of Service (percent of final average salary)	Type of System							
	All [a]		State-general		Local-general		Teachers	
	Systems	Employees	Systems	Employees	Systems	Employees	Systems	Employees
Single rates								
Total	39	2,520	17	1,380	9	156	20	1,545
1.00% but less than 1.5%	9	238	3	161	—	—	7	159
1.5%	6	208	4	174	1	9	2	109
1.51% but less than 1.67%	2	56	2	56	—	—	—	—
1.67%	5	284	2	149	2	40	3	139
1.68% but less than 2.00%	5	673	1	240	1	7	4	666
2.00%	9	917	4	530	3	27	3	402
2.01% but less than 2.50%	2	138	1	70	1	67	1	70
2.5%	1	6	—	—	1	6	—	—
Step rates—percentage when applied to $10,000 final average salary [b]								
Total	22	1,627	9	1,216	6	64	11	820
Less than 1%	3	146	1	77	—	—	2	69
1.00% but less than 1.5%	15	903	5	568	5	57	9	751
1.50% but less than 1.67%	1	30	1	30	—	—	—	—
1.67% but less than 2.00%	—	—	—	—	—	—	—	—
2.00% but less than 2.5%	3	548	2	541	1	7	—	—

Rates varying with length of service—percentage when applied to 30 years [c]

Total	9	398	6	265	2	76	2	85
Less than 1.5%	1	66	1	66	—	—	—	—
1.5% but less than 2%	4	173	3	116	—	—	1	57
2%	2	83	2	83	—	—	1	28
More than 2%	2	76	—	—	2	76	—	—

Rates for pensions where money-purchase annuities are added [d]

Total	15	760	5	280	3	159	8	396
Less than 0.83%	1	3	1	3	—	—	—	—
0.83%	1	63	—	—	—	—	1	63
0.84% but less than 1.00%	4	206	2	124	—	—	3	157
1.00%	3	145	1	83	—	—	2	62
1.01% but less than 1.50%	3	128	1	70	1	19	1	39
1.51% but less than 2.00%	—	—	—	—	—	—	—	—
2.00% but less than 2.5%	3	215	—	—	2	140	1	75

[a] These figures are not necessarily the totals of the detailed columns; a system covering both teachers and general employees is counted only once.
[b] "Step rates" refers to formulas with two rates: one percentage on a defined first portion of salary, generally identifiable with the Social Security tax base at some point, and a second on the excess portion.
[c] The benefit accrual rate depends on which year of service is involved: e.g., first 10 years, 1.0%; next 10 years, 1.5%; excess years, 2.0%.
[d] These rates account for only part of the retirement allowance.

these are "integration" formulas intended to shape the plan as a supplement to Social Security. Social Security has a cut-off on salary; the portion above that point is not used as the base for either contributions or benefits. A pension formula may be set so that there is one rate of benefit accrual on the portion of salary on which Social Security contributions and benefit computations are based and another— and higher—rate of accrual on the remainder or "excess" portion of salary. The idea has been to produce, in combination with Social Security, retirement income approaching a uniform percentage of pay. Typically, the breakpoint between the lower rate and higher rate is a past Social Security wage base, such as $4,800 or $7,800.[14]

To compare them with single-rate levels, the step-rate formulas have been applied to an employee earning $10,000 a year (a level realistic for 1972) and the results translated into a single percentage.[15]

Using this standard, step-rate formulas range from under 1 percent to over 2 percent, with the most significant concentration at 1 to less than 1.5 percent.

The most common salary "breakpoints" are $4,200, $4,800, and $7,800, each of which was a Social Security base for a number of years. None is higher than $9,000. There are six systems that define the breakpoint so that it changes automatically as the Social Security wage base changes.

Longevity Step-Rates

The plans that step up the annual rate of accrual for long-service employees have been made comparable by computing the single-rate equivalent for thirty years of service.[16] This type of formula may be found at both extremely high and low levels. The central cluster is from 1.5 percent to less than 2 percent (Table 2.8).

[14] There are, on the other hand, a few plans that step the rates in the other direction—they apply a higher percentage to the first part of salary and a lower percentage to the excess. That is a way of affording better treatment to low-salary employees. For example, the plan for general employees in Dallas, Texas, which does not have companion Social Security coverage, pays 2 percent of the first $7,800 of final average salary plus 1.67 percent of the excess.

[15] For example, if a formula credited 1 percent of the first $4,800 and 2 percent of the excess for someone with a $10,000 salary, it would credit an annual pension of $152 ($48 plus $104); that translates into 1.52 percent.

[16] For example, the Illinois plan, which credits 1.0 percent, 1.1 percent, and 1.3 percent for each successive decade of employment would, in effect, credit 1.13 percent for thirty years.

Pension-Plus-Annuity Formulas

In pension-plus-annuity plans, only the pension part can be readily compared (except in terms of representative illustrations presented in the next chapter). At this point we can only say that the typical plan of this kind still in existence was originally intended to produce half of the final average salary after twenty-five or thirty years. Of course, the actual result is considerably less.

Taking all of the final-average-salary plans with parallel Social Security coverage together, the median class is at, or somewhat above, the equivalent of a 1.67 percent formula. This will produce 50 percent of final average salary after thirty years of service.

Comparative Benefit Levels in Industry

On the whole, these formulas are higher than those prevailing among plans in private industry with benefits based on final pay. The Bankers Trust Survey (1965–1970) found that plans based on final average salary produced 36 to 40 percent of a $12,000 pay base after thirty years of service,[17] which amounted to about 1.25 percent per year, in contrast to the public plan median of 1.67 percent or better. The public plans based on final average salary have benefit formulas at least one-third higher than the corresponding type of plan in private industry.

Moreover, about 20 percent of these private plans were based on average salary over the last ten years of employment, a base considerably broader and therefore lower than the three- to five-year bases that stand out among the public plans. A five-year base produces results 10 to 17 percent higher than a ten-year base, if we assume annual wage increases of 4 to 7 percent.

A small part of the difference may be made up by thrift plans, supplementary employee savings plans with matching company contributions. Although they are popular among large companies, they affect as yet only a minority of workers covered by private pension plans.[18]

The typical plan will permit the employee to contribute up to 6 percent of pay, with 50 percent matched by the company. On the average, they do not cost the employer more than 2 percent of the payroll. That would provide a

[17] This refers to "conventional" plans, as distinguished from negotiated "pattern" plans. However, final-average-pay plans are more commonly found among the "conventional" plans.

[18] Bankers Trust Company, *Bankers Trust 1970 Study of Employee Savings and Thrift Plans* (New York, 1972).

pension, under typical circumstances, of less than one-half of 1 percent of career-average pay, obviously only a minor part of the difference between public and private plans.

SYSTEMS WITH SOCIAL SECURITY BASED ON CAREER-AVERAGE SALARY

The survey found nine systems with parallel Social Security coverage that paid benefits based on career-average salary (Table 2.9). The most common level—judging by the number of employees—is 1.5 percent. None of the formulas was higher than 1.67 percent.

SYSTEMS WITHOUT SOCIAL SECURITY

About a quarter of the systems do not have companion coverage under Social Security (Table 2.10). The formula levels cover a considerable span—with few exceptions, from 1.67 percent to 2.5 percent. They are all based on final average salary. The central tendency is clear—2 percent of final average salary, involving about half the employees. That is a higher level than for the aggregate of plans with Social Security added. The difference between the median of one and median of the other is on the order of 0.33 percent of final average salary. That is, however, only about one-third of the Social Security benefit for the average employee. It seems clear that, taking the systems in the aggregate, the jurisdictions that have Social Security coverage are providing higher combined benefits than those that do not.

Trends Over a Decade

In plans without companion Social Security coverage, benefit formulas have been rising sharply. In 1966, a large majority of employees not under Social Security were covered by formulas providing 1.75 percent or less. Now, the dominant rate is 2 percent or more. Employees covered by a 1.67 percent formula or less dwindled from 45 percent in 1966 to only 7 percent in 1972.

Table 2.9 ◆ **Normal Benefit Formulas Based On Career Average Salary** [a] **(Employees In Thousands)**

Benefit Accrual Rate per Year of Service	Type of System							
	All		State–general		Local–general		Teachers	
	Systems	Employees	Systems	Employees	Systems	Employees	Systems	Employees
Single rates								
Total	4	245	2	121	—	—	2	124
1.0 but less than 1.5%	1	6	1	6	—	—	—	—
1.5%	3	239	1	115	—	—	2	124
Step rates—percentage when applied to $10,000 final average salary [b]								
1.50 but less than 1.67%	4	58	1	29	—	—	3	29
Rates varying with length of service—percentage when applied to 30 years [c]								
Less than 1.5%	1	37	1	37	—	—	—	—

[a] All these systems have Social Security in addition.
[b] "Step rates" refer to formulas with two rates: one percentage on a defined first portion of salary, generally identifiable with the Social Security tax base at some point, and a second on the excess portion.
[c] The benefit accrual depends on which year of service is involved; e.g., first 10 years, 1.0%; next 10 years, 1.5%; excess years, 2.0%.

Table 2.10 ◆ **Normal Benefit Formulas Based On Final Average Salary: Systems Covering Employees Without Social Security (Employees In Thousands)**

Benefit Accrual Rate per Year of Service (percent of final average salary)	All		All state and local		Type of System — State-general		Local-general		Teachers	
	Systems	Employees	Systems	Employees	Systems	Employees	Systems	Employees	Systems	Employees
Single rates										
Total	20	1,104	19	1,099	4	362	6	75	12	727
1.67%	6	80	6	80	1	32	3	37	3	43
1.68 but less than 2.00%	2	170	2	170	—	—	1	8	2	170
2.00%	7	656	6	651	2	271	—	—	4	380
2.01 but less than 2.50%	2	56	2	56	—	—	1	5	1	51
2.5%	3	142	3	142	1	59	1	25	2	83
Step rates—percentage when applied to $10,000 final average salary [a]										
Total	2	23	2	23	—	—	2	23	1	16
1.67 but less than 2.00%	2	23	2	23	—	—	2	23	1	16

Rates varying with length of service —percentage when applied to 30 years [b]

	10	9	3,011	2	311	2	94	2	39	7	272
Total	10	9	3,011	2	311	2	94	2	39	7	272
1.5 but less than 2.00%	7	6	2,890	1	190	1	—	—	39	4	151
2%	2	2	96	1	96	1	69	—	—	2	96
More than 2%	1	1	25	—	25	1	25	—	—	1	25
Rates for pension where money-purchase annuity is added											
Total	2	2	79	—	79	—	—	—	—	2	79
0.83%	1	1	33	—	33	—	—	—	—	1	33
0.84 but less than 1.00%	—	—	—	—	—	—	—	—	—	—	—
1.00%	—	—	—	—	—	—	—	—	—	—	—
1.00 but less than 1.50%	—	—	—	—	—	—	—	—	—	—	—
1.50 but less than 2.00%	—	—	—	—	—	—	—	—	—	—	—
2.00 but less than 2.50%	1	1	46	—	46	—	—	—	—	1	46

a "Step rates" refer to formulas with two rates: one percentage on a defined first portion of salary, generally identified with the Social Security tax base at some point, and a second on the excess portion.

b The benefit accrual depends on which year of service is involved; e.g., first 10 years, 1.0%; next 10 years, 1.5%; excess years, 2.0%.

Definition of Final Average Salary

In the period from the 1920s to the early 1960s, common practice among public employee plans was to define final average salary as the average of five years—the last five, or any five consecutive years in the last ten, or any five years in the last ten. With inflation, the base has been shortened. Five years is still the dominant practice, but a three-year period, exceptional in 1961, is now very common (Table 2.11).

Final Pay Base in Industry

In private industry, plans based on final earnings generally use a five-year average. A small percentage use ten years.[19]

COMPULSORY RETIREMENT AGE

Most of the systems have established a compulsory retirement age (92 of the 129 systems). Two-thirds require retirement at 70 or later. In the others, the age ranges from 65 to 69. It is not always clear, however, what is meant by "compulsory retirement." Often it means a date when retirement is required—unless an extension is granted. Practices differ as to how readily extensions are granted.

Industry Practice.

In industry the usual practice is to require retirement at 65. That was the provision in almost half the large plans surveyed by the New York State Department of Labor in 1971.[20] *In the Bankers Trust Survey most plans required retirement at 65.*[21]

EARLY RETIREMENT BENEFITS

Eighty percent of the systems include early retirement benefits. The most common practice is to make reduced benefits available by age 55, generally with a requirement of at least five or ten years of

[19] Davis and Strasser, "Private Pension Plans, 1960–1969," p. 50.
[20] N.Y.S. Department of Labor, *Private Pension Plans in N.Y.S.*
[21] Bankers Trust 1970 survey, p. 26.

Table 2.11 ◆ Base For Computing Final Average Salary (Employees In Thousands)

	Type of System							
	All state and local		State–general		Local–general		Teachers	
Period	Systems	Employees	Systems	Employees	Systems	Employees	Systems	Employees
Total	118	6,884	44	3,614	31	663	63	3,940
Last pay	2	55	—	—	2	55	—	—
Last year	5	301	—	—	4	226	2	100
Two years	3	88	1	38	1	6	1	44
Three years	35	2,551	16	1,631	8	96	17	1,165
Four years	6	314	1	66	3	107	2	141
Five years	63	3,459	25	1,837	12	168	37	2,374
Ten years	3	74	—	—	1	5	3	74
Other	1	42	1	42	—	—	1	42

service (Table 2.12). When 55 is not the specified age, the early retirement age is fixed at 60. Another common practice is to allow early retirement benefits after twenty-five or thirty years of service, whatever the age. It might be noted, however, that a requirement of thirty years is less generous than an age 55 or 60 requirement; a large number of public employees reach age 55 or 60 before they have completed thirty years of service.

Table 2.12 ◆ Eligibility For Retirement Benefits: All State And Local Systems Including Teacher Systems

				Years of Service						
Age	Total	No mini- mum	Less than 5	5–9	10–14	15–19	20–24	25–29	30–34	35 or more
Total	139	23	3	12	21	9	18	22	27	4
Any	34	—	1	—	2	—	2	10	16	3
45–49	—	—	—	—	—	—	—	—	—	—
50	8	1	—	—	—	2	3	1	1	—
51–54	3	—	—	—	—	—	1	1	1	—
55	60	9	—	7	11	6	9	8	9	1
56–59	2	—	—	—	1	—	1	—	—	—
60	27	11	1	5	5	1	2	2	—	—
61–64	4	1	1	—	2	—	—	—	—	—
Other	1	1	—	—	—	—	—	—	—	—

A few public systems pay early retirement benefits at 50, generally with the proviso that the employee have at least twenty-five or thirty years of service. There are also a few that allow early retirement at any age; this is common with money-purchase plans, in which the benefit represents, in effect, disbursement of the accumulated employer and employee contribution accounts.

Trends in Early Retirement

Early retirement provisions have changed significantly since 1961. These benefits are virtually standard for general employees and teachers, particularly when the normal retirement age is 65. That was not true in 1961, when about 40 percent of the systems did not have early retirement provisions. And when early retirement was permitted in 1961, the age 55 requirement was generally contingent on twenty to thirty years of service. Now it is more often available after ten years.

Reductions for Early Retirement

Reductions for early retirement are of three kinds. The prevailing statutory provision reduces normal benefits actuarially—the reduction balances the expected longer period of payment. Second is a uniform reduction of 6 or 7 percent for each year that the retiring employee is younger than the normal retirement age. That amounts to converting the actuarial equivalent into a simple across-the-board percentage. A flat 6 percent a year is slightly advantageous to the early retiree. Third is a formula that gives the early retiree considerably more than actuarial equivalence would allow. For example, the Massachusetts law subtracts one-tenth of one percentage point from its age 65 formula of 2.5 percent for each year the employee is younger than 65. That amounts to a benefit reduction of only 4 percent for retirement at 64, when precise actuarial equivalence would require at least 7 percent. It amounts to only 5 percent from 60 to 59, which is still less than full actuarial adjustment. The cumulative effect is substantial—an employee who retires at 55 gets 60 percent of the normal benefit amount, while a more typical plan, with a 6 percent reduction, would pay only 40 percent of the full benefit. An even more generous plan covers the water and power employees of Los Angeles; it reduces benefits only 1 percent a year from 65 to 60 and by only 3 percent a year below age 60.

Early Retirement in Industry

Early retirement provisions are more extensive in industry than in public employment. Very few plans fail to provide for early retirement to some extent. At least half the plans in New York State provide, as of 1971, early retirement benefits by age 55 as a matter of right for the employee. Another 16 percent provide reduced benefits by age 60. An additional third of all private plans require company consent for early retirement, a provision inappropriate for public employment.[22] All in all, early retirement pensions are provided by

[22] The Conference Board, *Early Retirement Programs* (New York, 1971), p. 16. This report concerns a survey, as of 1970, of 841 plans among 641 manufacturers.

age 55 in about two-thirds of the plans and by age 60 in another 20 to 30 percent.[23]

However, the wider availability of early retirement benefits among private plans may not be particularly significant. It is balanced, probably outweighed, by the fact that the public plans have earlier ages for normal retirement. For example, the New York State systems have no early retirement provisions, but their full benefits are payable from age 55.

The prospects in the 1960s of plant shutdowns, extended layoffs, and reductions in force because of technological change stimulated higher early retirement benefits in private plans. Higher benefits before 65 mean less hardship for the man who finds himself unemployed at 60 or 62, and the new benefits encourage workers in that age bracket to vacate jobs for younger employees. Several different formulas have been adopted. One provides unreduced benefits if termination had company consent or resulted from layoff or plant shutdown. Another narrows the reduction for early retirement. A third adds a supplementary payment to make up for the absence of Social Security benefits before 65 or 62. A fourth, designed to meet an immediate problem of overstaffing, has been to offer a supplement to employees retiring within a fixed period, such as the next year or two. Still another, attributable almost entirely to union demands, is payment of unreduced benefits after thirty years, or after an age-service combination equal to eighty, or one equal to seventy, if the employee was at least 55.[24]

Public plans do not have the pre-Social Security supplements that are included in some of the private plans; on the other hand, they provide normal (that is, unreduced) pensions that are higher and normal retirement ages that are often lower. In general, the pensions provided by state and local government at 55 and 60 are not less liberal than those in private industry. The early retirement supplements in many private plans are a significant plus, except that public employment does not generally have the layoff problem that gave rise to this provision in industry.

VESTING

"Vesting" is the acquisition of a right, upon termination, to a deferred benefit. It is distinguishable from an immediate benefit,

[23] The Conference Board, *ibid.*, p. 8. The Bankers Trust survey arrived at approximately the same results—63 percent at age 55 and 20 percent at age 60.

[24] See The Conference Board, *Early Retirement Programs;* N.Y.S. Department of Labor, *Private Pension Plans in N.Y.S.;* and Bankers Trust 1970 survey.

which may be a normal, early retirement, or disability pension. Vesting is almost always included in the public plans.

In most systems, the practice is to vest on the basis of years of service, without regard to age. A majority require ten years of service, although a substantial number do so after five years. Others have varying requirements—age 55, sometimes with, sometimes without service requirements; or age 50 with ten or fifteen years of service (Table 2.13).

Table 2.13 ◆ *Eligibility For Vesting*

				Years of Service				
Age	*Total*	*No minimum*	*Less than 5*	*5–9*	*10–14*	*15–19*	*20–24*	*25–29*
				State systems—general employees				
Total	46	4	3	17	16	11	4	1
Any	39	1	3	16	14	10	4	1
Under 55	2	—	—	—	1	1	—	—
55 or older	4	3	—	—	1	—	—	—
Other	1	—	—	1	—	—	—	—
				Local systems—general employees				
Total	30	1	3	9	7	5	5	—
Any	27	—	3	8	6	5	5	—
Under 55	2	—	—	2	—	—	—	—
55 or older	1	1	—	—	—	—	—	—
Other	—	—	—	—	—	—	—	—
				Teachers				
Total	77	6	2	22	21	11	13	2
Any	66	2	2	21	18	9	12	2
Under 55	5	—	—	1	1	2	1	—
55 or older	5	4	—	—	1	—	—	—
60–64	—	—	—	—	—	—	—	—
Other	1	—	—	—	1	—	—	—
				All state and local systems (including teachers)				
Total	137	8	6	40	40	23	17	3
Any	119	3	6	37	34	20	16	3
Under 55	9	—	—	2	3	3	1	—
55 or older	7	5	—	—	2	—	—	—
Other	2	—	—	1	1	—	—	—

The vesting is generally full, rather than graduated or partial. Only ten of the surveyed systems had a vesting formula that was less than full. "Full" means that the regular benefit, for years of service credited, will be paid at the normal retirement age. Usually vested benefits, suitably reduced, are also available at the early retirement age, if the service requirements for early retirement have been met.

Since the plans are, with rare exception, contributory, the payment of a deferred benefit is contingent on the terminated employee leaving his contribution account on deposit. If he chooses to withdraw it, he forfeits his deferred pension.

Trends in Vesting

Vested rights are a recent but rapid development. In 1961, approximately 35 percent of the systems had no vesting at all and the thresholds for vesting were more often than not fifteen to twenty years of service.

Vesting—Private Plans

Although less prevalent among private plans, vesting is still quite extensive. As of 1969, 77 percent of covered workers were in plans that had some form of vesting. Almost one-third vested after five or ten years of service regardless of age; another large group required fifteen years. Many plans used an age threshold as well. Half of all the plans provided vested benefits for an employee who reached age 50 with fifteen years of service.[25] (Of course, under federal law enacted in 1974, virtually all private plans will be required to have vesting by 1976.)

DISABILITY PENSIONS

All but three of the surveyed plans provide pensions for permanent and total disability. Eligibility is set in terms of years of service, usually ten, or next most frequent, five. These provisions are found in about three-fourths of the systems. Thresholds are lower now than in 1961, when there were fewer plans using five years and more using fifteen.

Disability pensions are, in more than 80 percent of the plans, de-

---

[25] Davis and Strasser, "Private Pension Plans, 1960–1969," p. 49.

termined by a formula related to the normal retirement benefit. The most common provision is for the amount of the disability pension to be calculated in the same way as the normal pension, based on the employee's actual years of service. Some plans put a floor under the disability pension, such as 25 or 33 percent of the average salary used in pension computations. On the other hand, disability benefits in several plans are somewhat less than the normal benefit.

Another fairly common approach is to base the disability amount on the normal pension, but inclusive of the additional years of service the employee would have completed if his service had continued to normal retirement age. The logic is that disability interrupted a career or work-life that would have eventuated in a pension based on a fuller period of service and that benefit amounts are therefore equitable if they approach the normal benefits that would have been paid. However, formulas of this type do not generally pay 100 percent of the projected normal benefit; several use 90 percent and many use less.

A third method fixes the disability pension as a stated percentage of salary, generally less than 50 percent.

Disability Provisions—Private Plans

Disability pensions among private plans are difficult to compare with those of the public plans. Many private plans have no disability pensions. Those with disability pensions generally fix the benefits equal to normal retirement benefits or at a somewhat lower level. On the other hand, there are many collectively bargained plans that provide more than the normal benefit for disability, usually until Social Security becomes available. Also, many companies protect employees against disability through long-term disability insurance plans, rather than pensions. For the first several years of disability, the benefits under long-term disability insurance programs are often higher than those payable from pension plans.

Service-connected Disability Pensions

Most of the systems make no distinction between disability attributable to a job-connected accident and "ordinary" disabilities. However, about a third of the systems make special provision if the disability was attributable to a job-connected accident. The service required is generally minimal, and in most of these plans the benefit is higher than for ordinary disability. In half the systems with a special provision of this kind, the pension is 50 percent or more of the employee's salary and often 75 percent or more.

In the private sector, benefits for job-connected disability are provided through Workmen's Compensation. Public employees may also be covered by Workmen's Compensation and it may or may not be subtracted from disability pensions.

DEATH BENEFITS

About half the systems pay lump-sum benefits upon the death of a member in active service, either in addition to the total refund of employee contributions (generally with interest) or as an alternative, if the lump sum provides more.

The service required is minimal—less than five years and in many cases just a few months. However, the amount of payment is often dependent on length of service. For example, the California Public Employees' Retirement System provides one month's pay for each year of service up to a maximum of six years.

The death benefit schedule of a retirement system cannot be taken as a complete description of the life insurance covering its members, since there may also be a life insurance program, covering the same employees.

Survivors' Annuities

Half of the systems provide annuities for the widows and children of employees who die in active service. Such a provision is typical where the employees do not have Social Security coverage. Of the 32 systems *without* Social Security, only 6 do not have survivors' annuities. Most of the systems *with* Social Security coverage rely on Social Security for protection of dependent survivors. However, even among these, 40 percent have survivors' annuities in some form. The annuities provision is particularly common among the municipal plans. They are among the oldest plans for public employees and are likely to have included provisions for survivors before parallel protection was provided through Social Security.

It is understandable that the systems without Social Security

usually require only a short period of service—less than five years—
for an employee's family to be protected by survivor annuity provisions. The systems with Social Security—except for the large city
plans—require longer coverage for eligibility, most of them ten years
or more.

Since 1961, survivors' annuities have not become more common
among the public plans, but the service requirement has in many
cases been reduced to ten years. The annuity is not necessarily for
the full lifetime of the survivor or survivors. Benefits on behalf of a
child are likely to be discontinued at 18, or perhaps 22, if the child is
a student. Benefits to a widow are likely to be discontinued if she
remarries or, in some cases, when she no longer has a minor child
under her care. Annuities may in some plans be given to dependent
parents, if there is no dependent spouse or child.

Survivors' annuity amounts are determined by a wide variety of
formulas—as a percentage of the employee's accrued pension benefits, as a percentage of his salary, as a schedule of dollar amounts,
and as a combination of these formulas. Among the systems with
Social Security, a common provision is the survivor's portion of a
joint-and-survivor annuity, which means that the surviving spouse is
paid the same amount as if the employee had retired on normal
benefits appropriate to his years of service the day before his death
and had elected a 100 percent joint-and-survivor benefit. The benefit payable to the spouse of a person who dies in active service under
such a provision is usually at least 75 percent of the pension the employee would have received.

Among the systems without Social Security coverage, a schedule of
flat dollar amounts for survivors is more common. The amount generally varies with the number of minor children.

Survivor Benefits After Retirement

Most provisions for benefits to survivors payable on the death of
the employee after he retires do not properly fall within the category
of death benefits because provision for death is generally made in
the form of pension options—and these are at the expense of the
member rather than at the expense of the system. Almost all public-
employee pension plans include optional modes of benefit payment
at the choice of the employee.

The "normal" or "no-option" form of benefit, operative if the employee makes no choice, is usually a straight life annuity for the employee. In some cases, it is what the insurance industry calls a "modified cash refund"—a straight life annuity with the proviso that, if the benefits paid to the pensioner by the time he dies do not equal the amount of his own contribution account at retirement, the balance is paid to his beneficiary. The other options available all involve survivor or death benefits paid for by a reduction in the amount of the employee's own benefit.

The basic choices offered employees about to retire are the joint-and-survivor benefit, modified cash refund (see above), and return of reserve. The joint-and-survivor benefit guarantees that 100 percent, 75 percent, or 50 percent of the pension benefit received by the employee will continue to a surviving spouse for her lifetime. The employee's own pension, payable during his lifetime, is reduced actuarially to pay for the survivor pension.

In return-of-reserve, the lump-sum value of the entire pension (i.e., its reserve) is determined at retirement; if pension payments to the member do not add up to the reserve amount, the balance is paid to the beneficiary. Some systems allow as an option payment of a lump sum as a death benefit after retirement, balanced by a reduction in the benefit paid to the employee.

Death Benefits for Active Members Eligible to Retire

The survivors of employees who die while employed but eligible to retire have in many plans been given the protection of one or another of the retirement income options, as if the employee had retired. The most common arrangement is that if an employee who is eligible to retire dies, his spouse receives a life annuity as if the member had retired and chosen a 100 percent joint-and-survivor option or, under some plans, a 50 percent joint-and-survivor option. A variation is to permit the member to select an option, while still employed, and in the absence of an election, to presume that he chose a joint-and-survivor annuity. The statutes for New York City and for state employees in Pennsylvania include an option for full payment of the retirement reserve and presume that it was chosen, in the absence of choice to the contrary.

Survivor Benefits in Private Plans

It has also become common in the private sector for pensions to be provided to the surviving spouse of an active employee who dies when he is eligible for retirement. The Bankers Trust Company found (1965–70) that 56 percent of the plans it surveyed had such provisions. The spouse pensions generally amounted to 40 to 50 percent of the full accrued benefit under the pattern plans and to 30 to 50 percent under conventional plans.

AUTOMATIC POST-RETIREMENT ADJUSTMENTS

About half of the employees of state and local governments are covered by automatic post-retirement adjustments (See Table 2.14). They are of three major types.

Most common are automatic adjustments corresponding to changes in the federal Consumer Price Index, generally with a maximum limit on the annual increase. The maximum may be as little as 1 percent, but in most cases it is 3 percent or more.

Another sizable group of plans provide automatic fixed percentage increases, mostly 2 or 2.5 percent a year, regardless of changes in the cost-of-living index.

Other types are based on changes in the pay of active workers, the earnings of invested reserves, and other standards. For example, the Maine State Retirement System increases pensions by the same percentage as general salaries of active employees are increased (a practice more common among plans for policemen and firemen). Minnesota has an "Adjustable Fixed Benefit Fund" which makes automatic adjustments to the extent that the reserves for pensioners, invested half in fixed-income securities and half in equities, earn more than the basic assumed investment yield.

The term "automatic adjustment" has been strictly construed in this survey. It does not include one-time adjustments to correct for past changes in the cost of living, even if they are based on changes in the Consumer Price Index, nor does it include adjustments requiring annual legislative action. Thus, the cost-of-living formula adjustments in New York State are excluded since they depend on annual renewal by the legislature. Variable annuities, available at the

Table 2.14 ◆ Automatic Postretirement Adjustments: Systems Having Such Benefits (Employees In Thousands)

	Type of System							
	All state and local		State–general		Local–general		Teachers	
Type of Adjustment	Systems	Employees	Systems	Employees	Systems	Employees	Systems	Employees
Total	59	3,739	26	2,384	15	277	33	2,164
Automatic percentage increases								
Total	16	820	5	255	5	74	10	651
1 but less than 2%	5	184	2	110	—	—	5	184
2 but less than 3%	10	628	3	145	4	66	4	459
3% or more	1	8	—	—	1	8	1	8
Automatic increases according to C.P.I., with limit to following percentage								
Total	25	1,824	12	1,379	7	147	12	830
1 but less than 2%	8	604	5	433	—	—	4	246
2 but less than 3%	3	457	1	426	2	31	—	—
3% or more	14	763	6	520	5	116	8	584
Adjustment based on salary changes								
Total	1	32	1	32	—	—	1	32
Other	17	1,063	8	718	3	56	10	651

option of the member, are treated separately because the employee accepts the risk, as well as rewards, of common stock performance.

Automatic post-retirement adjustments are the most recent and most rapidly expanding changes among public systems. They began in 1959 when Illinois enacted an automatic 1½ percent pension adjustment and grew rapidly after Congress enacted a cost-of-living escalator for retired federal employees in 1962.[26] The 1961 survey of the Social Security Administration made no mention of provisions of this type, not through neglect but because there were none. The 1965 survey found only four state and local systems with Social Security that included automatic adjustments, apart from variable annuities. A survey in 1966 of 10 state and local systems without parallel Social Security coverage showed greater use of automatic adjustments. Interestingly, not one was tied to the Consumer Price Index.

Practice in Industry

Cost-of-living adjustments were, as of 1973, almost nonexistent among private plans. The New York State Labor Department's 1971 survey found only two plans with automatic post-retirement adjustments.

Employee Contributions

On the whole, the public systems require substantial employee contributions. Only six of the systems were found to be totally noncontributory (Table 2.15).

Contributions may take the form of a single uniform percentage of pay for all employees, or, in systems with "step-rate" benefit formulas, one percentage on the first portion of salary and another percentage on the remainder of salary, or a schedule of rates determined by age at entry into the employment, generally differentiated by sex and sometimes by occupation.

The latter type—schedule of rates—developed when the prevailing type of public retirement benefit was the pension-and-annuity combination. The idea was to have each part provide about 50 percent of the retirement allowance at normal retirement age. If so, an employee entering at 35 would have to contribute more than an employee entering at 25. Women and men might have to contribute at

[26] John P. Mackin, *Protecting Purchasing Power in Retirement* (New York, Fleet Academic Editions, Inc., 1971).

Table 2.15 ◆ Rates Of Employee Contributions

	Type of System							
	With Social Security				Without Social Security			
Rate	All	State–general	Local–general	Teachers	All	State–general	Local–general	Teachers
Total	97	45	19	48	32	6	10	22
Non-contributory	6	1	3	2	—	—	—	—
Uniform rate								
Total	46	25	2	25	28	6	7	21
3 but less than 4%	8	5	—	4	—	—	—	—
4 but less than 5%	18	11	1	7	5	—	2	3
5 but less than 6%	14	8	—	9	8	2	3	6
6 but less than 7%	4	—	—	4	10	2	—	9
7 but less than 8%	2	1	1	1	5	2	2	3
8 but less than 9%	—	—	—	—	5	—	2	3

Step rates—percentages when applied to $10,000 [a]

Total	29	15	8	13	—	—
Less than 1%	2	1	—	1	—	—
1 but less than 2%	1	—	—	1	—	—
2 but less than 3%	3	2	1	1	—	—
3 but less than 4%	8	1	4	3	—	—
4 but less than 5%	9	7	1	5	—	—
5 but less than 6%	5	4	1	2	—	—
6 but less than 7%	1	—	1	—	—	—

Schedule of rate—percentage for male, entry age 30 [b]

Total	16	4	6	8	4	3
Less than 2%	2	—	1	1	—	1
2 but less than 4%	1	—	1	—	—	—
4 but less than 6%	6	2	1	3	2	—
6 but less than 8%	5	2	2	3	2	1
8% or more	1	—	1	—	—	—
Other	1	—	—	1	—	1

[a] "Step rates" refer to formulas with two rates: one percentage on a defined first portion of salary and a second on the excess portion.
[b] The schedule determines a rate of contributions for each employee, according to age at entry and perhaps sex as well. For teachers, the rate included is that for a female entering at age 25.

different rates because retirement ages and life expectancies were different. When the pension-plus-annuity combinations were superseded by fixed-percentage formulas, the old-style variable contribution schedule remained in effect because it was assumed to represent an equitable sharing of the costs between employer and employee.

The uniform-contribution rates range from 3 percent (Indiana and Minnesota) to 8 percent (Missouri teachers). The median-rate class for systems with Social Security is from 4 to less than 5 percent. Among systems without Social Security, the median is much higher—7 to under 8 percent. Of course, the lower contribution rates for systems with Social Security are easily balanced by the fact that members of such systems must also make Social Security contributions.

Step-rates, measured by using contributions from an employee earning $10,000, fall mainly in the range of 2 to 6 percent. The median class is 4 to under 5 percent.

The schedules of rates according to age and sex can be tested fairly by using contributions required of a male entering employment at age 30. Most fall into the range of 4 to less than 8 percent; the median class is 4 to under 6 percent.

Employee Contributions—Private Plans

Employee contributions are almost as rare in private pension plans as they are prevalent in public plans. In 1969, almost 80 percent of workers under private plans made no contributions.[27] *A negotiated plan that requires contributions is exceptional. Moreover, in some of the contributory plans, employee contributions are voluntary in one sense or another. A common arrangement is to have what is in effect two plans, a basic noncontributory plan plus a supplementary plan or layer that requires an employee contribution. The basic plan may cover earnings equal to the Social Security tax base, the supplementary or "excess" plan adding benefits based on the remaining portion of salary. Some plans have voluntary contributions that, in effect, use the pension plan as a tax-sheltered vehicle for accumulating capital that is later translated into an additional pension.*

Where contributions are required by private plans, they are at a lower level than those required by public plans. The general level of employee contribu-

---

[27] Davis and Strasser, "Private Pension Plans, 1960–1969," p. 50.

*tions was summarized in the Bankers Trust study as two or three times the fu-
ture service benefit rate. The average benefit formula for larger private plans
in 1965–70 was about 1.25 percent for final salary plans and about 1.6
percent for career-average plans. If some weight is given to the probability
that the contributory plans have higher benefit levels than the noncontributory
ones, it is fair to conclude that the central level for employee contributions is 3
to 4 percent of pay, appreciably lower than the 4 to 5 percent contributions of
the public plans with Social Security.*

Summary

Adding up all these provisions, the retirement plans of state and
local government clearly provide more generous benefits than do
the pension plans of private industry. But, to make a comparison by
adding up the pros and cons of the plans can be misleading. We
have divided the plans into those for public employees and those for
private employees, an oversimplification that may obscure the very
wide differences among individual public plans.

For example, the South Dakota Public Employees' Retirement System pays a benefit at 65 equal to 1 percent of each year's salary up to
$6,000, with years of service before the system was established cred-
ited at only one half of 1 percent. By contrast, the employees of the
New York City Department of Sanitation can retire any time they
have completed twenty years of service on a pension of 50 percent of
final salary rate, plus additional amounts for additional years, so that
with thirty years of service the retirement income will exceed two-
thirds of final pay. Describing the *aggregate* benefit level of public
plans does not indicate the magnitude of the difference between
South Dakota benefits and New York benefits. Nevertheless, it is relevant to understand what general level of retirement income is provided for public employees and how it compares with that provided
for private employees.

In comparing the public and private sectors, certain differences
are obvious:

1. Half of the wage and salary workers in industry are not covered by a pension plan; almost all employees of state or local government are covered.

2. The age when full benefits are payable is distinctly lower in

public plans; most public plans make full benefits available by 60, in contrast to normal retirement at age 65 in most private plans.

3. Three-quarters of the public plans base retirement benefits on pay in the years close to retirement; this is true of fewer than 30 percent of the workers covered by private plans.

4. In determining final average pay, a large percentage of the public plans use a period of three years or less; among private plans of the "final pay" variety, the only significant departure from a 5-year base is a 10-year base.

5. The average benefit formula—the percentage of pay accrued with each year of service—is higher in public plans. Among the public plans based on final average pay with parallel Social Security coverage, the median rate is about 1.67 percent. Among large final salary plans in private industry, the corresponding median (1965–70) was approximately 1.25 percent.

6. Although early retirements are not very different overall, one notable difference is that many private plans provide special supplements that make up for the absence of Social Security if termination is involuntary or by mutual agreement.

7. Vesting provisions, now common in both sectors, are somewhat more prevalent in public than in private plans. (Of course, enactment of the Employee Retirement Income Security Act of 1974 will make vesting universal among the private plans by 1976.)

8. A little over half the state and local employees are protected in retirement by automatic adjustments; such adjustments are almost nonexistent in private plans.

The only respect in which the public plans are less favorable to the employees is that they require contributions. Eighty percent of the private plans are noncontributory, while the public plans are overwhelmingly contributory and require, on the average, contributions of about 5 percent of pay. Whether this contribution pays for the difference in benefits will be one of the questions answered in the next chapter.

3 ✣ Pensions as Wage Replacement

To identify the level of a pension plan, it is essential to consider its wage-replacement ratio—the extent to which its benefits replace the employee's final earnings—and also how that ratio is affected by Social Security.

Using these criteria, how do public plans compare with private plans?

How do the conclusions relate to public policy?

The findings in the preceding chapter do not provide the complete answer since they deal separately with each of the major features of pension plans. The variables of normal and early retirement ages and benefit formulas have somehow to be combined. This chapter will discuss the ultimate results of the plans in terms of their wage-replacement ratios for typical career employees both with and without Social Security benefits. The method of evaluation provides fairly precise comparisons, whether for judging a given plan in relation to prevailing levels or for evaluating more generally the public and private sectors.

For each plan the retirement benefit was computed as a percentage of salary in the final year of employment for twenty-seven typical career employees. These final-salary levels were used: $5,000 (the low-level employee); $10,000 (close to average as of 1972); and $14,000 (somewhat representative of public professional employees as of 1972). Results were developed for four retirement ages, with alternative assumptions about length of service, as follows:

age 65, with twenty, thirty, or thirty-five years of service;
age 60, with twenty or thirty years of service;
age 55, with twenty or thirty years of service; and
age 50, with twenty or twenty-five years of service.

Certain assumptions and choices had to be made in order to develop the results. To make fair comparisons among final-pay plans (using one- to ten-year averages), career-average pay plans, formulas wholly or partly of a "money-purchase" type, and flat dollar benefits unrelated to salary, it was necessary to assume some rate of salary increase. We assumed 4 percent a year, since that is the rate used for the same purpose by the U. S. Bureau of Labor Statistics, which found in 1970 that 4 percent was just slightly below the annual rate of increase over preceding periods of ten to thirty years.[1]

The New York State Department of Labor, which found it consistent with changes from 1950 to 1970 in the weekly earnings of workers covered by unemployment insurance, used the 4 percent rate in analyzing survey results among private plans as of 1971.[2] When compared with actual changes in the pay of public employees over the past two decades, the 4 percent assumption is low. To that extent, this analysis tends to overstate wage-replacement ratios for career-average and money-purchase plans. The same is true for final-pay formulas based on five- or ten-year averaging periods, although only by a relatively small margin.

Although the summaries deal with benefits as of January 1972, they are computed on each plan's current (or future) service formula, ignoring the somewhat different credits that may be provided for past service, since we are concerned here with what present statutes will provide in the future. The benefit summaries use the final-pay levels that were realistic for 1972, although future salaries will be higher. They illustrate what the typical employee would receive if he retired at the time of the survey (1972) but his entire employment was credited on the formula covering his 1971 employment.

The benefit summaries were prepared with (and without) Social Security as payable at age 65 under the law in effect January 1,

---

[1] Arnold Strasser, *Pension Formula Summarization—An Emerging Research Technique* (Washington, D.C., U.S. Bureau of Labor Statistics, December 1970).

[2] New York State Department of Labor, Division of Research and Statistics, *Private Pension Plans in New York State, 1971* (New York, April 1973).

1972. Therefore the effects of the July 1972 Social Security amendments, which increased benefits by 20 percent and established automatic escalation, are excluded. Social Security retirement benefits payable on January 1, 1972, ranged to a maximum of $216.10 a month for a man and $224.70 for a woman.

Inclusion of the Social Security amendments of July 1972 was not feasible. It would not only have required additional projections, but would also have made invalid the best available statistics on comparable pensions in private industry, particularly a survey by the New York State Department of Labor, which used precisely the same technique and basis for analysis.

For two of the systems, it was not possible, with the information on hand, to compute the wage-replacement ratios. Consequently, the analysis is based on 127 systems covering 7,174,000 employees.

All in all, the benefit summaries can most easily be described as those that would be paid under the provisions of law in effect January 1, 1972, if the typical employees retired on that date but were covered by the current service formula for all his years of service. While the individuals are, of course, hypothetical, they are fair samples and produce good representations of the benefits resulting from their plans.[3]

AVERAGE BENEFITS

The median retirement benefit among the public plans at age 65, after thirty years of service, is 49 percent of the final year's salary. This amounts to about 53 percent of the average salary over the last five years of employment. (See Table 3.1.)

Adding primary Social Security benefits as of January 1972, the median of total retirement payments for this employee—age 65 with thirty years of service and $10,000 terminal salary—is 68 percent of his final pay. (The increase is less than the amount of the Social Security benefit because these medians reflect the absence of Social Security for those jurisdictions without the dual coverage.)

Overall, system benefits provided about the same percentage of

[3] The appendix to this chapter gives fuller details on the methods and assumptions used to develop the representative wage-replacement ratios.

Table 3.1 ◆ *Mediun Pension Benefits Of General Employees And Teachers In State And Local Retirement Systems, As Percentage Of Final Year's Salary, As Of January 1, 1972* [a]

	Employee			Pension as Percentage of Final Year's Salary—Median	
Age	*Years of service*	*Final salary*	*Benefit alone*	*With primary Social Security at 65*	*Percent of employees ineligible*
65	20	$ 5,000	32.1	66.2	—
		10,000	32.4	53.7	—
		14,000	32.4	46.3	—
	30	5,000	48.1	80.1	—
		10,000	48.6	67.6	—
		14,000	48.6	66.2	—
	35	5,000	56.1	88.2	—
		10,000	56.7	74.6	—
		14,000	56.7	67.4	—
60	20	5,000	30.5	62.7	4.8
		10,000	31.7	51.9	4.8
		14,000	32.1	45.0	4.8
	30	5,000	47.2	77.3	0.7
		10,000	48.1	64.9	0.7
		14,000	48.1	59.9	0.7
55 [a]	20	5,000	22.8	61.1	43.5
		10,000	22.8	49.3	43.5
		14,000	23.9	40.7	43.5
	30	5,000	37.5	70.2	10.9
		10,000	36.5	59.2	10.9
		14,000	37.5	52.1	10.9
50 [a]	20	5,000	11.9	54.9	84.4
		10,000	11.9	42.4	84.4
		14,000	11.9	34.2	84.4
	25	5,000	22.2	58.7	75.8
		10,000	22.2	47.3	75.8
		14,000	20.3	38.3	75.8

[a] Benefits shown only for plans paying benefits at the indicated age; the fact that some plans do not pay benefits at these ages is not reflected in the medians.
Figures reflect Social Security before 1972 increases or escalation.

pay for terminal salaries of $5,000, $10,000 or $14,000. The picture changes, however, when the Social Security benefit is added, since that benefit is a higher percentage of salary for the lower-paid employees than for the better-paid. For example, the Social Security maximum (January 1, 1972) of $216 a month for a man was about 26 percent of a $10,000 salary, but only 18 percent of a $14,000 salary. With wife's benefits added, these amounts were 39 percent and 27 percent respectively.

For the hypothetical person with a history of 4 percent annual increases and a final salary of $5,000, the Social Security benefit was $166 a month, or 40 percent of final salary. With a wife's benefit, it was 60 percent. At the $5,000 salary level, the median system benefit at age 65 after thirty years was 48 percent; total benefits inclusive of primary Social Security therefore amounted to 80 percent of final salary; and, with a wife's benefit, close to 100 percent.

On the other hand, at the $14,000 final salary, primary Social Security added only 18 percent of pay (as of January 1, 1972), making combined median benefits (without the wife's benefit) 66 percent of final earnings.

Comparative Levels–State and Local Employees and Teachers

In the aggregate, the local (large-city) systems provide higher benefits than do the state systems or those for teachers (see Table 3.2). Teachers' benefits are on about the same level as those of general employees under state systems, except that a larger percentage of the teachers do not have companion Social Security coverage.

For retirement at 65 after thirty years, the local systems provide benefits higher by 7 to 11 percent of salary than the state systems. The median benefit of the local systems is 54 to 58 percent of final pay; with primary Social Security added, it is 74 percent of final pay at the $14,000 level, and 92 percent of pay at the $5,000 level. The local-government plans are also more generous for retirements at ages 55 and 60.

Comparison with Private-Industry Plans

A rather precise comparison with pensions in the private sector is possible because of a survey by the New York State Department of Labor that used the same method of analysis and the same assump-

Table 3.2 ◆ *Median Pension Benefits: General State Employees, State Systems And Local Systems, And Teachers, As Of January 1, 1972*

			Pension as Percentage of Final Year's Salary —Median					
			Without Social Security [a]			With primary Social Security at 65 [a]		
Employee								
Age	Years of service	Final salary	State	Local	Teachers	State	Local	Teachers
65	30	$ 5,000	46.6	54.7	48.1	81.7	92.4	74.8
		10,000	46.7	54.1	48.1	67.6	79.9	62.5
		14,000	46.7	57.7	48.1	62.5	74.3	57.7
	20	10,000	31.1	38.5	32.1	53.7	64.4	50.1
	35	10,000	54.5	63.1	56.2	74.6	84.4	69.0
60	20	10,000	30.0	38.1	27.8	52.6	66.4	49.0
	30	10,000	45.5	53.5	44.8	65.8	78.4	63.5
55	20	10,000	22.6	29.2	22.8	49.3	59.3	44.9
	30	10,000	34.0	43.9	34.2	59.6	74.9	55.5

[a] All plans are included, whether they had companion Social Security coverage or not. Social Security is included, however, only for those that had companion Social Security coverage.

tions. The New York survey embraced *all* pension plans in the state that covered approximately 1,000 workers or more; it included 278 plans with 1,498,150 members. The survey was more representative than it might first appear, because a collection of plans with 1,000 or more workers within New York State inevitably includes a large number of national companies. On the other hand, the New York survey covered a somewhat higher percentage of collectively bargained multi-employer plans than would a national sample. Multi-employer plans made up about 25–30 percent of national coverage, but they represented 40 percent of the New York survey sample. Although the state survey ended as of January 1, 1971, a year earlier than this survey, the one-year difference is not considered to have had a significant effect on the comparative findings.

In the aggregate, and for comparable individuals, the public plans provided pensions that were 50 to 100 percent higher than those provided by private plans. This comparison does not reflect the fact that about half the employees in private industry are not covered by pension plans at all.

The gap is not as wide, however, when Social Security is taken into account. Some of the public systems included in these findings did not have companion Social Security coverage. If the figures in Table 3.3 were adjusted to exclude such systems, the overall benefit levels of the public plans would be reduced a bit, but still a good deal higher than those prevailing in private industry.

Inclusive of the primary Social Security benefit, as of January 1, 1972, the combined retirement benefits for the public employees exceeded composite benefits for private-industry employees by 4 to 7 percent of pay at the $5,000 salary level and by 12 to 25 percent of pay at the $14,000 salary level.

Perhaps the single most significant comparison here is for the hypothetical employee who retires at 65 after thirty years of service with a final salary of $10,000. If he was covered by the average pension plan in private industry, his combined benefits (with Social Security), would be roughly half of his final pay. However, if he was employed by state or local government, his combined benefits would be about two-thirds of his final pay. This is an advantage of about one-third in favor of the public employee.

Benefits Financed by Employer

The public employee generally contributes substantially to his retirement system; the typical employee in private industry pays nothing. If the value of the employee's own contributions is subtracted, the two sectors come a good deal closer together.[4]

If approximate values of their own contributions are subtracted, employees who retire at 65 after thirty years of service receive, with

---

[4] The plans in our survey were subject to computations to determine how the benefits payable to the hypothetical public employees would be reduced if the value of their own contributions were subtracted. This computation was made by the following steps:

1. The contribution rate appropriate to the hypothetical employee was applied to his salary history to accumulate his contribution account, inclusive of 4 percent interest. For teacher systems, the employee was assumed to be female, with the appropriate contribution rate and life expectancy.

2. At the assumed retirement age, the accumulation was converted into a life annuity based on the Group Annuity Table, 1951, with a 4 percent interest assumption.

3. The annuity purchasable by the employee contribution was subtracted from the computed benefit.

4. The net amount was translated into a percentage of final salary. These findings are incorporated into several of the tables. They are summarized in Table 3.3.

Table 3.3 ◆ *Comparison Of Pension Benefits Of General Employees And Teachers, State And Local Government With Those of Employees Covered By Pension Plans In Private Industry, New York State, As Of January 1, 1972*

| Employee | | Final salary | Median Pension as Percentage of Final Salary | | | | Public employees' pensions, net of value of employee contributions |
| Age | Service | | Exclusive of primary Social Security | | Inclusive of primary Social Security | | |
			Public employees	Private employees	Public employees	Private employees	
65	20	$ 5,000	32.1%	22%	66.2%	62.1%	22.4%
		10,000	32.4	17	53.7	42.9	22.7
		14,000	32.4	17	46.3	35.5	22.7
	30	5,000	48.1	29	80.1	69.1	33.7
		10,000	48.6	24	67.6	49.9	34.1
		14,000	48.6	22	66.2	40.5	34.1

60 [a]	20	5,000	30.5	19	61.7	60.9	20.3
		10,000	31.7	14	51.9	42.3	22.2
		14,000	32.1	13	45.0	33.3	22.4
	30	5,000	47.2	28	77.3	69.9	32.0
		10,000	48.1	22	64.9	50.3	35.6
		14,000	48.1	20	59.9	40.3	35.6
55 [a]	20	5,000	22.8	13	61.1	56.0	15.1
		10,000	22.8	10	49.3	40.1	15.1
		14,000	23.9	10	40.7	31.5	15.7
	30	5,000	37.5	22	70.2	65.0	25.0
		10,000	36.5	17	59.2	47.1	15.0
		14,000	37.5	15	52.1	36.5	25.7

Source: For private industry: N.Y.S. Department of Labor, Division of Research and Statistics, *Benefits in Private Plans, New York State, 1971, Special Labor News Memorandum Number 148* (N.Y.S. Department of Labor, 1972). This was a survey of all pension plans covering approximately 1,000 workers or more in New York State as of January 1971.

For public employees: Survey by Twentieth Century Fund, as of January 1, 1972.

[a] Benefits shown only for plans paying benefits at the indicated age; the fact that some plans do not pay benefits at these ages is not reflected in the medians.

primary Social Security, the following percentages of their final salaries:

	Percentage replacement	
Final salary	*Public plans*	*Private plans*
$ 5,000	66%	68%
10,000	53	48
14,000	52	39

These figures are subject to important qualifications, including the difficulties of validly comparing the actual replacement ratios of flat-dollar private plans covering groups at different wage levels with percentage-of-pay public plans. (The higher flat-dollar private plans are not likely to be applicable to $5,000-a-year employees.) Nevertheless, they raise the possibility that some of the public plans may provide less in the way of *employer-financed* benefits for lower-paid employees than do private plans. It suggests, furthermore, that for the aggregate of public plans, the fact that benefits are substantially higher than under private plans is counter-balanced to a considerable extent by the much greater contributions of employees under most public plans. However, for at least the most significant wage and salary levels at retirement, the public plans provide greater benefits even after subtracting the value of employee contributions.

High and Low Levels in Public and Private Employment

Averages are useful as summaries, but the extremes—the high and low levels—are more pertinent, if the questions of public policy are to be well defined. The New York survey permits such a comparison between the public plans and those private plans which base benefits on earnings. Table 3.4 shows the results for employees who retire at 65 after thirty years of service if they last earned $5,000, $10,000, or $14,000.

On the low end, how many plans pay benefits of less than 25 percent of final pay to an employee earning $10,000? Only 5 percent of the public plans (six plans among those surveyed), in contrast to 37 percent of the private plans. With primary Social Security benefits added, benefits of less than 50 percent of final salary are paid to the hypothetical $10,000-a-year employee by 11 percent of the public plans and 29 percent of the private plans.

What about the high end? How many plans pay benefits equal to 60 percent or more of final pay to an employee earning $10,000? Ten percent of the public plans reach that level. None of the private plans surveyed in which benefits were based on salary paid as much (i.e., $500 a month) to the $10,000-a-year employee.

Combined benefits of 80 percent or more are provided to the $10,000-a-year employees by 15 percent of the public plans, which covered 26 percent of the employees. (See also Table 3.5.) By contrast, only 2 percent of the private plans reached that level of wage replacement.

If the comparison is made on the basis of the hypothetical employee whose final salary is $14,000, the contrast becomes more extreme, largely because the Social Security benefit is a lesser percentage of pay than it is for the $10,000-a-year employee. (See Table 3.6.) With primary Social Security, payments to such an employee of less than 50 percent of final pay are made by 17 percent of the public plans, but by 72 percent of the private plans.

For the low-wage employee earning $5,000 a year, Social Security benefits (as of January 1972) amounted to about 40 percent of pay. Added to system benefits, this produces high wage-replacement ratios in a large number of the public plans. (See Table 3.7.) Combined retirement income reaches 80 percent or more in 40 percent of the public plans. This was true of only about 16 percent of the private plans.

With primary Social Security, this low-paid employee reaches 90 percent or more of his or her final pay in 35 percent of the public plans; 5 percent of the plans provide at least 100 percent of final pay. (Table 3.7.)

Suppose one assumes that this low-wage employee is male and married, and suppose further that one takes account of his wife's Social Security benefits. Combined benefits total at least 100 percent of final pay in 40 percent of the public plans, which cover half the employees.

That picture is quite different, however, for better-paid employees; for example, for an employee with a final salary of $10,000. Even with the wife's Social Security benefits, 100 percent of final pay is possible in only five of the surveyed public systems, covering 4 percent of the employees. To maintain perspective, one should note

Table 3.4 ◆ **Extent To Which Public And Private Plans Pay Above Or Below Specified Levels In Relation To Final Salary, 1971–72, For An Employee Retiring At 65 After 30 Years Of Service**

Percentage of Plans Providing Pensions
Above and Below Specified Levels

Final Salary	State and local plans [a]		Private plans [b]	
	Without Social Security			
	Benefit level (percentage of final salary)	Percentage of plans	Benefit level (monthly amount)	Percentage of plans
$ 5,000	Plans paying less than 25%	9%	Plans paying less than $100	32%
10,000	Plans paying less than 25%	5	Plans paying less than $200	37
14,000	Plans paying less than 25%	4	Plans paying less than $300	43
5,000	Plans paying 60% or more	13	Plans paying more than $249	3
10,000	Plans paying 60% or more	10	Plans paying more than $500	0
14,000	Plans paying 60% or more	10	Plans paying more than $700	0

With Primary Social Security

5,000	Plans paying less than 50% 5	Plans paying less than $200 1	
10,000	Plans paying less than 50% 11	Plans paying less than $400 29	
14,000	Plans paying less than 50% 17	Plans paying less than $600 72	
5,000	Plans paying 80% or more 40	Plans paying more than $349 16	
10,000	Plans paying 80% or more 15	Plans paying more than $650 2	
14,000	Plans paying 80% or more 6	Plans paying more than $949 0	

[a] Twentieth Century Fund survey, plans as of January 1, 1972.
[b] N.Y.S. Department of Labor survey, all plans in which benefits are based on salary level, plans as of January 1, 1971.
Note: Dollar classifications of the New York State survey are the approximate equivalents of the percentage classifications of the Twentieth Century Fund survey.

Table 3.5 ◆ **Benefits, State And Local Systems: General Employees And Teachers At Age 65 With 30 Years Of Service, Final Salary Of $10,000**

Benefits as Percentage of Final Salary	Benefit		Benefit plus Primary Social Security		Benefit Net of Annuity Value of Member's Contributions	
	Systems	Employees	Systems	Employees	Systems	Employees
Less than 20%	3	24,900	—	—	13	333,500
20 – 24.9	3	89,600	—	—	18	964,700
25 – 29.9	10	364,200	—	—	21	884,600
30 – 34.9	15	412,800	—	—	27	1,491,100
35 – 39.9	13	1,052,600	—	—	18	1,200,000
40 – 44.9	14	513,600	2	16,900	12	1,020,000
45 – 49.9	23	1,335,700	12	196,000	8	216,300
50 – 54.9	13	464,700	18	728,500	2	17,500
55 – 59.9	20	2,248,900	18	1,027,500	4	790,000
60 – 64.9	9	378,300	19	1,198,700	3	242,000
65 – 69.9	3	145,400	17	639,800	1	14,000
70 – 74.9	1	142,000	17	1,400,300	—	—
75 – 79.9	—	—	5	100,400	—	—
80 – 84.9	—	—	12	1,500,000	—	—
85 – 89.9	—	—	4	158,200	—	—
90 – 94.9	—	—	2	193,400	—	—
95 – 99.9	—	—	1	14,000	—	—

Table 3.6 ◆ Benefits, State And Local Systems: General Employees And Teachers At Age 65 With 30 Years Of Service, Final Salary Of $14,000

Benefit as Percentage of Final Salary	Benefit		Benefit plus Primary Social Security		Benefit Net of Annuity Value of Member's Contributions	
	Systems	Employees	Systems	Employees	Systems	Employees
Less than 20%	3	24,000	—	—	13	333,500
20 – 24.9	2	61,000	—	—	15	847,300
25 – 29.9	9	369,500	2	16,900	24	926,800
30 – 34.9	12	401,900	1	8,000	27	1,566,300
35 – 39.9	20	1,098,500			18	1,189,000
40 – 44.9	12	479,100	6	243,200	13	1,050,000
45 – 49.9	24	1,365,700	13	285,800	6	129,900
50 – 54.9	11	446,300	25	810,300	2	72,800
55 – 59.9	22	1,930,200	27	1,973,500	5	802,100
60 – 64.9	6	634,500	18	640,900	3	242,000
65 – 69.9	5	220,000	13	1,137,400	1	14,000
70 – 74.9	1	142,000	5	390,800	—	—
75 – 79.9	—	—	10	910,300	—	—
80 – 84.9	—	—	5	675,200	—	—
85 – 89.9	—	—	2	81,400		

Table 3.7 ◆ Benefits, State And Local Systems: General Employees And Teachers At Age 65 With 30 Years Of Service, Final Salary Of $5,000

Benefits as Percentage of Final Salary	Benefit		Benefit plus Primary Social Security		Benefit Net of Annuity Value of Member's Contributions	
	Systems	Employees	Systems	Employees	Systems	Employees
Less than 20%	3	42,900	—	—	16	507,000
20 – 24.9	8	239,000	—	—	27	1,372,500
25 – 29.9	16	753,500	—	—	10	333,200
30 – 34.9	13	760,500	—	—	24	1,904,600
35 – 39.9	7	228,400	—	—	17	824,600
40 – 44.9	13	500,100	6	69,900	11	586,100
45 – 49.9	20	1,654,200	7	365,200	11	311,900
50 – 54.9	11	483,800	11	479,900	3	287,700
55 – 59.9	19	1,511,000	14	456,100	4	790,000
60 – 64.9	11	429,700	17	758,900	3	242,000
65 – 69.9	3	145,400	15	1,178,500	1	14,000
70 – 74.9	3	424,300	7	228,400	—	—
75 – 79.9	—	—	13	500,100	—	—
80 – 84.9	—	—	14	1,584,300	—	—
85 – 89.9	—	—	4	118,600	—	—
90 – 94.9	—	—	11	1,074,000	—	—
95 – 99.9	—	—	5	213,500	—	—
100 – 104.9	—	—	2	140,000	—	—
105 – 109.9	—	—	1	6,300	—	—
110 – 114.9	—	—			—	—

that retiring long-service public employees were no doubt closer in 1972 to averaging $10,000, than $5,000, a year.

Summary

To summarize, as of January 1, 1972:

Benefit levels of the public plans were, for the most typical employees, approximately double those prevailing in private-industry plans.

Public plans, with few exceptions, require employee contributions, while the private plans are largely non-contributory. In effect, for the aggregate of public plans, these contributions provide the margin for most of their superior benefit level. However, even after subtracting the value of employee contributions, the public plans provide an average level of benefits somewhat higher than those of private industry.

The average employee of state and local government who retires at sixty-five, after thirty years of service, receives a pension equal to 49 percent of his final year's salary.

Including primary Social Security benefit, the combination will provide from two-thirds to four-fifths of his final salary.

If a wife's Social Security is added, the combined retirement income ranges from 70 percent for someone retiring from a $14,000 salary to 100 percent for someone retiring from a $5,000 salary.

The most difficult questions of public policy are raised by retirement benefits that approach full pay.

For the employee retiring from a $10,000 job after thirty years of service, pension plus primary Social Security equals at least 80 percent of final pay in 15 percent of public plans covering over 25 percent of state and local employees.

Forty percent of the public plans, covering a majority of the employees, were set to provide a low-wage ($5,000) employee retiring at 65 after thirty years with a pension that, with Social Security, would replace at least 80 percent of his final earnings. If a wife's Social Security is added, replacement would come close to 100 percent of preretirement pay.

A relatively new question of policy is presented by the public plans which will provide full-career employees with total benefits, inclusive of Social Security, that reach or approach 100 percent replacement of salary. What dimensions that question is likely to assume is the focus of the next chapter.

APPENDIX

Methodology Used in Analyzing Pension Benefits as Replacement Ratios of Final Year's Salary

This method involves applying the terms of the plan to hypothetical individuals selected as representative. The cases chosen all involve long-term employees, with service ranging from twenty to thirty years. Only the plan's current service formula was used; different benefits for past service were disregarded.

If a system has more than one plan, only the plan covering the majority of employees was considered. If a system has companion Social Security coverage, it was counted for combined benefits, even though some members may not have elected Social Security coverage. If the system allows local unit option on Social Security coverage, the majority choice was used exclusively. Benefit variations for exceptional groups, such as public-safety employees, legislators, or judges, were ignored.

Social Security benefits are those payable as of January 1972. Subsequent increases and the present escalation provisions were ignored for these computations. Benefits based wholly or partly on money-purchase formulas were computed actuarially. The plan's rate of contributions for the money-purchase annuity was applied to the assumed salary history; interest earnings of 4 percent were accrued on the accumulation; and an annuity was calculated on the basis of the 1951 Group Annuity Table at 4 percent interest. In any given plan, a somewhat different set of assumptions is used by the system involved, with some difference in the results. However, those differences are not of sufficient magnitude, particularly when all of the plans are considered in the aggregate, to distort the survey results as fair representations of the benefit levels.

The technique used here is the same as that used by the U.S. Bureau of Labor Statistics, except that this analysis used round amounts of final salary (the amounts being relevant to 1972), whereas the B.L.S. has started with round amounts for the employee career-average salary, with consequently varying final salary amounts. For a study concentrating on the question of current replacement of final earnings, it seemed more appropriate to fix as assumed the final salary levels, and permit the career average to be the dependent variable.

The terminal salary figures represent the *last year* of employment, not the "final average salary" as defined by each plan. The average for the last five years is lower than the final salary by 7.4 percent, and the average for the last three years is lower than the final salary by 3.8 percent. Consequently, if a plan guarantees an employee with thirty years of service precisely 50 percent of his earnings in his last five or best five years, it is computed in this survey as paying only 46.3 percent of final pay (that is, 92.6 percent of 50 percent).

In computing Social Security amounts at age 65, it was assumed that an employee who retired before 65 went on to another job at which his salary was either the Social Security tax base or the salary from which he retired, whichever was lower. This assumption may not seem entirely realistic for someone retiring at sixty, who may not get another job, but since the Social Security Act allows up to five years of earnings to be disregarded in computing the average monthly wage, the assumption of undiminished Social Security at 65 is realistic, after all, for someone terminating his government employment at age 60.

4 ❖ Goals and Limits
for Retirement Income

As of late 1972 (following a 20 percent increase in Social Security benefits), about one-fifth of the state and local systems, covering about a quarter of the employees, will provide the $10,000-a-year employee who retires at 65 after thirty years of employment with a pension which, combined with primary Social Security benefits, will exceed 80 percent of his final year's pay (Table 4.1). If the Social Security benefit for a wife of age 65 is added, the 80 percent figure is exceeded under half the systems, covering more than two-thirds of the employees.

Net Income Before and After Retirement

The 80 percent level has special significance because at that point the retired employee of 65 is receiving at least as much net income as when he or she was working. In fact, for the unmarried employee or for the married employee earning $10,000 a year or more, that point is reached when retirement income equals 75 percent of gross pay.

That equation results from several factors:

1. Social Security benefits are exempt from federal and state income taxes.

2. The employee and his wife, if 65 or older, are entitled to double personal exemptions for income-tax purposes.

3. Since the public-employee pension is only a part of retirement income, the individual is in a lower tax bracket than he would be if the pension were his entire income.

Table 4.1 ◆ **State And Local Retirement Systems Providing Benefits Equal To 80 Percent Or More Of Final Year's Earnings To Employees Retiring At 65 With 30 Or More Years Of Service, September 1972**

	Systems		Employees Covered	
Final Salary	*Number*	*Percent of total*	*Number (millions)*	*Percent of total*
	With primary Social Security			
$ 5,000	57	45%	3.9	54%
10,000	24	19	2.0	27
14,000	13	10	1.3	18
	With primary and wife's Social Security			
$ 5,000	99	78	6.1	85
10,000	62	49	5.2	72
14,000	31	24	2.0	28

4. A portion of the retired employee's pension itself is not taxable, namely, that part attributable to his own contributions.

5. Several states exempt pensions paid by state and local government from state income taxes.

6. Social Security contributions cease.

7. Contributions to the retirement system cease.

A representative national picture is given in Table 4.2. The typical public employee with Social Security coverage, if 65 and single, would enjoy continuation of net income if his public-employee pension amounted to 30 to 57 percent of his final salary. The range is dependent on salary. For example, at the $10,000-a-year level, a pension of 41 percent of his final salary would suffice to continue full net income.

For the married man, the percentage required for continuance is slightly higher, because his income taxes before retirement were not as high as the single persons's. The percentages illustrated range from 34 percent at the $5,000 level to 61 percent at the $20,000 level. At the $10,000 salary level, 44 percent is required.

These figures ignore the wife's Social Security benefit. If her benefit is taken into account, on the basis of the reduced amount payable

Table 4.2 ◆ Retirement Benefits Required At Age 65 To Continue Pre-Retirement Net Income, As Of 1974

Item	Single Employee				Married Employee			
(1) Salary	$5,000	$10,000	$14,000	$20,000	$5,000	$10,000	$14,000	$20,000
(2) Federal income tax [a]	505	1,548	2,448	4,280	346	1,219	1,963	3,442
(3) State income tax [b]	54	244	420	720	34	195	370	670
(4) Social Security contribution [c]	292	585	772	772	292	585	772	772
(5) 5% system contribution [d]	250	500	700	1,000	250	500	700	1,000
(6) Net income [e]	3,899	7,123	9,660	13,228	4,078	7,501	10,195	14,116
(7) Net income as percentage of salary	78.0%	71.2%	69.0%	66.1%	81.6%	75.0%	72.8%	70.6%
(8) Social Security, primary insurance amount	2,293	3,254	3,295	3,295	2,293	3,254	3,295	3,295
(9) S. S. amount as percentage of salary	45.9%	32.5%	23.5%	16.5%	45.9%	32.5%	23.5%	16.5%
(10) Net required from system to continue net income [f]	1,606	3,869	6,365	9,933	1,785	4,247	6,900	10,821
(11) Pension required from system [g]	1,606	3,933	6,863	11,158	1,785	4,247	7,216	11,824
(12) Pension required as percentage of salary	32.1%	39.3%	49.0%	55.8%	35.7%	42.5%	51.5%	59.1%

(13) Wife's age 62 Social Security	—	—	—	955	1,356	1,373	1,373
(14) Pension required from system to continue net income, account taken of wife's Social Security	—	—	—	830	2,891	5,843	10,451
(15) Pension required as percentage of salary	—	—	—	16.6%	28.9%	41.7%	52.3%

a Computed on 1972 law with standard deduction of 15% of salary (but not more than $2,000) plus $1,300; personal exemption before 65 of $675, after 65 of $1,350.

b Computed on 1972 Virginia income-tax law, since it was close to median level for all states in 1972 (U.S. Advisory Commission on Intergovernmental Relations, State–Local Finances; Significant Features and Suggested Legislation, Report M-74 [Washington, D.C., 1972], p. 197). Exemption of $1,000; tax rate, 2% on first $3,000; 3% on next $2,000; 5% on excess. Exemption of state and local retirement benefits from income taxation by certain states ignored.

c As of 1974, 5.85% of first $13,200 of salary.

d Average rate of contribution as of January 1, 1972 for state and local systems with companion Social Security coverage.

e Salary less items (2) to (5).

f Item (6) less item (8).

g Computation includes federal and state taxation of system pension except for portion derived from the employee's contributions.

by Social Security at age 62, the amount required of a pension system to assure continuance of net income drops sharply (Table 4.2). At the $10,000 level, only 31 percent is required

The calculations to this point have not considered the fact that the employee who retires no longer has certain expenses incidental to working, such as transportation, lunches, union or association dues, and clothing expenses (the difference in style of dress related to work). Budget figures worked out by the Community Council of Greater New York involved these weekly allowances as of 1972.[1]

Lunches	$7.50
Transportation	6.00
Union or association dues	1.75
Clothing (difference between employed and unemployed	1.55
	$16.80

That amounts to 7.7 percent of a $10,000 annual income. Would this decline as a percentage if the salary were higher? That hardly seems likely. For someone earning, let us say, $20,000 a year, lunch undoubtedly cost more in 1974 than $1.50 a day in excess of what it would cost at home. Union or association dues may not be involved. On the other hand, extra cost for purchase and upkeep of clothing associated with the job would cost much more than $1.55 a week. It seems safe to assume that work-related expense accounted for a minimum of 7 percent of gross income.

Eliminating work-related expenses, the percentage of final salary required for a pension to replace net income would fall for the employee earning $10,000 a year by another seven points, dropping to 34 percent if single and 25 percent if married.

Retirement Income Sources and Goals

What is an appropriate goal for retirement income plans? Is there a standard of some objective validity? Are there outer limits?

For the first two or three decades of the Social Security program, it was customary to refer to retirement income as a matter of three tiers:

[1] The Community Council of Greater New York, *Annual Price Survey, Family Budget Costs* (New York, October 1971).

1. a floor of Social Security;
2. a supplement from pension plans; and
3. personal savings

If full continuance of income was visualized, it was only with very substantial reliance on the element of personal resources. Couper and Vaughn, referring in 1954 to the retirement income of a typical employee after fifteen to thirty years of service, inclusive of Social Security, suggested:

. . . total retirement income of approximately 50 percent of his final earnings, say 60 percent for low-income employees to about 40 percent for high-income employees. The fact that the majority of current plans do not achieve this objective does not detract from its validity as a desirable target. This standard may indeed derive from an unstated assumption that half a loaf is better than none. But it is based also on a conviction that much less would not be acceptable to employees and that much more might well be too burdensome to employers. A study in 1952 by E. C. McDonald of the Metropolitan Life Insurance Company revealed that 282 of 300 United States and Canadian corporations considered a pension equal to or better than 40 percent of compensation in the years immediately preceding retirement as a good workable arrangement which created no friction or resistance to retirement.[2]

Carson and McConnell summarized the approach implicit in most employer pension plans in 1956, with similar conclusions:

A benefit of 50 percent of average earnings of the last five or ten years, including the old-age and survivors insurance benefit, is considered an appropriate pension for a retired worker . . . [and] actually represents more than half of the employee's disposable income.[3]

McConnell revised the amounts in 1968 with respect to OASDI, private pensions, and personal savings:

This view of the three elements is reflected in the formulas used to determine the amount of private-pension benefits, since the private benefit is superimposed on the OASDI benefit to fulfill the popular formula which yields 65 percent of average wages for the low-income group scaled down-

[2] Walter J. Couper and Roger Vaughn, *Pension Planning—Experience and Trends* (New York, Industrial Relations Counselors, Inc., 1954), pp. 33–34.
[3] John J. Carson and John W. McConnell, *Economic Needs of Older People* (New York, Twentieth Century Fund, 1956), p. 299.

ward so that combined benefits will yield 50 to 35 percent for the various gradations of the high-income group.[4]

Indicative of the changing times, university professors found it appropriate over the course of a decade to raise their sights for institutional provisions of pensions. In 1957, a statement by the Joint Committee of the Association of American Colleges and the American Association of University Professors called for a retirement annuity, including Social Security, for a person who participates in a plan from age 30 to retirement "equivalent in purchasing power to approximately 50 percent of the average salary over the last ten years of service, if retirement is at 70, and a somewhat higher percentage if the fixed retirement age is younger." [5] Nine years later, the same group called for a contributory plan which, with Social Security, at an age such as 65, would provide a person who had thirty-five years of service with *two-thirds* of his yearly *disposable* income, after taxes and mandatory deductions, during the last few years before retirement, together with a continuance of 50 percent of that level for a surviving spouse.[6]

Personal Savings

The level of benefits now attained by most public employee plans raises the question as to whether personal savings are to counted on as part of projected retirement income. Savings are useful, but is there any compelling reason why policy decisions on Social Security and on pension plans should deliberately designate or carve out a specific sum, a segment of retirement income, which the individual is to provide out of personal savings?

The traditional individualistic approach is that a person ought to take care of himself, that there is no real need for collective provision of retirement income, that it is better to leave people independent to make their own spending-savings decisions. That view is now obsolete, essentially because of the uncertainty that characterizes the

[4] John W. McConnell, "Role of Public and Private Programs in Old Age Income Assurance," U.S. Joint Economic Committee, *Old Age Assurance, Part I,* 90th Congress, 1st sess. (Washington, D.C., U.S.G.P.O., 1968), p. 48.

[5] William C. Greenough and Frances P. King, *Retirement and Insurance Plans in American Colleges* (New York, Columbia University Press, 1959), p. 86.

[6] Greenough and King, *Retirement and Insurance Plans in American Colleges,* pp. 18–19.

economy. Technological change, the economic dislocation of areas, industries, and crafts, depressions and recessions, and continuing inflation at varying rates—each of these makes it unreasonable to expect a young man or woman to be able to make realistic decisions about how much to save for old age. The problem does not lie with the average level of income. If our society as a whole were less affluent, but each family had a secure, unchanging economic position that it occupied through generations, an individual could be expected to rely on personal or family arrangements for old-age security. However, rapid and unceasing change and the uncertainties of a working lifetime make individual planning for security essentially unrealistic. Economic security now depends on social or collective arrangements.

The depression of the 1930s set in motion the forces that produced both Social Security and the pension plan avalanche of the 1950s. The private pension plans that were established in the early 1950s responded essentially to the pressing needs of the workers in their sixties—who had been in their forties during the Great Depression. The years when these workers might have expected peak earnings had instead wiped out their savings. Neither good husbandry nor prudent management of resources made a difference. That twenty-year period made obsolete the idea that every individual could provide for his financial security in old age through lifetime savings.

When still more change is made by the introduction of social insurance and pension plans and by their repeated revision, the future becomes even more unpredictable and the idea of depending on lifelong individual husbandry of resources becomes even more unrealistic. For a young man (or woman) to determine how much to save for old age, he must know how much Social Security benefits will be at retirement, what sort of job he will have most of his life, what sort of pension plan the employer or union will have established, and how that might change for better or for worse by the time he is in his sixties. That is too much to expect. Nor is it essential that individuals be fully conscious of this long-range uncertainty. Modern conditions have developed an attitude, a style of spending, a set of relative values. And those styles have become standard. A large part of our society spends its current income relying on the prospect of Social Security and perhaps pension payments, and this reliance has an effect on everyone's way of life. A lifetime savings plan has become an outdated notion—even to those who are most insecure and unable to depend on any of the collective sources of future income.

In short, constant social change creates uncertainty for the individual; that uncertainty forces him to rely on social or collective arrangements for old-age security. In the light of all this, it has become impossible to lay down a rule that a specific portion of retirement income must be derived from personal savings. Individual savings are, of course, always useful. Savings allow leeway for personal preference, whether for immediate spending, future purchasing power, or building a legacy. They provide a means for meeting emergencies, or other situations that may seem more pressing than the need for ultimate retirement income. None of these benefits, however, *dictates* a conclusion that half, a third, or even a tenth, of retirement income must or should be expected to be provided by personal savings.

Moreover, if a significant segment of the population (such as some public employees) has achieved, through collective arrangements, continuance of net income after a specified term of work, it becomes more difficult to insist that the same goal is improper for others.

That is not to say that continuance of full net income is the appropriate goal for every public-employee retirement system. If there is no basic principle that proscribes full continuance, neither is there one that commands it. Rather, there is a wide area for different policies, each of which may be reasonable.

In considering which policies should be adopted regarding various benefit levels, a number of factors are relevant.

Prevailing Practice as a Standard

The fact that a given public system provides benefits higher than those prevailing in private industry is important to a public that is trying to weigh the equities, but it is by no means a conclusive or overriding standard. Certainly, some voters will ask why they should pay for better pensions than they themselves enjoy. A dramatic imbalance may be an irritant that generates a negative public attitude. On the other hand, the public is obviously willing to accept a wide margin of individual differences. Half the employees in the private sector have no pension coverage at all, yet they do not disapprove of pensions for public employees. In 1971, a substantial increase in a fairly liberal pension plan was voted for the Los Angeles police by a referendum that carried in black wards where pension coverage is relatively slight but sympathy for workers is high, even while it failed in some wealthy or middle-class districts. Most public systems provide permanent automatic cost-of-living adjustments, while they have been almost nonexistent among private plans. And the public probably approves of such provisions for government employees.

Clearly, the average voter does not insist on cutting everyone down to the level of his own benefits; he is willing to approve what he considers fair and desirable. In short, comparison with prevailing practice in industry is certainly relevant but it is by no means a determining factor.

Pensions vs. Salaries

Public employees have often defended the propriety of their higher pensions on the grounds that their pay is relatively low; consequently, the reasoning goes, they cannot be expected to save, and their pensions simply make up for their comparatively low current compensation. At times that argument has been persuasive; however, making up for low salaries through exceptionally high pensions is a questionable practice. For example, it may be bad policy in terms of the pension-pay relationship needed to manage and retain a work force. It could lead to additional difficulties if government salaries are later raised to the level of private industry.

A broad assumption that public-employee salaries are lower, always and everywhere, than those for corresponding jobs in private industry is not warranted. Occupational wage surveys by the United States Bureau of Labor Statistics in 1970 and early 1971 in nine major cities (Atlanta, Boston, Chicago, Kansas City, Los Angeles, Newark, New Orleans, New York, and Philadelphia) found that in seven of the nine municipalities, public-employee salaries were higher than those of private industry.[7]

Private wage-and-salary levels outstripped the public levels during

[7] United States Department of Labor, Bureau of Labor Statistics, *Wages and Benefits of Municipal Government Workers in the City of Newark, Middle Atlantic Regional Office, Number 24* (New York, November 1971).

World War II and its aftermath, but public employee pay has since recovered a margin of superiority. The turnaround came in 1967. The ratio of average earnings in state and local government to average earnings in all private industry has been as follows: [8]

1929	1.08
1939	1.18
1949	.95
1959	.94
1966	.98
1967	1.01
1971	1.15

Pensions and Personnel Management

If a pension induces employees to stay beyond the age when they are suitable for the job, then it is counterproductive for both the government-as-employer and for society itself. It is a poor utilization of human resources. For example, if a retirement plan helps to produce a police force or a fire department with an average age of 53, it is not good for the performance of the police or fire department. Similarly, if a retirement plan provides a strong incentive for a competent executive, technician, or skilled craftsman to leave his job at 55, when he may be functioning at a high level of efficiency, in order to take a position outside the government, it likewise represents poor management and inefficiency.

In short, considerations of effective management establish parameters for pension plans. For example, there should be a "normal retirement" age at which the level of benefits encourages retirement. For earlier ages, the level of benefits should represent a balance between making retirement possible and leaving sufficient incentive for remaining on the job. There should probably be a compulsory retirement age, perhaps with limited extensions for individuals. A pension should be provided for long-term or permanent disability. The disability pension should be high enough to provide a viable alternative to keeping a permanently disabled person on the payroll, yet not so high, whether by itself or in combination with other benefits, as to remove incentive for work.

[8] United States Department of Commerce, *Surveys of Current Business,* various issues, Washington, D.C.

These requirements or standards have nothing to do with prevailing practices or the evaluation of cost vis-à-vis other public needs. They are dictated by the objectives of the most effective performance of government functions.

Rate of Change

In changing a retirement plan, a relevant question is: how much change? It is possible to replace a wholly inadequate retirement plan, at one fell swoop, with an ideal plan. But that could also be a mistake. The impact of cost might be so steep that it produces a sharp reaction. A sudden increase in benefits might establish a precedent, building up hopes for similar increases in the future. In short, the rate of change is itself a factor that must be taken into account by decision-makers.

In summary, there are a number of considerations affecting the provisions of a retirement system for public employees, and they vary from system to system and perhaps from time to time. There are also limits to what a system should provide. Continuance of full net income appears to be a reasonable limit.

The 100 Percent Continuance Limit

It seems reasonable to say that the goal for retirement income should not exceed full continuance of net income for the retiring career employee. Three reasons can be advanced:

1. There does not, in general, appear to be any reason why the public should direct more income to a man when retired than he had when working full-time.

2. To provide an increase in net income upon retirement may seriously interfere with the productivity of society as a whole by making retirement too attractive at ages when continued employment would be socially desirable. If, for example, we assume that 65 is the normal and appropriate age for retirement, an arrangement that makes more than 100 percent of net preretirement income available may seriously weaken work incentives at 62 or 60 or perhaps even earlier. The pension at 60 or 62 may by itself be adequate for retirement; in many cases, any amount lacking could be made up from personal resources.

3. To be provided more net income after retirement than before

is so far beyond the lot of most workers in the private sector that it is asking too much of those who must pay the employer share of cost for the public employee retirement system. Although this seems like the argument of prevailing practice, it differs significantly from that position. If workers in private industry who are covered by pension plans can expect, after long service, 40 to 60 percent of final pay, they may readily tolerate payments to their counterparts in public employment of 50 to 75 percent of final pay. There is no sharp line that represents a threshold of grievance; there is no dramatic gulf. The situation is likely to be entirely different, however, if taxpayers recognize that the payments being made at their expense represent more net income than the public employee received in his last year of employment.

On the other hand, it should be recognized that continuance of full net income does not completely assure economic security. Two contingencies may not be provided for—inflation and the income needs of a dependent spouse who survives the employee.

When an employee retires, he abandons the bargaining power implicit in his labor. If there is serious inflation while he is employed, he can count on increases, resulting from bargaining or from the employer's need to retain staff or to keep pay levels in line. Failing all else, the worker can change jobs. However, if he is retired, he has no recourse other than to cajole, plead with, or pressure his public officials.

Over the period of retirement, inflation, even at a moderate rate, can have a devastating effect on purchasing power. One-half of those retiring at age 65 will still be living fifteen years (men) or eighteen years (women) after retirement. In that time, the purchasing power of a fixed-dollar pension that began at 65 will be reduced by 25 to 30 percent if the cost of living has advanced by as little as 2 percent a year, and it will be reduced by 40 to 50 percent if the cost of living has advanced by 3.5 percent.

A retiring employee may have much greater security on a lesser pension *with* a cost-of-living adjustment than on a higher pension *without* one. In relation to a fixed pension of $100 a month, a man of 65 will realize a greater lifetime income on a lesser pension if it is protected by an annual adjustment to the cost of living. The following figures are pertinent:

If the annual rate of inflation is:	The following pension amount, adjusted for the cost of living, will provide greater lifetime income than an unchanging $100 a month
2.0%	$80
3.5	65
5.0	58
10.0	32

For a woman, these figures for lifetime equivalence are even lower.[9]

The other problem is that of a surviving dependent spouse (normally the wife). The couple may have lived largely or entirely on his salary. If he dies, what does she live on? Social Security provides a widow's benefit equal to the full primary insurance amount, but that may not be enough. The retirement system may provide a survivor's annuity either at system expense or as an option at the expense of the retired employee. If it is at the employee's expense, he buys security for his wife only by reducing his retirement income while they are both alive.

If a system provides no protection against an increasing cost of living or no benefit for a surviving spouse, more net income in retirement than while working may represent no more than a margin for buffering these two contingencies.

However, it is better, if possible, for each to be provided for separately. The employee who will receive a higher net income by retiring than by working is likely to act on that immediate fact, without trying to determine what his position or that of his spouse will be some years later. The more-than-full-pay retirement income is vulnerable to public resentment, which will not be overcome by arguments about the future cost of living or the needs of a surviving spouse. Moreover, an overly generous pension favors the unmarried employee who has no need to lay aside income for a dependent spouse. Taking all these factors into consideration and without denying the real problems of inflation or of income for a surviving spouse, it seems appropriate to consider continuance of net income as a reasonable outside limit.

[9] These figures are based on total payments, without adjustment for investment yield on a hypothetical savings margin in the early years of the $100 payment.

Social Security Benefits

Perhaps we ought to reexamine our assumption that it is appropriate to measure retirement income in terms of the combination of Social Security and system benefits. That simple proposition is frequently challenged, but it is difficult to see what is wrong with it. The employee will get both. They both determine his income. They both influence his willingness to retire at one age or another. They both determine the adequacy of his wage replacement during disability and how his survivors are to be provided for. Both represent significant costs to the public and the employer. In fact, the public employer was asked to decide whether to join the Social Security system or not; private employers were compelled to join. Social Security is therefore as much a part of what state and local governments provide for their employees as their separate retirement systems are.

Age 65 with Thirty Years of Service

We have used, as a point of focus, retirement at 65 and a full career of thirty years. Why 65? Why thirty?

Neither standard is inevitable, but they are both reasonable and probably more so than any alternative. Sixty-five is the normal retirement age of the Social Security system and of most pension plans, public and private. It is still the age around which most voluntary retirements cluster. (This relates to the usual type of work. Different sets of standards should be expected for unusual positions, e.g., policemen or firemen.)

What would be an alternative standard? For example, can it be argued that a retirement program is acceptable because it provides 85 percent of net income at 62 and that its provision of 105 percent of net income at 65 is merely incidental to "postponed" or "postnormal" retirement? That is plausible, but it requires acceptance of 62 as the age when the typical employee should be expected to retire. That may or may not become the norm. Moreover, if it did become the norm, it would be questionable whether higher amounts ought to be provided for later retirement.

Furthermore, if benefits are excessive at 65, they may undermine work incentive several years earlier. A worker may be in a position to quit at 62 on 90 percent of his net income or stay until he is 65 and get 100 percent of his net income. It may not seem worthwhile to work for three years for 10 percent of net income plus an 11 percent addition to the pension.

Most fundamental is the fact that if age 62 were accepted as the norm, the basic problem of coping with Social Security benefits would still remain. Many of the public systems provide unreduced benefits at age 60, some even at 55. Social Security pays a benefit at 62 that is only 20 percent lower than at 65. Consequently, some systems are already providing greater net income for age 62 retirement than for working at that age. Although age 62 retirement is still less common than 65, one cannot assume that what we can now visualize as a problem for age 65 retirement will not also be a problem for age 62 retirement.

Why thirty years of employment? A full working life is a little over forty years.[10] Norms of thirty-five and forty were in fact used as the basis for establishing many of the early pension formulas. If pension plans were universal for all employment and if they granted vested benefit rights for all periods of employment, it would indeed be appropriate to use forty years as the norm. However, the actual situation is quite different. The early years are a time of turnover, trial-and-error, and relatively short-term employment, and few workers remain with one employer for forty years.

In the absence of universal pension coverage and of full and immediate vesting, it is appropriate for an employer that has employed someone for thirty years to assume responsibility for assuring him retirement income, without relying on pension accruals from another plan, other than Social Security.

To use fewer years as the norm may pose some difficulties. To reach a maximum in twenty or twenty-five years will often mean that there is no incentive by way of additional pension accrual for further employment. Also, a person who has worked for twenty or twenty-five years for one employer may have accumulated, or may still accumulate, pension rights with another employer. Fullest benefits after twenty or twenty-five years would mean that the man or

---

[10] Howard N. Fullerton, "A New Type of Working Life Table for Men," *Monthly Labor Review*, July, 1972, United States Department of Labor, Bureau of Labor Statistics, Washington, D.C., p. 21. Working-life expectancy at age bracket 20–25 for a person born in 1950 is 41.1 years.

woman who divides most of his working life between two jobs will ultimately have substantially greater retirement income in combination than the man or woman who stays with one job. Theoretically, this could also happen with thirty years, but under present practical circumstances it is quite unlikely. The norm of thirty therefore seems reasonable.

Present Plans and Outside Limits

That many public employees will be retiring with more net income than while they were working will probably come as a shock, not merely to the general reader, but to most public employees as well. Why?

First of all, a large proportion of the employees of state and local government have not worked as long as thirty years at age 65. In contrast to private industry, state and local governments hire large numbers of employees when they are in their forties, fifties, and even sixties. Civil service lists tend to eliminate age discrimination. Moreover, state and local government often represent the employer of last resort. If an employee retires after ten to twenty years of employment, he is of course far away from full continuance of his net income.

This is an aspect worth dwelling upon. About half of the employees in private industry are not covered by pension plans at all. Moreover, a great deal of attention has been directed in recent years to the fact that many of the workers covered by private plans do not acquire retirement benefits because they leave or lose employment before retirement age, without vested rights to deferred benefits. Public employment has undoubtedly picked up more than its proportionate share of these dispossessed or disadvantaged workers and has provided them with pensions more liberal, in relation to their remaining years of employment, than is provided by industry.

A second reason is that under many plans, years of past service earns less pension credit than do years of current service. In general, it is those who will retire in the future who will secure "full-continuance" levels.

A third, and perhaps the most important reason is that the employees and, to a large extent, the public, have isolated Social Security and pensions into separate mental compartments. Social Security has been thought of as a minimum program, provided by the federal government, and half-financed by employee contributions. What the state, city, or county should provide, as employer, has been thought of as something entirely separate. Even to measure the two in combination has often been rejected as inappropriate, yet it is inevitable that the two be considered together.

5 ❖ Social Security and the Need for Reform

The Social Security amendments of 1972 introduced automatic escalation of the wage base and of benefits. The wage basis—for contributions and benefit computations—will rise with the average wage covered by Social Security. The entire benefit formula will increase with the Consumer Price Index.

Sooner or later the combination of future Social Security and public-employee pensions will force radical revision of the retirement laws for public employees. The dynamics of the Social Security system itself will make that revision necessary.

The overwhelming majority of state and local employees are covered by both a staff plan and Social Security. The staff plan is enacted by the state, or sometimes local, government. Once adopted, it cannot, for constitutional or practical reasons, be decreased, except perhaps for new employees. Social Security, on the other hand, is enacted by Congress. It is not adopted for public employees alone; it is shaped to the overall needs of the country. Public employees therefore receive their retirement income from two independent sources: the federal government and the state or local government. The provisions of each are determined by independent legislatures, each responding to its own constituency and making commitments from which future retreat is difficult if not impossible.

The problem would not be pressing if Social Security were stationary, but it is not. Consequently, whatever a state or local system provides, if it is wholly independent of Social Security, is bound to result, in combination with future Social Security benefits, in something quite different from what state or local government now assumes or intends.

The 1972 amendments made this basic problem more visible, but the same ultimate result was predictable earlier. This point was made in 1963 in a review of New York City's retirement system: [1]

The need for a new system becomes overwhelmingly obvious when future developments are considered. The City participates in the Social Security system. Social Security benefits have increased vastly in the past 25 years. Now the present retirement benefits are entirely independent of Social Security, except where a member has reduced his annuity by diverting contributions from the retirement system to Social Security. Consequently, if the present systems were improved and made adequate now, they would inevitably become excessive in the future as Social Security changed. What the City provides for a new employee in 1963, it must be prepared to live with in the year 2003, when this employee may still be working, and in the year 2023 when he may still be drawing benefits. It is clear that one cannot fix an adequate retirement structure now without consideration of Social Security and expect it to make sense 10 years from now, much less 40 to 60 years from now.

Social Security in the Future

Under the cost-of-living escalation, in any year in which it is found that the federal Consumer Price Index has increased by at least 3 percent since the last benefit adjustment, benefits will be increased proportionately. The increase will apply not only to the benefit amounts then being paid to retired employees, but also to the entire benefit schedule. The monthly amount payable for a particular monthly average wage will be increased by the percentage change in the Consumer Price Index.

The wage base for 1974 was increased to $13,200, which was estimated to include the full wages and salaries of at least 85 percent of the covered employees. Thereafter, any time there is an upward shift in the benefit schedule, the wage base will be extended in proportion to the percentage change in national wage levels, since the last adjustment, as measured by the average Social Security wage.

Before an increase is made effective, the escalation procedure calls for a report to Congress—where it may be stopped, modified, or re-

[1] Martin E. Segal Company, Inc., *The Retirement Systems of the City of New York: Part Five, The Benefit Structure* (New York, 1963), p. 9.

placed by another form of adjustment. However, if Congress does not intervene, the escalation is automatic.

Projections of future benefits are startling, at least at first exposure. Assume that a person starts working in 1975 and retires forty years later, at age 65 in the year 2015. Assume that throughout he earns the maximum taxable wage ($13,200, as of 1974). Assume further that his earnings and the national average wage increase by 5 percent a year and that the cost of living goes up by 3 percent a year. When he retires, his Social Security benefit will amount to $33,200 a year.[2] If he has a wife, sixty-five or older, their combined Social Security will approach $50,000 a year.

However, this man's final salary will be $98,000 a year. Consequently, his Social Security will replace no more than 36 percent of his final earnings. The absolute magnitudes are startling only because of 5 percent annual increases, continued for forty years. It is not, after all, essentially different from what has happened over the past thirty to forty years.

The 36 percent replacement ratio is a figure we can readily accept as reasonable. It is appreciably higher than the 30 to 33 percent replacement ratio which Social Security has historically provided for workers at the maximum taxable wage. Moreover, the projection of 36 percent may be an overstatement. It is based on the assumption that the worker's wage increased over his work-life no faster than the national average. It is more likely that the worker enjoyed some progression—probably 0.5 to 1.0 percentage points faster, each year, than the increase in the national average. If this is taken into account, the 36 percent replacement ratio is reduced to approximately 28 to 32 percent, rather close, in short, to the traditional amount.[3]

For workers with lower earnings, the wage-replacement ratio will be higher. Assume that a worker always earns the *median* taxable wage ($7,681 in 1974). For the next twenty-five years, the primary Social Security benefit will replace 43 to 46 percent of his final earn-

[2] U.S. Social Security Administration, Office of the Actuary, *Actuarial Note Number 86*, 1974.

[3] In addition, the 36 percent ratio is higher than is projected for workers retiring in the next twenty-five years. In that period, for those who earn the maximum taxable wage, the primary Social Security is projected (on the 5 percent–3 percent assumptions) to range from 29 to 34 percent.

The estimates based on individual wage progressions exceeding the national average are derived from special projections furnished by the Social Security actuary.

ings; by 2015 it will rise to 48 percent.[4] If we adjust for individual wage progression greater than the national average by 0.5 to 1.0 percent annually, the replacement ratio will be about 35 to 42 percent by 2015. With a wife's benefit, that will amount to 56 to 63 percent.

For a worker with low earnings—$3,654 in 1975 and increasing with the national average at 5 percent a year—the replacement ratio will rise from 48 percent in the immediate future to 72 percent in 2015.[5] A figure of $5,000 a year is probably more realistic for a full-time low-wage public employee in 1974. At this level, and allowing for individual wage progression greater than the national average, the primary Social Security will replace from 50 to 60 percent of final earnings by 2015. With a wife of 65, these ratios will be 50 percent higher—that is, 75 to 90 percent.

These replacement ratios raise questions about whether a significant margin will remain for supplementation by staff pension plans. Even more crucial, however, is the *range* of possible replacement ratios under the Social Security law.

The 1972 amendments, including escalation of benefits and the contribution schedule, were based on actuarial estimates that projected annual wage increases of 5 percent and cost of living increases of 2.75 percent. These assumptions were based on experience over the preceding twenty years. However, in recent years, the rate of inflation has been greater. The figures quoted earlier were projected on 3 percent, instead of 2.75 percent, cost-of-living increases. That is, however, a modest change. The benefit escalation is sensitive to the rates of change in wages and living costs. What happens to the replacement ratios if these rates are moderately different from the central assumptions which have been made? The figures in Table 5.1 provide the answer.

If the cost of living increases by 4 percent a year and wages by 5 percent, primary Social Security will soon replace 50 percent, and in about forty years 70 percent, of the final earnings of the median worker. If a wife's benefit is added, replacement will approximate full wages. For a worker with less than median earnings, the primary benefit alone will exceed the wage. The worker earning maximum

[4] Social Security Department, Office of the Actuary.
[5] *Ibid.*

Table 5.1 ◆ Primary Social Security As Replacement Ratio Of Final Year's Earnings: Retirement At 65 In Selected Years

Year	Level of Earnings [a]	Assumed Annual Increases in Earnings and in Consumer Price Index						
		5.00–4.00%	4.00–3.00%	6.00–4.00%	5.00–3.00%	4.00–2.00%	6.00–3.00%	5.00–2.00%
1985	Low	.64	.62	.59	.58	.56	.54	.52
	Median	.50	.49	.47	.45	.44	.42	.41
	Maximum taxable	.37	.36	.34	.33	.33	.30	.30
1995	Low	.72	.67	.63	.59	.55	.51	.48
	Median	.55	.52	.47	.45	.43	.39	.37
	Maximum taxable	.40	.38	.34	.33	.31	.28	.27
2005	Low	.93	.80	.76	.69	.60	.57	.51
	Median	.63	.57	.51	.47	.43	.38	.35
	Maximum taxable	.46	.43	.37	.35	.32	.28	.26
2015	Low	1.06	.93	.83	.71	.63	.56	.48
	Median	.70	.62	.55	.48	.42	.38	.33
	Maximum taxable	.50	.46	.40	.36	.32	.29	.25
2025	Low	1.21	1.02	.89	.74	.62	.56	.46
	Median	.77	.67	.58	.50	.42	.38	.32
	Maximum taxable	.54	.48	.41	.36	.32	.29	.25

Source: U.S. Social Security Administration, Office of the Actuary, *Actuarial Note Number 86*, 1974.
[a] Low = $3,654 in 1974; median = $7,681 in 1974; maximum = $13,200 in 1974.

taxable wages will find that the replacement ratio rises from a present level of 30 percent to 50 percent; or to 75 percent, with the addition of a wife's full benefit.

The future replacement ratios are most sensitive to the rate of change in real wages, that is, the difference between the rate of wage increase and the rate of increase in the Consumer Price Index. It is secondarily sensitive to the level of annual increase in the C.P.I.

If real wages increase by less than 1 percent a year, or if the rate is maintained at 1 percent, but the cost of living goes up more than 4 percent a year, as it has in recent years, then Social Security replacement ratios will be even higher.

The basic problem is whether a goal for retirement income—*any* defined goal—can be fulfilled if provisions of a staff plan are fixed without taking Social Security into account. Suppose one were arbitrarily to choose 100 percent replacement of wages at 65 for the employee who has completed a full career, whether that is understood to mean twenty-five, thirty or thirty-five years of employment. Assume that the wife's Social Security benefit is disregarded. If one could be certain that the cost of living will increase by no more than 3 percent a year and wages will go up by 5 percent and that the Social Security Law will not be significantly amended for the next forty years, then a formula yielding 50–55 percent of final pay for the career worker would just about fulfill the goal of 100 percent replacement. Suppose then that such a formula is fixed and cannot be reduced for someone who is already hired but who will not reach 65 for another forty years. If the cost of living goes up by 4 percent, instead of the assumed 3 percent, that career employee will retire with 120 to 125 percent of final earnings; the plan will have overshot its goal by 20 to 25 percent.

One may anticipate that if the more extreme levels begin to develop, Congress will intervene to stop the process or to modify the formula. As noted, the Social Security Law includes a pause between the time the Social Security Administrator finds that an automatic adjustment is called for and the time it is effective, precisely in order to allow Congress to intervene if it so wishes. Can one predict with confidence whether, when, and how a future Congress will modify the results of escalation?

The Advisory Council on Social Security recommended in March

1975 that the escalation formula be changed to assure better control over the wage-replacement ratio. It called attention to the fact that the formula then in effect compounded benefit increases due to cost-of-living changes with increases based on higher wages and an escalated wage base and was likely to produce over the years vast changes, up or down, in the wage-replacement ratio. The Council suggested a "decoupling" by which the benefit formula would update wages in accordance with a general wage index and cost-of-living adjustments would apply only to those who had retired, not to the entire formula.[6]

Whether this sort of change or any other is made does not however eliminate the basic problem. Is there a predictable level at which the nation will hold Social Security? It is not possible to answer that question in the affirmative. The fundamental fact is that half of the employees in industry have no pension coverage at all and the progress in covering them has been so slow in recent years as to give no real hope that they will indeed be covered by voluntary plans. These workers depend almost entirely on Social Security. It will not be possible for Congress to cut back on Social Security to avoid excess in combination with existing pension plans, without imposing hardship on the non-covered half. Consequently, it is impossible to make any confident assumptions as to future levels of Social Security benefits.

Whether 100 percent replacement is the appropriate goal is actually somewhat beside the point. The essential problem is that *whatever* the goal may be in terms of retirement income, it cannot be fulfilled with any degree of confidence by a staff plan that is fixed without taking account of Social Security and its future dynamics or variability.

The same problem will face pension plans in industry. The issue is confronted sooner in the public sector because the benefits are higher.

Alternative Approaches to the Solution

In seeking solutions to the problem of an undirected combination of Social Security and public employee pensions, three alternative

[6] Advisory Council on Social Security, *Reports,* Washington, D.C., 1975.

approaches are possible. One is to reconsider Social Security for public employees. Should they ever have been part of the program? If they are not now, should they be? Should those now in the program remain in it? Should the application of the Social Security Act to public employees be changed? These questions will be considered in the next chapter.

A second approach is to modify Social Security to take into account the terms of the public staff systems. The third is to modify the public systems to take account of Social Security. These approaches will be explored in chapter 7.

6 ✤ The Merits of
Social Security Coverage

Social Security for public employees has been the subject of debate ever since the inception of the system in 1935. During the first fifteen years of the national system's existence, public employees were excluded from coverage; whether to admit them was debated. In 1951, they were given the option of joining on a restricted basis. By 1972, some 30 percent of all state and local employees had chosen to reject Social Security coverage, but the option is still open, and for many the problem is not yet resolved. In some jurisdictions, California, for example, the issue is constantly alive, and withdrawal from Social Security has been a lively issue.

The Growth of Social Security Coverage

When Social Security [1] first opened its rolls to public employees, it did so only for those employees not covered by state or local pension plans. In 1951 a state could elect Social Security coverage for all its employees or for all employees of some political subdivision or public corporation if those employees were not otherwise covered by a pension plan. The "not-otherwise-covered" provision was by-passed in eight states by a legal subterfuge: the existing law providing a public employee pension plan was repealed; Social Security coverage was elected; a new public employee pension plan was adopted. The

---

[1] To speak more precisely, that part of the Social Security program now known as Old-Age, Survivors, Disability, and Health Insurance (OASDHI), known earlier by shorter titles.

result: in these states employees now had both Social Security and a state pension.

Social Security was amended, effective January 1, 1955, to make coverage possible for public employees without subterfuge, that is, even if they were also covered by a state plan. The choice was up to the state, subject to the approval of a majority of the members of the system. If coverage was elected, *all* employees in the coverage group were included in Social Security, making it an "all-or-none" proposition. However, policemen and firemen covered by a public plan remained excluded and could not be brought into any part of the federal program.

A 1956 amendment made entry even easier. For specified states, employees who wished Social Security coverage could have it; those who did not were omitted. However, employees hired after the initial decision had to be covered. Originally applicable to nine specific states, this arrangement was eventually extended to a total of twenty states.[2] Limited coverage was also extended to policemen and firemen. Policemen can be covered by Social Security in nineteen states named in the statute [3] as well as Puerto Rico, but only if approved by a referendum of the uniformed group chosen by the state as appropriate. Firemen may be covered in any of the nineteen states on an all-or-none basis, subject to majority approval. In the other thirty-one states the state government must certify that the overall benefit protection for firemen will be improved if Social Security is added.

By 1961, about 60 percent of state and local government employees were covered by Social Security (see Table 6.1 and Chart 6.1).

Public employees entering Social Security as a group can receive as much as five years of prior service credit if the back contributions are paid. This retroactivity is significant in determining how soon the employees become insured for Social Security benefits. It is possible for a 65-year-old public employee to retire and then receive

[2] Alaska, California, Connecticut, Florida, Georgia, Hawaii, Illinois, Massachusetts, Minnesota, Nevada, New Mexico, New York, North Dakota, Pennsylvania, Rhode Island, Tennessee, Texas, Vermont, Washington, and Wisconsin.

[3] Alabama, California, Florida, Georgia, Hawaii, Kansas, Maine, Maryland, New York, North Carolina, North Dakota, Oregon, Puerto Rico, South Carolina, South Dakota, Tennessee, Texas, Vermont, Virginia, and Washington.

Table 6.1 ◆ Social Security Coverage: State And Local Government Employees, January 1951–March 1969 [a] (Numbers In Millions)

Employee Category	1951		1956		1961		1966		1969	
	No.	Pct.	No.	Pct.	No.	Pct.	No.	Pct.	No.	Pct.
Total employees	3.6	100%	5.0	100%	6.3	100%	8.3	100%	9.5	100%
Social Security	0.4	11	1.4	28	3.8	60	5.5	67	6.5	69
Social Security plus staff plan	—	—	n.a.	—	2.7	42	4.1	49	4.9	52
State employees	n.a.	—	1.3	100	1.6	100	2.1	100	2.6	100
Social Security	n.a.	100	0.4	34	1.1	68	1.5	71	1.9	73
Social Security plus staff plan	0.1	—	n.a.	—	0.9	55	1.3	62	1.6	63
County employees	n.a.	—	0.6	100	0.7	100	1.3	62	1.6	63
Social Security	n.a.	—	0.3	49	0.6	83	1.0	100	1.2	100
Social Security plus staff plan	0.1	—	n.a.	—	0.3	47	0.9	83	1.0	86
Other local employees	n.a.	—	3.2	100	0.3	47	0.6	55	0.7	57
Social Security	n.a.	—	.7	22	4.0	100	5.1	100	5.7	100
Social Security plus staff plan	0.2	—	n.a.	—	2.1	53	3.1	61	3.6	64
					1.4	36	2.2	43	2.6	46

Source: For period 1956–64: U.S. Social Security Administration, *State and Local Government under Old-Age Survivors Disability and Health Insurance, 1956–1965* (S.S.A., 1966). For period 1964–68, U.S. Social Security Administration, *State and Local Government Employment Statistics, 1964–1968* (S.S.A., 1970).

[a] Excludes Puerto Rico and Virgin Islands. Percentages approximate; data not for precisely the same periods.

Note: These coverage figures are at variance with those reported by the Census Bureau in its quinquennial survey, *Employee-Retirement Systems of State and Local Governments.* However, there is strong reason to believe that these Social Security estimates are more accurate.

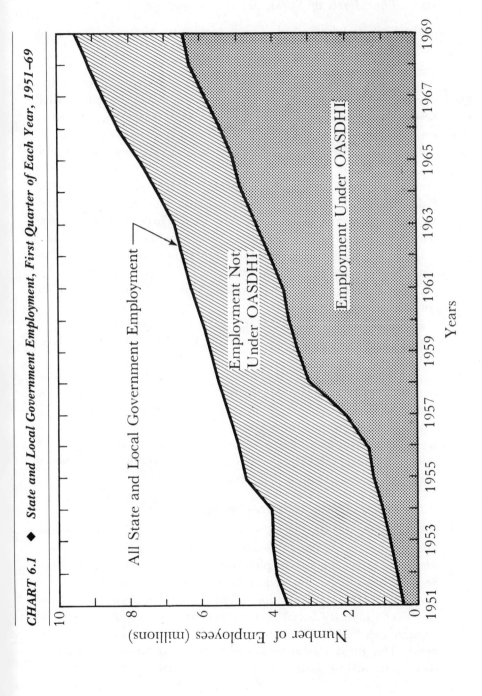

CHART 6.1 ◆ State and Local Government Employment, First Quarter of Each Year, 1951–69

Social Security benefits only a year or so after his public plan joins the system.

By 1972, Social Security covered members of 97 of the 129 systems in our survey; the systems covered included 5,500,000 employees—76 percent of the survey total. Members of the federal Civil Service Retirement System are not covered by Social Security; however, all members of the federal uniformed services are covered.

At the time of the survey, state employees in six states—Colorado, Louisiana, Maine, Massachusetts, Nevada, and Ohio—were not covered, nor were members of ten statewide teachers systems—Alaska, California, Connecticut, Illinois, Kentucky, Louisiana, Massachusetts, Missouri, Ohio, and Puerto Rico. Three general state systems not covered include teachers—Colorado, Maine, and Nevada.

In earlier years, the case against entry into Social Security centered primarily on these objections:

1. Social Security is a "social-welfare" program, not a "sound" or "proper" retirement system.

2. Social Security would take the place of the staff plan.

3. Entry would shift decision-making from the state or local level to the federal government.

4. After the state or local plan was adjusted, total benefits, in relation to contributions, would not be greater and possibly would be lower.

While some ground for argument remains, these particular considerations have, by and large, been swept aside by the positive results of the program. The general attitude of hostility toward Social Security has waned and is practically nonexistent now.

The Effects of Social Security Coverage

When entering the Social Security program, each system chose one of three paths. The first—then known as "supplementary"—was simply additive: the system plan was not changed at all, and Social Security was added. The second involved reshaping the state or local law as an "offset" or "envelope" plan; all or some proportion of the employee's primary Social Security benefit was subtracted from the amount specified by the system's formula to determine its net payment. The third was adoption of a so-called "coordinated plan" (known in private industry as an "integrated" formula). For example, a plan may provide a benefit, per year of service, of 1 percent of salary up to $4,800 (when that was the taxable wage under Social Security) plus 1.5 percent of the part of salary in excess of $4,800; this is a "step-rate" plan. Its advantage is that Social Security provides benefits on the first $4,800 of salary; therefore the system itself could provide a lesser benefit on that part and a somewhat higher benefit on the remainder of salary. The combination of the two would then represent a uniform percentage of salary or at least an approach to a uniform ratio.[4] Each of the three arrangements was tried by a number of systems. The net results were, in the aggregate, greater benefits than the previous system provided. A survey of state and local government retirement systems covering workers who also had Social Security coverage as of January 1, 1961, established the following: [5]

1. Of the 3.8 million state and local government employees then covered by Social Security, 2.7 million were also covered by a staff plan.

2. Over one-third—one million—of these employees were covered by a staff plan that was supplementary, that is, added to Social Security without reduction of the system's benefit.

3. For another third (about one million employees), the median system benefit payable at 65 was reduced by about 20 percent, but when combined with the Social Security benefit, it was substantially higher than the system's previous benefit.

There is evidence in the 1961 survey that the improvement in combined benefits was not entirely attributable to the addition of Social Security. Entering the Social Security program was apparently one facet of a general liberalization. For example, after Social Security coverage, eleven of the systems shifted to pensions based on final average salary, and systems with vesting provisions increased to seventy from fifty-five, although no aspect of Social Security coverage encourages vesting on the part of the staff plan. Obviously,

[4] The New York City systems offered a further alternative. The formula was not changed, but an employee was permitted to reduce his own contributions to the system to pay his Social Security contribution; to the extent of that diversion of funds, the money-purchase annuity part of his retirement allowance was reduced.

[5] Joseph Krislov, *A Survey of State and Local Government Retirement Systems, Covering Workers Also Covered Under the Federal Old-Age, Survivor, and Disability Insurance Program,* 1961 (Washington, D.C., U.S. Social Security Administration, 1962).

there was a wave of liberalization, a significant component of which was participation in Social Security.

In time, the practice of shaping the staff plans to the Social Security program was observed less frequently. The pressure was particularly strong against offset plans. When Social Security was increased, an employee in a 100 percent offset plan received no increase in benefits even though he may have had to pay increased Social Security contributions. Under a 50 percent offset plan he received only half the Social Security increase. Unless the plan made provisions to the contrary, the increase in Social Security benefit reduced the contribution required of the employer to the staff plan. That in turn raised the question of whether to reduce employee contributions or increase benefits. This problem could be met by freezing the amount of the offset in terms of earlier Social Security provisions. When this was tried, it ultimately resulted in a very complicated benefit plan. It meant that a retiring employee would receive a benefit that was offset not by some percentage of his actual Social Security award but by some percentage of an outdated Social Security formula.

There were other complications: how to adjust benefits payable at 55 or 60, before Social Security was available; what offset to make for an employee whose government employment accounted for only a part of his or her eligibility for Social Security; whether to make further changes if Social Security added benefits such as disability pensions at any age, etc. These complications—plus the continuing push for liberalization—led to the abandonment of offset plans. In both public and private employment, offset plans were far more widespread in the early 1950s than in the late 1960s.

Neither have the "coordinated" step-rate plans worked out as visualized. The formula becomes outdated as Social Security changes. Then either the system does not change the formula, which consequently fades into an increasingly remote relationship to the Social Security benefit; or the system makes changes in the formula, reducing the benefits payable out of system funds and making the formula unduly complicated.

For example, the Michigan state system calculates benefits, per year of service, at 1 percent of the first $4,200 of final average salary (highest five consecutive years), and 1½ percent of the portion of salary in excess of $4,200. The dividing line of $4,200 was adopted when that amount was the Social Security taxable wage and was the basis for its benefit formula (1957–1958). Now that the Social Security benefit will be based on $13,200 of annual earnings and successively higher amounts as average wages go up, the $4,200 figure has become meaningless. In 1971 the Virginia state system's formula accrued 1½ percent of that part of the five-year final average salary which exceeded $1,200. The first $1,200 was disregarded because the Social Security benefit formula had as its first component a high percentage of the first $100 of the monthly average wage. That is still true; however, because the Social Security wage base has changed so radically, the $1,200 subtraction lost its original significance and was eliminated in 1972.

A 1965 survey studied the effect of Social Security coverage and found that: [6]

1. Only a few systems (covering about one out of seven persons surveyed) still offset a member's normal retirement benefit, in whole or in part, by the amount of the Social Security benefit, and only one out of ten of the members was covered by a staff plan that had an offset against disability benefits.

2. Employees covered by "coordination" plans remained stationary at about one million. The most typical integration formula credited an extra one-half of 1 percent per year of service on that part of earnings which exceeded $4,200. At that point (1965) systems were drawing the step-rate line at $1,200, $3,600, $4,200, and $4,800. (How quickly this arrangement became outdated is obvious.)

3. The median benefit payable to a male employee retiring at 65 had increased slightly—3 to 5%—above the 1961 level (Table 6.2).

4. There was further liberalization with respect to vesting, early retirement, disability, and survivor benefits.

The retirement systems had become increasingly additive to Social Security. The systems with companion Social Security coverage provided total benefits higher by 10 percent to as much as 75 percent than the systems which shunned Social Security (Table 6.2).

---

[6] Joseph Krislov, *State and Local Retirement Systems, 1965—A Survey of Systems Covering Employees Also Covered by the Federal Old-Age, Survivors, Disability, and Health Insurance Program,* U.S. Social Security Administration (Research Report No. 15) (Washington, D.C., 1966). Data as of January 1, 1965.

Table 6.2   ◆   *Median Benefits, Male Workers, Age 65: Various Service Periods, Under State And Local Retirement Systems Before And After Social Security Coverage*

	Final Average Monthly Salary			
Length of Service	*$200*	*$300*	*$400*	*$500*
10 years:				
1961				
Before OASDI	$ 30	$ 43	$ 57	—
After OASDI	24	32	44	—
Combined with OASDI	105	135	163	—
1965				
Systems alone	—	34	46	$ 58
Combined with OASDI	—	139	169	181
1966				
General systems, no OASDI coverage	—	—	83	103
20 years:				
1961				
Before OASDI	60	90	114	—
After OASDI	51	69	90	—
Combined with OASDI	134	168	208	—
1965				
Systems alone	—	71	93	120
Combined with OASDI	—	176	216	243
1966				
General systems, no OASDI coverage	—	—	162	202
30 years:				
1961				
Before OASDI	100	132	171	—
After OASDI	79	106	135	—
Combined with OASDI	161	208	255	—
1965				
Systems alone	—	113	150	180
Combined with OASDI	—	218	273	303
1966				
General systems, no OASDI coverage	—	—	217	274

Sources: Joseph Krislov, 1961 and 1966 publications cited.
For 1966 data: Saul Waldman, *Retirement Systems for Employees of State and Local Governments, 1966,* U.S. Social Security Administration (Washington, D.C., 1967).

The existence of Social Security apparently also had a liberalizing effect on the systems that chose not to join it. Some added monthly benefits for widows and children.[7]

In short, those who predicted that state and local systems would continue in existence and that the benefits of the staff plan would not be reduced to the extent of Social Security benefits were proved right.

The Merits of Electing Social Security

About three million employees of state and local government are still debating whether or not to enter the Social Security system. That Social Security benefits are valuable—and increasingly so—is obvious. And since most Americans are covered by Social Security, why are so many public employees still skeptical about joining it?

For employees in the aggregate, OASDHI benefits are clearly worth what they cost: administrative expenses are very low (2 percent of benefits), and the program is devoted to desirable ends. For the nation they represent a massive source of basic financial security against the economic hazards of retirement, death or disability of the wage earner, and ill health in old age. However, it has not been possible to prove that the OASDHI program at any given moment is worth what it costs to each particular group of employees. On the contrary, it has been possible to identify specific groups of employees for whom the value of the required contributions would be greater than the value of the benefits earned, *if* one assumed continuation of the currently effective schedule of benefits. That was true, at least, before the 1972 Social Security amendments added benefit escalation.

Two major goals of Social Security benefits have been present almost since the beginning: to provide benefits related to wages and to help eliminate poverty. The first can be called the "insurance" element and the second, the "welfare" element. Since these two factors have separate purposes, they must be considered individually; Congress has always had to balance the two. The antipoverty-welfare element accounts for (1) the very high replacement ratios for employees with low average earnings (Table 6.3); (2) the wife's benefit

[7] Waldman, *Retirement Systems, 1966*, pp. 2–3.

Table 6.3 ◆ Social Security Benefits As Percentages Of Average Monthly Covered Earnings, February 1974

Average Monthly Earnings	Primary Benefit		Primary and Wife's Benefit *		Maximum Family Benefit	
	Amount	Percent	Amount	Percent	Amount	Percent
$76 or less	$ 93.80	123%	$140.70	185%	$140.70	185%
$100	120.80	121	181.20	181	181.20	181
$200	171.40	86	257.10	129	257.10	129
$300	214.40	71	321.60	107	351.70	117
$400	259.00	65	388.50	97	472.60	118
$500	299.40	60	449.10	90	549.30	110
$600	343.90	57	515.90	86	608.60	101
$700 †	380.20	54	570.30	81	665.40	95
$800 †	404.60	51	606.90	76	708.10	89
$900 †	426.80	47	640.20	71	747.00	83
$1,000 †	449.00	45	673.50	67	785.80	79

* Wife, age 65
† These average monthly covered earnings not achievable, because of past limits on the wage base, until after 1975.

(although that provision reduces substantially the value of Social Security to a working wife); and (3) benefits to the minor children and wives of disabled workers. It also accounts for the "fresh start" eligibility requirements of 1951 designed to make newly covered categories of employees quickly eligible and for the "special age 72" benefits that extended certain minimum benefits to aged workers who had had very little covered employment.

The structure is supported, with minor exceptions, by contributions that are the equivalent of payroll taxes on employees, employers, and the self-employed. A large portion of contributions is needed to support the "welfare" element, and that subtracts, of course, from what is available for the "insurance" element. Disregarding the employer contribution, it has been possible to argue that practically every worker would receive more than he contributed. But, adding the employer contribution, a case could be made that, for particular groups of employees, greater benefits could be produced by a combination of these contributions, without Social Security.

The case against entry has centered on the career employee, for whom a long period of contributions can be expected and for whom an advantageous set of separate benefits could be designed, since none of the contributions would have to be used for the "welfare" aspects of Social Security.

Calculations of that kind have almost invariably omitted the history of repeated liberalization of Social Security. A man, age 34 in January 1937, who assumed then that he would always be a bachelor, could have calculated that total Social Security contributions on his behalf would more than pay for full Social Security benefits. Technically correct, he would nevertheless have made a serious error of omission. A calculation has been made of the value of Social Security retirement benefits for a person who was 34 in January 1937 and who retired at the end of 1967, involving a comparison between what was paid for him (combined contributions) and the value of his retirement benefits, first on the basis of the 1939 law and then on the basis of what actually happened. For the single male, the commuted value of the benefits provided by the 1939 law was 5 percent less than the value of the total OASDHI taxes paid on his wages, assuming unchanging earnings. However, the total commuted value of his *actual* benefits was more than three times the commuted value of the contributions on his behalf (and therefore more than six times his own contributions).[8]

Paul Jackson found that over the period 1950–1968, Social Security benefits, Medicare aside, had increased at an annual rate of about three times the increase in the cost of living and 25 percent faster than weekly pay.[9]

Never valid, a static comparison has now been rendered wholly inappropriate by statutory escalation that makes the ultimate value of OASDHI benefits so much greater. Nor can further change in Social Security be ignored. The changes enacted in July 1972 were far-reaching, and yet only three months later, Congress made additional changes of great significance: widow's benefits increased from 82.5

[8] Joseph A. Pechman, Henry J. Aaron, and Michael K. Taussig, *Social Security: Perspectives for Reform* (Washington, D.C., The Brookings Institution, 1968), p. 170.
[9] Paul H. Jackson, "Future of Social Security Benefits and Their Impact on Integrated Plans," in *Committee on Public Employee Retirement Administration of the Municipal Finance Officers Association of the U.S. and Canada, 62nd Annual Conference, 1968*, pp. 13 ff.

to 100 percent of the primary benefits; retirement benefits increased 1 percent for each year of postponed retirement; Medicare premium increases were limited by the percentage increase in cash benefits; disabled workers were given Medicare coverage; and hemodialysis or transplant costs were covered for every covered employee and dependent suffering from kidney disease.

The significance of that last change may be vast. It is the first time the Congress has approved Medicare coverage based on a particular condition, regardless of the age or financial position of the person affected. He need only be covered by Social Security to the extent of either forty quarters or six of the last thirteen quarters, whichever is less. His dependents are also insured for this benefit.

The reason for taking that unprecedented step is that most renal dialysis can cost from $ 5,000 to $30,000 a year, an amount exceeding even the limits of major medical coverage. That this legislation may establish a precedent is also clear. Requests have already been made from the medical profession that coverage be extended to hemophiliacs for regular treatment to avoid emergencies. If this is approved, the question will arise, why then not cancer, congestive heart failure, and other illnesses that can bankrupt a family, even one with ordinary health insurance?

That Social Security may expand into some form of general health insurance is clearly a possibility, and these dynamics make it hazardous for any state or local government to promise benefits greater than Social Security will provide.

A fundamental influence in resolving the problem of whether to join the Social Security system is the fact that a large percentage—probably most—of those whose public jobs are not covered by Social Security will be entitled to Social Security anyhow.

This factor has been particularly persuasive with policemen, firemen, and teachers. Policemen and firemen are covered by retirement systems that provide substantial benefits with twenty or twenty-five years of service, at any age, or at 50 or 55. Typically, they take another job after retirement from the force and they have enough time left to earn Social Security coverage. It takes only forty calendar quarters ($50 each) to be fully insured. For firemen, "moonlighting" may also be a factor in assuring Social Security eligibility. True, their ultimate benefit amounts are less because of their years of noncoverage, but the minimum Social Security benefit is relatively generous. The Social Security amount is based on the worker's average monthly wage, which takes account of all taxable wages in the period after 1950 (or after age 24 if later) to age 62, except that the five worst years are dropped. Periods without Social Security coverage enter as zeros and pull down the average. On the other hand, the minimum primary insurance amount is $93.80. Moreover, the formula underlying the benefit schedule is heavily weighted in favor of the lower averages; directly after the July 1972 amendments, the percentages were:

108.10% of the first $110 of the average monthly wage, plus
39.29% of the next $290, plus
36.71% of the next $150, plus
43.15% of the next $100, plus
24.00% of the next $100, plus
20.00% of the remainder of the taxable wage.

Table 6.3 shows how Social Security benefits relate to average monthly earnings, and how much more liberal they are with respect to low wages than to average wages.

A man who averaged $7,680 a year of covered earnings earned a monthly benefit amount of $326.60. If another man averaged only one-third of that amount—$2,827—his benefit was $195.80, which is not much less than half of the first man's benefit. Social Security benefits for short or part-time careers are relatively high.

Teachers are affected by two special circumstances. A very large percentage of them are women who are married or expect to be. The husband may be employed under Social Security coverage, and the wife will therefore be eligible for wife's benefits—which is 50 percent of her husband's. All that her own coverage accomplishes for her—barring divorce or premature death of her husband—is eligibility for her own primary benefit, and since she probably will have earned less than her husband, the excess of her primary benefit over her wife's benefit is likely to be small or perhaps even nonexistent. That difference may not be worth her own Social Security contributions if she has many years of employment before age 62; and it is certainly unlikely to equal in value the combined employer-employee Social Security contributions on her wages.

The second factor affecting teachers is secondary employment, which permits many of them to establish Social Security coverage. The ten-month school year helps. All it takes to assure Social Security eligibility is one quarter of coverage ($50 a quarter) for each year after 1950 or after age 21 (whichever is later).

A new minimum benefit, added to the Social Security Act in 1972 to provide more adequate benefits for persons who have worked for twenty or more years at very low wages, may also make the system even more rewarding for those public employees who may be able to earn in a covered job one quarter of the maximum amount of taxable wages for more than twenty years. This special provision may be of particular interest to teachers not covered by Social Security in their teaching positions, if they can meet the minimum earnings requirements through covered summer employment and, in the case of college personnel, by lecturing, writing, or consulting. The new minimums will range from $1,122 a year for twenty-one years of credit to $2,040 a year for thirty or more years, but without benefit of cost-of-living escalation.

Illuminating figures on the extent of Social Security eligibility among exempt employees were developed in 1967 by the University of Illinois, which is not covered by Social Security. A canvass of its employees, with heavy responses, showed that the following percentages expected to be eligible for Social Security, whether as a retired employee or the wife of a retired employee: [10]

Academic—male	65%
Academic—female	61
Nonacademic—male	87
Nonacademic—female	87
Administrative—male	100
Average	77

Members of the Federal Civil Service Retirement System are another group not covered by Social Security. Nevertheless, more than half of its retirement beneficiaries in the late 1960s were eligible for Social Security benefits.[11] They earned their eligibility before or after their federal employment or concurrently, through a second job. The percentage may decline as fully insured status under Social

[10] Unpublished survey, University of Illinois.
[11] 1971 Advisory Council on Social Security, *Report* (Washington, D.C., U.S.G.P.O., 1971), p. 37.

Security approaches the ultimate requirement of forty quarters of coverage, but that is not true as yet—and the percentage is high to begin with.

While Social Security coverage is generally desirable, the fact that many of the public employees not now covered will enjoy Social Security benefits anyhow, either as wives or on account of private employment, is even today persuasive to several million that they ought to keep their government jobs out of Social Security.

Withdrawing from Social Security

A lively issue, in some states more than others, is the question of withdrawal from Social Security. The law provides that a public employee group can withdraw from Social Security coverage after seven years, provided the state has given the Social Security administration notice to that effect two years in advance. As of January 1973, withdrawal had been effected or the required notice given by 256 governmental units in seventeen states. Almost all of the units were small, affecting fewer than 25,000 employees altogether, and concentrated largely in California (117), Texas (44), and Louisiana (26).

Much of the argument for withdrawal has been that a group of employees who have been covered for ten years can retain their right to Social Security retirement benefits without paying anything more; and the money they and their employer can save can provide something more than any diminution in their future Social Security benefits. An advocate of this procedure, W. E. Groves, has been clear about this basis for withdrawal: [12]

The first step in initiating this plan is the realization that we are not contemplating the cancellation of Social Security. We are only talking about discontinuing payments to the Social Security Administration. The fact that practically all of our members will continue to be able to receive some Social Security benefits is an essential part of the plan.

Social Security provides for deferred benefits after an employee has worked in covered employment for forty or more quarters and these benefits are paid even though contributions may be discontinued in the meantime. This insures minimum benefits to practically all of our employees and also in-

[12] W. E. Groves, "A Plan for Replacing Social Security," *National Conference on Public Retirement Systems, Proceedings of the 29th Annual Meeting,* 1970, pp. 35–39.

sures their being eligible for Medicare. In this plan we are concerned with supplementing these deferred benefits and guaranteeing that no one will get less than he would have had he continued under Social Security.

Social Security up until the present time has been an excellent vehicle for unloading a large part of the costs of the retirement plan on the federal government but the turning point has been reached and unless we get out now, we will eventually have to pay back all the savings we have so far realized and will even have extra costs added on.

What is then usually proposed is that all or part of the discontinued contributions be used to provide additional benefits that would more than make up the diminution of the Social Security benefit, plus a guarantee that any employee, except one who withdraws from the program after relatively short employment, will not receive lesser benefits than if Social Security coverage had continued. A proposal of this kind can look attractive to public employees who have had at least ten years of Social Security coverage and whose employment has been long enough to qualify them for the retirement benefits of their own system. The proposal takes advantage of the fact that forty quarters of coverage allow an employee permanent entitlement to Social Security's old-age, survivors, and hospital benefits, and that the benefit formula favors those whose average covered wage has been low. Consequently, if a public employee drops out of Social Security when he is 40 or 50 he will still be entitled to Social Security retirement benefits and if he suffers a reduction in his average monthly wage, the benefit will still be a relatively rewarding amount.

From the standpoint of *national* policy, there is of course nothing that can be said in favor of withdrawal. It is based on a frank appeal to the self-interest of a specific group of employees at the expense of the rest of the country. As Groves points out, entry into Social Security was an advantage in the first place. A staff pension plan carries the financial burden of paying for benefits attributable to past service; that is, years preceding establishment of the plan. Entry into Social Security solves the problem very inexpensively—benefits are available very quickly and the cost is spread over all employment covered by Social Security. After unloading that cost on all other employees and employers and after acquiring through ten years of coverage permanent fully insured status under Social Security, the idea is to avoid paying any more and to use the money saved for additional benefits while retaining benefit rights under the Social Security Law that are relatively generous because of its emphasis on abolishing poverty. Clearly, the moral basis for withdrawal is weak.

The public employee who has been covered by Social Security for ten years and who now withdraws will always enjoy for himself and his immediate family the coverage for renal dialysis and kidney transplants—and in the future perhaps for other catastrophic illnesses. However, the cost burden is shifted to those who continue to contribute to the system.

However, discontinuing Social Security is not without difficulties for the employee group itself:

1. The employee who leaves without rights to retirement benefits suffers a loss; he has impaired his status under the Social Security law. If he does not pay Social Security for five years, it will take him another five years to regain insured status for disability benefits. If he did not become fully insured (ten years of Social Security coverage) and he has been out of Social Security for a little over three years, it will take him a year and a half to regain insured status for death benefits whether in lump sum or as monthly income for the benefit of a surviving child or children, as well as his widow, if she is caring for them. His retirement or disability benefit will be diminished to the extent of the absence of covered earnings (unless it is merely part of the five years of lowest earnings that may be disregarded in the Social Security benefit calculation).

2. The guarantee that the benefits paid by the local plan will never be less than the amount that would have been paid if Social Security coverage had continued is an insecure one. If it includes future changes in Social Security retirement benefits, it is impossible to say, at the present time, what it will mean or how expensive it will be and whether the contribution rates now made available will be adequate to meet such changes. In fact, considering inevitable escalation, it is dubious that such a guarantee would be valid at all.

3. Employees with less than ten years of Social Security coverage will not retain, and employees hired in the future will not earn, the right to deferred Social Security benefits. For them, the local plan would have to replace *all* of Social Security, if it is to be fair.

4. The group of employees who withdraw from Social Security

may not be able to participate in any enlargement of the Social Security system.

5. A decision to withdraw may mean that a new employee may never have Social Security coverage—whatever it may be—and may never be able to receive it. A decision to withdraw therefore carries a very heavy burden of responsibility for employees with low seniority and those not yet hired.

6. Another important variable would be a shift in the financing of Social Security. There have been many proposals to finance a significant part of Social Security out of general revenue, at least with respect to those elements of eligibility and formula that represent the social welfare emphasis as distinguished from an "insurance" relationship among benefits, covered wages, and contributions.[13]

Social Security benefits would become a much better "buy" in relation to employee and employer payroll taxes than now; it would then be even more difficult for a group of employees to receive more benefits by using the same contributions outside the Social Security system. Moreover, employees who were not included in the system might nevertheless be called on to pay, through income taxes, for the general revenue part of Social Security financing.

There has been repeated criticism of the Social Security tax as regressive. It is on that basis that partial financing from general revenues has been suggested. However, there have also been other proposals that would coincidentally cut the ground from under those public employees who see an advantage in withdrawal. Pechman, Aaron, and Taussig have suggested at least two. One would be to allow a full or partial credit for the Social Security payroll tax against the personal income tax liability of the individual.[14] To make up for the loss in general revenue would mean compensating adjustments in the income tax schedules. However, low-income families would then pay the Social Security payroll tax as part of their income taxes,

[13] See Joseph A. Pechman, Henry J. Aaron, and Michael K. Taussig, *Social Security, Perspectives for Reform* (Washington, D.C., The Brookings Institution, 1968); and Bowen, Harbison, Lester, and Somers, eds., *The American System of Social Insurance, Its Philosophy, Impact, and Future Development; The Princeton Symposium* (N.Y., McGraw-Hill, 1968).

A contribution from general revenue was advocated by the Committee on Economic Security in 1935 and by the 1938 and 1948 Social Security Advisory Councils. The 1971 Council recommended one-third financing from government revenues of both the hospital and medical portions of Medicare.

[14] *Social Security*, p. 213.

thereby suffering no increase in taxes. And, if this were so, would the same treatment be extended to the retirement contributions of public employees not covered by Social Security? That is doubtful, or at least speculative. If not extended to them, then the participant in Social Security would have a clear advantage, in terms of current net income, over the nonparticipant.

The second possibility that has been advanced is to introduce the personal exemptions used for income tax purposes into the Social Security payroll tax.[15] This could be done either by having the employer recognize the exemptions in the same way they are recognized for income tax withholding or else by leaving the Social Security contribution unchanged, but allowing the worker to receive equivalent credit or a refund in connection with his income tax filing. This proposal simply means that the Social Security contribution would be treated as a federal tax, which indeed it is. In fact, it has become the second highest federal tax, and for millions of workers it is the highest tax they pay. Consequently, the proposal is not at all unrealistic.

Still another possibility for transforming Social Security would be created if Congress were to enact some sort of income maintenance program *outside* of Social Security. Consider this possibility in the simple and limited terms of an income floor for the aged, whether covered by Social Security or not, and without reference to whether other portions of the population are included or not. A program of this kind could be (1) a "demogrant" of $X a month, (2) a minimum income, or (3) a negative income tax. There are four countries—Canada, Denmark, Norway, and Sweden—which provide both "universal pensions" (flat amounts payable to every aged citizen) and social insurance (graduated amounts based on contributions or earnings).[16] In these arrangements the universal pension is a demogrant to the aged; it separates the "welfare" aspect from the "insurance" aspect. A guaranteed minimum income would certainly require the Social Security formula to move sharply toward closer correspondence with earnings. Otherwise Employee A, who contributed to the system for a full working lifetime, might receive benefits only

[15] Pechman, Aaron, and Taussig, *Social Security*, pp. 191–95.
[16] U.S. Social Security Administration, Office of Research and Statistics, *Social Security Programs Throughout the World, 1971*, Research Report No. 40 (Washington, D.C., U.S.G.P.O., 1971), p. xii.

slightly, if at all, higher than Employee B, who did not contribute at all but drew the guaranteed minimum income. A negative income tax is simply a variation on that theme. It would provide, in effect, a minimum payment to those who have no other income, plus certain amounts to those who have modest incomes, graduated inversely with income.

Any of these arrangements, if financed through general revenues, whether within the Social Security program or not, would inevitably shift the program's benefit schedules into greater correlation with employer-employee contributions. The result would completely undo the arithmetic of those who have figured that they are better off leaving the Social Security system.

Fundamentally, the situation amounts to this: Social Security is a large and growing national institution and for a particular group to pursue a separate course is not only to avoid what should, in the national interest, be a universally shared program; it also means that they risk being shunted aside and ultimately disadvantaged, no matter what the immediate attractions of disaffiliation may appear to be. Moreover, judgment of the ultimate impact requires recognition of the fact that if a group of state or local employees withdraws, the same employee unit, whether comprised of the same or different individuals, may never, under present law, rejoin the Social Security system.

Closing the Withdrawal Loophole

The provision in the Social Security Law that permits a unit of public employees to withdraw, while retaining eligibility and favorably weighted benefits, was clearly a mistake, a lack of sufficient caution as to what the long-run consequences might be. The mistake ought to be corrected. The Social Security system was not designed for voluntary coverage. The equities and the benefit-cost relationships of a mandatory system are bound to be very different from those of a voluntary system; one cannot design a benefit plan on the assumption that membership is mandatory and then allow groups to opt out.

If Social Security coverage were made mandatory for public employees, the problem would of course disappear. However, that step is plainly far broader than plugging the loophole of withdrawal. We will return to mandatory coverage later.

It is conceivable that the law could be amended to eliminate the right to withdraw, but that would be difficult on the moral, and possibly the legal, grounds that it was a right on the basis of which the state and its employee units decided to enter the system in the first place.

However, it should be possible to attach tough-minded but reasonable consequences to withdrawal that would sufficiently protect the system from being taken advantage of. This is particularly true with respect to more generous benefit provisions enacted after a new group enters. It is anomalous in the extreme for cost-of-living escalation, increases for postponed retirement, greater widow's benefits, permanent coverage for renal dialysis, and a long list of similar liberalizations to apply to a unit of employees who have chosen not to help pay for the additional benefits. That is the current law, and it is, to say the least, overly generous. It should be possible to shut off benefit escalation and perhaps a number of other recent liberalizations for those employees who withdraw from coverage. Another possibility would be to include in the law, with respect to groups withdrawn from coverage, decrements in benefits or subtractions from already credited years because of the years of noncoverage attributable to withdrawal.

Excluding Public Employees from Social Security

We return at this point to our original question—whether the inherent difficulty of achieving a desired retirement policy through two independent arrangements, federal Social Security and state retirement laws—can be resolved by withdrawing from Social Security.

It should be clear by now that this author's answer is no. Social Security is a bedrock of security for the nation. The great majority of the employees of state and local government are covered. It protects a worker, no matter how mobile he may have been. Not only should it remain, it should be made universal for public employees.

Mandatory Social Security Coverage

There is no fundamental reason to allow public employees exemption from Social Security. It would be desirable to extend coverage on a mandatory basis.[17]

---

[17] Also proposed by Pechman, Aaron, and Taussig, *Social Security*, p. 220.

Originally there was no doubt as to the constitutionality of mandatory coverage (although the decision not to include public employees was actually made on the ground that it would be bad politics). Now, three decades later, it seems likely that mandatory coverage would be held constitutional. The step would amount to taxing state and local employees on the same basis as other employees, and their employers on the same basis as other employers. The purpose of covering public employees would be the same as that of covering private employees.

The case for universal coverage rests on three premises: the equity of universal financing, the desirability of eliminating duplication, and the value of full vesting or portability.

Financing the welfare aspects of Social Security should be a widely shared obligation. It is difficult to see exemption as other than a privileged tax position. To be sure, public employees not covered by Social Security pay substantial rates of contribution to their retirement systems, but none of it helps to support the relatively generous Social Security benefits for those who have had the lowest earnings in the nation.

A second purpose would be to eliminate the payment of relatively liberal Social Security benefits to workers who seem, in OASDHI records, to have suffered from exceptionally low earnings or irregular employment, but who were really working most of the time in public employment on the basis of which they qualified for relatively good staff pensions.

A third purpose would be to protect the worker who goes through many jobs by crediting his public employment, however short, toward his Social Security eligibility for retirement, disability, and death benefits.

If all public employees were covered, including the federal government, there would of course be large additional contributions coming from the public units affected. That would not be inequitable. On the part of the federal government, it would amount to some financing of the welfare aspects of Social Security out of general revenues.

A major difficulty with mandating employee coverage would lie in the integration of Social Security benefits with the staff retirement plans now in effect. State and local units without Social Security have created retirement plans designed on the basis of its absence. The benefits and the employee contributions are usually higher than in other plans. To add Social Security on top would be excessive. Moreover, the state and local plans cannot readily be reduced; in fact, in some states they are constitutionally guaranteed against diminution.

The problem might perhaps be handled by establishing, for all groups brought in by the mandate, maximums for the total of Social Security and staff-plan benefits. The Social Security law has a small precedent for that type of provision in its maximum limit on disability benefits; in combination with Workmen's Compensation, they may not exceed 80 percent of final earnings. The law goes on to provide that the Social Security benefit is reduced, as necessary, unless the state's Workmen's Compensation Law makes the offset. An analogous set of provisions, but on a much larger scale, could perhaps be written into the Social Security law, to avoid excess as a result of mandating public employee coverage. However, if the state or local system did not adopt the offset, the effect of such a maximum on Social Security benefits might be regarded as grossly inequitable.

A simpler way to handle the problem of integration might be to mandate Social Security coverage only for all *new* employees hired approximately two or three years after enactment. That would avoid established state guarantees, put the states and localities on notice, and give them a chance to work out a new plan for new employees that would give recognition to companion Social Security coverage. It would quickly accomplish the goal of protecting short-term employees and eventually achieve complete coverage.

Social Security for Federal Employees

The federal government is a large part of the problem. Those covered by the Federal Civil Service Retirement System are not covered by Social Security. Congress could act on integration of the two systems at the same time. New employees could be given both Social Security and a staff plan so that the combination would provide appropriate total benefits. No employee would lose out, except that there would be no future counterpart to the career employee who now manages to add an unduly generous Social Security benefit to his civil service pension. Other employees—particularly those with short service—would get better protection than they now have. Employee contributions would not have to be increased. In fact, the employee's Social Security contribution could simply come out of his present contribution under the federal staff plan, in which event the entire change-over would be a liberalization of federal employee benefits, except for those new employees who would otherwise have been in line for future windfalls.

Federal authorities have, from time to time, concerned themselves with the possibilities that federal employees with relatively short service might fall between Social Security and the federal staff retirement systems. Several proposals for integration of Social Security and federal retirement plans, involving changes in both, have been made. One of the more recent proposals stemmed from a request in 1967 by the House Ways and Means Committee and the Senate Finance Committee to the Social Security Administration to study the problem of filling gaps in the cash benefit program and of establishing a satisfactory relationship between Medicare and the Federal Employees' Health Benefits program. The Social Security Administration was also asked to review the problem of federal retirees with annuities based on substantial salaries who also qualify for Social Security benefits. Robert Ball, then Social Security Commissioner, offered a three-point answer to the problem of the employee who falls between the two programs: [18]

1. *Transfer of credits to Social Security.* If a federal employee was not insured by the staff system for death, disability, or retirement, credits would be transferred to Social Security, which would be reimbursed for the extra cost from the employee contributions to the staff plan.

2. *Guaranteed minimum benefits.* A federal employee covered for death, disability or retirement benefits would be guaranteed that these benefits would be no less than the OASDHI benefits payable if his federal employment had been covered by Social Security.

3. *Medicare coverage for federal employees.* Federal employees would be covered by Medicare; supplementary insurance would be made

[18] *Social Security Administration, Relating Social Security Protection to the Federal Service— A Report Requested by the Committee on Ways and Means, U.S. House of Representatives and the Committee on Finance, U.S. Senate* (Washington, D.C., 1969), pp. 38–39. A similar recommendation was made by a Cabinet Committee on Federal Staff Retirement Systems. *Federal Staff Retirement Systems, U.S. Senate, 90th C., 1st S., Doc. No. 14* (Washington, D.C., U.S.G.P.O., 1967).

available for bringing coverage up to the level of the Federal Employee Health benefits.

Along the same lines, the 1971 Advisory Council on Social Security recommended that Congress consider favorably the idea of transfer of credits to and from Social Security so as to protect a federal worker or his beneficiary who would otherwise be ineligible.[19]

These proposals would fill out the gaps, but they would not touch the windfall benefits of career employees who also manage to qualify for Social Security, nor would they involve contributions toward the general financing of Social Security. Moreover, if special arrangements of this kind were implemented for federal employees, there would be no reason why they should not be extended to state and local employees—not only to those still not participating in the Social Security system, but also to those now covered by it. And, in turn, why not an arrangement for private industry by which Social Security would serve, not as an independent layer of protection, but as a minimum benefit purchasable by transfers of credits for those workers who need it?

A better answer—although more far-reaching—is outright Social Security coverage for new employees, with recasting of the staff plans. Simultaneously, it might be reasonable to enact, for current employees, reciprocal credit and funding arrangements along the lines proposed by Ball or the 1971 Advisory Council on Social Security. That would bring additional security for present employees, plus universal OASDHI coverage for future employees, whose benefits would be integrated with Social Security.

In summary, the problem posed by dual coverage should not be solved by eliminating Social Security for public employees. On the contrary, its coverage should be expanded. The system should be made less vulnerable to groups that want to withdraw after establishing coverage. These groups should be barred from unpaid-for privileges.

Social Security should be made mandatory for all public employees hired in the future. That future date should be fixed with sufficient lead-time for the states and the federal government to accommodate their staff plans to universal Social Security coverage.

[19] S.S.A., *Report,* pp. 37–38.

7 ❖ Integrating
with Social Security

The problem is to establish and implement a policy of retirement income for public employees in the face of the fact that their benefits are determined by two independent authorities, one federal and one state. If one takes the position that Social Security benefits should not be curtailed for public employees, what are the alternatives for overall policy?

A Layer of Mandated Pensions

One possibility for accommodation is for Congress to mandate a layer of pensions on all of private industry.[1] The mandated layer would be a basic amount, fully vested and fully funded: a minimum pension analogous to a minimum wage. If an employer's plan already met that requirement, it could remain unchanged. Otherwise, an employer would have to match the minimum, either through contributions to a government fund, such as Social Security or some other fund, or through a private plan fulfilling the mandated level of benefits.

This proposal has been advanced basically as an answer to the problem posed by the fact that about half of private employment is not covered by pension plans. These workers are unlikely to get coverage by voluntary action. If their needs were adequately met by Social Security alone, then Social Security will have reached levels excessive in combination with private-plan benefits. Another pur-

[1] Robert D. Paul, "Pensions: An Issue that Won't Retire," *The New York Times,* October 22, 1972, Editorial Section, p. 3.

pose of the proposal is to avoid inequity when vesting and funding are required of private plans, but nothing more than Social Security is asked for the most unprotected of all—that half of the work-force without private-pension coverage.

The concept can also be viewed to mean that those employees who would otherwise have no pension-plan coverage would be more adequately protected than they are now, without increasing Social Security for those who may already enjoy an adequate combination of benefits from Social Security and a private plan.

While this proposal was conceived for the private sector, it has possible relevance for public employment. If enacted, it would entail relatively minor revisions in existing public-employee plans, with early vesting of limited benefits, and would not require additional increases in Social Security, which might otherwise compound the total benefit problem of many cities and states.

However, this proposal comes at a time when it may be too late as a solution for the problem of public employee benefits. The benefits already established by the public plans, in combination with Social Security and its escalation, already present us with a major problem for the future.

It has not been suggested that any part of existing Social Security be split off as the mandatory layer so as to leave a reduced remainder; such a solution seems neither desirable nor feasible.

It does not appear, then, that the problem of control over the totality of benefits can be achieved by accommodation on the part of the Social Security program. In fact, it seems generally inappropriate for the larger system—Social Security—to accommodate to the peculiarities of the many federal, state, and local staff plans. Instead, the latter should adapt to the Social Security program.

Accommodating a Staff Plan to Social Security

As we have said, if Social Security were stationary, the problem of setting up a staff plan to produce a desired totality of benefits would be simple. In the light of Social Security, a completely independent set of benefits could be established so that the two taken together would produce whatever result were desired. The problem for a state that has established an independent formula is that its formula remains fixed, while Social Security changes in ways that are neither controllable by the state nor entirely predictable. That has been the difficulty with past efforts to integrate with Social Security.

Integration Formulas

Historically, the most popular way of dealing with the problem has been a step-rate or integrated formula—one percentage benefit on the part of salary subject to Social Security and another—and higher—percentage benefit on the remainder or "excess portion" of salary.

By 1971 the Social Security wage base had been changed six times, from $3,000 to $9,000; integration formulas had lost their logic even before escalation became part of the program. It was useless for a plan to step up its benefit formula on the amount of salary over $3,000 or $4,800 if later the Social Security base became $9,000. The 1972 escalation amendments made it explicit that step-rate integration formulas were obsolete. It will make little sense for a plan to step up its benefit formula over a fixed breakpoint of $13,200 (the 1974 base for Social Security) if twenty years later the Social Security base is $36,000.

One could, perhaps, design a plan with an automatic shift in the salary "breakpoint" to match changing Social Security maximums, although it might become complicated. If one has a plan based on final average salary (as distinguished from a career-average salary), each time the breakpoint goes up, the benefit from the plan goes down. For example, suppose the plan credits, for each year of service, 1 percent of the part of salary currently taxable under Social Security plus 2 percent of any excess. When the tax base moves up, the rate of accrual on the increment goes down by 1 percent (from 2 to 1 percent). Social Security moves up simultaneously, to be sure, but to a much lesser extent. Since it is based on career-average salary (except for a drop-out of five years) the additional piece of salary is averaged in with all past taxable earnings and therefore has a very minor effect on benefits in any immediate terms. This fault could be corrected. One can visualize an alternative design: a career-average formula, such as Social Security's, but modified by an index of wage and/or cost changes, so that the benefit from the staff plan would not go down any more than Social Security would go up. That would certainly be new and different and possibly complicated in some respects, but it might be manageable.

A second difficulty, however, is that an integration arrangement takes account of only one dimension of change, namely, increases in the wage base. Social Security benefits will change, however, not only through the present escalation formula but also through further legislation. Congress may change eligibility terms, age thresholds, accruals for postponed retirements, reductions for earlier retirement, the retirement work-test or the age when no test is applied, payments for disabilities, etc. Combining all of these provisions with the terms of the staff plans determines the total result, and it is the total result toward which public policy and law should be directed.

A second alternative for state or local legislation is more theoretical than practical. If retirement statutes were so flexible that they could be amended, with increases or decreases each time Social Security changed, accommodation would be possible. However, that much flexibility would please no one and unsettle many, and would be an unwise choice.

A third alternative lies in the direction of a staff plan that will provide an all-inclusive benefit; that is, the plan would:

1. Establish—guarantee—the totality of benefits desired;
2. Identify the employee's Social Security benefit as fulfilling part of that guarantee; and
3. Make the payments necessary to fulfill the remainder of the guarantee.

For example, a statute could be written to guarantee an employee retiring after thirty years of service at age 65 retirement income equal to 80 percent of his final average salary, including his Social Security benefit. Each qualifying employee would receive the amount required, with his Social Security, to equal the 80 percent. If final average salary were $10,000, the guarantee would be for $8,000. If his Social Security were $2,200 the plan would pay $5,800; if $3,100, the plan would pay $4,900.

A plan of this kind would not be without problems. If Social Security is increased, the career employee would get no benefit from it, except that a larger percentage of his retirement income would be subject to the cost-of-living escalation provided by Social Security and survivor benefits might be greater. At the same time, his contributions might be increased. It may therefore be necessary to consider employee contributions on some overall basis (Social Security and system combined). Also, if an employee terminates with a vested right to a deferred pension, the equity of subtracting a future Social Security amount from a total benefit amount frozen at termination well in advance of a retirement age is debatable. A guarantee of total retirement income, inclusive of Social Security, may therefore have to include some sort of cost-of-living adjustment.

The concept of an all-inclusive guarantee is radically different from prevailing practices and is therefore not apt to win easy acceptance. Those who are accustomed to benefits fixed independently of Social Security are apt to look upon an all-inclusive design as "taking away Social Security." Yet the arrangement adds something to Social Security and guarantees that total result. The real question, ultimately, is whether the total benefits and total employee contributions represent a fair and desirable goal.

That a design is inclusive of Social Security does not necessarily mean that the state or local system will pay out greater or lesser benefits than with a formula that is independent of Social Security. Consider, just as an example, a plan geared to produce the following benefits, *inclusive of Social Security,* for an employee who retires at 65 after thirty years of service:

(1) 70 percent of final average salary, plus
(2) Continuance of half that amount for a surviving spouse, plus
(3) Full adjustment to the cost of living after retirement.

How would the total payments under that plan compare with a plan which would pay that employee 70 percent of his final average salary *independently* of Social Security, if the latter plan did not include the cost-of-living guarantee or the spouse continuance feature? Let us assume that Social Security would amount to 30 percent of final pay, so that the combination amounts to 100 percent of final earnings.

The answer depends on what happens to the cost of living and to Social Security. If the cost of living remains stable, the illustrative all-inclusive plan would pay less. However, assume that Social Security continues to provide approximately 30 percent replacement of wages. Assume further that the cost of living goes up by at least 3.5 percent a year. Under those circumstances, the all-inclusive plan would provide substantially greater lifetime income and security. While the independent formula starts off the employee's retirement with combined income equal to full pay, that fact would in time be overshadowed by the cost-of-living adjustment and spouse annuity of the alternative formula. In terms of assuring a lifetime of economic security, this particular inclusive formula would be clearly better than the alternative.

Another problem is that the rules of the federal Treasury Department have not permitted full offset by Social Security from uniform percentage-of-pay benefit formulas, on the theory that this means that employer-financed benefits would be greater for the higher-paid than for the lower-paid employees. However, if an all-inclusive formula can be designed with benefit and contribution formulas that would provide the lower-paid employees with equal or better treatment (in toto) than the higher-paid, it is difficult to see how this could be denied acceptance under the Internal Revenue Code.

More common than full offsets have been plans that offset half or some similar percentage of Social Security. The logic is to offset only what the employer has paid for and to let the employee enjoy the benefits of any increases in the other half. For example, assume that a plan is designed to assure total benefits of 80 percent of final average salary at age 65 after thirty years of service. If we assume that the primary Social Security benefit will provide, let us say, 35 percent for the average employee, the staff plan would then furnish 45 percent. If the staff plan prescribes 62.5 percent minus half the Social Security benefit, it will pay the necessary 45 percent $(62.5\% - 17.5\% = 45\%)$.

This kind of arrangement has generally been more acceptable to employees, but it is also less certain to accomplish the retirement income goal. If Social Security turns out to differ from the amount assumed, the goal is missed—by half of the difference. On the other hand, if there is confidence that the federal government will keep Social Security within certain broadly predictable limits, the chance of a 50 percent miss may be tolerable.

Some public systems have approached an inclusive formula by providing that plan benefits may not, when added to primary Social Security, exceed a certain figure, such as 80 or 85 percent of final pay. That means that an independent formula operates freely until Social Security reaches the point at which the maximum begins to be applied. To the extent that the maximum applies, the plan becomes one that guarantees a designated amount, inclusive of Social Security.

Plans inclusive of social security are in essence "offset" or "envelope" plans. They were tried in the early days of pension growth in the 1950s and for the most part discarded. Is there any reason to expect that approach may be revived? There is. Current circumstances are quite different from those of the 1950s. Originally the idea served three major purposes. First, it made a small pension payment sound generous. It was common to find a private plan that paid a long-service employee $100 a month, offset by half his Social Security. This might mean a payment by the plan of about $60 a month, but $100, including the employer-financed part of Social Security, sounded better.

Second, an offset formula was one way of providing proportionately higher payments from the plan to the higher-paid employees. A plan might provide a percentage of pay per year of service, offset by half or some other percentage of the Social Security award. For the lower-paid employees, the offset would amount to a relatively large percentage of the total benefit; for the higher-paid, it would be a relatively small percentage and the payment from the plan would therefore be commensurately greater.

The third reason was that future increases in Social Security would reduce plan payments and therefore employer costs.

When Social Security was increased, employers with offset plans enjoyed sudden reductions in cost, reductions which proved to be temporary, however, since labor recognized the result and demanded the elimination of offsets. Their benefits were being increased anyway with each round of negotiations. Reducing or eliminating the offset was simply another way of increasing benefits. Furthermore, once the benefit level was increased, there was no longer any need to make it sound larger than it really was.

In none of the 1950s plans, however, did any question arise as to whether for some employees the totality of benefits might be inappropriate. In that decade it was simply a question of shifting from a combined wage-replacement ratio of 35 percent to 40 or 50 percent, or perhaps occasionally to 60 percent. Fundamentally, it did not matter much whether this liberalization took the form of a change in formula, an elimination of the offset, or both. Moreover, if an employer wanted to, it remained possible to help the higher-paid employees—those earning more than the Social Security base—by shifting to some sort of step-rate integration formula. Also, offset plans carried a burden of complexities, mentioned earlier.

For these reasons, the offset plans of the 1950s almost disappeared. However, in the late 1960s they began to reappear in large numbers in private industry, under the pressure of the successive changes in Social Security that made it increasingly apparent that change was the constant and that the traditional step-rate formulas, as a way of integrating with Social Security, were becoming ineffectual and obsolete.

Even those negotiated private plans that have avoided offset or step-rate integration formulas have recently shown increasing evidence that they are being designed as complements to Social Security. The Auto Workers' agreements provide special early-retirement benefits which include extra amounts payable up to the age when full Social Security benefits are received. Also, a "bridge" survivor income benefit is provided to pay benefits to a widow if she was at least 45 or 50 when the employee died; the benefit is payable until the widow's Social Security benefit is available. These do not involve offsets, but by adding amounts when Social Security is lacking, they have a similar effect. Moreover, direct offsets are quite common in disability provisions, to avoid exceeding net income while at work.

The question of all-inclusive or offset plans occurs now under new circumstances. Many of the public employee retirement systems face a more compelling pressure. Their benefit levels are, in most cases, higher than in private industry. Under future Social Security benefits, most of the employees of state or local government who retire at 65 after thirty or more years of service are likely to realize greater net income after, than before, retirement. The difference between a wage-replacement ratio of 35 percent and 65 percent is 25 percentage points, but it is only a quantitative difference; no principle is involved. The difference between a wage-replacement ratio of 80 percent and 100 percent is arithmetically less—only 20 percentage points—but it is a qualitative difference, and it raises important questions of basic objectives and policy.

This much is clear and undeniable: when limits or well-defined objectives have to be adopted and effectively implemented, the features of staff plans will inevitably be pressed, one way or another, into a mold increasingly complementary to the Social Security system. Inevitably, state and local plans will be reshaped in that direction. Considering the long-range nature of pension commitments, the appropriate action should be taken as soon as possible.

8 ✧ Funding

Pensions for public employees are sometimes voted with no consideration of the ultimate cost, which is put off by pay-as-you-go financing to a future generation of taxpayers. That is not typical, however. Ultimate cost is usually taken into account and, at least to some extent, financed. Generous benefits with pay-as-you-go financing make headlines and create a general public impression; the more common practice of actuarial funding does not and is therefore less recognized.

A variety of practices are followed; they run the gamut from pay-as-you-go to vigorous pursuit of full actuarial funding. Early financing methods were either pay-as-you-go or the earmarking of certain revenue sources (such as taxes on fire-insurance companies) totally unrelated in yield to the plan's needs. About 1920, there was massive movement toward actuarial reserve systems. Today, pay-as-you-go, where it exists, is defended, not as a virtue, but as a necessity. Massachusetts has been an exception to this rule; in 1948, on recommendation of a study commission, the state adopted pay-as-you-go as a matter of policy. More often, however, the practice is simply inherited, and the authorities have lacked the determination or the budgetary margin to change it. The practice is most apt to be followed by the older plans, particularly in cities with limited funds.

Movement is in the direction of funding. Delaware legislated funding for its state employees' system in 1970; Connecticut in 1971; and California for its teachers' system in 1971. The process is by no means complete, and it may never be, but change is largely in that direction.

The question of funding is not entirely settled by accepting or rejecting pay-as-you-go. The *extent* of funding is another question.

What funding goals are appropriate for government plans? Should they differ from the funding schedules for pensions in the private sector? What are the implications of the claim that the government is a continuing institution with the power to tax to meet its obligations?

Next to establishment of benefit goals and levels, funding is probably the most significant of the perennial questions affecting the public systems.

Pay-as-you-go and Reserve Funding

"Funding" may be an ambiguous term. In its broadest sense, it can refer to any schedule or plan for financing a retirement system.[1] More commonly, "funding" refers to a systematic schedule of contributions based on long-term needs (thus the other frequently used terms: "advance funding," "reserve funding" or "actuarial funding"). That is the sense—as distinct from pay-as-you-go—in which funding is used here. "Pay-as-you-go" means that the plan is financed by the appropriations necessary to meet the system's current expenditures (benefits, refunds, expenses). As used here, the term will also include the accumulation of such limited assets as those representing accumulated employee contributions or reserves for short-term contingencies. Pay-as-you-go systems typically accumulate member contributions; the employer pays the *employer's* share of current pension payments. The idea of using the contributions of active employees to pay current pensions is generally frowned upon, even by those who defend pay-as-you-go policies. Also, some systems that are essentially pay-as-you-go maintain contingency reserves—on the order of one or two years of benefit payments—to cover a temporary shortfall in government appropriations.

With funding there are systematic contributions in excess of what is required for the system's current expenditures in consideration of long-term needs. A long upward curve of expenditures characterizes almost all pension plans. It takes a pension plan about thirty-five years to "mature." When a group of active employees is first covered by a plan, the beneficiaries will at first be few, then increase for thirty-five to forty years, and level off when the number of pensioners dying equals the number of retiring employees. Moreover,

---

[1] "Funding" has also been used to refer to the method of underwriting, that is, whether the plan is implemented through an insurance contract, uninsured trust, etc. That meaning does not apply here.

the projections hold only theoretically, that is, in the highly improbable case in which the size of the employee group, salaries, and benefits provisions do not change during the maturing period. If the employee group increases, or benefits are liberalized or rise because of salary increases, the leveling-off time is postponed—it is as if a new plan has been added to the old and a new upward curve added to the old.

Table 8.1 and Chart 8.1 illustrate the disbursement curve, shown under the heading of "pay-as-you-go." In this theoretical case, benefit payments in the fortieth year are thirteen times benefit payments in the fifth year. Constancy of the employee group and of benefit levels has been assumed. In reality the upward curve of disbursements is, of course, much sharper and longer. The New York State Employees' Retirement System, during a fifty-year period, dramatically illustrates how benefits can rise.[2] In the fortieth year, benefits were 250 times their level in the fifth year.

Fiscal years ended March 31	Retirement allowance payments and postretirement supplements (thousands)
1921	$ 18
1926	550
1931	1,293
1941	4,327
1951	10,281
1961	36,602
1971	141,884

A funding schedule determines contributions in anticipation of the upward curve of expenditures. This does not mean that contributions for the current year are set at the projected disbursements for the fortieth year; contributions may be greater or less than that ultimate level of payments, depending on the specific funding plan.

PAY-AS-YOU-GO VERSUS FUNDING

Pay-as-you-go financing has been defended with a variety of reasons.

[2] New York State Employees' Retirement System, *Annual Reports, Comptroller*, Albany, New York. All figures include those for the Policemen's and Firemen's Retirement System, which became a separate system in 1966.

The Case for Pay-as-you-go

The arguments for pay-as-you-go financing can be summarized as follows:

1. It involves the lowest immediate appropriation.

2. Increasing cost can be met more easily in the future, when dollars will be softer and the tax base larger.

3. Reserves are not necessary. Public authorities are bound to fulfill benefit commitments. Federal, state, and local governments are perpetual institutions that can tax to raise the money ultimately needed.

4. Reserves will only serve as a standing invitation to enact benefit increases that will absorb them. At some future time someone is bound to argue that the reserves are unnecessary or at least too large and persuade the authorities that they can give benefit increases without increasing contributions.

Enforcing Responsibility

The most important single consideration in favor of funding, in the author's opinion, is that it helps to enforce responsibility. Pay-as-you-go financing offers the temptation to adopt benefit changes while passing the cost on to the future. It becomes too easy for the cost to be passed off as the problem of another administration or legislature.

Sometimes there is open recognition that future costs will be greater, even when no current payment is made toward those costs. That is not generally an adequate guarantee of responsibility. Explanations and reservations do not affect the public the way an appropriation or tax does. Real discipline for public policy is exacted only by the need to pay now for benefits enacted now.

In several states, any bill for pension change must be accompanied by a fiscal note giving its cost. That is a step toward responsibility, even though questions may still remain as to who does the estimating and how realistic it is.

A 1970 enactment in New York is another illustration of a step taken to make sure contributions are commensurate with benefits. Although the New York systems have for decades been on a funded basis, the City of New York secured a number of pension increases and, by one stratagem or another, postponed funding them for a year or two. The state therefore enacted a law forbidding benefit improvements unless the budget simultaneously reflected the funding cost.

It is true, as defenders of pay-as-you-go have sometimes claimed, that large assets can be "raided" for seemingly painless benefit increases. However, that danger is minor compared to the constant invitation which a pay-as-you-go policy extends for benefit increases without current contributions reflective of the ultimate cost.

Benefit Security

Historically, pay-as-you-go was abandoned for two persuasive reasons: to enforce responsibility and to assure security for present and future pensioners.

Before the 1920s, financing generally took one of three forms:

1. Simple pay-as-you-go.

2. Member contributions, such as 1 or 2 percent of pay, or a dollar amount, or deductions from pay for absences or disciplinary penalties—none of it being related to benefit costs. The remainder was met by the public employer on a pay-as-you-go basis.

3. The yield from an earmarked tax, such as pistol permits, taxes on foreign fire-insurance carriers, charges for boiler inspections, etc. There was of course no connection between these yields and costs.

A Commission on Pensions of the City of New York summarized the local situation in 1916 as follows: [3]

Lack of knowledge of the extent of future obligations and oblique methods of financing fund requirements were the main characteristics in the establishment of the city's pension funds.

A rough guess was first made of the probable amounts required to meet currently maturing pension claims for a few years ahead. The next step was to assume that these demands would remain stationary forever thereafter or, at worst, increase in equal ratio with the annual payroll. The goal of the procedure was to secure an income preferably through the automatic diversion to the fund of more or less obscure miscellaneous city revenues. In the selection of such revenues, care was generally taken that the proceeds would net some margin of safety over and above the guessed annual pension demands.

[3] Commission on Pensions, City of New York, *Report on the Pension Funds of the City of New York,* Part I, *Operation of the Nine Existing Pension Funds* (New York, The Commission, 1916), p. 50.

While the whole procedure deserved condemnation, its principal fallacy is the optimistic expectation of a stationary or only slightly increased pension change. The persistence in this misconception, even to the present day, is unfortunate and surprising. It continues to lay the foundation for future disaster of newly established funds and greatly handicaps the introduction of sane methods of financing pension systems. The great number of object lessons furnished by the experience of pension funds abroad, as well as in the United States, has been in the past and is at present ignored.

Because the fixed revenues proved inadequate and demands on city and state budgets increased rapidly, there was a massive trend, starting in New York in 1917, toward actuarial reserve systems.

Employees welcomed funding because they saw that their pension plans were running short of funds and might discontinue payments. In addition they worried about taxpayer resistance to rapidly increasing demands on general revenues; they liked the security of financing through systematic contributions, with accumulation of reserves specifically allocated toward benefit fulfillment.[4]

By and large, that attitude continues. Most employees want an adequate funding schedule and bitterly resist underfinancing. Employee groups have gone to court to enforce funding standards. For example, in 1970 the Governor of Washington cut the appropriation to the Teacher's Retirement System because of a shortfall of revenues. This had no immediate or short-range effect on benefits. The Washington Education Association won a decision from the state's Supreme Court that appropriations in accordance with the retirement-system law were a contractual right of the employees, constitutionally guaranteed.[5]

The employees, as well as the taxpayers, have often been concerned with the notion of burdening future generations; they worry that those future generations may try to avoid the liability and imperil payments.

That concern is real, but it should be put in reasonable perspec-

---

[4] The term "reserve" is often used in actuarial and insurance literature to identify a calculated *liability*. Some writers have therefore found it desirable to use two terms: "reserve assets" and "reserve liabilities." However, in most *pension* literature, the term "reserve" is identified with assets; the term "liability" is used for "reserve liability." This text adopts the single terms "reserves" and "liabilities" as simple and sufficiently clear.

[5] Mae Weaver *et al.* v. Daniel S. Evens *et al.*, 41851, Washington Supreme Court, 1972.

tive. Public authorities have rarely if ever run out on pay-as-you-go obligations, even when they became very costly. They may sometimes close down an unfunded plan and replace it with a funded system for new employees, but they have almost always met the old obligations. Moreover, it is not as if funding a plan avoids heavy future contributions. Investment yield on the reserves of a funded plan may reduce ultimate contribution requirements by 25 to 50 percent, but if a future generation rebels against the pension costs it has inherited, even a funded plan may not be entirely safe from attack.

Perhaps a fair summary is that if pay-as-you-go financing leads to extravagance and abuse because payment can be deferred, then there is an extra element of danger that the generation facing the bill may regard it as the cost of an undue privilege and resist paying it. A funded system is somewhat safer.

The Power to Tax

Those who defend pay-as-you-go argue that a government does not have to fund because it has perpetual life and the power of taxation. Although there is a good deal of merit to that argument, which draws a valid distinction between government and private funding, the point can be carried too far. The distinction between public and private funds is by no means hard and fast. Some political jurisdictions (counties, cities, towns, villages, special-purpose districts, authorities, agencies) can shrink to a point that makes the continued financing of their pension plans impossible. A ghost town can do very little for its pay-as-you-go pensioners. Moreover, a great many local governments are hedged in by statutory or constitutional limits on taxation and debt. Their future ability to pay is by no means certain or unlimited.

What will happen if there is a taxpayer's revolt, a general economic depression, actual or potential bankruptcy or a serious slump or dislocation in the economy that drastically reduces revenues? What if a compelling need arises for expenditures judged to have priority over pension rights—war, widespread and acute want, domestic turmoil, or a natural catastrophe? These possibilities make it hard to be smug about the continuation of legislative policy. The question has also been raised as to whether court decisions or constitutional provisions forbidding diminution of pension rights are enforceable if the legislature refuses to appropriate the funds.[6] In the face of these uncertainties, there is reason to put significant value in terms of employee security on the funding of public plans.

The very fact that some jurisdictions find it difficult to appropriate enough money to put their pension plans on a funded basis is significant. One might promulgate a principle for both public and private plans—the more difficult to fund, the more necessary. If it is difficult now, why should it be easier in the future? Unless there is a clear and convincing answer to that question, the logical inference is that it may be even more difficult in the future than it is now. Funding may therefore be necessary for the sake of security.

If a system faces the prospect, even on a long-term basis, that it may not be able to meet contribution requirements, then reserves provide desirable security. At least they will reassure the beneficiaries. Newark, New Jersey, claims to be close to bankruptcy. At this writing, New York City is in danger of default. What is the pensioner or older worker to think? Reserves to guarantee pension payments may reassure every pensioner that the assets for his lifetime pension are already on hand and to prospective retirees that their benefits are secure.

The Analogy to Social Security

The Social Security system is financed essentially on a pay-as-you-go basis with a contingency reserve of only about one year's benefit payments. There is fairly wide agreement that this is entirely appropriate and, further, that to fund the system with much greater reserves would be economically unsound for the nation. It is recognized that each generation of beneficiaries will be supported by its contemporary generation of active employees and their employers.

Why should not state and local governments follow the same policy? The answer has two aspects, each of which helps to clarify the reasons for funding in state and local systems.

The first point is that the Social Security system is relatively mature. Its provisions have been designed quickly to encompass as large a percentage of the aged as possible. The result is that the percentage of payroll required to meet current Social Security payments

[6] Rubin G. Cohn, "Public Employee Retirement Plans—the Nature of the Employees' Rights," *Law Forum*, Spring 1968.

is theoretically close to the percentage of payroll expected to be required for its ultimate support. The Social Security system does not ignore long-term costs. On the contrary, its contribution schedule is based on a seventy-five-year projection. Moreover, the entire financing basis for future Social Security is embodied in the law. For old-age, survivors, and disability benefits it is (as of 1974) a combined employer-employee rate of 9.7 percent, declining to 9.6 percent in 1978, and rising to 11.7 percent in 2011. This is fixed now and it is obviously not a sharply escalating cost. The equivalent for the seventy-five-year period of projection would be 10.6 percent. True, an escalation of the wage base is also built into the law. Nevertheless, the essential point is that the ultimate cost is faced and honestly reflected in the legislated contribution schedule.

If a public employee plan were mature, in the sense that benefits had reached a stable percentage of payroll, it would provide rationale for not funding. But cases of that kind are rare, and consequently, that parallel to Social Security is inappropriate.

The second difference is that Social Security can look to the entire nation and its economy for its support, while individual states, cities, counties, and other governmental units are exposed to a greater hazard of economic change or natural disaster. The degree of funding desirable is directly proportionate to the uncertainty of future ability to pay.

Cost Accounting for Government Activities

A funding schedule allocates cost to the time when the benefit is being accrued, that is, to the period of employment, not the period of retirement. That permits proper cost accounting for a public project or activity. A state or local government frequently has to know what a particular operation costs, e.g., running a power or water utility, a transportation system, a hospital, garbage collection, etc. For this purpose, the attendant pension cost should be charged to each year of employment; employment costs are thus paid by the generation that enjoys the services, not by a future generation.

Effect of Investment Earnings

Investment earnings on pension reserves will reduce future contribution requirements. On the average, investment earnings equal 26 percent of the total receipts of state and local retirement systems.

Marples has calculated that if a typical plan is fully funded and earns 4 percent interest, its investment yield will ultimately pay about 50 percent of the benefits, thereby cutting the contributions otherwise required in half.[7] The illustrative figures shown in Table 8.1 were developed on a low-interest rate of 2½ percent, but even they show ultimate contributions for a fully funded system to be 43 percent of the contributions required under pay-as-you-go financing.

Funding, over the years, means a lesser total outlay of public funds. This is an impressive, but not conclusive, argument. Confronted with the same choice, a businessman would ask what else he could do with the money. Could his company invest the contribution difference in some way that would earn more? If it could, then that might be a cheaper way of paying for the ultimate pension costs. Of course, the parallel is not exact. The alternative "investments" for a state or local government are generally of a social nature or at least very diffuse in their economic results so that it would be difficult to determine whether the government would in fact be better able to meet its ultimate pension costs by alternative "investments" in place of present funding contributions.

It may all come down to this. A pension fund represents one of the few means by which a state or local government can realize investment yield, which is a painless source of income to meet pension disbursements. That income will serve to reduce the upward pressure on future tax rates. Moreover, the investment yield of a public pension fund is held in trust for the pension plan; it therefore offsets costs, not for government in general, but specifically with respect to the pension plan. Holding that particular cost in check helps to assure continuation of the commitment.

Paying in "Soft Dollars" or "Hard Dollars"

Advocates of pay-as-you-go argue that the relatively "soft dollars" of the future will make it easier to contribute. Why, they ask, should "hard dollars" be paid in now in order to meet future commitments that will be paid in depreciated dollars? Won't the money lose its real value while it remains an asset of the retirement system? Won't it be easier to pay later?

[7] William F. Marples, *Actuarial Aspects of Pension Security* (Homewood, Illinois, Richard D. Irwin, Inc., 1965).

Part of the response is the argument that invested assets can keep pace with inflation. Over long periods, they generally have. The Wall Street rule of thumb is that high-quality bonds will yield 3 percent plus the expected annual rate of price inflation. Stocks, over long periods of time, have yielded more. History offers justification for the expectation that diversified investments will keep pace with price levels.

Another part of the answer is to pose this test: what sort of pension financing would be in order if the long-term costs are to be met by a constant rate of taxation on the public's personal income? If one adopts as a fair standard the idea that the cost of a public plan should be so spread that it will always amount to the same percentage of taxpayer income, would this argue for funding or pay-as-you-go?

The answer is not difficult to find. The average government salary has, broadly speaking, at least kept pace with average income. Consequently, contributions to public employee pensions determined as a long-term level percentage of their pay will not represent a greater proportionate burden for present taxpayers than for future taxpayers. If anything, the contrary is true—because the government sector has been increasing, funding that approximates a level percentage of payroll will, in fact, be an increasing burden to the public. A schedule that does not demand of the present generation of taxpayers a greater percentage of income than will be demanded of a later generation cannot be fairly accused of paying "hard dollars" for "soft-dollar" disbursements. Level percentage-of-pay funding does not therefore impose unfairly on the present generation of taxpayers.

VARIETIES OF ACTUARIAL FUNDING POLICIES

Funding policies vary greatly from one to another. A goal and a schedule by which to reach it must be chosen. Moreover, funding rests on anticipated experience, which in turn raises the important question of what should and should not be taken into account in projecting the future. In this chapter, we will consider the basis of funding policy for public employee plans; in the next, the questions of policy involved in actuarial assumptions as to future experience.

Funding is based on the actuary's projection of what the plan's experience will be—benefit payments, administrative expenses, investment yield, payrolls, and employee contributions. There is a wide choice of funding goals and a further choice of the period of years and the contribution schedule by which to achieve the desired goal.

Although some actuaries may demur, it is our view that there is no formula that is the only "correct" basis for actuarial funding. The choice is a matter of policy. We will review the options, define the concepts involved, and evaluate their role in the financing of public systems. In that process, we will formulate a number of principles which should, in our opinion, govern funding policy.

Terminal Funding

For any particular year, a contribution is made equal to the total value of the benefits awarded in that year (except as that total is off-set by the accumulated contributions of the beneficiaries). The entire obligation, whether for a lifetime or otherwise, is taken into account. That liability is not the simple sum of the expected payments. Payments are discounted for the expected investment yield on the sum of money involved over the period of its disbursement. The immediate liability is therefore equal to the "present value" of the future series of payments. In other words, the sum of money set aside is sufficient to meet the payments if the unexpended balance of that sum earns interest at the assumed rate. "Commuted value" is synonymous with "present value"; "discounted value," as used in business literature, has essentially the same meaning.

Although "present value" is no doubt already a familiar concept, it still warrants explanation because of its central position in funding. Suppose a man age 65 is awarded a pension of $300 a month. According to a currently used mortality table, his benefits will probably total $57,240. If we assume investment yield of 4 percent, it requires only $38,112 at the point of his retirement to make all of the payments. That last figure is the "present value" of his pension at the point of his retirement.

"Present value" also applies to a sequence of payments *into* a fund. Consider that same man: suppose there were no advance funds for him, but it was decided to meet the total obligation by making contributions in five equal annual installments, each made at the beginning of each year starting with his retirement. How much is needed? The installments, once made, will earn interest for as long as they are not paid out in benefits. The actuary has to solve for five equal first-of-year future payments with a "present value" of $38,112. That comes to $8,232 a year; over the five years $41,160 will be contributed.

Terminal funding results in erratic contributions from year to year. The contribution in a particular year is determined by the number, age, and benefit rights of those who retire in the year, items that can fluctuate by a substantial margin. Contributions generally increase over a period of years because an employee group will typically produce an increasing number of retirees for a substantial period of years. (For illustrative figures, see column 2 of Table 8.1, and refer to Chart 8.1).

Terminal funding entails maintenance of modest reserves— precisely enough to see the current pensioners through without further contributions. In the theoretical model, investment earnings reduce ultimate annual contributions below pay-as-you-go levels by 20 to conceivably 40 percent.

Terminal funding does not answer the need for a funding plan that will fully reflect long-term costs; it reflects the long-term needs only if those who are already beneficiaries and not the needs of future benefit recipients. Moreover, changes in the plan that may involve increased future disbursements are not reflected in terminal funding contributions. For example, the rate of benefit accrual for future service (service after the change) could be increased, let us say, from 1 percent of final average salary to 1.5 percent. For someone retiring thirty years later, it would probably affect all service credits and represent a 50 percent increase in pension. Terminal funding would reflect only the negligible immediate impact on pensioner liability. For decades, the contributions would be forced upward.

Terminal funding has not been widely used by public plans because: contribution requirements vary from year to year, a fact difficult to reconcile with government budgeting; it does not provide an actuarial foundation for systematically sharing costs with the employees; and it does not take account of all ultimate costs.

Table 8.1 ◆ *Illustrative Projections Of Traditional Funding Schedule*

Years	(1) *Pay-as- you-go*	(2) *Terminal funding*	(3) *Unit credit, interest only*	(4) *Entry age normal, interest only*
Beginning of year:		*Contributions (000's)*		
1	None	None	$ 36.9	$ 43.2
2	$ 0.8	$ 10.2	37.9	43.2
3	2.1	15.2	38.8	43.2
4	3.5	18.5	39.6	43.2
5	5.3	23.1	40.2	43.2
10	17.3	39.0	42.3	43.2
15	30.0	42.3	43.4	43.2
20	40.6	44.1	44.4	43.2
21	42.4	44.4	44.5	43.2
25	48.2	45.3	45.2	43.2
30	54.4	55.8	45.5	43.2
35	63.0	63.4	44.0	43.2
40	65.6	50.4	43.6	43.2
50	64.2	49.2	49.9	43.2
Limit	63.0	50.8	44.1	43.2
End of year:		*Funds (000's)*		
1	None	None	$ 37.8	$ 44.3
2	None	$ 9.5	76.8	88.9
3	None	23.2	116.3	133.2
4	None	39.1	156.1	177.3
5	None	58.3	195.8	220.5
10	None	178.2	380.6	417.3
15	None	289.0	528.1	570.9
20	None	364.7	638.1	682.4
21	None	375.9	656.3	700.4
25	None	410.1	719.6	760.8
30	None	455.0	781.3	815.6
35	None	528.2	803.5	834.6
40	None	536.1	793.6	826.6
50	None	501.0	770.1	806.3
Limit	None	502.1	775.0	810.6
Ratio of fund at limit to:				
(a) year's benefit payments	0	8.0	12.3	12.9
(b) liability for pensioners	0	1.0	1.5	1.6
(c) value of accrued benefits	0	0.4	0.6	0.7
(d) value of all future benefits	0	0.3	0.4	0.5

Basis: A hypothetical plan and employee group. The group consists of 1,000 active employees, distributed from age 30 to 64, assumed to be replenished with new entrants each year, and with no retired persons initially. The benefit is $420 annually payable at age 65; the investment yield is assumed to be 2½%.

Table 8.1 Continued)

(5) Unit credit, 20-year amortization	(6) Entry age normal, 20-year amortization	(7) Attained age normal, 20-year amortization	(8) Aggregate	(9) Individual level premium
		Contributions (000's)		
$ 53.4	$ 68.5	$ 77.9	$ 95.6	$ 126.5
54.4	68.5	75.9	89.9	112.4
55.3	68.5	74.1	84.7	101.5
56.1	68.5	72.5	80.0	92.8
56.7	68.5	71.0	75.7	85.1
58.8	68.5	65.3	59.2	57.2
59.9	68.5	61.5	43.3	42.0
60.9	68.5	58.9	37.7	34.1
34.0	27.1	31.5	36.9	33.0
34.7	27.1	30.2	34.0	30.0
34.9	27.1	29.1	31.6	27.9
33.5	27.1	28.4	29.9	27.1
33.1	27.1	27.9	28.9	27.1
33.4	27.1	27.4	27.9	27.1
27.1	27.1	27.1	27.1	27.1
		Funds (000's)		
$ 54.7	$ 70.2	$ 79.8	$ 93.0	$ 129.7
111.0	141.3	158.8	191.7	247.2
168.3	212.9	236.5	281.1	355.3
226.3	284.8	313.1	366.5	455.6
284.7	356.6	388.3	447.8	548.7
570.0	707.3	737.4	794.1	918.6
831.3	1,035.1	1,039.1	1,090.1	1,160.8
1,070.1	1,343.7	1,302.0	1,251.7	1,315.9
1,088.3	1,361.7	1,323.5	1,277.3	1,339.2
1,151.5	1,422.1	1,395.2	1,362.7	1,413.8
1,213.2	1,476.9	1,459.7	1,438.8	1,475.9
1,235.4	1,495.9	1,484.8	1,471.4	1,495.9
1,225.5	1,487.9	1,480.7	1,472.0	1,487.9
1,202.0	1,467.6	1,464.6	1,461.0	1,467.6
1,206.9	1,471.9	1,471.9	1,471.9	1,471.9
19.2	23.4	23.4	23.4	23.4
2.4	2.9	2.9	2.9	2.9
1.0	1.2	1.2	1.2	1.2
0.7	0.9	0.9	0.9	0.9

Source: Charles L. Trowbridge, "Fundamentals of Pension Funding," *Transactions, Society of Actuaries*, Vol. 4, 1952. (Radios added.)

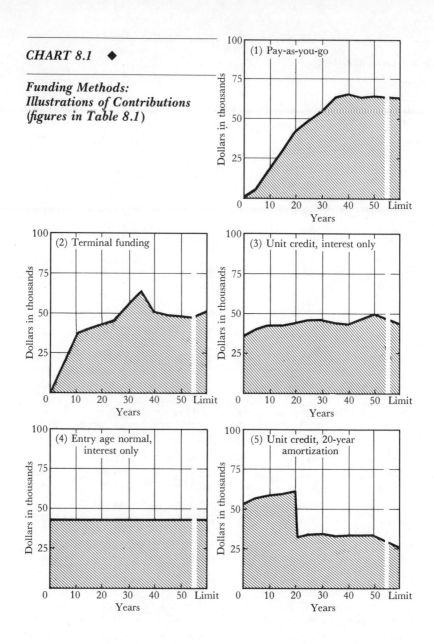

CHART 8.1 ◆

Funding Methods:
Illustrations of Contributions
(figures in Table 8.1)

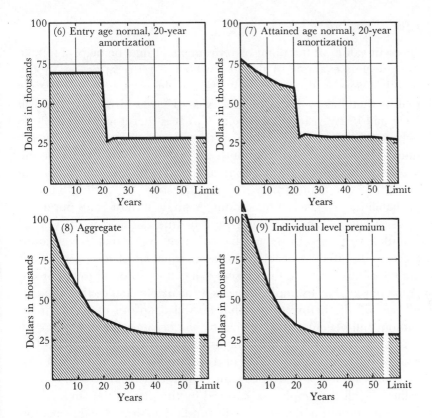

Unit Credit Funding

"Unit credit" funding is somewhat in the same category. It is not much used by public plans but worth describing if only because of the usefulness of the concepts.[8]

Under this method, the contribution for a particular year has two components—a current service contribution and a past service contribution. The current service part is determined by identifying the amount of benefits attributable to the current year of service of the covered employees; the present value of those accrued benefits is the "normal cost." The sum of those present values is the current service contribution requirement.

"Present value" is taken at the point of benefit accrual (service) and involves more discounting of the future payments than does the

[8] In an effort to create clearer pension terminology, a Committee on Pension and Profit-Sharing Terminology, under the auspices of the Commission on Insurance Terminology and of the Pension Research Council of the Wharton School, has developed a set of terms. "Unit credit" funding is called the "accrued benefit cost" method. The older terms are used in this text because they are better known.

"present value" at the point of retirement. It may be helpful to take the previous example of the man who will retire at 65 on $300 a month. Consider the funding of that benefit when he is 55. Assume that he then has twenty years of service. (He was hired at 35 and will have had thirty years of service at 65.) It is therefore reasonable to say that his one year of service, in the year when he is 55, earns for him a pension of $10 a month ($300 ÷ 30 = $10). What is the present value (at 55) of $10 a month payable for life starting at age 65? There are many answers to that question, depending on what probabilities are taken into account. A single sum of $848 put in reserve at age 55, and earning 4 percent (the assumed yield) will accumulate to $1,270 by 65 and be sufficient to pay that $10-a-month piece of the lifetime benefit. However, when *all* of the probabilities are taken into account, the present value at 55 is found to be considerably lower. For example, there is a calculable chance that the employee will die before 65, or that he will drop out of employment without full benefit rights, or that he will become disabled.

In short, an array of actuarial assumptions comes into play. The result, with one illustrative set of assumptions, is a present value of $604 instead of $858, for that same benefit accrual. The sum of such values for all the employees covered by the plan is the current service contribution under unit credit funding. Cost under this method changes with the employee's age. When the same employee was younger, the same unit of benefit required a lesser contribution, because of a longer period of interest earnings lay ahead and because there was a greater probability of his falling by the wayside before maturing for benefits. This means that as an employee group gets older, on the average—after weighting for relative benefit amounts—the current service contribution under unit credit funding increases, up to the point when the weighted average age stabilizes. (That effect is noticeable from column 3 of Table 8.1.) Initially, unit credit funding is likely to be an understatement of subsequent contribution requirements. The fact that it does not level contributions is, in fact, one of the principal deficiencies of this funding method for public employee retirement systems.

Past Service Funding

A past service contribution is the second part of unit credit funding as it is of many other funding schedules. That contribution would not be necessary if a pension plan had been in effect, with all of its present provisions, since the earliest time that any member (employee or pensioner) started to work in creditable employment. If that were true, with unit credit funding, the funds on hand would at any point exactly equal the present value of all benefits accrued on account of service to that date. (In this sense, it should be understood that a benefit is "accrued" even if benefit rights are contingent on some additional employment.) However, at the time a pension plan starts, it gives benefit credits for service before it began. The present value of those past service benefits is the past service liability under unit credit funding. That obligation is commonly amortized over a period of twenty to forty years.

"Amortization" is a concept used repeatedly in actuarial funding. It is analogous to mortgage payments—a series of level or otherwise regular payments that pays off the principal plus the interest accruing over the period of payment. Of course, the longer the period, the smaller the annual payment. Once the past service liability is completely amortized, the fund is said to be in a "fully funded position." With unit credit funding, the plan then has on hand assets equal to the then-present value of all future benefits to pensioners and other beneficiaries plus the value of all future benefit rights accrued by nonretired employees to the point of valuation. (Column 5 of Table 8.1 illustrates the contributions and assets of funding on a unit-credit basis with twenty-year amortization of the initial past service liability.)

Contribution requirements drop abruptly once the past service liability has been amortized; but that change is liable to be more theoretical than real. Changes in the plan and actuarial losses, due, for example, to salary increases in excess of those calculated, add to the accrued liability and generally require additional periods of amortization. In the theoretical model, however, any funding schedule with a fixed period of amortization entails a drop in contributions when amortization is completed. (See Table 8.1 and Chart 8.1.) At that point, it is considered "fully funded," which simply means it no longer needs contributions on account of the past service liability or, to use a broader term, the "supplemental liability."

It is possible (although uncommon) to fund on a unit-credit basis, but to pay interest only (at the assumed rate) on the past service liability. (See column 3 of Table 8.1.) That would mean that at any time in the future the fund would have reserves equal to the value of all benefits accrued *except* for the benefits attributable to service before the funding began. Problems associated with "interest only" payments on past service liability will be discussed later in connection with "entry-age-normal" funding, a method much more widely used.

Unit credit funding has frequently been used in connection with insurance contracts. Contributions amount to the annual "purchase" for each employee of the benefit he has accrued by virtue of his current year's employment. It is, therefore, also known as "single premium" or "deferred annuity" funding.

Unit credit funding is not common, certainly not among the larger public employee retirement systems. One reason is that insurance contracts are rarely involved. Another is that the technique is not readily applicable to plans based on final salary, which require projections to the future; unit credit tries to deal with readily identifiable segments of benefits already accrued. Still another reason is the fact that cost increases with age.

Entry-Age-Normal Funding

Entry-age-normal funding is widely used. It comes closest of all the traditional methods to developing level contribution requirements, whether expressed in dollars or as payroll percentage (except at the end of the amortization period, when contributions drop).

Entry-age-normal funding is comprised of "normal cost" and a contribution on account of the unfunded supplemental liability (also called the "accrued" or the "past service" liability).[9]

Normal cost is determined when the actuary answers the following question:

> How much would have to be contributed each year for each covered employee as a level amount or percentage of pay, from the time he started creditable service, for the value of his pension to be accumulated at the time he is expected to retire?

Consider our example of the man who is 55, has twenty years of past service, and will retire at 65 on $300 a month. From the time he entered the employment (at 35) until age 65, an annual contribution of $349 would provide an accumulation of $38,112, equal to the

---

[9] The Committee on Pension and Profit-Sharing Terminology refers to this method as the "projected benefit cost method, individual, with supplemental liability."

value of his pension at his retirement. Since this normal cost is level from entry to retirement, the annual contribution exceeds the present value of the current benefit accrued while the employee is young and is lower than the value of the current benefit accrued when he is comparatively old.

The aggregate of entry-age-normal costs for each of the employees is the normal cost of the plan. It does not increase if the average age of the employees increases. (It does increase, however, if the average hiring age increases.)

Funding the Accrued Liability

In addition to normal cost, the supplemental liability must be taken into account, since normal cost was not in fact contributed during the period of employment preceding the plan, or else it was contributed on the basis of a less liberal plan or much lower salary levels (and therefore lower projected benefits). The supplemental liability is equal to the assets that would have accumulated if present normal costs had been contributed all along, that is, ever since any member of the plan was first employed.

While often referred to as the "past service liability," that term is not precisely accurate. The amount is normally greater than the then-present value of benefits accrued on the basis of past employment. As we have pointed out, entry-age-normal funding levels the normal cost from employment entry to retirement and therefore accumulates reserves through the early years of employment greater then the value of the benefits accrued. It is these reserves which permit the normal cost contribution to be held level over the remainder of employment. It is therefore more precise to refer to the "accrued liability" or "supplemental liability" under the entry-age-normal method.

The unfunded accrued liability must be dealt with in one way or another, whether by a policy of amortization—twenty- to forty-year periods are common choices—or by paying interest on it at the assumed rate of yield. Table 8.1 illustrates the results of amortizing over a twenty-year period (column 6) or of paying the interest only (column 4). (See also Chart 8.1.)

The accrued liability is calculated as the excess of the present value of all benefits for the present members, active and retired (and their beneficiaries) over the present value of all future normal cost contributions. It is recalculated with each valuation. That liability is offset by existing assets; the remainder is the *unfunded* accrued liability and it is that which is subject to further amortization or interest payments.

The Fully Funded Plan

Once the accrued liability has been amortized, the plan is in a "fully funded" position. As indicated, "full funding" by this method represents greater assets than with unit credit funding; the reserves equal more than the present value of all accrued benefits. In Table 8.1, note that the final fund with entry-age-normal and amortization of the accrued liability is 21 percent higher than under unit credit funding.

Discussion of pension financing often involves the question of whether a plan is "on full funding." That does not mean that it has achieved a fully funded position; it means that it is on a schedule intended to achieve that goal.

The Method and the Calculation of Employee Contributions

Whatever the funding, a calculation using the entry-age-normal method is strongly indicated for a contributory system in which the rate of employee contributions has been fixed so as to pay for some desired portion—for instance one-half or one-third—of the pension cost. That situation is very common among the public systems. In determining employee contribution rates, the benefit attributable to past service is usually disregarded. After all, it would be an unfair burden for an employee to pay for his past service credit; he would have to pay much more than a new employee who was hired at the same age. Furthermore, for someone close to retirement, the rate of contribution would be impossibly high. The entry-age-normal method permits the employee's share to be determined on the basis of a level normal cost, without reference to the supplemental liability.

If member contribution rates are determined by the entry-age-normal method, it does not necessarily follow that employer contributions are fixed by the same method. The employer has to meet essentially three costs: (1) the portion of normal cost (under the entry-age method) not borne by the employees; (2) payment on account of the unfunded accrued liability as calculated upon establishment of the plan or of any plan modification, and (3) payment on account of any additions to the unfunded accrued liability because of actuarial losses. These costs may be met be a number of other funding schedules, even though employee contribution rates may have been determined by the entry-age-normal method.

Entry-Age-Normal, "Interest-Only" Funding

This funding method has been advocated by some as particularly relevant for public employee retirement systems where permanence can be taken for granted and reserves adequate to fulfill all pension obligations without further contributions are not regarded as essential. With some modification, it is the basic method written into the statute governing the federal Civil Service Retirement System.

The contribution consists of two components: normal cost, as developed by the entry-age method, and interest at the assumed rate on the unfunded accrued liability.

The method has two major advantages: it prescribes an entirely level contribution, in contrast to a drop when amortization is completed, and contributions are lower than with amortization, to the extent, obviously, of the omitted amortization payment. Of the methods shown in Table 8.1 and Chart 8.1, it is the only one with level payments. Interest is paid because otherwise the calculated unfunded accrued liability would increase and the fund would ultimately be unable to meet disbursement needs.

The reserves produced are of course lower than an amortization program would provide—lower, of course, by the amount carried forward unamortized. In the typical case, reserves may be expected to cover the liability for annuitants and something more for still-active employees. The hypothetical case in Table 8.1 (column 4) shows a reserve always greater than the liability for pensioners.

Some Shortcomings of "Interest-Only" Funding

In the long run, however, "interest-only" funding has some shortcomings, even where system permanence can be presumed and a goal of less than "full funding" reserves is acceptable.

If interest-only funding is applied to a mature group, that is, one with a fully developed roster of beneficiaries and active employees with a stationary age distribution, it is the equivalent of pay-as-you-go financing.[10] In fact, the reason "interest-only" funding generally produces reserves is that the plans are immature—they start off with few beneficiaries in relation to the ultimate numbers. At a later point in time, the group may be mature or nearly so. If at that point benefits increase, whether through plan amendments that include pensioners or through salary increases greater than assumed, normal-cost-plus-interest-only funding may no longer suffice to produce reserves equal to the liability for pensioners.

It is also possible to be saddled with what we might call, for lack of a better word, an "over-mature" group. This would be a retirement system that has produced a large crop of beneficiaries, but whose active employees have decreased in number. In a situation of that kind, paying normal cost on the active employees and interest only on the accrued liability may not even match benefit disbursements. That situation is not theoretical: it has happened.

In short, interest-only funding can suffice, provided that at the appropriate time a fuller funding schedule is substituted. Congress did this in 1969 for the funding of the Civil Service Retirement System partly because some of the shortcomings of "interest-only" funding began to appear. With a history of insufficient appropriations, the deficiency reached $43.4 billion by June 30, 1965, and interest alone amounted to $1.5 billion a year or 9.1 percent of payroll. Congress established a graduated schedule of appropriations so that full interest on the deficiency will be paid by the 1980 fiscal year. More to the point, however, was a provision authorizing appropriations based on thirty-year amortization of any liberalized benefits, of any extension of coverage to a new group, and of any benefit increases resulting from statutes increasing salaries. In short, Congress found it desirable to meet extra cost increments on an amortization basis, rather than add to the established accrued liability on which only the interest would be paid.

The problem is that a transition of this kind is hard to make. The question of stepped-up funding comes at a time of benefit increase and it appears to be a disproportionately high cost for the proposed

[10] Demonstrated mathematically by Trowbridge, "Fundamentals of Pension Planning," *TSA* IV, p. 24.

change. A further disadvantage is the arbitrariness involved in drawing the line between the part to be amortized and the part to be left unamortized; the process introduces confusion as to the ultimate funding goal and makes it more vulnerable to further change.

"Interest-Only" Funding and Pricing Benefit Changes

A second potential difficulty with interest-only funding is that it may put a misleading price tag on particular benefit changes.

An important criterion for the funding policy of a public employee system is that it should furnish an adequate price tag for every contemplated change. The various formulas do not furnish the same cost estimates. If a particular change affects the accrued liability but not the normal cost, it is liable to be underpriced by the interest-only method. An increase limited to current annuitants is a typical example. Since it does not affect active employees, it does not change the normal cost. It increases only the unfunded accrued liability, on which this funding method requires payment of no more than interest. It therefore looks like a very inexpensive benefit, compared to what might be done for still-active employees.

An extreme but simple illustration would be a one-time additional payment to current annuitants of, let us say, $1,000,000. What additional contribution would "interest-only" funding require? If the interest assumption is 4 percent, the answer is $40,000 a year, which seems strange as the price tag on the expenditure of $1,000,000. Moreover, if the interest assumption were shifted to 5 percent, the quoted cost would then become $50,000. Again, it seems peculiar that if it is assumed that the fund *improves* its earnings, the extra benefits become *more* costly rather than *less* costly. There is an explanation of the anomaly. Expenditures of $1,000,000 would diminish the reserve position of the system; its future earnings would be diminished by $40,000 or $50,000 a year, depending on the interest rate assumed. It is this income loss that the extra contribution, levied in perpetuity, would make good. However, an explanation of that kind is too complex for public debate or for any layman's grasp. In essence, part of the price is a hidden cost in terms of a diminution of the reserve position or funding of the system. A more desirable system for pricing a change is one that would include an appropriate allowance for restoration of reserve position.

An alternative is to determine *total* contributions on one basis (e.g., interest-only funding) but to quote price tags on specific changes in other terms (e.g., entry-age-normal cost with thirty-year amortization). That is, in essence, what Congress has prescribed for the federal Civil Service System. But that may be a complicated and confusing procedure. It is better to have a policy that provides cost appraisals of possible changes on the same basis as is used to determine contributions. Interest-only funding cannot always meet that criterion.

Perpetual Period of Amortization

It may be possible to compromise between amortization over a fixed period of time, such as twenty, thirty, or forty years, and non-amortization of the accrued liability, by amortizing over a perpetually renewing period, such as thirty or forty years. For example, such a schedule would start with contributions necessary to fulfill forty-year amortization. The next year, the contribution amortizes the un-funded accrued liability, not over the remaining thirty-nine years, but over a new forty-year period, with similar renewal of the amortization period in each successive year. The Virginia state system, among others, uses a funding plan of this kind.

The formula pursues a fully funded position, but at a measured pace that assures it will never get there. It may build up reserves falling between those of fixed-period amortization and those of "interest-only" funding; that depends however on the actuarial assumptions used and the precise way in which the method is applied.

Sometimes a system which has been on a fixed amortization period for a long time finds that it is forced to take on some characteristics of the renewing period. With a fixed amortization period, there is inevitably the problem of what to do about a large increase in the unfunded accrued liability when the plan has been substantially amended. Suppose this happens when the system is facing the twenty-first year of thirty-year amortization. Should the additional liability be priced and funded over the remaining twenty-one years, or should a new period of thirty years be used? The latter expedient has sometimes been adopted. To be sure, it can be confusing to split the accrued liability and follow two different amortization schedules. And if a new period is selected several times, it may amount, *de facto,* to an irregular equivalent of a policy of perpetual amortization.

Theoretically, with a perpetually renewing period for amortization, the contribution should gradually decrease. However, the experience is that this is usually counterbalanced by increases in the accrued liability because of benefit liberalization or actuarial losses, that is, experience more costly than anticipated, so that the expected reduction in contributions may not materialize.

Individual Level Premium Funding

This method is probably not used by public plans except perhaps for some small systems underwritten through insurance contracts, for which it was designed.[11] It ignores the distinction between current service and past service, starting with employees at whatever age they are *at the beginning of the plan,* projecting the pension on which each one is expected to retire, and then determining the annual contribution as the level amount necessary to fund each person's pension over the period from his *attained* age to his retirement age. If the pension amount is increased because of a salary increase or a plan change, it entails an additional piece of level annual premium from the new attained age to retirement age.

This method results in a very high initial cost followed by a sharp downward slope (Table 8.1, column 9, and Chart 8.1). For individuals close to normal retirement age, the funding is obviously very costly, and that is what produces the high initial cost. Each contemplated plan change involves high next-year cost all over again. Ultimately, the total annual contribution requirement and its reserve position are exactly the same as with entry-age-normal funding with full amortization.

Aggregate Funding

This method is widely used among public employee systems. In effect, it takes the accrued liability as computed under the entry-age-normal method and amortizes it over approximately the average future service period of the current employees. It does not, however, actually require an entry-age-normal computation. Cost is determined as follows:

1. The present value of all future benefits is determined. (Employees not yet hired are not included.)

[11] Called by the Committee on Pension and Profit-Sharing Terminology, the "projected benefit cost method, individual, without supplemental liability."

2. The existing fund, if any, is subtracted. The remainder is, of course, the *unfunded* present value of benefits.
3. The unfunded present value is divided by the present value of all future salaries. (Employees not yet hired are not included in the total for future salaries.)
4. The result is the percentage of salary to be contributed.

The required contribution starts higher than that of any other method except individual level premium funding, or, in typical cases, a schedule with amortization of less than twenty years. It declines thereafter and, in the theoretical model, ultimately reaches the same contribution level and the same reserves as those of entry-age-normal with full amortization. This tendency is liable to be counteracted by liberalizations of the plan or by actuarial losses, such as greater salary increases than anticipated. The result is that the contribution rate often does not decline. In effect, the relatively high level of contributions in the early years has frequently acted as a hedge against actuarial losses. This net leveling-off helps to account in part for the endurance of aggregate funding.

The strong appeal of aggregate funding for public systems is that it has a definite and understandable principle on which to stand; namely that the funds required for pensions should be accumulated by the time the employees are eligible (or likely) to retire. The contribution requirement may be comparatively high—more, in the typical case, than entry-age-normal with twenty-year amortization and certainly more than with twenty-five, thirty, or forty-year amortization. The reserves accumulated may sometimes be more than the security considerations of a public system require.

However, with a fixed amortization period, the choice of any one fixed period is, to some extent, arbitrary; reasonable perhaps, but arbitrary. This may be unsettling for a public employee retirement system, because if an arbitrary period is chosen, another arbitrary period can be substituted and the sanctity of adequate funding or consistent pricing may in time be compromised. Aggregate funding has the attractiveness of providing what seems to be a defensible line, a precise principle on which a firm stand can be taken. That is a valuable attribute for public systems, because of the pressure and political debate to which they are subject.

Attained-Age-Normal Funding

This is essentially a modification of aggregate funding.[12] The portion of the present value of benefits attributable to *past service,* as initially calculated, is segregated as a supplemental liability. It is funded on a separate schedule while the remainder of benefits is met through aggregate funding (Table 8.1, column 7). The initial contribution will be lower than that of aggregate funding, if the amortization period chosen for the supplemental liability is shorter than the average remaining period of service of the employees. Ultimately, assuming that the supplemental liability is amortized, the contribution becomes the same as for entry-age-normal or aggregate funding, and so do the reserves.

Frozen Initial Liability

The supplemental liability may be "frozen" at an initial amount so that, as gains or losses are experienced, they are reflected, not in changes in the supplemental liability but in changes in the normal cost computed by the aggregate funding method. This method is used fairly widely. It has the advantage of spreading actuarial gains and losses over a perpetually renewing period approximately equal to the future work-time of the members, instead of amortizing them within some fixed, and perhaps short, period of years.

The funding methods described above are traditional, in the sense that each has achieved wide and long-continued usage in the financing of pension plans generally. The unit credit and individual level premium methods are relatively uncommon among public plans except perhaps for small systems underwritten through insurance contracts. Neither is terminal funding popular. The traditional methods do not, however, exhaust the possibilities.

Fixed-Period Projection Methods

The computer has made it possible for the actuary to add another type of funding, a family based on year-to-year projections of benefit payments, employee contributions, employer contributions, expenses, investment yield, and fund balances. He can therefore solve

[12] Called by the Committee on Pension and Profit-Sharing Terminology, the "projected benefit cost method, aggregate, with supplemental liability."

for a contribution level that will produce at the end of "n" years any desired relationship among assets, liabilities, contributions, and benefits. For example, he can determine which contribution will produce, after twenty years, reserves equal to accumulated employee contributions, plus the liability for future payments to all persons then on the benefit rolls. If desired, he can add reserves to match the liability for benefits vested at that point. With assumptions about new entrants, he can project for forty or fifty years. An assumption can be made as to the likely growth or shrinkage of the covered group.

There are some disadvantages to the method. Choice of a period involves some degree of arbitrariness. If price tags on particular changes are to be produced on the same basis as the overall contribution requirements, the procedure may be unduly laborious, even with a computer. Then there is the hazard that a projection for any given year may turn out to be quite different from the actual experience. The layman may be tempted to judge the reliability of the method by just such a short-run test, even though the ultimate cumulative results may be more dependable than a single one-year slice of the projection would lead one to suppose.

The Unfunded Present Value Family of Funding Formulas

Trowbridge has proposed a method that would determine the annual contribution by applying a predetermined percentage to the total unfunded present value of all future benefits.[13] The percentage is not applied to the unfunded accrued liability, which is based only on that part of the benefit liability which is attributable, in one sense or another, to the period preceding the valuation. It is applied to the much larger figure that includes as well the present value of benefits which present employees will accrue through future service.

The percentage can be chosen so that it accomplishes whatever may be selected as an ultimate objective. That goal may be fixed at reserves equal to any percentage of the value of all benefits; it may be fixed at matching the ultimate liability for annuitants. The value of the accumulated contributions from still-active employees may be added to the reserve goal. Similarly, the then-present value of vested

[13] Charles L. Trowbridge, "The Unfunded Present Value Family of Pension Funding Methods," *Transactions, Actuarial Society*, XV, 1963, p. 151 ff.

benefits may be added, if a higher "security ratio" is desired. By selecting the appropriate percentage, the method can approximate the goals of any of the older methods.

The percentage chosen has to be something more than the assumed interest rate. Just how much more is calculable for a particular plan, depending on the funding objective chosen.

The method would seem to be very simple to apply and to explain. It would have the merit of erasing the usual distinction between past service and current service, normal cost and supplemental liabilities. Discussions of past service liability, prior service liability, accrued liability and how these might differ from one to the other, and how any of these is to be funded, can be confusing even to those who are close to the situation and relatively sophisticated. The proposed method would cut through all of this confusion by dealing only with the unfunded portion of the present value of *all* benefits. Actuarial gains or losses would be reflected automatically in the unfunded present value and therefore spread through future contributions in the same way as any other cost.

There might be a remaining problem for systems which divide the normal cost in some ratio between employees and employer if the employees are not to share in the financing of past service. In such cases, it might be necessary to develop by another method, such as entry-age-normal, a contribution requirement for current service, from which the fixed rate or rates of employee contributions could be derived. However, the total contribution could still be calculated annually by the proposed method.

One of the principal attractions of the method is that it could be used to establish the practical equivalent of perpetually level funding without the shortcomings that develop with "interest-only" funding. The first difficulty we described was that with a "mature" or "overmature" group, contributions may be insufficient. The "unfunded present value method" would seem to solve that problem. If the contribution is a fixed percentage of the unfunded present value of all benefits, the level of contributions will automatically and in appropriate degree accommodate to the maturity of the group. If the unfunded value increased, so would the contribution.

The second problem with "interest-only" funding, we may recall, is that it sometimes results in a misleading price tag where proposals affect largely past service. The proposed method would seem to eliminate the problem by ignoring the past service distinction. If extra benefits are added, they increase the present value of benefits in direct proportion and the contribution similarly. So, as an example, we refer back to the hypothetical case we used earlier of a one-time extra benefit payment of $1,000,000. If 4 percent is the assumed interest rate, interest-only funding would lead to a cost quotation of $40,000 a year, in perpetuity. The Trowbridge proposal would apply a percentage, perhaps 7 percent, and would quote a first year cost of $70,000. To be sure, the second year's cost would be somewhat less—7 percent of the balance, after its adjustment for interest—or about $67,000. Cost would gradually decline. Nevertheless, $70,000 is a more balanced price tag than $40,000 for the simple reason that it would be arrived at in precisely the same way as for any other type of benefit change. It would price proposals for recently hired employees and proposals for current annuitants on precisely the same basis.

It has been noted previously that these two shortcomings of interest-only funding can also be remedied by freezing the amount of liability to be carried forward unamortized. However, that method involves a degree of arbitrariness either in the amount to be frozen or, if that is fixed equal to the initial amount of unfunded accrued liability, in the degree of funding that will result. By comparison, the Trowbridge proposal is simple.

It has been suggested that the method could be adapted so that rather than being a fixed percentage of the unfunded value, the applicable rate could be a calculated series, determined in advance so as to produce a level percentage of payroll.[14]

It has also been suggested that results approximating those achieved by the Trowbridge proposal can be secured by resorting to a perpetual or moving amortization period, described earlier. Also, goals could be established with the more traditional methods by selecting a portion of the value of benefits *not* to be funded. For example, it is possible to use one of the older methods and amortize 50 or 75 percent of the supplemental liability.[15]

[14] William A. Dreher, in discussion of the Trowbridge article, *T.A.S.*, XV, 1963, p. 183.

[15] Discussion by Cecil J. Nesbitt and Malcolm D. McKinnon of Trowbridge article, *T.A.S.*, XV, 1963, pp. 170–77.

It is true that approximately the same ultimate reserve positions can be developed through other calculations or funding schedules. However, for public plans, there is a heavy premium on a method of funding that is simple, that is totally directed toward a readily describable and defensible goal, and that applies the same basis for pricing particular aspects and changes as it does to the plan as a whole. It is a particular charm of the Trowbridge proposal that it holds out the prospect of accomplishing all of these objectives.

Although proposed ten years ago, the method has not been used. One reason is that for private plans there has been the question whether such a method would win acceptance by the Internal Revenue Service. I.R.S. has thus far defined its limits in terms of traditional funding formulas with past-service amortization as a key element. However, this question need not concern public plans, since there are no upper limits on government contributions to public plans. Another reason for lack of application is the fact that private plans are not under the same pressure as public plans for a funding policy that can endure political debate. Moreover, private plans generally want a flexible funding policy; public plans want—or need—a firm one.

As for the public plans, application of the method has probably been held back by inertia, whether on the part of the actuaries or of others, by attachment to the older formula methods, and by the understandable advantage, in public discussions, of methods that have been sanctified by tradition and general practice. The method deserves, however, to be thoroughly explored for application.

CHOICE OF FUNDING METHOD

It should be clear by now that a wide variety of funding methods is available. Although it is often assumed that there is only one correct funding policy and that the actuary should define it, the situation is actually more flexible. A funding goal can be established as a matter of policy; an actuarial formula can be designed to fulfill that goal.

Recognition of that fact opens a certain freedom of decision for the governmental policy-maker. That freedom is not an unmixed blessing. To break away from a course followed through tradition or respect for authority presents the troublesome question of which of many alternatives to choose.

Criteria for Funding Policy

Clearly, choosing a funding policy is different for a public plan than for a private plan. In the first place, governments are, in most cases, perpetual and they do have the power to tax, even though in some instances their future ability or willingness to pay may be subject to question. Secondly, governments need, far more than corporations, a constant or stable basis for contributions. Third, governments need a funding policy that can withstand public debate, whereas corporations need only convince their officers and directors and sometimes a union.

A number of standards, most of them already implied, should, in the author's opinion, be used to choose a funding method for public plans:

1. All elements of long-term cost should be taken into account.

2. Contributions should approximate a level percentage of the payroll.

3. Additional funding should be provided only to the extent that security is needed against the possibility of future incapacity of the government to pay.

4. The funding method should provide fair and realistic cost estimates for benefit proposals.

5. The funding method should be one that can be firmly maintained in the face of political pressure and debate.

Level Cost

All elements of long-term cost should be taken into account. That aspect is developed in the next chapter.

A level percentage of payroll is desirable because it provides a fair spread of cost between generations and between present and future price and income levels.

Full Funding

Substantial reserves will accumulate if contributions are made as a level percentage of pay and if they reflect recognition of all elements of cost. Additional funding is desirable if, under the circumstances, future ability to contribute is questionable and reserves are therefore desirable to protect present and future beneficiaries against curtailment of financing. This objective is quite different from the appropriate standard for private plans. For a typical pension plan in private industry, the proper goal is a fully funded position—assets equal to the accrued liability.

Mandatory minimum funding standards were imposed on private pension plans by the Employee Benefit Security Act of 1974, as follows:

1. Normal cost plus amortization of unfunded accrued liabilities over thirty years, except that forty years is permissible for the liability on the effective date of the law (and throughout for negotiated multiemployer plans), plus—

2. Amortization of actuarial gains or losses over fifteen years (in the case of negotiated multiemployer plans, twenty years).

In any event, the objective decreed is full funding. The logic is that the fund should be able to pay all accrued benefits if the plan is terminated.

But if termination is not a real danger, if a state or other unit of government can reasonably assume perpetual life and ability to pay, then achievement of a fully funded position is a questionable standard.

This position is quite different from many widely held views on what is necessary for the "actuarial soundness" of a public plan. There are many advocates of the view that the *only* proper course for a public employee system is to follow a schedule directed to full funding. By that they mean that the past service, accrued, or supplemental liability should be completely amortized within some reasonable period.

The term "full funding" has a normative ring to it, an implied sense of value judgment, as if something less than "full" funding is bad. In our opinion, that judgment is not necessarily valid. The term has been used here despite its normative cast, because it also has an objective meaning, and it hardly seems worthwhile to quarrel over words or to introduce an alternative term.

Those who regard full funding as sacrosanct often make use of other value-colored words. The unfunded accrued liability is often referred to, in reports or headlines, as the "deficiency" or "deficit."

The impression conveyed is that it is an item of fiscal unsoundness, that it must not increase, and that it should be eliminated as soon as feasible. It is easy enough to see how an unfunded liability can be re ferred to, in a sense, as a "deficiency" or "deficit." Furthermore, it is understandable that a finger of accusation should be pointed at a situation in which the "deficiency" or "deficit" is supposed to be eliminated by the funding method adopted but instead grows in absolute numbers and in relative significance. On the other hand, there is nothing *necessarily* improper or unsound about a continuing (but not growing) unfunded liability.

Full funding advocates have sometimes gone to the extent of attempting to secure court enforcement of full funding as the only concept consistent with actuarial soundness. There have been discussions about seeking judicial determination that the unfunded accrued liability of a public employee system is equivalent to public debt, to be charged against the municipality's debt limit. It is not in fact comparable to bonded indebtedness. A public employee system can continue in perpetuity, can discharge all its obligations, and can be financed on a level contribution rate fully reflective of its ultimate disbursement needs, without ever achieving or attempting to achieve a "fully funded" position, as that has traditionally been defined. If there is any reason for doubt about the future fiscal position of the governmental unit, then concern for the security of the employees may dictate accrual of appropriate reserves. But judgment on that score will differ to the same degree that the federal government is different from a small city, county, or public authority with an uncertain future.

Many systems aim at full funding but few achieve it. Liberalization of benefits and experience losses, including salary increases greater than assumed by the actuary, have the effect of stretching out amortization schedules beyond the fulfillment dates. In fact, if the objective is full funding but the actuarial assumptions are not quite realistic, then the system is doomed to perpetual striving toward a goal that always manages to stay beyond its grasp. It is, as we have said, a hedge against inadequate projections. To some extent, there is logic to that. If full funding is solidly accepted as the proper goal, it may be more sensible to pursue it, even with inadequate assumptions that make its achievement elusive, than to shift to some lesser funding policy. Changing from an established course may put the policy-makers in a difficult position by opening up too many choices, debates, and occasions for pressure.

Moreover, if a public system accumulates greater reserves than it really needs, it may not be doing any harm. It will be earning a return on the excess amount. Furthermore, if the government unit is at the same time borrowing money for other purposes, it will in fact be making a profit out of the difference between the interest it pays on its tax-exempt bonds and the higher rate it earns on its retirement fund investments.

If we focus on the state or other government unit that can safely assume perpetual life and ability to pay, then we narrow the most appropriate funding policy down to those which call for level percentage-of-pay funding without reaching for full funding. That would include:

1. Entry-age-normal cost with interest-only on the unfunded accrued liability.

2. Using the "unfunded present value" system with a schedule of percentages that establishes a level percentage-of-pay contribution.

3. A projection method over a long period of years, solved for a level percentage-of-pay contribution with no reserves beyond what the levelling process produces.

4. Amortization of the unfunded accrued liability or of some predetermined portion of it over a properly selected perpetually renewing period.

5. Leaving a designated portion of the accrued liability to remain unfunded.

6. Entry-age-normal funding with amortization over a sufficiently long period so that a fully funded position is always a fairly distant goal.

The first three prescribe a more or less level percentage-of-pay contribution; the remaining three may approximate it.

In summary, funding policy should be chosen to fulfill a carefully chosen goal. Actuarial formulas can and should be designed to implement policy. Policy should be readily defensible in legislative forums. It should reflect all long-term costs and be applicable both to the determination of contributions and to the realistic pricing of plan changes. Funding policy should enforce responsibility by requiring current payment for current decisions.

Contributions based on long-term costs will also result in the accumulation of some reserves, which will help to reassure the pensioners of their ultimate security and produce investment earnings that will substantially reduce cost to the government. However, to the extent that a governmental jurisdiction can realistically presume perpetual life and ability to pay, it need not accumulate those levels of reserves which private pension plans need in order to provide security for employees and pensioners against the possibility of plan termination.

PRESENT STATE OF SYSTEM FUNDING

Public employee systems run the gamut of funding. The New York State Teachers Retirement System, which is quite old, had assets of $3.7 million on June 30,1972, at least 24 times the amount of its annual benefit payments. At the other end of the spectrum is Pittsburgh, with assets of $42,000 (1970–71) and annual benefit payments of $3.6 million; it has been using the contributions of active employees to pay benefits to retirees because city contributions do not meet annual benefit payments.

Sound judgment of the adequacy of system funding requires actuarial calculations. That is not feasible for the aggregate of public plans. With that *caveat,* it may be possible to learn something of their funded position from certain financial ratios and how they have changed over a period of years.

For system fiscal years ending in the period July 1, 1971, through June 30, 1972, system revenues were 2.6 times disbursements. Employer contributions alone exceeded benefit payments by 40 percent. Assets were almost 17 times the level of annual benefit payments. Investment income accounted for almost 28 percent of total revenue (Table 8.2).

Measured against 1942, there has been noticeable progress toward funding. Revenues in 1942 were only twice disbursements and government contributions barely exceeded benefit payments. In 1942, there was heavier reliance on employee contributions. Since then, assets have grown to 17 from 12 times benefit payments, and investment income now provides almost 28 percent of total revenue, rather than 19 percent.

State-administered systems are more fully funded than locally administered systems. For all state systems, receipts were almost three times payments; the ratio for municipal systems was a little less than two times payments. Assets of the state systems were 18 times benefit payments; for the municipal systems the ratio was only 12 (Table 8.3).

Ratios of contributions and assets to benefit payments can be misleading if the systems are very young. Their benefit payments are bound to be comparatively low, and even meager funding can still show a large excess of revenues over disbursements and a seemingly high reserve. We have therefore sought to isolate the relatively mature systems. Among all large state and local systems (all of those with at least 2,500 members as of 1966–67) the median had 15 to 20 annuitants for every 100 active members. For local systems other than those for policemen and firemen, the median was 20 to 25 annuitants per 100. Among the police and firemen's funds the median ratio was at least one annuitant for each two active employees. Using these medians as the minimums to define *relatively* mature systems, we can make the following findings as to current financing ratios:

1. State-administered plans—typically, the government contributes at least 50 percent more than benefit payments and reserves are equal to 20 to 25 times benefit payments. In a fully mature system with retirements at 62–65, assets equal to about 8 or 8.5 times benefit payments would generally be sufficient to match the liability for pensioners. The excess is a reserve for future pensioners.

2. Local systems (other than policemen's and firemen's) are typically not as well financed. Government contributions are often less than benefit payments and, in the average case, not as high as 50 percent more than the payments. The median ratio of assets to benefit payments is in the bracket of 15 to 20 times. Most significant is the fact that among systems where government contributions are the least—less than benefit payments—the reserve for half the cases is less than 10 times benefit payments.

3. The large local systems for policemen and firemen are usually financed at an even lower level than other city systems. Their ratios

Table 8.2 ◆ ***Finances And Financial Ratios: State And Local Retirement***

Fiscal years ended in	Total revenue	Contrib'ns by government	Contrib'ns by employees	Ratio, gov't to employee contrib'ns	Investment income	Percent investment income of receipts
1971–72	$12,620	$5,750	$3,400	1.7	$3,471	27.5
1970–71	11,310	5,241	3,159	1.7	2,910	25.7
1969–70	9,848	4,600	2,788	1.6	2,460	25.0
1968–69	8,558	3,976	2,440	1.5	2,142	25.0
1966–67	6,580	3,055	1,960	1.6	1,565	23.8
1965–66	5,771	2,630	1,771	1.5	1,370	23.7
1964–65	5,260	2,418	1,626	1.5	1,216	23.1
1963–64	4,787	2,256	1,466	1.5	1,065	22.2
1963	4,394	2,100	1,361	1.5	950	21.6
1962	3,997	1,883	1,288	1.5	827	20.7
1961	3,724	1,806	1,201	1.5	717	19.3
1960	3,393	1,652	1,140	1.5	601	17.7
1959	2,974	1,403	1,073	1.3	498	16.7
1958	n.a.	n.a.	n.a.	n.a.	n.a.	n.a.
1957	2,455	1,200	899	1.3	357	14.5
1952	922	387	350	1.4	185	20.1
1942	332	158	111	1.4	63	19.0
Ratio, 1971–72 to						
1962	3.2	3.1	2.6	—	4.1	—
1952	13.6	14.8	9.7	—	18.7	—
1942	38.0	36.3	30.6	—	55.0	—

Source: U.S. Census Bureau.

of reserves to benefits seem to be about the same, but because the policemen and firemen retire earlier than other employees, their reserve ratios actually should be higher if the same degree of security is to be provided.

The fact that the local systems are not as well financed as the state systems is not surprising. We have been considering large systems only, and we are therefore essentially comparing the large cities with the states. Large-city plans are frequently older, with larger annuitant rolls, and they are often more generous in their terms. Moreover, compared with the states, they have suffered from a lesser abil-

Systems, Fiscal Years Ended In 1942 To 1971–72 (Dollars In Millions)

Benefit and withdrawal payments	Benefit payments	Ratio, revenue to benefits and withdrawals	Ratio, gov't contrib'ns to benefit payments	Cash and security holdings	Ratio, assets to benefit payments
$4,768	$4,121	2.6	1.4	$68,760	16.7
4,155	3,524	2.7	1.5	61,603	17.5
3,638	3,037	2.7	1.5	54,918	18.1
3,202	2,638	2.7	1.5	48,873	18.5
2,609	2,103	2.5	1.5	39,265	18.7
2,219	1,859	2.6	1.4	35,262	19.0
2,008	1,686	2.6	1.4	31,814	19.0
1,844	1,518	2.6	1.5	28,639	19.0
1,690	1,368	2.6	1.5	25,929	19.0
1,567	1,259	2.6	1.5	23,294	18.5
1,383	1,133	2.7	1.6	20,875	18.4
1,264	1,010	2.7	1.6	18,539	18.4
1,145	921	2.6	1.5	16,340	17.7
1,073	n.a.	n.a.	n.a.	14,555	n.a.
941	725	2.6	1.7	12,834	17.7
530	n.a.	1.6	n.a.	6,406	n.a.
169	147	2.0	1.1	1,785	12.1
3.0	3.2	—	—	2.9	—
8.9	—	—	—	10.7	—
28.2	28.0	—	—	38.5	—

ity to pay. As we said earlier, funding is most needed where it is most difficult.

We can supplement that observation now by saying that funding is in fact poorest where it is most needed.

We have said that the drift over the years has been away from pay-as-you-go to funding. But some highly funded systems have felt pressures for increasing benefits and holding down contribution rates. That has often meant lowering the funding goal through less demanding funding formulas, lengthened amortization periods, or less conservative actuarial assumptions. The overall aggregates show

Table 8.3 ◆ **Finances And Financial Ratios: State And Local Retirement Systems Separately, Fiscal Years Ended In 1972–73
(Dollars In Millions)**

Item	State Administered Systems	Locally Administered Systems		
		Total	Municipal	Others
Receipts	$11,148	$ 3,730	$ 2,795	$ 938
Government contributions	4,715	1,934	1,510	424
Employee contributions	3,334	832	562	270
Ratio, government to employee contributions	1.4	2.3	2.6	1.5
Investment income	3,099	965	721	244
Percent, investment income of receipts	27.7	25.9	25.7	26.0
Benefit and withdrawal payments	3,930	1,882	1,534	348
Benefits	3,279	1,668	1,372	297
Ratio, receipts to benefit and withdrawal payments	2.8	1.9	1.8	2.7
Ratio, government contributions to benefit payments	1.4	1.2	1.1	1.4
Cash and security holdings	58,499	19,919	15,473	4,447
Ratio, assets to benefit payments	17.8	11.9	11.2	14.8

Source: U.S. Census Bureau, *Finances of Employee-Retirement Systems of State and Local Government in 1972–73* (Washington, D.C., March 1974).

remarkable stability over the years. The gradual disappearance of pay-as-you-go financing has probably been matched by a softening of funding policies of systems that once followed the most rigorous and demanding schedules.

The cases most in need of attention are the systems of the financially distressed urban centers and of the many smaller cities and counties that have no real assurance of future ability to pay. It is their fiscal difficulties that have kept many on pay-as-you-go, and that is precisely why they should begin to fund on an actuarial basis—so that they will confront the long-term implications of their pension decisions and help assure the ultimate security of their employees.

9 ❖ *Actuarial Assumptions*

Actuarial assumptions are as important as the funding method in determining the amount of contributions necessary to support a pension plan. Using the same funding method, one set of assumptions may show a cost figure 50 to 100 percent higher than another set of assumptions.

The policymaker should have some understanding of the nature of the assumptions and should be involved in some of the choices. True, it is the actuary who usually plays the key role—often the exclusive role—in selecting assumptions. After all, assumptions are technical in content and in their mathematical expression; judgment of the validity of most assumptions requires specialized knowledge; testing and refining them in the light of a plan's experience require actuarial expertise; and it is the actuary who understands the cost implications of one choice or another. Still, on a number of key assumptions, including salary projections and investment yield, the judgment of the laymen who are responsible for the well-being of the system is appropriate. In essence, questions of fiscal policy are involved. Economic and financial judgments may be required.

The extent to which trustees, administrators, and other officials actually share in the process of setting actuarial assumptions differs widely from system to system. Sometimes the actuary adopts assumptions with only minimal discussion or consultation with system officials. In other cases there is full discussion before the actuary proceeds with assumptions of broad interest, such as investment yield and salary progressions. In some systems each assumption is subject to official adoption by the trustees (e.g., the New York systems). Never, however, is the actuary excluded from the process; on the contrary, in most cases, he is in fact the principal decision-maker.

Assumptions are projections of experience, founded on knowledge of past experience both with the employee group involved and with similar groups under similar circumstances. Obviously, experience never fulfills the projection precisely. The differences between projection-assumption and experience give rise to actuarial gains (increases in assets, decreases in liabilities, or both) or actuarial losses. When gains or losses are incurred, they are taken into account for future contribution requirements. If differences persist between assumptions and relevant experience, there is reason to reevaluate the assumptions in light of the experience in a feedback process by which experience refines assumptions and projections are made more accurate.

Despite this ongoing process of corrections, many actuarial assumptions are chosen with at least a small margin of "conservatism," that is, on the financially pessimistic side of probable experience. This is appropriate, so long as it is not overdone. Understandably, the actuary does not want to be in the position of assuring adequate future financial resources simply on the basis of the probable; there is always a chance that things will not turn out as projected. Consequently, assumptions are often somewhat more cautious than past experience would suggest.

The Mortality Assumption

Mortality tables are used to project life expectancy after retirement, and deaths for which death benefits will be payable. The most commonly used of these tables for pension valuations is the 1951 Group Annuity Table and a variety of modifications derived from it. Certain of the derived tables involve projections of continuing mortality improvements. Until now, the most dramatic reductions in mortality have been in the younger ages, but the diseases now receiving most research attention are the major causes of death among older people. If the research is successful, mortality tables used by pension actuaries may need overhauling.

The mortality assumption rarely creates difficulty, at least in determining contributions. Mortality is fairly predictable; good data are available; and the assumption can be tested against experience. The possible difference in projected cost for retired persons based on differing mortality assumptions is apt to be narrow—generally 5 percent, rarely as high as 10 percent. Mortality before retirement is of relatively minor importance, liable to be overshadowed by the larger effect of turnover. Unless there are substantial death or survivor benefits, precision on preretirement mortality is not especially significant.

Turnover

The turnover assumption, on the other hand, can have a drastic effect on pension cost. Cost based on a low turnover projection can be twice as high as cost based on a high turnover assumption, absent vesting. With a liberal vesting provision, however, cost reductions that would otherwise stem from turnover will be limited.

Turnover rates vary with length of service (at least for the first few years), age, and sex. A single turnover rate for a group is virtually valueless; a schedule of turnover rates, generally arrayed by sex and attained age, is required. A more precise, though complex, assumption is a schedule of rates by age and service, in which higher rates of turnover are projected for each of the first three or five years of employment.

Turnover rates can be derived from experience—either that of the group covered or of a similar group—and they can be tested against the future experience of the covered group. But they are not as predictable as mortality; in fact, they are subject to radical change. Even changes in the retirement plan itself can change turnover experience; lowering the early retirement age to 55 may eliminate turnover after 50. Introduction of a full vesting provision may increase turnover after the vesting threshold but decrease it for those who are just shy of the necessary years of service. A labor shortage encourages turnover; a job shortage discourages it.

Turnover among public employees is also affected by factors unique to public service. Establishment of a strong civil service in place of a patronage system will drastically reduce turnover. Unionization, with job protection for incumbents, may do essentially the same. In Pennsylvania, the traditional pattern was a huge turnover among state employees with each change in state administration; increasing civil service regulation and union strength have cut the turnover drastically. The result will be a substantial increase in pension costs.

Because of these special factors, past experience of the particular group is by no means the most reliable guide to future turnover. Judgment is required as to the extent by which past turnover rates may have to be discounted to arrive at a safe actuarial valuation. Knowledge of current and historical experience of other groups under similar circumstances is naturally relevant to the proper choice.

Retirement Rates

That employees *can* retire on full benefits at 60 or at 65 does not mean that they *will* retire at these ages.

If retirement at full benefits is possible at 65, postponement by an average of one year—in a situation in which there is no concomitant increase in benefit amount—may reduce cost by 7 to 8 percent. If postponement is accompanied by the accrual of additional benefits because of the additional service, without significant change in the salary used to compute benefits, the saving is less—but still substantial. If the benefit is based on final average salary, and the postponed retirement is accompanied by an increase in salary, the base for computing benefits also increases and the reduction in cost is diminished further.

Usually a retirement age assumption is made in the form of a table of percentages of eligible employees expected to retire at each age, or else it is the weighted average age at which retirement is assumed. Although the single average age is much easier to use in calculations, it may lead to misunderstanding. It lacks precision, particularly in fixing cost estimates of particular proposals that will influence retirement rates. For example, average retirement age may not reflect adequately the cost impact of reducing the compulsory age from 68 to 66, or the cost of providing full benefits at 60 instead of 65. A tested set of retirement rates appropriate to each year of age will more accurately show the impact of these changes.

The retirement rate assumption can be vital in projecting the costs of unreduced benefits after twenty or thirty years of service regardless of age, or at age 50 or 55 with twenty years of service. Employees retiring under such provisions generally do not withdraw from the labor market; they leave their public jobs for other jobs. Experience of these plans indicates that there is greater willingness to retire (shift jobs) in the 40s than in the 50s. And if there are relatively few retirements under a provision of unreduced benefits after thirty years of service, regardless of age, it does not mean that experience will remain the same if the service requirement is dropped to twenty-five or twenty years. With the thirty-year requirement, employees are 55 to 60 when they become eligible; with twenty or twenty-five years, employees may be 40 to 50 and much more willing to change jobs.

Retirement experience may shift even without change in age or service eligibility. A retirement rate assumption that may have been valid for many years may become invalid directly after a substantial increase in benefits. A 20 percent increase in the benefit accrual rate may increase cost by 23 percent mainly because employees may retire earlier.

Retirement may also occur earlier because Social Security benefits increase. When Social Security retirement benefits were made available at 62 there was a noticeable increase in the willingness of employees to retire at 62 rather than 65. Retirements may also be affected by economic conditions or by program changes: if there are layoffs, eligible employees may decide to retire; changes in school administrations or populations may make teachers and principals eager to retire early. Inflation may impel employees to cling to their jobs.

Plans that base benefits on the final rate of salary or on final year's salary may show periodic increases in retirements timed to union agreements or legislative acts; employees will tend to postpone retirements to, and retire soon after, the time when substantial wage increases are put into effect.

For all these reasons, assumptions about when retirements will occur cannot be confidently predicted solely on the basis of past experience, since dynamic elements affect the projection.

Disability Rates

Assumptions about the rate of incidence of long-term or permanent disability are difficult to set with any degree of confidence unless the system is quite large or the validated experience of a very similar situation can be applied. There are just too many variables to make projections with any certainty.

Defining disability is itself a problem. Is it inability to do any work whatsoever or merely inability to continue in the present job? Then strictness of application is another factor. If a 58-year-old employee finds it physically difficult to continue at his job and is probably too old to get another job, there is a human—and humane—tendency to agree if he claims to be disabled and therefore eligible for a pension.

Whether an alternative pension exists is also a factor. If an early retirement pension is available at ages 50 to 59, the inclination to apply for a disability pension is reduced. But the first $100 a week of disability pension is exempt from federal income tax up to normal retirement age, a consideration which may cause employees who have a choice of disability or early retirement pensions to choose the former. (A large percentage of U.S. military officers retire on disability pension because it is tax-exempt.)

Other factors affecting this assumption include the benefit level, the availability of Social Security disability benefits in addition to system benefits, and the rules regarding permissibility of other work while receiving a disability pension.

Personnel policy about substandard employees may be a key factor. An employee may be working at low efficiency and it may be awkward, undesirable, or impossible to transfer him to any more suitable job. The agency for which he works may be anxious to get a disability pension for him. Should they be required to keep him on the payroll? Should they have to seek his discharge? Should they be able to get a disability pension for him?

Availability of a service-connected disability is another factor. If the disability is service-connected, the pension may be payable after a short period of employment, while an ordinary disability pension may require five to ten years of service. The level of benefits may be higher than for ordinary disability or for normal retirement. Administration of the provision may be demanding or it may be relaxed. There are police and firemen's systems that have many service-connected disability pensioners but exceedingly few ordinary disability pensioners. The District of Columbia retires three-quarters of its policemen on service-connected disabilities. That experience is in utter defiance of the laws of probability; obviously, it is a system in which retirement on service-connected disability has simply become the way that things are done.

Difficulties are further compounded by the fact that the more generous the granting of disability pensions, the more the average award will cost, because more of the disability pensioners will have the average life expectancy of a non-disabled person.

Survivors' Annuities

If a plan provides annuities for the widow, minor children, and other dependents of a deceased employee or pensioner, it becomes necessary to make a set of assumptions about the probability of there being eligible survivors on the death of an employee, the ages of such survivors, the life expectancies of such survivors (or their attainment of a disqualifying age, such as 18 or 21, and about the possibility and timing of remarriage if the widow's benefit is discontinued on her remarriage. (The reference is to survivors' annuities at the expense of the plan, not to survivors' annuities payable because the pensioner chose an optional form of retirement income at the expense of an actuarial reduction in his own pension.) All of these elements may be combined into one average actuarial factor.

New Entrants

An assumption as to the rate of growth (or decline) in the active employee group may be necessary, depending on the type of funding and cost calculation involved. In special circumstances, an assumption about the entry ages of the new employees may be required. For example, new employees may be older when first employed than former employees; this has, in fact, been the long-term trend. And, not unusual as government expands, a new agency may have to hire experienced personnel—generally middle-aged and older—to fill its roster; later employees will probably be younger on the average. Each of these can affect the cost calculations and so require projection.

Salary Projections

Public employee retirement systems typically calculate the pension benefit as a percentage of salary; in most cases as a percentage of final salary, however defined. This makes it necessary to project probable future salaries; and that raises a basic problem which has been argued for a long time: Are salaries to be projected in terms of the progress of the individual employee up the rungs of a stable salary and job ladder, or is the assumption also to include future general increases in the salary levels?

The traditional approach, developed in the decades before steady inflation was taken for granted, has projected individual salary progressions without allowance for general increases. The argument for this approach holds that funding now in anticipation of future general salary increases is, in effect, paying the costs now for pension increases incidental to salary increases not yet decided on. Projecting general salary increases is objected to on the grounds that it leads to using today's "hard dollars" to pay for tomorrow's "soft dollar" benefits. Funding for the individual's expected progression up the salary ladder, on the other hand, merely recognizes the inevitable consequences of commitments already made, that a certain rate of merit increases plus promotions is statistically inevitable.

There is a persuasive case on the other side of this question. Realistic projections require some recognition of general salary increases. Contribution requirements of a pension plan are calculated as a percentage of payroll rather than as level dollar amounts. This spreads the cost of pensions over future payrolls—which will reflect future inflation. Concern about putting today's "hard dollars" into the pot to pay tomorrow's "soft dollar" benefits should be mitigated by recognition of the fact that the same percentage of payroll will be contributed then as now. As we have said earlier, this will mean no greater proportionate burden on future national income, except of course to the extent that public employment grows more rapidly than total employment.

Omission of general salary increases from the salary progression assumption can lead to serious error in pricing proposed benefit changes. The New York City retirement systems, which continue many actuarial assumptions based on experience before 1920, use an assumption projecting practically no increase in salary in the last five years before retirement. This may have been a safe assumption thirty or forty years ago, when an employee of 55 or 60 could be assumed to have reached his peak position and peak salary. But it is not a safe assumption today, nor does it appear safe for the future. On the City's assumption, the cost difference between basing pension on final salary over five years, three years, or the last year alone is negligible. Yet if salary levels increase at the rate of 6 percent a year—a modest rate for many jurisdictions—final average salary—and benefits will be 6 percent higher as between five and three year averages, and 12 percent greater as between five years and one year.

There are more dramatic examples. Suppose a retirement law has a salary cut-off of $30,000—that is, any salary in excess of $30,000 is not taken into account in determining benefits—and the question is asked: "What will it cost to remove the ceiling?" With a salary scale allowing for individual progressions only, there might be very few employees projected as earning more than $30,000 at the point of retirement. Consequently, the cost of canceling the maximum would be quoted at a negligible figure. However, an assumption based on 5 percent general salary increases would project tripled salary levels in only twenty-three years and therefore show a very substantial cost for the new provision.

One way of dealing with the problem in cases of this kind is to price a change by *special* calculations that include general salary projections, separate and apart from the calculations that determine current contributions. It is, in fact, the only honest way of reporting the cost implication of a change affected by salary projections, if the cost is not to be reflected in immediate contributions. Yet the difficulty is that this procedure amounts to saying the following:

> The change proposed will probably add "n" percent to the cost of the plan. However, that will not have to be paid now. It is not reflected in contribution requirements. It will certainly have to be contributed in the future, as it becomes apparent that the contributions were made without regard to general salary increases.

Unfortunately, that amounts to putting a price tag on a change but telling the authorities that they do not have to pay it, at least not in the immediate future.

It is not only a question of salary projections. The same problems come up in connection with cost-of-living adjustments. They may prove to be costly, and what they may cost should be made clear, but the question arises whether government contributions should be made now to fund for cost-of-living changes that have not yet taken place.

Salary Levels and Interest Rates

Salary projections are often tied in, quite logically, with the interest assumption. The interest rate assumed may be anywhere from 3 to 6 percent. Let us say it is 4 percent. If it is proposed to fund now in contemplation of future salary increases, the argument goes that with inflation the investment yield of the fund will exceed 4 percent. It may turn out to be 7 to 9 percent. If that sort of return is realized, it may entirely offset the effect of the general salary increases. Consequently, if general salary increases are to be included in the projection, then so should a 7 to 9 percent investment return. The alternative, it is argued, is to leave out the general salary increases and keep the interest assumption at a non-inflationary level in the expectation or hope that if salaries exceed salary assumptions, investment return will commensurately exceed the interest assumption.

The cost effects of inflation could, to some extent, be offset by the market value of investments that share in rising price levels. This has meant, to many, common stock investments. Whether particular portfolios in fact provide that hedge against inflation is another question.

To assume general salary increases and also some inflationary level of investment return is by no means a simple decision. Calculating costs on a projection of high investment returns (for example, 6 to 10 percent; some consider 5 percent high) may be hazardous for a retirement system. The assumption must be valid both for money invested now and for investments to be made twenty or thirty years from now. A high-rate assumption exposes the system to the hazard that the assumed investment return will not be realized for many years, during which the system's officials will be recording actuarial losses and perpetually explaining that they are looking to the future.

Of course, salary increases and investment yields may not move in tandem. There may be periods when wages go up, but investment yield is relatively low; and other periods, although less likely, when yields are high but wages relatively stable.

As a result there are cases in which two alternative valuations are made. The first makes no projection of general salary increases and uses a conservative interest assumption. The second projects general salary increases and a higher rate of interest assumption, which may be 6 to 9 percent. The purpose of having cost ascertained both ways is to put the more traditional valuation (the first) on the official record and to make the annual contributions on that basis, while at the same time establishing, for purposes of policy guidance, what will actually happen if general wage and price levels continue to rise. This practice of two calculations has been used by some private plans, but rarely by public plans, which could often use it to advantage.

A reasonable answer might well include not only an alternative calculation but also a range of possible results with respect to any cost estimate that will be affected by the future dynamics of salaries, prices, and investment returns. An extreme case presents the most convincing illustration. Suppose it is proposed that a retirement system provide a permanent post-retirement adjustment keyed to the Consumer Price Index, without maximum limit. What will it cost? A single figure—any one— is not likely to be a complete answer. The *range of possibilities* is at least as relevant. Consequently, the proper basis for decision is an estimate of the cost range, involving a spread of inflationary rates and a spread of rate assumptions as to future investment returns (including asset values). Uncommon today, the practice should be more general.

Contributions should be made on safe long-term assumptions. These may include some minimum rate of general salary increase (and in the cost of living, where pertinent) plus an assumption as to the appropriate investment yield. Variability should be reflected through cost projections based on a range of possible experience.

Interest Rates

The interest assumption is a projection of the rate of earnings on the fund's assets. (Although the term "interest assumption" is traditional, it is understood to include all investment income.) This assumption is not supposed to represent what the assets are earning currently; it is supposed to be a very long-range assumption as to what funds already invested, or now awaiting investment, or yet to be invested in future years will earn. It is, therefore, generally a conservative view of investment yield; at least, it should be.

However, at any one time, judgment as to future interest earnings tends to be conditioned by current investment yields and those of recent years. In the early 1950s, when a great many pension plans were set up, assumptions of 2.5 percent or 2.75 percent were common and considered quite respectable. Examination of interest levels in the 1940s and early 1950s shows why. From January 1936 through August 1956, a period of twenty years, long-term high-grade corporate bonds did not pay as much as 3.5 percent and for twelve years straight did not yield as much as 3 percent. They did not climb to 4 percent until September 1958 and they reached 5 percent only in June 1966 (Table 9.1). The hard question facing those who must select an interest assumption is what investment yields on high-quality securities will be like in the future. Recent, comparatively high interest rates and improved yields for pension funds have encouraged public systems to revise their interest assumptions upward, from about 3 percent to 4 percent, in many cases to 5 percent, and even higher in a few instances. The California Public Employees' Retirement System changed its interest assumption seven times from 1945 to 1971, starting with 2.50 percent and ending with 5.75 percent. In 1972, large corporations generally assumed 4 to 6 percent.[1] The higher rates were adopted for the most part after 1968.

The upward trend was also encouraged by the rapid movement of public system money into stocks. Although a representative group of listed stocks provided short-term dividend yields of only about 3 percent since 1961, total return including appreciation has, for long periods of time, been much higher. In the seven-year period from the beginning of 1966 to the end of 1972, stocks in Standard and Poor's Index yielded an average of 6.9 percent a year in dividends and appreciation. In the period from January 1926 to December 1960, the stocks listed on the New York Stock Exchange yielded, dividends and appreciation combined, the equivalent of 9 percent a year.[2] Experience in the most recent period has been less encouraging.

These figures are very important, because the interest assumption has great leverage on pension costs. When the interest assumption is moved up by one-quarter of one percent, cost is reduced by about 4

---

[1] Chase-Manhattan Bank, *Survey 2 on Pension Fund Financing* (New York, 1972).
[2] Lawrence Fisher and James H. Lorie, "Rates of Return on Investment in Common Stocks, *"Journal of Business,* XXXVII, a, January 1964.

Table 9.1 ◆ Bond Yields, 1900–1970: Standard And Poor's Composite High-Grade Corporate Bond Index

Year	Yield	Year	Yield
1900	4.49%	1940	2.92%
1901	4.38	1941	1.84
1902	4.34	1942	2.85
1903	4.52	1943	2.80
1904	4.49	1944	1.78
1905	4.28	1945	2.61
1906	4.38	1946	2.51
1907	4.72	1947	2.58
1908	4.76	1948	2.80
1909	4.51	1949	2.65
1910	4.60	1950	2.59
1911	4.58	1951	2.84
1912	4.60	1952	2.95
1913	4.78	1953	3.18
1914	4.75	1954	2.87
1915	4.83	1955	3.04
1916	4.73	1956	3.38
1917	4.99	1957	3.91
1918	5.47	1958	3.80
1919	5.51	1959	4.38
1920	6.18	1960	4.41
1921	6.03	1961	4.36
1922	5.17	1962	4.29
1923	5.22	1963	4.24
1924	5.07	1964	4.37
1925	4.93	1965	4.47
1926	4.77	1966	5.13
1927	4.65	1967	5.53
1928	4.63	1968	6.05
1929	4.86	1969	6.93
1930	4.71	1970	7.84
1931	4.55	1971	7.38
1932	5.28	1972	7.26
1933	4.69	1973	7.56
1934	4.14	1974	8.25
1935	3.61		
1936	3.34		
1937	3.30		
1938	3.20	**Note:** Yield is yield to maturity,	
1939	3.02	monthly average for the year.	

to 6 percent if the system is well funded; if funding is marginal, the cost reduction is somewhat lower.

Because of its effect, increasing the interest assumption seems to accomplish a miracle. Benefits can suddenly be increased without requiring greater contributions; inadequate contributions can be suddenly pronounced adequate. The temptation is great. Of course, the interest assumption should be increased if the increase is supported by well-informed, carefully considered judgment. But high current yields should not dictate overly optimistic projections. The decision as to interest assumption is an important policy decision requiring broad knowledge and contributions from the economist, the actuary, and the investment advisor.

The decision is particularly hard to make now, and will probably be harder tomorrow. If the historically high interest levels of 1969–74 continue much longer, the problem of creating a sound policy on interest assumption is apt to become acute. Judgments on the question tend to be molded by recent experience; the greater gap between recent experience and the longer historical record, the more ground there is for debate. Neither the recent record nor the historical average is necessarily controlling. The real question is the long-range future. Those now making conservative judgments will be accused of clinging too long to the past; those making optimistic judgments will be accused of taking too much risk on the basis of a temporary phenomenon. The answer may lie in developing new ways of dealing with the interest assumption, so as to reflect the full value of current high interest rates without automatically assuming those high rates for future investments.[3]

Yield depends in part on what asset value is assigned to a fund's investments. In most cases, fixed-income investments are carried at cost or at cost adjusted for the amortization of the premium, or accrual of the discount, involved in the purchase. The real problem is in the area of equity investments. How to reflect the unrealized market appreciation of equities is a major problem. If stock is valued at cost, unrealized increases in market value are ignored, and realization of a gain, through sale and reinvestment (or even literal

---

[3] One method answering that need would be to value debt securities on the basis of the actuarial present value of the future income stream they will produce. This method of valuation would show proportionately higher book value for any security with a projected yield exceeding the basic interest assumption.

repurchase), can result in a sudden write-up of assets, achieving an asset gain without real change of position, unless the sales proceeds are transferred away from stocks.

Investment yield should include appreciation or depreciation in equity securities. The relation to market values need not be immediate or full, but there should be some consistent way of safely reflecting market values in determining both investment yield and asset values.

The Accounting Principles Board had this to say with respect to the pricing of stocks in private plans:

Unrealized appreciation and depreciation in the value of investments in a pension fund are forms of actuarial gains and losses. Despite short-term market fluctuations, the overall rise in the value of equity investments in recent years has resulted in the investment of pension funds generally showing net appreciation. Although appreciation is not generally recognized at present in providing for pension cost, it is sometimes recognized through the interest assumption or by introducing an assumed annual rate of appreciation as a separate actuarial assumption. In other cases, appreciation is combined with other actuarial gains and losses and applied on the immediate-recognition, spreading, or averaging method.

The amount of any unrealized appreciation to be recognized should also be considered. Some actuarial valuations recognize the full market value. Others recognize only a portion (such as 75 percent) of the market value or use the effects of short-term market fluctuations. Another method used to minimize such fluctuations is to recognize appreciation annually based on an expected long-range growth rate (such as 3 percent) applied to the cost (adjusted for appreciation previously so recognized) of common stocks; when this method is used, the total of cost and recognized appreciation usually is not permitted to exceed a specified percentage (such as 75 percent) of the market value. Unrealized depreciation is recognized in full or on a basis similar to that used for unrealized appreciation.

The Board believes unrealized appreciation and depreciation should be recognized in the determination of the provision for pension cost on a rational and systematic basis that avoids giving undue weight to short-term market fluctuations.

An important consideration is that a sound method should not give a realized gain any advantage over unrealized appreciation, except perhaps as the proceeds are applied to the purchase of debt securities. Otherwise, there is an incentive to sell when no investment purpose is served and the assets are worth no more after the transaction than before. Pension Fund A may have bought IBM common stock at 200 and its price may have gone up to 300. Whether to sell it or hold it should depend entirely on how good an investment it is for the future, considering its current price of 300. To sell it in order to buy something else with no better future prospect than IBM accomplishes nothing. It would be equivalent to selling the IBM stock and repurchasing it immediately. Yet an asset valuation policy that credits *realized* gains but not unrealized gains provides an accounting and actuarial reward for an entirely superficial reshuffling. It is for that reason that stock or equity assets should be valued by a reasonable and systematic process that takes account of all gains and losses, realized or unrealized.

With rare exception, the public employee retirement systems have yet to develop appropriate asset valuation policies.

Assumptions and Zero Population Growth

Growth in the number of active employees reduces the cost of a pension plan as a percentage of payroll. Most actuarial calculations ignore that factor by making, implicitly, the traditional assumption that the group will remain the same size. However, there are certain funding plans, based on computer projections and described in the previous chapter, that may include an assumed rate of growth in the number of active employees. However, that assumption may lose its factual foundation if birth rates decline and the population of the country grows less rapidly or perhaps not at all. Zero population growth will clearly make retirement plans more expensive as a levy on the population that is actively employed.

That effect on public employee systems may be compounded. Zero population growth would change the age distribution within the labor force by cutting down on the young contingent. It would therefore increase the proportion of older workers. As it is, government hires a disproportionately high percentage of older workers. (The military is an exception). There are large percentages of the employees of state and local government who enter their jobs in their 50s and 60s. With zero population growth and a generally older total labor force, the ages at which employees enter public employment will probably be even higher, resulting in an increase in retirement cost beyond anything now anticipated.

Assumptions and Full Funding

It is common to find a public retirement system in which these two basic facts coexist:

(1) Full funding is considered essential—that is, the goal established is to amortize the unfunded accrued liability, in many cases on the comparatively rapid schedule of aggregate funding; and

(2) No increase in the *general* level of salaries is projected or in some other major respect the assumptions do not realistically anticipate the future.

The result is that the funding schedule is not fulfilled, at least not at the pace originally intended. For example, a system may be funded on the basis of aggregate funding, which would ordinarily mean a high contribution (as a percentage of payroll) for the first year and decreasing percentages thereafter. General salary increases incur an actuarial loss and in turn keep the percentage at least as high as the first year's. Combining the two may therefore amount to a roughly level percentage, about equivalent to using an assumption reflective of general salary increases with a funding formula less demanding than aggregate funding.

There are at least two difficulties with this balancing process. One is that the two effects may in fact not balance. Either salary increases may push up cost as a percentage of payroll or the aggregate funding arrangement may dictate an unnecessarily high contribution in the early years. The other disadvantage has to do with the pricing of changes, for which there is no substitute for a set of assumptions, each of which is independently realistic. It is hazardous to rationalize an underestimate of one aspect of experience by arguing that there is a compensating margin with respect to another aspect of the experience or that the funding schedule will compensate.

It is not difficult to understand why full funding is stressed even where it is being frustrated by inadequate assumptions. Full funding was established as a desirable goal for public systems in the years before persistent inflation challenged the adequacy of salary assumptions. It is a case of inertia—the old principle persists while the pressure of new circumstances is resisted. And—to be realistic—full funding plus recognition of general salary increases produces contribution requirements so high that few are willing to face them.

Even conservative actuaries are liable to blanch at the results. A projected rate of general salary of even 2 to 3 percent a year, if added to a full-funding calculation, can easily dictate a doubling of the employer's contributions.

On balance, however, it would seem preferable to include among the assumptions *all* reasonably safe projections and simultaneously to fix a contribution schedule on what is truly essential for the retirement system without absolute and inflexible insistence on "full funding." This may mean that the assumptions should include realistic projections and that the funding formula should recognize all long-term costs without trying to accumulate reserves beyond the system's actual needs, based on the particular risk—or remoteness—of possible termination or of future limitations on ability to pay.

10 ✢ Portability of
Pension Credits

Portability of pension credits in both the private and the public sectors has been the subject of public debate for more than a decade. For public employees the ability to transfer credits among government units is particularly important. Increase of population mobility and the loosening of community bonds has affected all forms of employment. The increasing employment of women means that one employed spouse may have to leave work when the other transfers. As long ago as 1947–1948, a survey found that about 30 percent of teachers had been employed in more than one state.[1] In certain government occupations, movement from one governmental unit to another is the norm—as with city managers, fiscal officers, and other professional and technical employees. Many broad governmental programs—among them health, education, health insurance, agriculture, social services—are either joint federal and state projects or require employees to shift from one governmental level to another. Under these circumstances it is difficult to insist that the employee forfeit accrued pension rights. Similar situations exist among state, county, and city levels.

There have been serious complaints that loss of pension credits acts as a restraint, preventing public employees from accepting employment that would advance their careers or meet pressing personal needs.[2] The Municipal Manpower Commission objected that

[1] National Education Association, Research Division, *How to Provide Reciprocity in Teacher Retirement* (Washington, D.C., January 1959), p. 10.

[2] Advisory Commission on Intergovernmental Relations, *Transferability of Public Employee Retirement Credits Among Units of Government* (Washington, D.C., March 1963), pp. 5–6.

"in the vast majority of states and urban governments . . . retirement credits have turned into an anchor, and operate as a real deterrent to the easy interchange of middle and top-level APT (administrative, professional, technical) personnel." [3]

Countering these complaints is evidence that for a large percentage of those who leave government jobs, the possible loss of pension rights is not in fact a central consideration. When offered a choice, upon termination, between a vested deferred pension and a lump-sum payment of accumulated member contributions, these employees overwhelmingly choose the refund, even though it is worth much less actuarially than the pension.[4] Three-quarters of federal employees who leave after qualifying for a vested deferred benefit elect to withdraw their contributions and cancel their benefits.[5]

Despite the apparent contradictions, these two factors are actually both valid in different ways. Most job-changing takes place when employees are comparatively young or have relatively few years of service. At that point the promise of a pension is decades away and far outweighed by the attractions of present employment. But to middle-aged or older employees, loss of pension rights is a very serious consideration—they have substantial benefit accruals at stake. The older employee offered an out-of-jurisdiction job is also likely to be a professional, technician, or executive. The gross number of job changes is not therefore the controlling consideration. A serious problem is presented by employees with valuable skills who may not be able to use them to best advantage for themselves or for public administration because of fear of losing pensions. To this group must be added those who are forced to change jobs because a program was transferred from one political jurisdiction to another or because the spouse took a job in a new location.

The problem of pension forfeiture may be an acute problem for only a minority of those who leave government employment, but for them it is indeed serious. Moreover, there is the agency that cannot fill key positions with the best people because the potential employees feel frozen at their current positions.

[3] *Government Manpower for Tomorrow's Cities,* 1962, p. 78.

[4] See Harold Rubin, *Pensions and Employee Mobility in the Public Service* (New York, The Twentieth Century Fund, 1965).

[5] Joseph Krislov, "Characteristics of Persons Separating and Withdrawing Contributions from the Federal Civil Service Retirement System," U.S. Department of H.E.W., Analytical Note No. 6–61, June 1961.

From the standpoint of the employee, there is every reason to seek complete transferability of pension credits. This may also be true of the "importing" employer, although the cost of protecting the employee against loss of accrued pension benefits may be an obstacle. It is the agency that will lose the employee that takes a dim view of any action that would facilitate transfer. The unit in danger of losing an experienced employee is inclined to stress an older concept of the purpose of a retirement plan, namely, to stabilize employment (hold employees). From that view, making payments to an employee who leaves before retirement may be expensive and may not represent the best use of the employer's resources. That attitude was well expressed by the director of the South Carolina Retirement System.[6]

The wealthier States can afford to attract teachers and other employees by offering higher salaries, to the disadvantage of the poorer States. It would be dangerous for the poorer States to compound this disadvantage by an outright preservation of pension credits.

New York . . . will agree to transfer reserves to the retirement system of another State when a teacher leaves New York to work in the other State, but the law also provides (and this is most equitable) that transfer of reserves must also be made when a teacher moves in the opposite direction. We in South Carolina would not want to enter into this kind of agreement with New York (and no other State either) because our citizens fail to see any sense in losing a good teacher to New York and at the same time sending a substantial reserve fund to New York.

While the arguments continue, public-employee plans have developed many methods of preserving the pension credits of employees who leave public jobs. These methods include vesting, participation in Social Security, allowance for the purchase of credit for related service, a variety of reciprocal arrangements for crediting related employment, and the consolidation of separate plans.

Vesting

In both public and private pension plans, vesting is the principle means of protecting the pension rights of a terminating employee. And, as observed earlier, the last decade was marked by substantial liberalization of vesting in public systems, generally in the direction of earlier vesting. One advantage vesting has over other methods of

[6] Quoted in Rubin, *Pensions and Employee Mobility in the Public Service,* p. 79.

protecting pension credits is that it is applicable without regard to the kind of job the employee transfers to—whether public or private. And most job skills are as useful in private industry as in government.

However, vesting has three shortcomings as the total solution to the problem: salary base, qualification for the first pension, and qualification for the second pension.

A vested deferred benefit is based on the employee's salary with the first employer, not his salary with his last employer. Since most public plans compute benefits on some version of final average salary, there will be a considerable difference between a vested benefit based on a final average salary for employment ten or twenty years before, and final average salary just before retirement. The employee therefore loses income, for he receives much less from the two sources than he would have received had he been employed only by his last employer.

Second, vesting is likely to require ten or fifteen years of employment. The claim of an employee who has shifted from one government unit to another, particularly within the same state, should not depend to the extent it does on his length of service with the first employer.

Third, service with the earlier employer does not count toward the employee's eligibility for pension benefits with the next employer. The final employer may require ten or fifteen years of employment for benefit payments at a particular retirement age; the employee's years of service with the earlier employer have no effect.

The employee may also be at a disadvantage if one of the plans graduates the rate of benefit accrual according to years of service. For example, the federal system and plans in Illinois and Rhode Island accrue lesser pensions for each of the first ten years than they do for subsequent years; plans in New York and Puerto Rico jump the rate of accrual for all years when twenty or thirty years of service have been completed.

In effect, then, vesting falls short of equalizing benefits for the employee who transfers; he is by no means in the same position he would have been in had he remained in the same job.

Vesting among public employee plans generally requires that the employee not withdraw his contributions. But since the great majority of terminating employees do withdraw them (usually with interest), suggestions have been made that the option be stricken, that the deferred benefit be mandatory. This is debatable on two grounds: how paternal the state should be and how far the law should go in protecting an employee against making a choice that may be to his ultimate disadvantage. And is a deferred benefit always the best choice? A young woman who wishes to help pay for a home or start a family may withdraw a lump sum instead of waiting for a deferred pension right. That choice is difficult to debate. If she put the amount into a home, it might be difficult to prove that it was a poor investment when compared to the value of her deferred pension.

Costs may increase enormously if the option to withdraw is eliminated or if employee contributions are drastically reduced or eliminated. In a system with a liberal vesting provision and a vesting-or-withdrawal option, as many as 80 percent of employees entitled to a deferred benefit may divest themselves; if employee contributions are eliminated, all eligible employees who leave will retain rights to deferred pensions. The result is an unexpected escalation in the cost of deferred benefits.

Teachers Insurance and Annuity Association

State laws frequently provide the teaching staffs of public colleges and universities with the option of pension coverage by the Teachers Insurance and Annuity Association in lieu of the state's own benefit provisions. About 25 percent of these staffs are covered by T.I.A.A., which is a specially chartered non-profit insurance organization that provides fully vested, fully transferable annuities for the employees of educational organizations. The annuities are of the "money-purchase" type, the ultimate benefits depending entirely on what the employee and each employing institution has contributed, plus the investment earnings credited by T.I.A.A. (If the member chooses, contributions are credited with the changing market values of a companion common stock fund, the College Retirement Equity Fund.) This successful institution has gone far toward solving the question of pension portability for teachers in higher education. A similar plan, the National Health and Welfare Retirement Fund, covers health and social workers but does not cover a large number of public employees. A national plan for all public employees has been discussed—as has one that would cover specific categories, such as teachers or policemen. But the feasibility of such a plan is sharply reduced by diversity of jurisdictions, benefits, capacity to pay, entrenched arrangements, etc.

Social Security

Participation in Social Security gives the public employee—as it does the private employee—complete credit for all his covered employment. Obviously this is only a partial answer—it is only as adequate as the Social Security benefit and does not protect the staff system pension. Nevertheless, membership in Social Security mitigates potential pension loss from job transfer. Although this point is obvious, it is pertinent to any discussion of portability for public employees, since many are not covered by Social Security.

Unilateral Credits for Other Employment

A number of plans allow credit for related employment. For example, many teachers' plans allow a member to purchase credit for out-of-state teaching service. This purchasable credit may be limited to a fixed number of years and it may also be tied to the number of years of new employment—to avoid incurring costly obligations for very new employees. The employee may be expected to pay only the scheduled member contribution or he may be required to pay the employer contribution as well, if out-of-state service is to be credited. Once paid, the full formula of the new plan is generally applied to the extra years credited.

In some states arrangements of this kind may encounter constitutional problems regarding the right of the state to make payments based on out-of-state employment. Yet retirement laws do credit military service. Similarly, credit is sometimes given for other precisely defined employment considered to be in the interests of the state or locality. A modification of this idea is to grant leaves of absence for other approved employment and to grant pension credit for the leave time if the employee makes the required contributions for that period.

Statewide Plans

The problem of intrastate transfers usually disappears if all the employing units participate in a single retirement system. A number of states have a single system for all employees, state and local. Service credits accumulate regardless of job transfers within the limits of the system.

The establishment of a single system does not necessarily provide an adequate answer to the question of what benefit is to be paid to the employee who has shifted jobs within its scope. A unitary system may encompass several plans of benefits for different employers and the pension for someone who has been in more than one plan can be based either on the last plan or on a combination of the two plans. If the entire benefit is based on the last plan, there may be a question as to which employer pays the difference. Some systems have different plans for various occupational groups—police, clerks, teachers, legislators, etc. Movement from one occupational group to another also raises the question of which benefit is to be paid, the best, the last, or a blend? And how should the cost be allocated among the various employers?

Because states do not readily consolidate local plans—or even plans for teachers, universities, police, etc.—into single statewide systems, the portability question still has to be solved without amalgamation. And regardless of the ability of statewide plans to solve the problem of *intra*state portability, the issue of *inter*state portability remains.

Reciprocity

Reciprocity covers a wide variety of arrangements by which two or more systems agree to recognize years of employment under the allied system. The arrangements vary from shifting funds to paying benefits entirely on the basis of the last final average salary or entirely on the basis of the provisions of the last plan.

In New York State, for example, reciprocity involves transfer of funds. An employee can transfer his credits from the system he is leaving to the system he is entering, in which event an appropriate reserve is transferred from the first to the second. The employee's pension is calculated as if he had always been covered by the second system.

The fund-transfer arrangement is impractical between states and even within some states when both state and localities are involved, because of differences in funding, in the actuarial bases for computing reserves, and because one system may profit unduly if reserves are transferred far in advance of retirement. (It is unrealistic to assume that the transfers will flow equally in both directions; the net flow may in fact move consistently in one direction.)

Kentucky has had a reverse transfer arrangement. If an employee shifts from the State Employees' or Teachers' System to the County Employees' System, he can remain covered by the original system, to which both he and the County System contribute. All three systems are administered by the state. The limited nature of this arrangement indicates that it was apparently intended to prevent a decrease in benefits because of transfer to county employment.

Reciprocity provisions that recognize the related or "sister" service, but make no transfers of funds, at least not before retirement, are more common than the Kentucky system.

Massachusetts, which has many systems but a uniform plan, mandates complete portability. The systems share the ultimate benefit costs in accordance with years of service under each.

In Michigan there is a reciprocal retirement act with voluntary participation by state and local units. This act provides that eligibility for benefits in each system is to be determined by the total of recognized service, that each system pay the benefit called for by its plan on the basis of years of employment within its scope and using the final average salary from its employment. Although this arrangement keeps a transferring employee from falling in between two or more plans, it does not of course provide the employee with the entire pension he would get from continuous service at one job. His benefit from the first plan is based on his salary at that time and perhaps on an older benefit formula that has since been changed.

Illinois has the same program but adds an alternate provision intended to credit all years of service on the basis of the final average salary and the benefit formula covering the employee when he retires.

A reciprocity system that recognizes all service within a state and requires each system to pay a benefit consistent with its own plan, but prorated on the years of service directly within its scope, is readily feasible. Such a plan requires a number of decisions: minimum service requirements under each plan, how much to pay if the retirement eligibility ages differ, what to pay in the event of disability or death, how to prorate the pension, and the extent to which the final average salary and the benefit formula at the point of retirement should govern the aggregate payment.

In his report on the subject, Harold Rubin suggested five-year vesting, plus a provision by which the final retirement plan would supplement inadequate vested benefits by raising them to the level paid by the system.[7]

Federal Intervention

Most difficult of the reciprocity problems is that of devising an acceptable system operable among states and between states and the federal government. A job offer from an importing state often attracts employees even if it does not grant out-of-state service credits. The exporting state is not inclined to add to its personnel troubles by continuing his benefits. Suggestion has been made for federal subsidy which will underwrite a national reciprocity arrangement and make adherence desirable. The National Council on Teacher Retirement, affiliated with the National Education Association and representing teacher retirement systems, has sponsored a federal "Mobile Teachers Bill" which would provide federal money to help meet the cost of assuring pension portability for teachers.

Study Recommendations

A study on portability for police pensions made the following recommendations: [8]

1. . . . . All local plans within each state should be included in a single "law enforcement officers' retirement system. . . ," if not in full then at least with respect to a minimum benefit.
2. Reciprocity among the state systems, with federal payment of part of the costs of reciprocity.

The Advisory Commission on Intergovernmental Relations recommended the following:

1. Merger of systems within a state where feasible.
2. Enactment of intrastate reciprocity provisions.
3. Vesting after five years of service, if member contributions

---

[7] *Pensions and Employee Mobility in the Public Service*, p. 84.

[8] U.S. National Institute of Law Enforcement and Criminal Justice, *Portable Police Pensions—Improving Inter-Agency Transfers* (Washington, D.C., U.S.G.P.O., 1972), pp. 62–64. This report was prepared for the Institute by Geoffrey N. Calvert.

are not withdrawn. Whether the vesting should be uncondi-
tional is a matter worth considering.

4. Consideration should be given to extending Social Security to
those who do not already participate.

Recommendations

Amalgamation of systems within a state would help solve the portability problem. However, that solution also involves other and perhaps weightier questions.

Every state with more than one system should have a reciprocity
provision requiring recognition of an employee's total public service
in the state and obligating each system to provide a fair prorated
benefit. If possible, total benefits should be based on average salary
before retirement and on the provisions of the plans updated to the
time of retirement.

This would mean greater portability within the public service of
the state than if transfer were to another state, to the federal government, or to private industry. Why not equal portability everywhere?
The answer is that if public employee pensions are legislated by a
state, then it is anomalous for the state to penalize an employee who
shifts from one form of state (or local) employment to another when
both are covered by a state-enacted retirement law. The same moral
claim does not apply, at least not with equal force, as between different states or between a state and the federal government.

Social Security should be universal. There is an inconsistency in
principle between asking for portability and rejecting Social Security
coverage.

The states and the federal government should recognize the needs
of employees whose work involves transfer among jurisdictions, joint
projects, or shifts in employment to the advantage of the state. Employees thus affected should be protected in their pension rights.

Liberal vesting is in general desirable, particularly at the ages and
after the periods of service that make ultimate pension payments a
matter of serious concern. Deferred benefits might well be conditioned on nonwithdrawal of employee contributions. Of course, as
with all provisions, the cost of vesting has to be weighed against
other demands on the systems and their financing.

The Federal Employee Retirement Income Security Act of 1974

omitted public employees from its mandatory vesting and funding requirements, but provided for a two-year study of the question whether and to what extent regulation on those aspects should be extended to the public systems. This issue is therefore on the national legislative agenda.

11 ✤ Investment Policies
and Procedures

     Investment yield is important in determining the contributions required by a retirement system. The weight of that influence depends on the size of the system's assets in relation to its actuarial liabilities. In a pay-as-you-go system, increased investment yield has little importance; in a fully funded plan, an increase of one percentage point in investment yield may reduce contribution requirements by 15 to 20 percent, or pay for a commensurate increase in benefits if the level of contributions is maintained.

Within the limits of broad economic movements, investment yield depends on how well investments are handled. Comparing public systems with all pension funds, some public systems rank among the best in terms of investment management; others among the poorest. In the 1950s, investment management of public-employee systems was generally poor; since then it has improved remarkably. However, as of 1972, many of the systems were still not being managed in accordance with standards of good investment policies and procedures.

The historic limitations placed on public-employee systems are responsible, to a great extent, for this situation. In the 1950s and 1960s, public-system investments were severely restricted by statute to certain types of fixed-income securities, restrictions similar to those applied to savings banks and insurance companies. Assets were invested in corporate bonds, U.S. government obligations, municipal bonds, and mortgages, in that order of importance. Only 2 percent of total assets were in the form of stocks as late as 1960; for many systems they were entirely forbidden. Investments were made through "in-house" decisions by staff and system trustees; professional counsel was used, if at all, only for periodic advice rather than for discretionary management. To sell one security in order to buy another—in other words, to trade—was considered improperly speculative.

Many of the systems have changed remarkably since then. Investment leeway has been broadened and many states are now able to invest in stocks. In several cases legal restrictions have been abandoned in favor of the "prudent-man rule," which gives flexibility to those with investment authority, limited only by what the courts might hold to be imprudent. A radical change occurred between 1957 and 1973 (Table 11.1).

> State and local obligations have been reduced from 26 to 2 percent of assets.
> Federal obligations have been reduced from 40 to 4 percent.
> Corporate bonds have increased from 26 to 55 percent.
> Mortgages have increased from 4 to 9 percent.
> Corporate stock has increased from 1 to 22 percent.

Investment decisions are now frequently delegated to professionals, sometimes by giving discretion within prescribed policy limits to outside investment managers or to in-house staffs of full-time professionals. There is a wider recognition that market changes may dictate selling as well as buying; portfolio turnover, once virtually unknown, is a more common practice.

Investment Restrictions

Among four states that did not permit investment of public-employee retirement funds in common stock as of early 1972, the situation was as follows:

> Florida limited investments in corporate bonds to 50 percent; 39 percent of the state fund was in U.S. government obligations.

> In Mississippi, 9 percent of the fund was in tax-exempt bonds and 16 percent in U.S. bonds.

> South Carolina's system held $37 million of the state's bonds.

> Wyoming limited corporate bonds to 60 percent; issues of the U.S. government and its agencies composed 44 percent of the portfolio.

Table 11.1 ◆ *Investments Of State And Local Retirement Systems, By Type Of Security, 1957 Through 1972–73*

	Period: Fiscal years ended in			
	1957	*1962*	*1966–67*	*1972–73*
Type of Security	*All Systems*			
Total amount (billions)	$12.8	$23.3	$39.3	$78.4
Percentage distribution:				
Cash and deposits	1.7%	1.2%	1.1%	1.4%
Federal obligations	40.0	26.2	16.9	4.4
State and local obligations	25.6	17.4	6.2	1.9
Nongovernmental securities	32.7	55.1	75.7	92.3
Corporate bonds	26.3	40.9	51.6	55.3
Corporate stock	1.4	3.0	6.1	21.8
Mortgages	3.5	8.8	12.4	8.7
Other	1.5	2.5	5.7	6.5
	State Systems			
Total amount (billions)	$ 8.1	$15.5	$27.7	$58.5
Percentage distribution:				
Cash and deposits	1.4%	1.0%	0.9%	1.0%
Federal obligations	44.4	26.7	16.6	3.7
State and local obligations	18.5	11.1	2.5	0.6
Nongovernmental securities	35.7	61.3	80.0	96.7
	Local Systems			
Total amount (billions)	$ 4.8	$ 7.7	$11.6	$19.9
Percentage distribution:				
Cash and deposits	2.1%	1.7%	1.7%	2.7%
Federal obligations	32.3	25.3	17.7	6.6
State and local obligations	38.1	30.1	15.0	6.0
Nongovernmental securities	27.5	42.9	65.6	84.7

Source: U.S. Census Bureau, *Census of Governments* (various), and *Finances of Employee-Retirement Systems of State and Local Governments in 1972–73* (Washington, D.C., March 1974).

Investing in Tax-Exempt Bonds

For a tax-exempt pension fund, investing in tax-exempt state or local obligations is, with rare exception, senseless. A yield differential between taxable and tax-exempt bonds of comparable quality and maturity is almost inevitable because of the special advantage of tax-exempt income to a taxable institution or individual. When a high-grade corporate bond yields 7 percent, a high-grade tax-exempt bond of similar maturity may yield 4.5 percent. If a pension fund, which is tax-exempt, buys the latter, it is in effect losing 2.5 percent a year.

In fairness, it should be noted that in some cases the tax-exempt bonds bought by the systems were issued by small communities that would have had difficulty in selling their bonds even at comparatively high interest rates. The political appeal of providing subsidies is obvious; nevertheless, there was usually a yield differential in favor of corporate bonds or mortgages. That the government was paying for the lesser yield was not immediately obvious and was not made an issue at the time.

Although now it is generally recognized that a retirement system should not buy tax-exempt securities, getting rid of those already acquired has been a very slow process, often a matter of redemption rather than sale. Because the transaction would show a capital loss, many systems shy away from selling these bonds—a reluctance that, ironically, leads to a very real loss of investment income. For example, the Chicago Municipal Employees Fund held $64 million in municipal bonds as of 1971, although the disadvantage of such holdings had been acknowledged for some time.

The Bond Swap Problem

Unwillingness to "swap" bonds is not limited to tax-exempt securities; it also applies to trading U.S. government bonds for corporate bonds or mortgages and to trading one corporate bond for another. Bond market dynamics cause constant change in the relationship between deep-discount bonds and high-coupon bonds, between new and outstanding issues, and between short- and long-term bonds. These changes make switches profitable. When interest levels are changing, lengthening or shortening maturities is advantageous.

Swapping one corporate bond for another does not yield annually more than a fraction of one percent, but when millions of dollars are involved, the cumulative results are significant. Yet even today most public systems are reluctant to swap bonds because of the fear of showing a loss.

A loss is recorded because of the fact that the past decade has been one of rising interest levels. When general interest levels rise or fall, market values of outstanding bonds change automatically. If a thirty-year bond, paying a 5 percent interest coupon, is issued at par ($1,000) and a year later general interest levels are higher, so that a bond of equivalent quality and maturity can be sold only at a 6 percent yield, then the price of the first bond will have fallen by about 15 percent. These price swings, which have been substantial, are totally unrelated to the quality of the investment. A thirty-year U.S. Treasury bond issued in 1953 and paying 3¼ percent interest had gone up more than 8 percent within one year; by 1969, when the market yield of such a security was 7.5 percent, its price was 36 percent below par and 40 percent below its high of 1954. Systems often hold bonds that were acquired when interest rates were comparatively low. This is particularly true of tax-exempt bonds and in the late 1960s and early 1970s they could be sold only for substantial discounts from what had been paid for them.

When such a bond is sold, the usual accounting system requires the difference between the book value and the sales price to be shown as a loss. The book value of bonds—the basis on which they are inventoried as assets—is generally cost or adjusted cost. "Cost" means the original cost; "adjusted cost" is cost adjusted each year for accrual of any discount at purchase, or amortization of any premium at purchase. If general interest levels have gone up since a bond was bought, its market value is inevitably lower than its current book value. If sold, the difference is recorded as a realized capital loss and that inhibits swapping.

When a bond swap would be advantageous, it can be established through fairly straightforward arithmetic that the "loss" will be more than made up over a reasonable period of time, to the ultimate advantage of the fund. For instance, Table 11.2 demonstrates a bond swap showing a bookkeeping loss of over $265,000, but a real gain of over $962,000.

Demonstrating the advantages of swapping does not suffice for the trustees of many public systems, who, even if they see the ultimate advantage, are afraid of how it will look to the public, the membership of the system, or the legislature—and that fear is not groundless. Political points have been scored repeatedly with accusations that the trustees (or the controller or treasurer) "lost money"

Table 11.2 ◆ Bond Swap

Trade date: July 1, 1971
Sold: $1,000,000 par value, U.S. Treasury bonds, 3½% due November 15, 1998—selling price, $726,406.25.
Bought: $1,000,000 par value, A.T.&T. 37-year debentures, 4¾%, due June 1, 1998—purchase price $697,500

	Issue Sold	Issue Purchased
	Calculation of bookkeeping loss	
(1) Book value [a]	$ 991,961.70	—
(2) Proceeds of sale (principal only)	726,406.25	—
(3) Capital loss (1–2)	265,555.45	—
	Calculation of ultimate results	
(4) Par value	1,000,000.00	1,000,000.00
(5) Purchase price (principal only)	——	697,500.00
(6) Cash remaining (2–5)	——	28,906.00
(7) Interest at 6% to July 1, 1998, on cash [b]	——	113,719.00
(8) Interest (coupons) to be received to July 1, 1998	945,000.00	1,282,500.00
(9) Interest at 6% to July 1, 1998, on interest (coupons)	1,349,906.00	1,832,016.00
(10) Total results at maturity (4 +7 +8 +9) [b]	3,294,906.00	4,257,141.00
(11) Total gain from transaction (difference in Item 10 between issue sold and issue purchased)	$962,235.00	

[a] The bond had been bought at a discount; reported here is its book value (adjusted cost) as of the time of sale.
[b] It is assumed here that income received after the trade date will be reinvested at 6%. A lower assumed reinvestment yield would still show an advantage in favor of the trade; a higher assumed yield would show a greater advantage.

on investments. This is an important difference between public and private pension funds. The corporate fund can trade bonds to advantage without worrying about an unsophisticated or demagogic attack; a public fund cannot. The concern is so widespread that many investment advisors and managers cater to it; they assume that a swap is not to be suggested if it means showing a loss, and they make little real effort to educate the trustees or provide them with adequate buttressing against uninformed criticism.

Holdings in tax-exempt securities are the most extreme example. As of 1972, state and local systems held about $2 billion in tax-exempt securities. It is safe to estimate that, through failure to act on these securities, the systems were then losing, in the aggregate, about $40 million in annual yield.

Another element is that many systems credit interest to employee accounts on the basis of yearly earnings, earnings that are reduced if the accounting reflects realized capital losses.

The problem has led to a number of suggestions for other methods of assigning book values to bonds. One method, "historical cost," assigns to the new bond the last book value of the bond that was sold, assuming the two are of similar type, quality, and maturity. A more popular proposal amortizes the bookkeeping gain or loss over the life of the old bond or of the new bond, whichever is shorter.

These accounting arrangements have helped to free some systems for advantageous trading, but they do not provide ideal or complete solutions. Perhaps a better basis for assigning asset value to a bond is the present or commuted value of the income stream it will produce. This is not the context in which to explain the method, except to point out three principal virtues. First, it would value every fixed-income asset on a basis precisely parallel to the method by which an actuary determines the present value of future benefits. Second, if a bond is sold for an advantageous reinvestment in another bond of equivalent maturity, this basis shows no loss—on the contrary, it should show a capitalized gain appropriate to the advantage. Third, this asset value is an excellent indicator as to when a trade would be advantageous. This method is used in England, but not yet, unfortunately, in the United States.

Whatever the accounting procedure, officials who fail to make a bond exchange when such an exchange will demonstrably improve the income flow of the fund may be guilty of imprudence. It is doubtful that the courts would in fact at this time hold failure to make such a trade to be imprudent. They may do so, however, at some time in the future. It boils down to a question of how clearly a court would understand the situation and how much sophistication those responsible for the investments would be expected to have. Should trustees be presumed to know that real loss will result from refusal to swap bonds? Is refusal to act justified by concern about appearances?

Among investment professionals, there is no question about the correct investment decision. If the professional viewpoint came to be widely shared, then there may come a time when accountability as a prudent trustee may include the obligation to trade-in bonds when advantageous. The fact that trading transactions may be attacked by those who are uninformed or demagogic may not be an adequate defense. The obligation of the trustees (or whoever makes investment decisions) should include the creation of an adequate record of justification for the transaction, with appropriate support from investment advisors, actuaries, and accountants.

Mortgages

Many systems are heavily invested in mortgages, which produce a higher yield than bonds. (Fourteen state funds reported more than 20 percent mortgage assets.) [1] In this respect, public systems have an advantage over most private pension funds, which are usually not large enough to warrant placing the large dollar amounts needed for good mortgage investment, or able to command the staff work usually required.

Inactive Management

With notable exceptions, public systems buy to hold and do not actively manage their portfolios; they are unaccustomed to deciding whether and what to sell.

An investment policy that buys to hold is usually considered conservative, and a policy that buys to trade, speculative. This is often an oversimplification. Assume, for example, that a pension fund buys to hold. In time there are economic changes, shifts in market values. What the fund bought at one point may not be worth buying several years later. If a particular security is no longer worth buying, then selling is worth considering. A decision to hold is not in fact readily distinguishable in principle from a decision to buy. That being the case, even a fund that never intended to secure short-term trading profits should perpetually reassess its holdings.

[1] Securities Industry Association, *State and Local Pension Funds, 1972* (New York, 1972), p. 8.

The rate of portfolio turnover indicates whether the investment managers recognize this factor. "Turnover" means selling to buy something else; specifically, it is the ratio of sales or purchases, whichever is less, to the average value of the portfolio. Annual turnover should, for example, probably be at least 10 to 15 percent within the stock portfolio and 5 percent within the bond portfolio. These ratios are far below the turnover rates of institutional investors, such as mutual funds, insurance companies, or common trust funds, yet a great many public funds do not sell even that much. The point of course is not that any particular rate of turnover is a virtue *per se,* but rather that persistent lack of turnover under changing circumstances is prima facie indication of lack of active portfolio management.

Nonprofessional Control

In many public systems, the power to decide on investments rests in the hands of trustees who are not equipped to make investment decisions. The board frequently consists largely of public officials and employee representatives who do not have the relevant background—yet they are generally legally required to make the decisions.

Three procedures are commonly used to make up for this discrepancy. First, if the system is large enough, it may have an investment staff that recommends transactions. One difficulty with this solution is that, except for the very large systems, the investment staff is apt to be small and have limited resources. Moreover, the civil-service salaries available cannot compete with those of the investment industry. Young men and women on the investment staff who prove competent are apt to be enticed to the private sector, stripping the public system of its first-rate talent.

A second procedure is to establish an investment committee, consisting of a small group of trustees with particular expertise. They may make recommendations to the full board, or be empowered to act on investment decisions according to the policy adopted by the full board. Decisions may be subject to approval by the trustees; authorizing the committee to proceed entirely on its own may not be possible if the statute assigns investment responsibility to the entire board. Moreover, much depends, as one might expect, on the quality of the investment committee itself. Sometimes it is too small a group, operating too privately and without adequate checks and balances, or it may be only slightly better equipped for the task than is the board as a whole.

Third, investment counsel may be engaged—either a trust company or an investment advisory firm of one sort or another. This relationship is generally advisory only. The board of trustees does not commonly contract with a trust company or other investment organization as a "discretionary account," which would give the contractor the right to buy and sell without specific prior authorization by the board.

The merely advisory relationship is not ideal. Investment decisions are made only at periodic intervals, and the board has to meet to review and act on recommendations of the advisors. Quick action is impossible—and yet it may be essential. This was proven in a case involving the Illinois State Universities System, which was advised on March 31, 1971, by the Harris Trust Company to sell its 9,200 shares of Abbott's Laboratories because the company was going to be sued on grounds of an allegedly contaminated product. The executive director of the system tried to reach the board members for a vote to approve, but he could not complete a vote until twelve days later, on April 12. On March 31 the shares could have been sold at a gain of $280,000; on April 12 they were sold at a loss of $29,000.

Speed in decision-making is also essential when acquiring an attractive new issue of bonds or making an advantageous swap. Quarterly or monthly meetings severely limit action.

The process of acting on the investment advisor's recommendations is not likely to be a joint consideration by equally qualified representatives. Consequently, review is apt to be either entirely perfunctory or marked by sporadic dialogue, with the amateurs generally endorsing the recommendations of the professionals more because of their own inability to judge than genuine agreement.

The several methods of bridging the gap between professional expertise and trustee's knowledge may be combined. There may be professional investment advisors on contract, plus some investment experts on the staff of the system, and perhaps an investment committee as well. The "approved list" is one device that has been used to give power of immediate decision to the investment manager while retaining investment responsibility with the trustees, who approve a list of securities and authorize the managers to buy and sell within that list.

If the final responsibility for deciding on each transaction rests with a board of trustees it is unlikely in most cases that an optimum investment policy will be followed. Trustees are burdened with responsibilities which, in most cases, they are not trained to fulfill. A misuse of talents results: the investment advisor does not assume legal responsibility and the trustees assume legal responsibility for decisions actually made on someone else's judgment.

The Trend Toward More Professional Investment Management

The trend toward greater professionalism may take the form of greater use of professional advisors, wider delegation of the right to buy and sell without prior clearance, and concentration of investment in a special agency. There has also been a healthy tendency to publicly disclose how investments are handled. In some cases, the quality of investment management is periodically measured by monitoring comparative performance.

The concentration in a single state agency of investment management for several systems is a significant development, occurring in Wisconsin, New Jersey, Minnesota, New Mexico, Oregon, and Illinois, among other states. Although concentration alone does not assure good or even active management, creation of a central agency has often been an integral part of a series of changes aimed at a more active investment policy. Accompanying changes have included more adequate professional staffs, fuller employment of outside counsel or management, greater facility of decision-making, more flexible investment policies, monitoring of results, and fuller disclosure of information. The typical centralized arrangement involves a board made up of individuals with investment experience plus representatives of the systems. The board gives general direction and supervision to the investment program, leaving day-to-day decisions to the professional staff.

The same style and results can be achieved by any large or even moderate-size fund, given the same impetus for active management. For example, the California Public Employees' Retirement System is in itself a conglomerate, with total assets close to $8 billion in 1973.

Employees of most of the political subdivisions of California are covered, as well as those of the state government. Its staff also handles investments for the Teachers' Retirement System.

Investments for the California P.E.R.S. are made in a wide variety of securities, including bonds, mortgages, and stocks, within limits prescribed by law and by policies adopted by the system's board of administration. The system has an investment staff and also retains investment counsel. The right to buy is delegated to the system's executive officer, who may in turn delegate it to certain staff members. The investment committee receives weekly reports of transactions and meets once a month to review current investments and approve a list for stock investments, usually from recommendations by the investment advisors. While free to buy within the list, the staff may not sell more than five equity issues between committee meetings. Each published annual report lists every security transaction and every recipient of commissions and the amount involved. Investments for the California Teachers' System are handled essentially in the same way by the same staff, except that the Teachers' System has its own investment committee, and there are some differences in investment policy.

In New York State, the comptroller's office occupies the same position, handling the combined assets of the Employees' Retirement System and of the Police and Fireman's Fund, totalling about $5 billion. The comptroller decides on all investments, aided by an unpaid Investment Advisory Committee consisting of leading members of the financial community, and by an unpaid Mortgage Advisory Committee composed of ranking experts. The Investment Advisory Committee meets regularly, reviews investment policy, and receives periodic reports itemizing each transaction. As of 1973, seven institutions were retained as investment advisors on stock transactions; they submit monthly recommendations and execute the transactions if approved by the comptroller. No mortgage investment is made without the Mortgage Advisory Committee's approval. There are external as well as internal audits, periodic examinations by the superintendent of insurance, and a history of *ad hoc* management surveys.

In 1968 the New York City Teachers Retirement System established a variable annuity fund based on voluntary allocations by the members and wholly invested in common stocks. The board of trustees engaged two investment managers—one a bank and the other an insurance company—and gave them freedom to invest the $250 million income, to buy and sell within an approved list. In 1973, having grown to a billion dollars, large enough to split without undue expense, the fund was divided among nine investment managers, and there has been constant monitoring of the results each produced. Handling a growing common-stock fund of more than $100 million is sufficient to engage the full talents of an investment-management firm, and the trustees have the advantage of instant nine-way comparison of results judged over whatever time frame they consider adequate.

Performance Analysis

In recent years a number of public funds have commissioned studies to compare their investment results with those of other funds, other institutional investors, and market indices. These performance measurements were used by corporate funds long before they were adopted by public funds, in part because the motivation for such studies may have been different. Corporations commonly consider their pension funds as profit centers; in effect, pension funds are seen as mutual funds that produce lower pension contributions if the rate of return is good and higher pension contributions if poor. Eventually the results affect corporate profit-and-loss statements.

In government systems such direct profit motive does not exist. If investment yield is superior, it is not generally clear who will profit: the public employer (by way of an abatement of contributions), or the employees (perhaps because the extra yield is credited to employee-contribution accounts, or because any extra margin is often considered an appropriate basis for benefit improvements). In any case, no one party is as strongly motivated as the corporate executive to improve investment yield. A public board may be as much interested in a performance review to establish a record of due diligence as it is in its contribution to future decision-making.

Performance comparison has limited use for public funds because fixed-income investments typically account for 80 to 85 percent of their portfolios. Performance analysis has not yet been made as useful a tool of analysis for bonds and mortgages as it has been for common stocks. In fact, the typical investment performance study of fixed-income securities may be confusing. The customary analysis is based on market value changes as well as on income. Bond prices fluctuate with changes in general interest levels. When interest rates are rising, a rate of return that includes price changes will be low or even perhaps negative. The typical analysis makes it seem as if the fund lost money, although it can afford to hold its bonds to maturity and realize an unimpaired flow of funds. A bond portfolio acquired to yield 6 percent will, over the years, yield 6 percent, notwithstanding years when its market value may have gone down. It is the assured long-term yield, not the changing market value, that forms the basis for a decision on an actuarial interest assumption and on the means for meeting future liabilities. Consequently, it may be confusing for a public board of trustees to be confronted with an analysis of performance that seems to indicate that the trustees lost money on their bonds, when the principal remained intact and the rate of yield continued unchanged.

Performance studies have, however, been generally useful to trustees in monitoring and illuminating the work done by their investment managers, particularly on equity securities, by giving trustees the kind of cross-check they need in dealing with their professional managers and advisors. The resulting dialogue has often had useful results.

Local Interests

Investment policies of public systems are often influenced by a desire to keep the money in the local economy. Sometimes this means simply that transactions are restricted to local brokerage firms; but it may also influence the nature of the investment. Mortgage investments in particular tend to favor the local area.

Both the Hawaiian and the Puerto Rican systems invest in home mortgages for their members, because, in each area, housing is in great demand and commercial mortgage rates are comparatively high. Mortgages are given to members at bargain rates with liberal down-payments. In a sense, the investment program represents an additional benefit to the members. On the other hand, even the bargain rates represent a good rate of return for the fund and they have been quite secure since the mortgagee has been a civil servant with a steady job. In Puerto Rico, mortgage payments are made through payroll deductions. In Hawaii, the system does not actually handle the mortgage: it puts up the money for certain designated banks to give mortgages to members on the favorable terms prescribed by the system.

Corruption

The possibilities of corruption in the handling of investments cannot be ignored. The opportunities are ever-present: large sums of money, a constant stream of transactions, the involvement of many outside interests—bankers, brokers, advisors, agents, underwriters, borrowers. Given these circumstances, there is a great deal of pressure, to which some trustees or administrators may succumb. A number of such incidents have come to light. In one case, a trustee took a kickback for favoring a particular investment; in another, an influential trustee was an officer of a bank in which the system maintained for years large deposits without interest.

But, on the whole, few cases of corruption have come to light. Of course, the cases that have been publicized may be only a fraction of the total—which is still not to imply that corruption is extensive. But opportunities are ever-present and checks and balances and disclosure practices are not as extensive as they should be. The small number of cases of malfeasance that have been disclosed may be due to scrupulous administration of the systems, but they may also be attributable to a low rate of discovery.

Proper perspective requires recognition that a double standard exists. What may be condemned as corrupt or unethical practice on the part of a public official may be accepted as common by a corporation official. If a public administrator uses his cousin as the system's broker, a scandal may result even if no price disadvantage was involved. If a company president does the same, it is taken in stride. That does not excuse the public official, who is guilty at least of favoritism.

Preventing corruption requires a system of accountability by those who make the decisions, full record-keeping, reporting and disclosure, and a system of independent audits and evaluative reviews.

The Question of Social Policy

A fund holding stock in a particular company may be confronted with the question of what to do about the company's social policy. Several American corporations have faced criticism from the public and stockholders on pollution and other environmental problems, hiring and promotion of minorities, business activity in South Africa, Angola, or Communist countries, product safety, manufacture of napalm and other weapons, and public or minority representation on boards of directors. What is the role of a public pension fund with investments in such companies? Two basic decisions are involved: whether to buy or hold a particular stock involved in such a social issue, and whether and how to vote the stock if an issue of social policy is presented at the annual meeting of the corporation.

The question is not academic. The College Retirement Equity Fund, which, with its companion Teachers Insurance and Annuity Fund, provides pensions for a large percentage of the college staffs of the nation, has never invested in liquor or tobacco stocks because of the social principles of some of the supporting educational institutions.[2] The Methodist Board of Missions dropped a bank because it entered into a financial consortium in South Africa. The United Church of Christ, the United Presbyterian Church, and the Episcopal Church were prepared to exert similar pressure.[3]

Selling a stock because of social policy may not always be easy for a large institutional investor; its holding may be too large to be salable without unduly depressing the price. This would be particularly true if there were many institutional investors who reacted at the same time in the same way.

Action may be taken on votes on stockholder proposals to change corporate policy. The best known is Campaign GM, initiated in 1970 by the Project for Corporate Responsibility. It proposed that General Motors add three public directors and establish a shareholders' committee on corporate responsibility. While the proposals drew only 3 percent of the vote, the type of response was indicative of what is possible. Twelve college endowments, including Amherst, Boston University, Brown, Iowa State, Oregon, and Tufts, voted for the proposals. Several public retirement funds voted similarly— Iowa, Wisconsin, New York City, San Francisco, and Boston. Some of these votes—for example, Boston's—became a political issue.

[2] Clarence E. Galston, "Fiduciary Responsibilities of Institutional Investors" (New York, Association of Life Insurance Counsels 1968), p. 853.
[3] Phillip I. Blumberg, "The Politicization of the Corporation," *The Business Lawyer,* Vol. 26, No. 5, July 1971, p. 1568.

A committee appointed by Harvard University to study the question concluded that the university "may properly, and sometimes should, attempt to influence management in directions that are considered to be socially desirable." William C. Greenough, Chairman of the Teachers Insurance and Annuity Association of America–College Retirement Equities Fund, expressed his viewpoint this way: [4]

Just a year ago, General Motors stated that a "corporation can only discharge its obligation to society if it continues to be a profitable investment for its stockholders." But it is time to rearrange these priorities: a corporation can only continue to be a profitable investment for its stockholders if it discharges its obligations to society.

The San Francisco retirement system authorized a review of its portfolio to see whether it had any holdings in companies guilty of pollution. A board member particularly active in advocating adoption of a resolution that would forbid such holdings became a candidate for mayor.

Interesting variants were provided in 1971 by the Los Angeles City Board of Pension Commissions. It disapproved of remarks on marijuana made by a television comedian and protested to the drug company sponsoring the talk show, mentioning that it owned $500,000 of the drug company's stock. The same board expressed concern to an oil company in which it had invested more than $1 million about reports that the company intended to contribute to candidates in a forthcoming city election.

Proxy voting or buying and selling by public retirement systems on the basis of social issues is a practice that can mushroom. A public system cannot brush aside public policy questions, despite the political problems entailed; system trustees may soon confront an entirely new set of policy questions.

Company Ownership

Theoretically, a public retirement system could buy control of a company. However, most statutes would not allow it for they restrict the percentage of stock ownership in any one company. It has probably never been attempted or even seriously suggested. In a novel

[4] *The New York Times,* May 3, 1971.

approach, when the trustees of the Employees' Retirement System of the State of Hawaii found that they owned 16 percent of the stock of the Hawaiian Independent Refinery, Inc., they successfully nominated a company director who reports regularly to the system trustees on the company's progress.

The Board's Function

The typical board is not well equipped for buy-and-sell decisions. It often assumes responsibility without the commensurate capability. It should instead devote itself, not to managing the portfolio, but to structuring the management of the portfolio. The board should carefully select its investment managers—whether in-house or outside professionals, or some combination of the two—and give them authority to buy and sell. In addition, the board should define the boundaries of the discretionary authority and, in broad terms, define the degree of risk the fund should assume—the extent of common-stock investment, the degree of flexibility in that boundary, the general types of stocks to be acquired, the quality of fixed-income obligations, etc. It should define what relation, if any, there should be between the investments of the fund and the local economy, and should determine policy on questions affecting social policy or the voting of proxies. Within these broad boundaries, the board should delegate the power to decide. To do this may require amendment of the statute, and if so the statute ought to be amended.

The trustees should also be concerned with the accountability of their investment managers, whose transactions and performance should be reported and monitored. There should be external, as well as internal, audits. In short, the trustees should concern themselves with establishing a system of checks and balances in order to assure both complete integrity and sustained high quality of management. Accomplishing all of this is not a simple task, but it is a much better approach than merely rubber-stamping the recommendations of investment advisors.

Summary

In the past two decades, public systems have radically improved their investment policies and procedures. However, too many are still burdened by overly restrictive and outdated limitations on their investments.

Even more prevalent is the continuing absence of active management, despite a growing number of notable exceptions. Most systems do not give sufficient consideration to the possibilities of selling as well as buying. Advantageous bond sales are inhibited, if not foreclosed, by the fear of showing a loss, although prudent management should require bond swaps when clearly indicated and creation of a record of justification sufficient to fend off political attack.

Systems may find themselves suddenly confronted with major questions related to the social responsibilities of corporations that may affect either buy-and-sell decisions or proxy voting.

An important question is whether the systems will be able to anticipate future developments and adjust their investment policies accordingly. Clearly they have not kept pace with the best professional investors. As the economy changes, investment styles change. As institutions accommodate to these changes, public systems on the whole have been slow to respond, lagging behind private pension funds and other institutional investors. This is a dangerous position. The last to accommodate to change is the most likely to be adversely affected. Public systems need to revise their policies so that they can respond quickly in line with changes in the economy and investment markets, and compete favorably with other institutions in active management of their investments.

The statutes should authorize system trustees to delegate decisions on investment transactions to professionals, while holding the trustees accountable for the investment arrangements, including prudence in fixing the basic investment policies and in delegation, establishing procedures, providing organizational checks and balances, and maintaining surveillance and review.

12 ❖ Pension Plans for
Policemen and Firemen

Pension plans for policemen and firemen are usually quite different from the pension plans for other public employees—they resemble the retirement plans for military personnel, intended to keep the public safety force youthful by providing substantial pensions at comparatively early ages.

These plans are among the most expensive, sometimes reaching 50 percent of payroll. Serious underfunding is a common phenomenon. Much more often than with the plans for their general employees, cities and countries are committed to relatively expensive benefits, the full cost of which is not reflected in present budgets but will inevitably have to be confronted ten or twenty years from now.

In 1971–72, a total of 344,108 policemen and firemen were covered by 1,511 state and local systems.[1] The great majority of these systems were small—fewer than 200 members.

Our survey of public employee pension plans included 42 systems for policemen and firemen, covering over a quarter of a million employees as of January 1, 1972. This survey therefore reports on about 80 percent of the policemen and firemen. About two-thirds of the systems are local; the others are state-administered. Included are most of the systems in the largest cities and eight plans for state police. Since large public employee systems tend to pay higher benefits than small systems, and the survey covered the largest systems,

[1] U.S. Department of Commerce, Bureau of the Census, *Employee Retirement Systems of State and Local Governments, 1972 Census of Governments* (Washington, D.C., U.S.G.P.O., December 1973.

the benefits shown are higher than for small jurisdictions and do not precisely represent a true cross-section.[2]

A Typical Plan

Based on the features most common to these plans, a typical (though hypothetical) policemen-firemen pension plan can be described as follows: [3]

Normal benefit payable at age 50 or 55, after twenty to twenty-five years of service.

Normal benefit is 50 percent of final pay, plus 1.67 percent for each year of service over the minimum service required for a normal pension. Final pay varies from pay in the last year to the average of the last five years.

There are no early retirement benefits; a vested right to a deferred pension is acquired after fifteen years of service.

Disability benefits are payable after five years of service, equal in amount to one-third to one-half of final salary if disability is not service-connected; half to three-quarters of salary, if service-connected.

Annuities are provided widows and surviving minor children ranging from 25 to 50 percent of pay if death is not service-connected, up to two-thirds final pay if service-connected.

There is no automatic cost-of-living adjustment of pensions.

Employees contribute about 6 percent of pay to the plan.

There is no companion Social Security coverage.

Normal Retirement Benefits

About a quarter of police and firemen's plans provide full benefits after twenty or twenty-five years of service regardless of age. The prevailing pattern, however, is full benefits at age 50 or 55 with

[2] A survey that distinguished plans in cities of 100,000 or more population from those of small communities established that, on the average, larger communities had slightly more liberal plans. International Association of Fire Fighters, *Fire Department Pension Profile* (Washington, D.C., The Association, April 1966). A 1970 national survey of U.S. municipalities found that "the largest cities pay the highest benefits and the smallest cities the lowest benefits." Labor-Management Relations Service of the National League of Cities, United States Conference of Mayors, and National Association of Counties, *First National Survey of Employee Benefits for Full-Time Employees of U.S. Municipalities* (Washington, D.C., 1973).

[3] Within the same jurisdiction, plans for policemen are generally, though not invariably, the same as for firemen.

twenty or twenty-five years of service. And a few plans do not pay
unreduced benefits until age 60 or 65 (Table 12.1).[4] The single

Table 12.1 ◆ *Eligibility For Normal Retirement Benefit: Policemen And Firemen—Number Of Systems*

Age	Total [a]	No minimum	Less than 20 years	20–24	25–28
			Years of Service		
Any	12	—	—	7	5
50	11	2	—	4	5
51–54	5	—	—	2	3
55	17	4	3	6	4
56–59	1	1	—	—	—
60	3	—	2	1	—
61–64	1	—	1	—	—
65	5	1	1	2	1
Total	55	8	7	22	18

[a] Numbers do not equal number of plans in survey; plans with more than one eligibility provision are entered more than once.

most common requirement is age 55, but when weight is given to the plans that pay normal benefits after twenty or twenty-five years, regardless of age, the pattern closest to average is a normal retirement age of 50.

Normal benefits are typically 50 percent of salary after twenty-five, sometimes twenty years of service (Table 12.2).[5]

[4] Similar findings have been made by two other surveys. One, covering 122 plans for policemen as of 1971, found that 30 percent had no age requirement, but 63 percent required attainment of at least 50. U.S. Department of Justice, Law Enforcement Assistance Administration, National Institute of Law Enforcement and Criminal Justice, *Portable Police Pensions—Improving Inter-Agency Transfers* (Washington, D.C., U.S.G.P.O., 1972), p. 7.
The 1966 survey by the International Association of Fire Fighters found this distribution among 463 plans:

No minimum age	19 percent
Age 50	28 percent
Age 51–52	15 percent
Age 55	30 percent
Other	8 percent

[5] The 1966 survey by the Firefighters Association found that, of the plans reporting a flat percentage benefit, 92 percent paid 50 percent; of the plans reporting a percentage per year of service, 69 percent had a 2 percent formula, which is equivalent to 50 percent after 25 years.

Table 12.2 ◆ *Normal Benefit Formulas: Policemen And Firemen—Number Of Systems*

Formula for First 20 or 25 Years	Total	Nothing	Formula for Years in Excess of First 20 or 25						
			Less than 1.5 percent	1.5–1.66 percent	1.67 per-cent	2 per-cent	2.5 per-cent	More than 2.5 percent	Other
20 years									
Less than 50 percent	6	3	—	1	—	1	—	—	1
50 percent	10	1	1	1	2	1	1	1	2
25 years									
50 percent	14	6	3	2	1	1	—	—	1
More than 50 percent	1	—	—	—	—	—	—	1	—
Other [a]	11	—	—	—	—	—	—	—	—
Total	42	10	4	4	3	3	1	2	4

[a] Includes flat dollar amounts, step-rates, and a variety of other benefit formulas.

Additional service usually accrues additional benefits. The rate of accrual for these extra years is generally less than the 2.0 to 2.5 percent accrual rate for the first twenty or twenty-five years of service. A common pattern might be 2.5 percent for the first twenty years (that is, providing 50 percent at retirement after twenty years) plus 1.67 percent for each additional year of service. This provides about two-thirds of salary after thirty years of service.

Almost all pensions for police and firemen are based on final pay. A sizable group uses the last year of employment as the measure of final pay, but the largest group uses the average of the last three to five years [6] (Table 12.3).

Early Retirement and Vesting

Most plans for police and firemen do not provide reduced benefits for earlier-than-normal retirement. Even those that do usually

[6] The Firefighters 1966 survey found that 39 percent of the plans used the last year's pay, but 57 percent used a period of three years or more. The single most common provision was a five-year period.

The 1970 survey for the National League of Cities, as cited in footnote 2 above, found that the three-year average dominated among its responding plans; on the other hand it reported no plan with a shorter base than three years.

Table 12.3 ◆ **Base For Computing Final Average Salary: Policemen And Firemen (Employees In Thousands)**

Base	Systems	Employees
Pay of the position [a]	3	5
Last pay	4	20
Last year's pay	9	82
2 years	1	1
3 years	7	79
4 years	3	7
5 years	12	60
Total	39	254

Note: Two plans pay flat dollar amounts.
[a] These plans adjust the pension amount, after retirement, according to the current pay for the position from which the employee retired.

require twenty or twenty-five years of service (Table 12.4). But most of the plans surveyed do vest deferred benefits if the employee leaves before earning a normal pension. However, the period of service needed for vesting—fifteen to twenty years—is appreciably

Table 12.4 ◆ **Eligibility For Early Retirement Benefits: Policemen And Firemen, Systems With Early Retirement Provisions—Number Of Systems**

Age	Total [a]	Years of Service					
		No minimum	10–14	15–19	20–24	25–28	30 or more
Any	4	—	—	—	2	2	—
50	10	1	4	—	2	3	—
51–54	0	—	—	—	—	—	—
55	2	—	—	1	1	—	—
56–59	—	—	—	—	—	—	—
60	1	—	—	—	—	1	—
Over 60	0	—	—	—	—	—	—
Total	17	1	4	1	5	6	0

[a] Numbers do not equal number of plans in survey; plans with more than one eligibility provision are entered more than once.

higher than in private plans or even in plans covering other public employees (Table 12.5). The extent of vesting among the larger

Table 12.5 ◆ Eligibility For Vesting: Policemen And Firemen, Plans With Vesting Provisions—Number Of Systems

Age	Total [a]	No minimum	Less than 5	5–9	10–14	15–19	20–24
			Years of Service				
Any	25	1	2	3	4	7	8
40–54	1	—	—	1	—	—	—
55–59	1	1	—	—	—	—	—
Total	27	2	2	4	4	7	8

[a] Numbers do not equal of plans in survey; plans with more than one eligibility provision are entered more than once.

police and firemen's plans covered by this survey apparently does not hold for smaller plans. A survey which included many more small plans found that over half of the police plans had no vesting provisions.[7]

As in other public-employee plans, most police and firemen's plans have a compulsory retirement provision. Of the 42 surveyed, 16 set the limit at 65 or older and 14 used an age between 60 and 64 (Table 12.6).

Table 12.6 ◆ Compulsory Retirement Provisions: Policemen And Firemen

Age	Systems
Under 60	5
60	8
61–64	6
65	14
Over 65	2
No such provision	7
Total	42

[7] Labor-Management Relations Service of the National League of Cities, et.al., *First National Survey,* p. 67.

Rates of Salary Replacement

The median policeman's and fireman's pension at normal retirement age after twenty years of service is slightly less than half of the final year's salary.

There is a problem in adequately evaluating *total* retirement benefits, that is, system pensions plus Social Security benefits. Most policemen and firemen will retire from their public employment ten years or more before becoming eligible for unreduced Social Security benefits. In the ten-year period between retirement from public employment (if retirement is at 55) and age 65, general wage levels will have increased so that the salary with which total benefits may then be compared will have become obsolete.

That makes it difficult to relate combined retirement income at 65 to final pay. About two-thirds of police and fire employees covered by the survey will, if they retire at 55 after thirty years of service, receive combined benefits—system benefits plus primary Social Security—of at least 60 percent of final pay; half of them will receive at least 70 percent of final pay (Table 12.7). However, the "final pay" figure is by age 65 at least ten or fifteen years old.

Disability and Death Benefits

Pensions provided in the event of disability generally require a minimum of five or ten years of service unless the disability arose from the employment (Table 12.8). Pensions for ordinary disability cluster around half-pay. If disability is service-connected—"duty disability"—the amount is generally higher, often two-thirds to three-quarters of pay (Table 12.9).

Most police and fire plans provide annuities for the survivors of officers who die while employed—whether death is attributable to employment or not. Payments made to the wife and children fall in the range of half to three-quarters of the accrued pension or else 50 percent of the deceased officer's salary (Table 12.10). If death was service-connected, the typical benefit is an annuity to the widow equal to 50 percent of salary; in many plans there is an additional benefit of a fixed monthly amount or 10 percent of salary for children.[8]

[8] International Association of Fire Fighters, *Fire Department Pension Profile*.

Table 12.7 ◆ **Benefits, State And Local Systems, Police And Firemen; Retirement At Age 55 With 30 Years Of Service, Final Salary Of $14,000**

Benefit as Percentage of Final Salary	Benefit		Benefit plus Primary Social Security at 65 [a]		Benefit Net of Annuity Value of Members' Contributions	
	Systems	Employees	Systems	Employees	Systems	Employees
Ineligible	—		—		—	
Not applicable	1	1,200	1	1,200	1	1,200
Less then 20%	2	7,100	2	7,100	2	7,100
20 – 24.9	—	—	—	—	1	2,600
25 – 29.9	—	—	—	—	1	1,400
30 – 34.9	1	2,600	1	2,600	2	2,200
35 – 39.9	—	—	—	—	7	33,000
40 – 44.9	—	—	—	—	12	55,300
45 – 49.9	5	13,300	4	5,000	3	10,300
50 – 54.9	8	26,700	6	24,300	4	16,000
55 – 59.9	10	52,700	9	45,000	3	23,700
60 – 64.9	5	53,900	3	10,900	3	68,000
65 – 69.9	4	59,100	4	27,400	2	41,800
70 – 74.9	3	37,700	5	40,100	—	—
75 – 79.9	2	8,300	2	8,300	—	—
80 – 84.9	—	—	1	7,700	—	—
85 – 89.9	—	—	2	43,000	—	—
90 – 94.9	—	—	1	40,000	—	—
95 – 99.9	—	—	—	—	—	—
Total	41	262,600	41	262,600	41	262,600

[a] Reflecting January 1972 Social Security and only for those systems which have Social Security coverage.

Table 12.8 ◆ **Eligibility For Ordinary Disability Benefits: Policemen And Firemen**

Years of service	Systems [a]
Any	12
Fewer than 5	3
5	11
6–9	0
10	9
More than 10	3
Other	0
Total	38

[a] Four systems do not provide ordinary disability benefits within the framework of the retirement system.

Table 12.9 ◆ **Benefit Amounts For Service-Connected Disability: Policemen And Firemen**

Formula	Systems [a]
Flat amount	1
Percentage of normal benefit	
Less then 90 percent	—
90 percent or more	1
Based on projected service	1
Percentage of salary	
50 percent	9
More than 50 but less than 75 percent	10
75 percent	2
More than 75 percent	7
Varying percentage	3
Same as for ordinary disability	7
Total	41

[a] One system does not provide ordinary or occupational disability benefits.

Table 12.10 ◆ Amount Of Survivors' Annuities, Ordinary Death In Active Service: Policemen And Firemen

Formula	Systems with Social Security	Systems without Social Security
Flat amount	—	4
Percentage of employee's pension amount		
50 but less then 75 percent	1	6
75 but less than 100 percent	—	2
100 percent	—	—
Percentage of salary		
50 but less than 75 percent	—	8
75 but less than 100 percent	—	—
Other	2	9
Total	3	29

Postretirement Increases

Most plans for policemen and firemen do not provide for automatic increases in pensions after retirement (Table 12.11). Among those with cost-of-living increases, the most common provision is an automatic increase in accordance with the Consumer Price Index, with a cap of 3 percent, possibly more, per year. A few plans in-

Table 12.11 ◆ Automatic Postretirement Adjustments: Policemen And Firemen

Formula	Systems	Employees (thousands)
Automatic percentage increase		
1 but less than 2 percent	2	6
2 but less than 3 percent	2	8
Automatic increases according to C.P.I.		
2 but less than 3 percent	1	9
3 percent or higher	7	38
Adjustment to pay of the position	5	13
Other	1	19
Total with adjustments	18	93

crease pensions for policemen and firemen as the pay of the position increases. Adjusting pensions to changing wage levels is so strikingly different that there is a widespread impression that this is typical of plans for policemen and firemen. Actually, it is unusual; it was more common fifty years ago than it is today.

Employee Contributions

With rare exception, the systems are contributory. Employee contributions are fairly substantial, particularly since Social Security contributions are not usually required. The most typical rate is between 6 and 7 percent of pay (Table 12.12). If the value of the employee's

Table 12.12 ◆ ***Rates Of Employee Contributions: Policemen And Firemen***

Rate	Systems with Social Security	Systems without Social Security
Noncontributory	1	2
Uniform rates		
Total	1	27
3 but less than 4 percent	—	1
4 but less than 5 percent	—	1
5 but less than 6 percent	—	4
6 but less than 7 percent	1	9
7 but less than 8 percent	—	8
8 but less than 9 percent	—	3
9 percent or more	—	1
Step-rates—percentage when applied to $10,000 [a]		
Total	2	—
1 but less than 2 percent	1	—
2 but less than 3 percent	—	—
3 but less than 4 percent	1	—
Schedule of rates—rate for male, entry age 30 [b]		
Total	3	3
Less than 2 percent	2	—
2 but less than 4 percent	—	—
4 but less than 6 percent	—	—
6 but less than 8 percent	—	1
8 percent or more	1	2
Other formulas	—	2
Total	7	34

[a] "Step-rates" refers to one rate on a first portion of salary and another on the remainder
[b] "Schedule of rates" refers to contribution rates determined according to the entry age.

contribution is subtracted, the average policeman or fireman retiring at 55 after thirty years of service receives an employer-financed benefit equal to 55 to 59 percent of final pay (Table 12.7).

Social Security Coverage

Only 17 percent of the fire and police systems surveyed (38 percent of the men) have companion Social Security coverage. Were the survey more comprehensive, it would be found that even a lower percentage has coverage.

Most policemen and firemen have opposed Social Security coverage. Originally, their concern was that participation might eventually undermine their special pension provisions. Now, however, probably the most important consideration is the fact that most policemen and firemen expect to be eligible for Social Security anyhow through other employment, without having to contribute while working as a policeman or fireman. Most employees leave police or fire departments early enough to earn Social Security coverage. Some—particularly firemen—may even have coverage through moonlighting in a second job. All it takes to qualify, as we have noted, is 40 calendar quarters of coverage (with earnings of at least $50 a quarter).

On a short work-span covered by Social Security, the benefit is relatively liberal. If a man had left police or fire employment not covered by Social Security in 1960, worked for the next twelve years in a job covered by Social Security, and applied for Social Security benefits at age 65 in 1972, he would have been entitled to 70 percent of the benefit amount he would have gotten if his police or fire employment had been covered by Social Security, yet he would have contributed perhaps as little as half as much. Similarly, if retirement occurs in the year 2000 with only the last ten years in covered employment, the Social Security benefit will be at least 50 percent of what it would be if all employment had been covered, although contributions by the employee would have been only about 25 percent as much. The opposition of many police and fire groups to Social Security coverage is therefore not surprising.

We have noted that the Social Security Act restricts participation by policemen and firemen. Policemen under a retirement system are not permitted to participate, except in 19 states listed in the Social Security Act (and Puerto Rico) and then only if the employees approve by referendum. Firemen may be covered in any of the states, subject to approval by referendum, with the proviso, however, that in any but the 19 named states, the governor must certify that the step will improve the overall benefit protection of the firemen.

In appraising the pensions of policemen or firemen whose jobs are not covered by Social Security, it is by no means clear that the existence of Social Security should be disregarded. Certainly, if a man works from age 25 to 60 as a policeman or fireman and his job offers no special opportunity for "moonlighting," then Social Security should indeed be disregarded. If, however, he quits the service at 45 or 50, he has enough time left to earn Social Security coverage. In that case, the possibilities for early retirement from a police or fire job include an advantage that is not immediately obvious, namely, the opportunity subsequently to acquire Social Security coverage at a high ratio of benefits to contributions. The critical question then is whether the men will as a matter of fact usually be in a position to earn Social Security benefits apart from their police or fire jobs.

PROBLEMS OF POLICE AND FIREMEN'S PLANS

Retirement Policy

It is fair to ask whether there are cities, counties, or states that have systematically considered a policy for the retirement of their police or firemen. Do they know at what ages they want the men in the several ranks of their safety forces to retire? If so, do they know why? If they have an objective, have they actually directed their retirement plans toward its accomplishment?

This much at least is true—there has been very little *articulation* of policy or factual backing for it. The pattern of what is done may amount to a policy, but it is unlikely that the pattern has often been thought through in terms of whether it really serves the efficiency of the force and the security of the men.

Discussion of police and fire pensions has generally revolved around the hazardous and arduous nature of the work. There are really two ways of looking at it: one from the standpoint of the men, and the other from the standpoint of public administration. The men stress the demanding nature of the job. They would like to be *able* to retire early, without being *forced* to do so. They would like to have greater benefits for staying on longer. On the other hand, for the sake of public safety, it may be necessary to have a large percentage of comparatively young men in police and fire jobs.

The two viewpoints are not necessarily different, nor do they necessarily coincide. Management may want to consider a compulsory retirement age, a maximum hiring age, a maximum on benefits after twenty-five years of service, a tapering of the formula with long service, or a number of other possibilities. The employee attitude is different in this respect: it stops short of limiting the benefits or the job tenure of any of the men.

That the efficiency of public agencies is involved is significant in another respect. There are other jobs that are hazardous and physically demanding, but from which the public safety element is missing. These jobs have not, as a matter of fact, won equivalent treatment. The man who collects garbage is a good illustration. Going out in all kinds of weather and lifting heavy cans and other refuse is not a job to be recommended to someone who is 55. It is arduous and the accident rate is high. The same observation might be made about someone who maintains city sewers. However, with rare exception, these jobs are not given special consideration for retirement. What is missing is the appeal to the public in terms of public safety; physical demand alone has not been a sufficiently persuasive factor.

When should a policeman or fireman retire? Is there a particular age bracket that is suitable? Is the stress on youth overdone? Does the right age depend on the particular job that the man has in the force? Precisely how much of the force is actually involved in work that requires youthful stamina and reactions? Is there a valid distinction between the men in the ranks and the officers? Does the job of the officer call more for judgment, knowledge, and qualities of personality than for physical capacity? These are questions which have rarely been systematically confronted.

It is common for a police department to transfer men according to their capacities. A man with diminished vigor or a physical impairment is often shifted to a desk or light-duty job. If that course is not available and the man is not yet eligible for service retirement because he has not put in twenty or twenty-five years or reached 50 or 55, he may take disability retirement, with the consent or even advice of his superior officers. He may even be able to retire on a service-connected disability pension, which may pay more than any other type of benefit and carry partial or complete exemption from income taxes.

Certain patterns have become noticeable. If a police or firemen's retirement plan has a high age or service requirement for normal benefits, it is apt to develop a high incidence of disability requirements. That is entirely understandable—the man wants out and the department would like to see him out. Probably, in most of the cases, he really does have difficulty in meeting the physical or psychological demands of the job. Some systems that have resisted the early provision of normal retirement benefits may find that they pay heavily in terms of disability pensions.

If a policeman or fireman retires before age 60, certainly before 55, he almost invariably takes another job. Yet policy on retirement benefits does not seem to take that distinction into account. Consideration is not given to the fact that at early ages "retirement" means retirement for another job; at later ages, retirement means just that. This means that the man who retires early has one or two decades in which his pension will supplement job income, followed by a later period of years when his pension will play a much larger role in his economic security.

The possibility of a second career has a great deal to do with maintaining a high ratio of young men on the force and with the ultimate economic security of the employees.

Someone who has the right to a pension in his forties is much more likely to retire than someone who does not acquire that right until he is in his fifties. In his forties, he is more energetic and daring, he has a better chance of getting a good job, he has much more incentive for further education and retraining, and he has many more years in which to develop and enjoy the rewards of a second occupation. However, if he is in his fifties when this opportunity first appears, he may conclude that it is too risky to shift and that he had better stick it out as long as he can for the sake of the income, to build up a better pension, and to reduce the period of time when he will have to rely on his pension. When he does retire, it will be either for total retirement or for some marginal or mediocre job providing a comparatively modest income.

If in fact it is important for a police or fire-fighting force to have a high ratio of young men (let us say, ages 25 to 45), then it may be important to allow attractive benefits when they are in their forties. It may simultaneously achieve management's goals and allow the men second careers they can fruitfully continue much longer than their police or firefighting work. It would be desirable to recognize that some policemen and firemen do—and should—retire for another career, while others stay in the force for essentially all of their work-life.

Shaping the pension benefits of policemen and firemen to two objectives—transition to a second career and income for full retirement later—is a simple enough concept once it is described, but it has not as yet been given explicit recognition in shaping the systems. The typical discussion centers on a single lifelong benefit and argument over whether it is or is not enough to live on and whether the age threshold is too high or too low. The concept of shift to a second career may raise an entirely new set of questions. Should there be education or retraining benefits for retirement in the forties? Should the retirement benefit payable while the man is in his forties and fifties be a form of guaranteed income, from which a percentage of subsequent earnings is subtracted? Should a different kind of pension be provided for the presumed total-retirement years?

The point here is not to advocate any particular answer, but to suggest that the provisions of police and fire plans could be rethought to the advantage of both the employees and the efficiency of public safety services.

Cost

Pensions for policemen and firemen are relatively expensive, because of comparatively early retirement, liberal disability benefits, and frequent provision of annuities for survivors. New York City contributes 28 percent of pay for its police; New York State 40 percent for its highway patrol; Los Angeles 48 percent and Minneapolis 43 percent for its firemen. These figures are not particularly the chance results of particular funding schedules; in fact the Minneapolis figure is very close to the system's pay-as-you-go costs. The benefits in these cities may be above average, but even lesser percentages would still be substantial.

There are many cities with roughly equivalent benefits that are contributing far less; generally, it is because they are seriously underfunded. A survey of 122 police and fire funds found that 56 were on a pay-as-you-go basis.[9] They will ultimately find that contributions will have to be increased to 30 percent or more of payroll.

Transferability

Pension provisions for policemen and firemen discourage shifts among forces from one city to another. This interferes with development of superior officers with professional training and ability to move from one community to another.

The problems of transfer within a state can be solved by a state-wide system or by state legislation mandating reciprocal arrangements between or among the several systems, with or without transfer of funds. All of that still leaves unsolved the problem of interstate transfers. A study for the National Institute of Law Enforcement and Criminal Justice recommended partial federal subsidy for systems providing transferability.[10] There are, of course, institutional obstacles to such a development. The agency which might lose officers if transfer were easier is likely to resist. Moreover, there is a traditional feeling that promotion ought to come from the ranks, not by the lateral movement of officers from elsewhere. Nevertheless, the increasing need for officers with technical and managerial capacity argues for some arrangement to permit the best men to be employed in key positions regardless of geography.

Disability Pensions

As noted, disability retirement may become a substitute for service retirement if the age or service requirements for a normal pension have not been met. Generally, it need only be established that the employee is unable to fulfill the duties of his position. No distinction is made between disability for the job and a more general type of disability. A policeman who has lost the use of his trigger finger is not generally differentiated—as to benefit rights—from a policeman who has become blind.

Retirement on the basis of service-connected disability is a per-

[9] National Institute of Law Enforcement and Criminal Justice, *Portable Police Pensions*, p. 11.
[10] *Ibid.*, pp. 62–64.

vasive problem. As noted earlier, about three-quarters of the police of Washington, D.C., retire on service-connected disability. This is a little extreme, but it is symptomatic of what happens, to some extent, in many police and fire departments. The statistics obviously raise a question whether every one of the disabilities is in fact attributable to the job. Clearly, in some departments, retirement on service-connected disability has become the standard operating procedure. The benefit is attractive; service requirements are usually negligible, and so someone who wants to get out long before he is eligible for a normal pension may consider the disability route. He may need the cooperation of his superiors, but there is often a mutuality of interest and little concern over the cost to the retirement system. Moreover, the benefit for service-connected disability is almost always better than for normal retirement. Finally, if the service-connected disability pension is in lieu of workmen's compensation, it is tax exempt. It is also pertinent that there is generally little or no concern—statutory or administrative—with whether the disability pensioner takes another job outside the government.

In part, the overutilization of disability provision is attributable to the fact that managerial personnel find it convenient and are not directly affected by the cost impact. In fact, if the payroll has become top-heavy with light-duty assignments, the efficiency of the force can be improved if some light-duty men can be induced to take disability retirement. There may not be much net saving to the community, but cost is transferred from the department's payroll to the retirement plan.

Several states and cities have adopted provisions that if a policeman or fireman is affected by a heart disability, it is presumed to be attributable to the job. A similar presumption is sometimes made as to a fireman afflicted by lung disease. Without benefit of a statutory presumption, a California policeman won a court decision that his alcoholism was attributable to the tensions of his job.

Summary

The distinctiveness of police and firemen's pensions is not new. They were among the first to be covered by pension plans. The earliest patterns were half-of-final pay after twenty or twenty-five years. A similar pattern, half-pay after a specified period of service, was followed by the earliest plans for other public employees. For police-men and firemen, that pattern has persisted. In some respects, the benefits for these employees are less generous than they were fifty and seventy years ago, when it was common to find plans providing half-pay pensions that escalated after retirement with the base pay for the rank held at retirement. It was only when the cost of such escalation began to become apparent that many of these provisions were dropped.

Nevertheless, pensions for policemen and firemen are clearly more expensive and generous than for other employees, except per-haps for judges and legislators. The men in the safety forces are deeply convinced that they are entitled to that special niche. And the record is that in this regard they have generally had the support of the public.

These plans are the result of a long historical development, plus pressures from the men, who are effectively organized and per-suasive both with legislators and the public, notwithstanding the cost implications of their plans. However, there has been no systematic effort to shape the provisions of these retirement systems to the employment, staffing, and retirement needs of a present-day police or fire department. If maximum effectiveness for public safety is to be achieved, retirement policy should be brought in line with public need for efficient police and fire-fighting services. Attention ought to be focused on the role of the retirement plan in relation to a sec-ond career as well as in relation to an adequate full-retirement in-come.

13 ❖ Several General
Policy Questions

Legislators, Judges, and Executives

Normally, judges receive far more liberal pensions than do other public employees. A pension of two-thirds to three-quarters of final salary at age 60 or 65 is standard. Service requirements are modest—ten or fifteen years. Many states pay this amount at younger ages or at any age for service of twenty to thirty years. In some judges' plans, benefits after retirement increase with salary. Judges normally contribute, and when their benefits are higher than for other employees, they contribute at a higher rate. In some states, however, judges are covered by the same benefit formula as other employees.

With Social Security, which most judges receive, most judges probably retire with greater after-tax income than they enjoyed while on the bench. The plan for the federal judiciary provides full pay at 70 after ten years of service, at 65 after fifteen years, or upon disability after ten years of service; it is basically non-contributory.

With few exceptions, there has been no visible resentment of the liberal retirement benefits of judges. The public is apparently accustomed to thinking of the judiciary as a special group which should be placed above concern about future economic security. Because their numbers are small, the total cost has not created alarm. Nor, in general, have pensions for judges been generally used as precedents for other and larger groups of public servants.

Executives are generally covered by the same plan of benefits as other state employees. Sometimes elective or appointive officers are made eligible for vesting after relatively few years in recognition of the fact that they may lose their positions as the result of an election.

Legislators in some states have voted themselves much higher pensions than are provided for the rank-and-file. They sometimes justify it to themselves on the grounds that they are underpaid, that the voters will not stand for increasing their pay, and that therefore, they must resort to the indirect and less noticeable route of increasing their pensions.

Pennsylvania has provided a notable example of a legislator's pension plan far above that of the ordinary employee. For state employees generally, Pennsylvania provides at age 60 a benefit equal to 2 percent of final average salary (five-year average) per year of service, which amounts to 50 percent after twenty-five years. In addition, if the member so elects, he receives another 2 percent of that part of career-average pay which exceeds the current Social Security tax base. Employees contribute 5 percent, plus another 5 percent on the excess if they have chosen the Social Security "integration credit." Members also participate in Social Security, and their retirement income is exempt from state and city income taxes. Regular state employees and executives, with thirty years of service, receive at 65 substantially more net income than before retirement.

The legislators, however, have a special slot: they can collect full benefits from age 50 (instead of 60). At the expense of an actuarial reduction they can begin drawing at any age if they have had at least six years of legislative service. The full allowance is 7½ percent of final average salary (instead of 2 percent) for each year of legislative service. For that they contribute 18.75 percent of pay, which is steep but does not pay for more than a third of total cost. Their pay, when this plan was adopted, was $7,200 a year. A maximum of $12,000 a year was set on the pension, but with a catch. The $12,000 limit was on the annuity *after* choice of option. A retiring legislator could qualify for a pension of $16,000 a year or more and bring it within the maximum by choosing a joint-and-survivor option that would pay him only $12,000 in exchange for an income guarantee to his beneficiary.

In addition, legislators are covered by Social Security, and they can choose the Social Security integration option. This benefits only legislative leaders, however, because ordinary legislators are restricted to credit for a $7,200 salary, which is within the Social Security tax base.

This plan has been highly controversial. In 1972, legislators' salaries were increased to $15,600, but the law provided that only the old $7,200 was to be used for pension purposes. This freeze was put into effect in order to allow for correction of their overly liberal benefits. As of mid-1973, that freeze was still in effect.

Even with the freeze, total retirement benefits, including Social Security, for a typical legislator (sixteen years of service) comes to 125 percent of the $15,600 salary, and his retirement income net after taxes amounts to 195 percent of his salary.[1]

Rhode Island offers another, though essentially quite different, example. Its legislators are paid a mere $5 a day for a session of 60 days. A pension plan effective in 1975 will pay legislators retiring at age 55 after six years of service a pension of $300 per year of service. In other words, the pension is to be $2,400 for eight years and $6,000 for twenty years. The disproportion between salary and pension is glaring, but no more so than the inadequacy of paying $5 for each session day.

New York and California have other variations. Salaries for state legislators are not low in comparison with other states. Their pensions are also more favorable than for typical state employees.

Some states make no distinction in favor of legislators (e.g., Massachusetts), although it would seem reasonable at least to provide earlier vesting in view of uncertainty of tenure.

Different pension provisions for legislators are warranted in some areas—as, for example, early vesting—but not in all. Many legislators are badly underpaid because voters tend to measure their salaries by the number of days in the session. That may be a valid standard for a poor representative; for a good one, it is not. It would seem better practice to set the salary on the expectation that a good job of representation will be done. The poor pay in many states has made the enactment of special benefits for legislators seem more reasonable; however, it remains difficult to justify voting higher pensions to get around a public that disapproves higher salaries. The result may be an abuse of legislative power that tends to undermine respect for the

---

[1] Pennsylvania Economy League, Inc., *Retirement Benefits for Pennsylvania State Officials* (Harrisburg, Pa., October 1972).

democratic process and to establish poor standards for others to follow.

Tax Exemption for Public Pensions

Several states exempt state and local pensions from the state income tax. New York goes so far as to include such a provision, indirectly, in its constitution.

This privilege is difficult to justify. It is nothing more than a carry-over from the days when pensions were considered a type of charity for the impoverished schoolteacher and other faithful but underpaid civil servants.

An income tax exemption has precisely the same effect as a benefit. There is no reason why public employees should be given a subsidy denied other state residents. In fact, the inequity is compounded since the exemption gives the greatest benefit to those pensioners who have the highest family incomes.

Consolidation

Consolidation (or "conglomeration") of systems is gradually being accepted, generally in the form of a state-administered system for localities in which participation may be voluntary or, sometimes, mandated. The system may be for general employees, for policemen or firemen or both, or for all of these groups. This pattern developed early for teachers—a single statewide system and plan for all teachers except those in large cities. Further consolidation for teachers now centers mainly around possible merger with a general state employees' system.

Consolidation is variously attractive to different groups. Its major objective may be uniformity of benefits, with high or average levels. The level is not likely to be low, compared to the supplanted local plans. A uniform state-prescribed plan eliminates whipsawing future benefit demands and puts the provisions beyond the immediate influence of any particular local group. Also, it becomes easier for the legislature to understand the plan and to keep track of it. Without a statewide plan, changes in one locality or for one group can create a precedent for other localities and groups. With a statewide plan, the implications are obvious to all who are ultimately affected.

One major problem with a statewide plan is the level at which to fix benefits in relation to the local plans being supplanted. A statewide plan may be a means of raising benefit levels for small cities, towns, and counties, even though consolidation into one system does not necessarily imply a single benefit level. Distinction may be made according to the size of the city or county, or several optional levels may be offered. Even so, a leveling process takes place; the result may approximate an average or be equal to the most generous of the plans already in effect.

Of course, uniform benefits can be mandated without a centralized system. Massachusetts uses that approach throughout, Pennsylvania for classes of cities and counties, and Illinois for its downstate police and firemen. However, uniformity is more commonly tied to a single system, with its appeal of efficiency, easy tranferability of credits, etc.

Contributions can be uniform or varied. Cost to each employing unit for a given plan of benefits may be a uniform percentage of the covered payroll, a different percentage—to a point where each unit pays its own way—or it can be a compromise formula. For example, all participating units may pay the same "normal cost" but differing contributions for "past service" or for the "deficiency" between normal cost and full cost for the participating unit, the idea being to reflect a difference in initial costs but ultimately to reach a point at which all units contribute the same percentage of covered payroll.

Theoretically, if participation or termination is voluntary, then each group should somehow pay its own way. If the group does not, there is always the possibility of adverse selection against the state plan because, with a uniform rate, the most costly groups will choose to come in and stay in, and the least costly will stay out or drop out. However, events do not always follow the actuarial rule book, and there are some voluntary statewide plans that manage without strain to establish and maintain a broad range of participation, notwithstanding their exposure to adverse selection.

With mandatory coverage, cost uniformity is, of course, readily possible. Amalgamation may lower costs to expensive groups at the expense of higher costs to inexpensive units. Bleakney has made the point that a multi-agency system can be the victim of a form of anti-selection. A participating unit may raise salaries at the terminal point of a career, so as to increase pensions for its people, while relying on the cost being spread among all units.[2] The same possibility is also inherent in statewide teacher systems and other large state systems. Moreover, it is somewhat dependent on whether benefits are calculated on final average salary over five years, three years, or one year. Obviously, a one-year formula invites deliberate changes, especially because the particular employer does not have to pay for the benefit consequences.

Supporting consolidated plans is the efficiency of a larger system—in management, computer applications, actuarial services, informational programs, and investment handling. Against them are arguments that a very large portfolio may be more frozen into its investments, and concentrate too much power; that a uniform plan may not accommodate well to local circumstances and needs; and that it may preclude valuable experience with a diversity of answers.

The trend toward consolidation will continue if only because states will now and then create statewide plans, but are not likely to reverse the process. And the existence of many small systems—competitive in benefits beyond any requirements of responsiveness to special needs, inefficient in administration, and laggard in the handling of investments—suggests that the trend toward amalgamation of plans under state sponsorship will continue.

Uniformity or Diversity

At the same time, there has also been a tendency in some states for multiplication of plans through distinctive benefits for particular groups. For example, the number of different plans within the N.Y.S. Employees' Retirement System and its Policemen's and Firemen's System multiplied in the 1960s. The trend was related to collective bargaining. If the police of Nassau County negotiated a special package, it was provided through a special plan within the system. If someone else negotiated the computation of pension on final pay, instead of a three-year average, it was offered as an optional variation for each participating employer. In New York City, if prison guards, sanitationmen, and transit workers negotiated three different plans, they were accommodated within the City Employees' Retirement System. A special niche was created for a host of

[2] Thomas P. Bleakney, *Retirement Systems for Public Employees* (Pension Research Council) (Homewood, Illinois, Richard D. Irwin, Inc., 1972), pp. 20–22.

specific city jobs deemed physically demanding. There has been a tendency for a variety of law-enforcement personnel—marshals, sheriffs, park police, wardens—to secure benefits intermediate between the average employee and policemen and firemen. In several cases this type of accommodation has also been extended to workers in hazardous jobs, whether public safety is involved or not; for example, attendants in mental hospitals and electric linesmen. Although these special benefits have been the result of pressure from the interested employees, they have not generally been achieved by collective bargaining *per se*. Nationally, the trend toward uniformity has probably outweighed the trend toward diversity.

Complete uniformity of benefits does not resolve all equity problems. Public employment encompasses a great and diverse array of jobs; inevitably, claims for special-pension provisions arise; many have merit. Complete uniformity for all categories of employees within a state is therefore neither realistic in all cases nor necessarily equitable. A more appropriate goal is a rational structure, completely uniform where it can be uniform and differentiated to the extent that the facts establish a genuine case for variation.

The Internal Revenue Code

In 1972 the Internal Revenue Service [3] declared that a public employee pension trust fund and the benefits thereunder are entitled to the special tax treatment for qualified pension trusts and their beneficiaries only if they meet the qualifying standard requirements of the Code.[4] Theoretically this could have far-reaching consequences. If a trust does not qualify:

1. Its investment income is subject to federal income taxes. (However, an argument would ensue over whether a trust established by a state or local government could be taxed.)
2. The employee is subject currently to income taxes on employer contributions made after the employee has passed the point of vesting.
3. The employee may be currently taxable on subsequent interest credits on his contributions.
4. Lump-sum distributions are not entitled to the more favorable treatment accorded qualified plans.

[3] Revenue Ruling 72-14.
[4] Sections 401(a) and 501(a).

The trouble is that the Internal Revenue Code was not written with public systems in mind. Its principle concern was to define the extent to which a company could secure recognition of pension contributions as a legitimate business expense. The essential thrust of the Code is to avoid abuse of the privilege of making tax-exempt contributions. It imposes a limit on how rapidly a pension may be funded, and limits the fund's use to pensions and properly incidental purposes. A central concern is that the plan not discriminate in favor of company officials, executives, or other highly compensated individuals. These requirements have given rise to elaborate regulations, rules, and interpretations.

For public plans, the question of deductibility of contributions does not come up at all, since state and local governments are not taxable. What remain are the questions of tax-exemption for the trust itself and favorable tax treatment for the employees and certain beneficiaries.

Some difficulty arises when rules designed for corporate pension plans are applied to public plans. However, with rare and only very recent exception, the rules have in fact not been applied, except when question has been formally raised. The answer is given, at least in the first instance, by the local director of the Internal Revenue Service. Consequently, answers differ from one state to another, as is to be expected when a complex set of rules written to assure even-handed treatment of corporate executives and the rank-and-file in private industry is applied to public plans. Many public systems have never asked for rulings as to whether their plans qualify; they and their members have simply assumed that there is no problem.

Nonenforcement by the Internal Revenue Service has in fact been the rule. If enforcement were attempted, it would confront the question whether to assess most state and local judges for thousands of dollars of back taxes because of their superior benefits. Awkwardness has arisen—at least until 1973—only for those system trustees or officials meticulous enough to ask for a ruling.

The proper answer to the problem is for the Treasury Department or the Congress to face the dilemma honestly and work out for enactment an appropriate adaptation of the Code for application to the public employee retirement systems.

Moreover, Treasury rulings on Social Security integration should be changed. The law itself does no more than forbid a benefit formula that discriminates in favor of the higher-paid. The regulations do not permit a full offset of primary Social Security, on the logic that an employer-financed plan is discriminatory if it subtracts the portion of Social Security which the employee's own contributions have financed. Yet it is possible to have an "all-inclusive" or 100 percent offset plan under which the combined benefits, together with the combined contributions, represent not merely equal treatment for all wage and salary levels but discrimination in favor of the lower-paid. It is difficult to understand how such an arrangement can violate the anti-discrimination rule of the Internal Revenue Code. The regulations should be revised to accept that fact and permit 100 percent offset if the combined results do not discriminate in favor of the higher-paid.

Post-Retirement Adjustments

At least half of all public employees are covered by automatic post-retirement adjustments. In that respect, as was clear in chapter 2, their pensions are very different from those in private industry.

The states and localities without automatic adjustments have generally made *ad hoc* adjustments. The need to which all of these legislative enactments respond is obvious. For someone who retired on January 1, 1963, on a fixed pension, the dollar was worth only 71 cents ten years later. For someone who retired in 1953, the purchasing power of the dollar had declined by 1973 to 63 cents.

The great majority of public systems start off with the advantage of basing pension payments on some version of final salary, in contrast to flat benefit amounts or benefits based on career-average earnings. This design results in automatic accommodation to changing salary levels during the period of active employment. The rapid inflation of the last few years has in fact stimulated a shortening of that salary base in many plans from what used to be a standard five-year period to periods of four years, three years, or occasionally one year.

It is the post-retirement period that occasions special provisions. Whether to enact automatic post-retirement mechanisms or to make *ad hoc* adjustments is a much debated issue. *Ad hoc* adjustments are flexible in the sense that they can be designed—in terms of fixed dollars or percentages or minimums—in any way the legislature decides. A price can be attached. Since it does not involve the long-term and perhaps uncertain commitment of an automatic adjustment, it allows the legislature to change its mind on the next round, and also gives it several opportunities to grant benefit increases instead of concentrating all of its good works into the one enactment of an automatic mechanism.[5] The objection, of course, is that *ad hoc* adjustments do not reassure the pensioner as to future changes.

Automatic adjustment is normally based on increases in the Consumer Price Index from year to year. These laws generally contain a limit—2 or 3 percent—on the extent of benefit change in one year. The higher the limits the more uncertain the cost.

The third type of adjustment is a strictly automatic percentage increase without reference to the Consumer Price Index. This provides a much more ascertainable cost and permits the cost to be shared by the employees, where desired.

A number of states—including Arizona, Minnesota and Mississippi—have adopted various forms of pension supplements that depend on actuarial gains. By and large, these depend on the extent to which the pension fund has earned investment yield in excess of its assumed rate. These results may have a rather chancy, haphazard relationship to cost-of-living changes and they may exercise an extraneous influence on actuarial assumptions and investment decisions.

A few systems, such as Wisconsin, New York City Teachers, Oregon, and New Jersey, have established variable annuity programs in which employees are given the option of participating. The variable annuity is based on an accumulation in a common stock fund and benefit payments are subsequently varied with the changing unit value of that fund. In every case, only a portion of the employee's pension may be secured through the variable annuity, the theory being that it is safest to have a combination of fixed-dollar income and variable income, and that the two together will by and large cope with cost-of-living increases. In certain years the stock market has gone down while prices have gone up, but the long historical record has provided ground for the belief that a combination of fixed income and an income variable with common stocks will,

[5] For full discussion of post-retirement adjustments, see John P. Mackin, *Protecting Purchasing Power in Retirement* (New York, Fleet Academic Editors, Inc., 1971).

over the long run, provide a shelter against the erosion of living standards through inflation.

Except for a few pension funds for police and firemen, Maine is unique in providing for post-retirement adjustments proportionate to general salary increases for active employees. Of course, salary increases are almost invariably greater than cost-of-living changes. Over the past twenty years, real earnings (earnings adjusted for cost-of-living) have increased at a rate of about 2.2 percent a year. The theory of an adjustment to wage levels is that higher living standards ought to be shared with those who have retired.

Collective Bargaining

Many states have recognized the right of public employees to collective bargaining. Retirement benefits are obviously part of remuneration and of the conditions of employment and unless specifically excluded, they may become the subject of bargaining. As yet, retirement benefits are rarely set through collective bargaining.[6]

Collective bargaining raises an awkward but fundamental question: Which takes precedence, the right to collective bargaining or the right of the legislature to legislate?

If a municipality has home rule on pensions it can negotiate pensions to a definitive conclusion, assuming the executive who negotiates has effective power to commit the municipality's legislative body. A public authority might also have the independence to decide its pension arrangements. However, in all other cases, there is always the question of whether the legislature that must vote on pension changes will accept what a public employer and a public employee's union have negotiated. If the legislature does not accept the package submitted to it, then the negotiated agreement is not consummated; it was only an agreement to recommend or to seek a particular legislative act.

New York's recent history provides the classic case. In 1970 the mayor of New York City reached agreement with the union representing the largest unit of city employees. A key part of that agree-

[6] The term "collective bargaining" refers here to negotiation on the terms of employment between the employer and authorized representatives of the employees. This does not include lobbying or any form of campaigning for legislation, although successful lobbying sometimes involves some type of "negotiating" between employee organizations and legislators, governors, or mayors.

ment was for a more liberal pension plan. It was practically taken for granted that the legislature would approve—but it did not. So, for more than two years, the union campaigned and lobbied with the governor and the legislative leaders, to no avail.

In short, if the legislature refuses to accept a prepared package and asserts the right to legislate independently, then the collective bargaining process becomes less than full collective bargaining—the "negotiations" shift from the "employer" to the governor and the legislature. At this point, the process has become far removed from a bargain arrived at between two parties across a table. Several additional stages have been added; several more parties have intervened. Even the voter may get involved.

Theoretically, there are alternative possibilities. One is to eliminate pensions from legislation and authorize each public employer to set its own pension plan in the same way a city or county authority can fix salaries or hours of work. That would mean a tremendous increase in the number of different pension plans and more competitive leapfrogging than ever before. It would also mean that pension provisions could change, up or down, with each negotiation. Therefore it does not seem to be a suitable answer.

Another possibility, theoretically, is to require the legislature to enact whatever is negotiated. Pennsylvania has come close to that. Its constitution has provided since 1966 that

. . . the General Assembly may enact laws which provide that the findings of panels or commissions, selected and acting in accordance with law for the adjustment or settlement of grievances or disputes or for collective bargaining between policemen and firemen and their public employers shall be binding upon all parties and shall constitute a mandate to the head of the political subdivision which is the employer, or to the appropriate officer of the Commonwealth, if the Commonwealth is the employer, with respect to matters which can be remedied by administrative action, and to the lawmaking body of such political subdivision or of the Commonwealth, with respect to matters which require legislative action, to take the action necessary to carry out such findings.[7]

This authorization by the constitution has been implemented in two different ways. For public employees generally, the Public Employee Relations Act provides for voluntary agreement for binding arbitra-

[7] Article 3, Section 31.

tion, but with the qualification that "the decisions of the arbitrator which would require legislative enactment to be effective shall be considered advisory only." However, a separate act, applying to policemen and firemen, states that if the appropriate lawmaking body does not approve an agreement reached by collective bargaining or if the bargaining reaches an impasse, the issues are to be submitted to arbitration by a three-man board. The decision of the arbitration board is final and binding:

No appeal therefrom shall be allowed to any court. Such determination shall constitute a mandate to the head of the political subdivision which is the employer, or to the appropriate officer of the Commonwealth if the Commonwealth is the employer, with respect to matters which can be remedied by administrative action, and to the lawmaking body of such political subdivision or the Commonwealth with respect to matters which require legislative action, to take the action necessary to carry out the determination of the board of arbitration.

This provision is clearly mandatory on all localities. As to the state itself, a 1974 act made it clear that the legislation was not subject to change through collective bargaining agreement.

Collective bargaining on pensions involves still another problem. Public employees can be highly influential in electing (or deposing) their bosses—through direct electoral activity, through contributions, and through helping to raise or lower the image of an official. That observation applies to the legislative process as well, but it makes a noticeable difference in the tone of contract negotiations.

Collective bargaining can be an instrument for employee pressure for more benefits, but it is certainly not the only source of employee pressure. New York's laws in the late 1960s developed out of collective bargaining; California's did not. Yet, except for its substantial rate of employee contributions, California has a more liberal state employees' retirement system than New York.

Pensions as Contractual Guarantee

The laws of several states make retirement benefits for public employees contractual rights which may not be diminished or impaired. That means that benefit rights, whether accrued for service completed or yet to be accrued on future service, may not be diminished for anyone who is already a member of the system. Less advantageous benefits may be enacted only for persons who are hired or who become members after the date of change.

New York, Florida, and more recently Illinois have constitutional provisions to that effect. Massachusetts has accomplished the same result by providing in its retirement statute that its terms for superannuation retirement are to be contractual obligations, not subject to reduction. It is difficult to see how the statutory language in Massachusetts has any different result from the constitutional provisions in the other three states, except that it does not apply to ancillary benefits such as disability pensions, and new provisions could be exempted from this contractual commitment.

The same effect, although in less rigorous form, has been achieved in a number of other states by court decisions that hold pension provisions to be implicit contractual obligations. The California Supreme Court has ruled since at least 1955 that pension rights may not be diminished for those who were members of the system prior to the change, except if the amendment was necessary for the integrity of the system or was counterbalanced by benefit increases. Its most momentous decision along these lines almost stripped the system for Los Angeles policemen and firemen of its assets. Before 1925 the system's pension payments fluctuated after retirement with the pay for the position from which the man had retired. A new charter in 1925 discontinued that postretirement increase for persons not yet retired. The court held in 1958—thirty-three years later—that the change could only be made effective for persons hired after the change and summarized the judicial rule as follows:

An employee's vested contractual pension rights may be modified prior to retirement for the purpose of keeping a pension system flexible to permit adjustments in accord with changing conditions and at the same time maintain the integrity of the system. Such modifications must be reasonable, and it is for the courts to determine upon the facts of each case what constitutes a permissible change. To be sustained as reasonable, alterations of employees' pension rights must bear some material relation to the theory of a pension system and its successful operation, and changes in a pension plan which result in disadvantage to employees should be accompanied by comparable new advantages. In the present case, it appears that . . . the amendment substantially decreases plaintiff's pension rights without offering any commensurate advantages, and there is no evidence or claim that the changes enacted bear any material relation to the integrity or successful operation of the pension system.[8]

There are probably a few more states—perhaps as many as four— in which the courts have held retirement benefits to be contractual rights that may not generally be diminished for those already employed.

A 1969 survey by a New York State Commission found that in most states—at least 35 at that time—benefit accruals based on prospective service could legally be reduced. Six did not permit reductions in benefits already accrued and four limited the ban to annuities already in process of payment.[9]

The Supreme Court of the state of Washington has held the funding plan called for by the statute to be a contractual right akin to the benefit rights.[10]

In Pennsylvania the judicial precedent is that the provisions may not be changed for anyone already employed "except where the changes bear some reasonable relation to enhancing the actuarial soundness of the retirement system." Changes such as lengthening the period of service, increasing the retirement age, or increasing the contribution rate are considered relevant to actuarial soundness, but in no event is it considered legal to change adversely the rights of someone who has fulfilled the age and service requirements for retirement.[11]

A federal court has held that Congress has the constitutional right to amend the provision for retired pay to officers of the armed services. The case involved an amendment eliminating post-retirement escalation in accordance with the changing pay for the rank and grade from which they retired.[12]

The reasoning behind a ban on diminution of benefits is fairly plain. A person takes a job partly in reliance on the future benefits.

[8] Abbot v. City of Los Angeles, 50 A.C. No. 11; 1958.
[9] N.Y.S., The Governor's Committee to Study the State Employees' Retirement System, *Report,* June 1969. The six states listed as banning reduction in benefits accrued were Alaska, Hawaii, Iowa, Kansas, Michigan, and Washington. The four limiting the proscription to pensions begun were Kentucky, Minnesota, Nevada, and Wisconsin.
[10] Mae Weaver, et al. v. Daniel S. Evans, et al., 41851, Washington Sup. Ct., 1972.
[11] Levy Anderson, "Vested Rights in Public Retirement Benefits in Pennsylvania," *Temple Law Quarterly,* Vol. 34, No. 3, 1960–61, pp. 255–277.
[12] A. L. Abbot, et al. v. The United States, U.S. Court of Claims, No. 785-71, January 8, 1973.

Expectations for retirement income are built on that basis. His services are consideration for that promise. Hence, the conclusion is that benefits should be treated as a contract right that may not be impaired.

Even without constitutional or judicial limitations, state legislatures and local councils have in fact been extremely reluctant to reduce benefits already promised, which is as it should be. However, a prohibition on legislation that would in any respect reduce the future benefit accruals of any present employee is fraught with difficulty.

The most detailed experience with such a complete and inflexible guarantee is that of the New York State system. It is described in the next chapter. There, the provision has had far-reaching consequences. Statutory language running to more than 200,000 words is frozen, except as it may be liberalized. The words have often been written under eleventh-hour pressure of a legislative log-jam or of collective-bargaining negotiations under circumstances that permitted scrutiny by, at best, no more than two to four people. That is not, of course, unusual for technical legislation at the state level. What is unusual is that, under the guarantee, whatever is written into a permanent retirement statute might as well have been written into the constitution itself. If a provision or a phrase turns out to have been a mistake or leads to an unintended or unanticipated result, nothing can be done about it with respect to anyone who is already a member. It is even difficult to plug a loophole or correct a mistake for *new* members, because the process would clutter the statute with a sequence of corrections, each applicable only to persons who joined the system after the respective effective date of the changes.

Equally serious is the fact that long experience with the guarantee led the State of New York to avoid it by enacting numerous temporary laws, which automatically expire unless renewed by the legislature. The result, in short, can encourage the opposite of the long-run security the guarantee was supposed to assure.

Rationalizing Pension Statutes

Public employee pension systems have sought ways of assuring responsibility and consistency in pension legislation. This demand has been met in part by funding, which dampens the temptation to liberalize now and pay later. The idea of splitting cost between employer and employee has been similarly motivated. To the same end, some states require every pension bill to carry a fiscal note stating the cost of the change; at least one state requires that funding of a benefit change begin as soon as the change is effective. One taxpayers' group—the Pennsylvania Economy League—proposed at one point that the unfunded liability of the public pension system be counted as part of the public debt in the application of debt limits.

In several California cities, pension proposals must be voted by referendum as amendments of the city charter. Popular referendum is certainly not a suitable technique for adopting proposals as technical and complicated as pensions. If proponents expect that popular vote will result in less expensive benefits, they should consider the willingness of the Los Angeles electorate to vote liberal benefits to its policemen and firemen.

Permanent Commissions

Pension commissions have often been resorted to as a way of trying to introduce some order into an otherwise unruly scene. A pension commission may also be created to consider a major change in benefits, funding, investment, or administration. It may be conceived as a vehicle for pushing a particular change, or as a buffer against it, or as a proper way of considering its merits.

A study commission can bring together legislators of both houses and parties, government executives, and outsiders as well. By "outsiders" we mean persons who are neither legislators nor government officials. These laymen may enjoy a degree of insulation from political pressure, particularly if they represent organizations or if they have a public stature to protect, and may help to move the basis for decision from expediency toward principle. These individuals should represent a mixture or balance of viewpoints and not be dependent on government officials. Independence is necessary, whether through public reputation or through connection with a broad constituency.

The real question at issue is whether a state should establish a *permanent* commission. An ad hoc commission presents no great policy problem. If the issue of the moment suggests the advisability of a study commission, it can always be set up. Its recommendations can be accepted, rejected, or modified. But a permanent commission may tend to limit the freedom of action of the executive or of the legislator, except if it happens to be part of a desired balancing process.

Permanent commissions are in operation in Massachusetts, Illinois, Wisconsin, Minnesota, Ohio, Washington, and (very recently) New York. Their influence varies. The first few have been particularly effective in getting the legislature to go along with its recommendations.

The merits of an ongoing commission may be several. First, pensions are a specialized subject requiring a degree of expertise or knowledge; once acquired, it should continue to be available, as it can through a commission. Second, there is need for continuity of policy—which is lost if successive pieces of pension legislation are considered by entirely different people. Naturally, change of policy should always be possible, but it should be accompanied by knowledge of the past. Third, a continuing commission can apply a consistent policy to the perpetual stream of pension bills; legislation is more apt to get into ultimate disarray through a long sequence of piecemeal changes than through a single large enactment.

The value of pension commissions cannot be judged solely by those that have survived. That way of judging is selective: successes survive and failures die. Many commissions have proved unproductive. Chief executives and legislative leaders often view a commission as an inhibition on their power. If there is a settled power arrangement that the authorities are happy with, they have little incentive to set up a possible source of interference or competition. In some states, the effective decision-makers on pension matters are a few key legislators or the governor or a member of his cabinet. In several states the trustees of the state retirement system or of several of the systems act as reviewers and proposers of legislation. Some are effective with the legislators; others are almost ignored as partisans.

A commission may founder for any number of reasons. It could be weak; its membership may not embrace sufficiently varied viewpoints; it may lack public stature; its recommendations may be faulty; it may not know how to convey the significance of its proposals; it may fail to engage public support. Important legislators may not want to spend time on a pension commission, which deals after all with only one among many legislative subjects, one that is neither the most glamorous nor urgent. On the other hand, recommendations from an unimportant legislator may be ignored. Timing is important too. A commission of high quality with merits on its side may find that its recommendations are too far out of line with the political or social balance or the trend of the moment. Several commissions in Massachusetts recommended a uniform state law with no practical result for many years, although the idea was ultimately enacted. A prestigious commission in New York State worked for two years on a new law only to find that the state had shifted pension policy to collective bargaining. The Illinois permanent commission is highly effective, but not in winning consolidation of the many tiny funds for police and firemen (because of the opposition of local banks and other interests), nor in securing adequate funding.

Success in the establishment of continuing policy through a standing commission rests ultimately on the arts of statemanship—working out a set of principles, securing their implementation, knowing both what is ideal and what is possible and how they can be blended with integrity. The individual abilities of a commission's membership are obviously important ingredients.

At the very least, a commission can identify the essence of a proposal, attach to it an appropriate cost, spell out some of the implications, and offer an informed viewpoint. Hopefully the commission will be one that is accepted by the public and by government officials, as representing a span of responsible opinion.

There is, in any event, widespread need for governmental mechanisms for developing, maintaining, and changing the policy of a state or local government with respect to its retirement systems. A great deal of pension law grows by patchwork, yielding in time to favoritism and special pressures. An articulated policy that is subject to review is necessary to developing and maintaining a fair and effective law.

14 ❖ New York State

An historical review—a longitudinal study—of the retirement systems of a state reveals a good deal about the dynamics of the institution, how it developed, what progress has been made, what mistakes have been repeated, and what may account for order or disarray in its public policy. Solving today's problems requires not only an idea of the appropriate answer, but also an understanding of the forces that effect changes in the institution.

New York provides a good case history, not because that history is typical (although in many respects it is), but because it is longer than in most states. New York has faced many problems and anticipated others that some states have yet to meet.

New York State has eight retirement systems—five in New York City, three for the rest of the state.[1] Such division is common within states, particularly those with large cities. Their municipal pension plans generally predated the state plans and, when the latter were created, the legislatures usually respected the separateness of the major cities.

There are three statewide systems that omit New York City:

1. The New York State Teachers' Retirement System covers all teachers in the state and has only one plan of benefits. School boards must participate.

2. The N.Y.S. Policemen's and Firemen's Retirement System covers these safety employees whether employed by the state or by local government. It has a variety of benefit plans, optional to the employer.

3. The N.Y.S. Employees' Retirement System covers all other em-

[1] New York also has a number of closed systems for discontinued plans that still pay benefits but have little or no active membership.

ployees of the state and of local governments. If a unit of local government provides a retirement plan, it must do so by joining the state system; a choice of plans is available.

THE NEW YORK CITY SYSTEMS

The five New York City systems are: the N.Y.C. Teachers' Retirement System; the Board of Education Retirement System, covering the noncertified personnel of the Board of Education; the Police Pension Fund; the Fire Department Pension Fund; and the N.Y.C. Employees' Retirement System. The latter is the largest, covering all other employees of the city and of city-related agencies, such as the N.Y.C. Transit Authority. It has essentially four benefit plans for separate employee groups—transit and housing police and correction officers; uniformed sanitationmen; transit workers; all others.

All of these systems are governed by state legislation. Although New York City has "home rule" in a broad sense, the state legislature reserves to itself the right to make changes in the retirement systems, excluding two limited areas in which local option is permitted: supplementary benefits for already retired persons and other existing beneficiaries and employer contributions which substitute for otherwise-required member contributions. However, the state constitution requires the city to consent to changes in the Employees, Police, or Fire Systems, unless the legislature acts by general law applicable to a broad class of municipalities. This limitation does not apply to the Teachers and Board of Education Systems since the school system is legally under direct state jurisdiction. In practical effect, any position taken by the City's officials is significant in determining state legislation on all five of the City systems, but it is the state legislators and the governor who have the ultimate authority to decide. Outside New York City, the only local autonomy is the right to choose one of several state system plans.

Each of the systems is subject, under state law, to periodic audit and review by the state insurance department.

New York City Plans Before 1920

The first law in the country to provide retirement benefits for public employees was a New York state law passed in 1857 to provide for New York city's policemen. Thus, New York City's plans predated state plans: a pattern typical of much of the country. In general, the earliest pension plans were for cohesive groups able to exert the necessary pressure—policemen, firemen, and teachers.

The earliest provisions were rudimentary. The 1857 plan covered only policemen injured in the performance of duty, for which a lump-sum and later a pension was provided. Firemen got the same protection in 1866. It took another twenty-one years—1878—before the city's policemen were able to retire without proof of incapacity—half final pay at age 55 with twenty-five years of service. Firemen got a more generous plan—half of final pay after twenty years.[2] Note that half of final pay after twenty years is not a recent innovation; it was one of the earliest patterns.

Employees of the city's health department got a pension fund in 1894. Manhattan teachers got their first plan the same year; Brooklyn teachers the next year; and the two were consolidated when the Greater City of New York was created in 1901. The teachers plan was financed by salary forfeitures on account of absence; an attempt, typical of many plans in that era, to avoid special appropriations or contributions by the teachers themselves.

"In 1905," the city's Commission on Pensions reported in 1916, "a law was passed for the retirement for disability after thirty years' service, of employees of the department of finance, and the first beneficiary, a bookkeeper of the chamberlain's office, for whose benefit the law was drafted, retired on January 1, 1906. Known as the 'Grady Law' this plan was extended in 1911 to all city employees not provided for by existing pension plans." [3] There is nothing wrong with broad legislation sparked by one man's plight, but the fact that for five decades the law was known by the name of its first beneficiary has the charm of another era about it.

Separate plans followed for the street cleaning department and for two judicial districts. As of 1916, a study commission found that New York City had developed a tangled mass of conflicting provisions, a description encountered again and again in the history of public retirement plans.

[2] City of New York Commission on Pensions, *Report on the Pension Funds of the City of New York*, Part 1 (New York, 1916).
[3] *Ibid.*, p. 3.

The benefit provisions of these early plans were simple. The standard provision was half of final pay; the miscellaneous mass of employees covered by the Grady Law could get these benefits only if disabled and after thirty years of service. Half of final pay at early ages or at any age was not limited to policemen and firemen. Employees of the health department and of City College could get half-pay after twenty years, any age. Strangely, at the same time, New York City policemen had to wait until 55, after twenty-five years of service; teachers had to have thirty years of service, any age; and street cleaners, age 60 and twenty years of service. Firemen were eligible for service-connected disability pensions after any period of service, but policemen and street cleaners only after ten years. This curious relationship reminds us not to take any pattern for granted.

Typical of pre-1920 plans in New York and elsewhere were contributions that took no account of the long-term needs of the plan. Moreover, these early plans required little in the way of employee contributions. Employee contributions were required of police (2%), and teachers, employees in the health department and in one judicial district (1%); the others were non-contributory. Every effort was made to get painless income, some earmarked source that would not offend the taxpayers nor require annual appropriation. Several plans got the income derived from disciplinary and absence deductions from employee pay. Two plans received unexpended salary appropriations. The police fund got the income from pistol permits, boiler inspections, and masked ball permits; the firemen's fund from a tax on foreign fire insurance carriers and the sale of condemned property; the street cleaning department fund got the receipts from the sale of ashes, garbage, and refuse. Some of these may sound quaint, but earmarked special revenues of this kind are still part of the financing of many municipal funds for policemen and firemen, including to this day the pre-1940 "closed," but still functioning, systems for New York City policemen and firemen.

The 1914–1918 Review

Rapid escalation of the city's costs, abuse of some provisions, and inequities among the various groups of employees led to overhaul of the pension arrangements. The mayor established a Commission on Pensions which functioned for four years (1914–1918) and led to the establishment of the present actuarial reserve systems for teachers and all city employees except policemen and firemen.

The Commission found that the plans were inadequately financed. Disbursements had increased from $291,000 in 1870–74 to $21 million in 1910–14. It reported that funds dependent on limited revenue sources would soon be exhausted, that the Teachers' fund was already in that position, and that the Health Department fund was within a few years of disaster. The Commission predicted that the policemen's and firemen's funds, able to draw on city appropriations, would in time require contributions of 35 or 45 percent of payroll.

The Commission found that although the plans permitted retirement of many employees before 50, they were, at the same time, ineffective in eliminating superannuated employees. Because policemen had to wait until 55 to retire, and street cleaners until 60, both resorted to the half-pay disability pensions available to them after ten or twenty years of service. Consequently, a very high percentage of those on the rolls were disability pensioners—65 percent of retired policemen, 25 percent of retired firemen, 92 percent of retired street cleaners. In most of the current public employee systems the figure is 5–20 percent. These figures dramatically illustrate the point, made earlier, that a high threshold for age retirement may induce over-utilization of a disability provision. It is a conclusion that some legislatures, even today, have not yet learned.

Pertinent, in the light of recent developments, is the criticism leveled by the commission against the use of final pay as the base for determining the pension: [4]

This arrangement results in unduly increased pension to those whose retirement follows soon after a change in salary schedule and gives the beneficiaries an unwarranted advantage. . . . Finally, there is always the possibility of unwarranted promotion of an employee to a higher paying position shortly before retirement for the purpose of granting a larger pension.[5]

The laws provided that police, fire, and street cleaners funds pay pensions of "not less than" half-pay. The fire and street cleaning

[4] New York City plans now compute benefits as a percentage of final pay or final year's pay, instead of average pay over a five-year period, a practice continued until recently and still the most prevalent nationally.

[5] N.Y.C. Commission on Pensions, *Report,* p. 22.

commissioners (but not the police commissioner) availed themselves, selectively, of their discretionary authority. More than half pay was granted to 26 firemen, all except 4 of whom were officers, and to the 3 employees of the Street Cleaning Department who happened to be its highest-ranking officers.

Retirement on pension, followed by reemployment on full-time jobs by other branches of municipal government, was a frequent abuse among policemen and firemen—even though most of the former had retired for disability.

The case of Thomas Mulvey, a patrolman for the old City of New York (Manhattan), was well publicized at the time. Mulvey retired in 1893 on a pension of $1,000 a year. He immediately found a job as captain of police for the suburban town of New Utrecht. When New Utrecht was absorbed by Brooklyn he became a Brooklyn policeman; when Brooklyn merged with old New York to become the Greater City of New York, Mulvey found himself back on the N.Y.C. police force four years after he had retired—on a salary of $2,000 and a pension of $1,000. He retired finally in 1913, claiming a second pension. He was awarded only one, this time at $1,125. He sued, but lost.

Establishment of Funded Systems

The report of the Commission on Pensions resulted in enactment of new actuarial reserve retirement systems, in 1917 for teachers and in 1920 for city employees, with the exception of policemen and firemen, for whom actuarial reserve systems were not established until 1940. The Commission, aided by George B. Buck as actuary and an advisory committee of several insurance company actuaries designated by the Actuarial Society of America, performed a monumental task. The staff gathered a huge mass of data on city employees over the six-year period, 1908–1914, and developed from it the actuarial foundations for funded systems in New York and elsewhere. It created a plan of benefits that was subsequently widely followed throughout the country (sometimes referred to as the "Buck Plan"), with a basic design that despite considerable modification over the years is still somewhat in evidence fifty years later.

The basic plan was designed to provide an employee who retired after long years of service with a retirement allowance equal to one-half of his salary in the period of years close to retirement. Basing pensions on final average pay is an old concept for the public plans; it is relatively new for private plans.

Cost was to be shared; that was a relatively new concept. The idea was for the city to provide half of the "retirement allowance" and for the employee to pay for the other half. The employer's part was a "pension" that accrued, with each year of service, as a fixed percentage of pre-retirement salary. The employee-paid part was an "annuity" resulting from his accumulated contributions, with interest, converted upon retirement into a lifetime benefit computed actuarially on the basis of life expectancy and assumed interest earnings—in short, the employee's contributions paid for a "money-purchase" annuity. The employee contribution was fixed as a percentage of pay in accordance with a schedule which varied the rate according to sex, age at entry into membership, and, in one system, the occupational grouping of the employee's position (clerk, mechanic, or laborer). This schedule of contributions was originally worked out on the theory that if everything proceeded normally, the employee contribution account would provide, upon normal retirement, an annuity equal to the pension amount; consequently, after the appropriate number of years of service, the two taken together would provide a retirement allowance approximating half-pay. As things turned out, this design did not accomplish its planned purpose—it could not cope with the rapid escalation in the last several decades. The annuity portion, accumulated out of a percentage of each year's salary, failed to provide the expected 25 percent of the final average salary.

In the N.Y.C. Teachers System the retirement allowance was planned at half of final average salary at 65 for a teacher with twenty or more years of service, or at any age if the teacher had been employed for at least thirty-five years. That half-pay goal was to be achieved through a pension equal to 25 percent of final average salary plus an annuity from member contributions that was expected to supply the other 25 percent.

The plan established for general city employees had various normal accrual rates, depending on job category:

laborers and unskilled workers could retire at age 58 and accumulate $1/132$ of final average salary per year of service;

mechanics and skilled workers, age 59 and $1/136$ of salary;

clerical, administrative, professional, and technical workers, age 60 and $1/140$ of salary.

Each fraction was fixed to provide a pension of 25 percent of salary (therefore, half-pay for the *total* retirement allowance) for an employee who entered employment at 25 and retired at normal retirement age. Interestingly, the Commission did not arrive at this age schedule—58 to 60—by the logic that heavy work required an earlier retirement. Instead, the ages were derived from a decision as to an acceptable rate of employee contributions. Actuarial tables had been constructed separately for each group, based on its own experience; half-pay was selected as the objective to be obtained, with the annuity part to provide half of that; then 4 percent was selected as a tolerable rate of contribution for a new employee, age 25. From that combination of decisions, the retirement age was determined as the age at which the typical employee of the class would accumulate an annuity of 25 percent. That age became the normal retirement age for the occupational class. That, at least, was the official rationale; it may perhaps have been a convenient justification for choosing retirement ages older than some employees had come to think appropriate.

The new systems had certain important characteristics:

1. They were funded. The annuity, being the end-product of a savings-account accumulation, was always fully funded. Its benefit liability was, by definition, equal to the assets on hand. The pension part was to be funded over the future service of the employees, taken in the aggregate. Funding was considered an important element of security for the employees since the new systems were established to supplant plans that were financially shaky.

2. They fixed a full-career pension at 50 percent of final average salary, with lesser amounts for lesser service and, to some extent, greater amounts for greater service. Half-pay was by then an established goal, but it had previously been on an all-or-nothing basis—nothing less for lesser service, nothing more for greater service.

3. They combined a fixed-formula pension paid by the employer with a money-purchase annuity from employee contributions.

4. They defined final average salary in terms of five years in a deliberate effort, as the result of previous experience, to get away from using the final salary.

5. They provided disability and death benefits, and the return of contributions in the event of preretirement termination.

6. They were contributory, based on the principle that the employees were to pay half the cost. Employee contributions were far higher than had been required in the earlier plans, which had involved no employee contributions, or at most 2 percent. The new plans required most employees to contibute in the range of 4 percent to 8 percent of salary. The new levels of employee contributions were accepted by the employees and for several decades were almost an article of faith because they gave assurance of future security and because in some respects—though not in all—they provided broader benefits. On the employer side they had the attraction not only of helping to pay the benefits, but of restraining increases, for which it was long assumed the employees would have to pay half. The commission said:

> The commission recommends, not as the only just method, but as a just method which best meets present conditions, that the cost be concurrently shared by the city and its employees. Through the responsibilities thereby developed for the provision and retention of benefits equitable to both parties, there would be a natural check on over-liberal interpretation and legalized liberalization of the provisions which would make the system unduly costly to either party.
>
> .   .   .   .   .
>
> The preceding compromise plan of dividing the cost of the retirement system between the employees and the city is suggested in order that both city and employees will come to realize and consider in concrete values the benefits which are being paid from the retirement system.[6]

The new systems involved some cutback on benefits. For example, they substituted five-year average salary for final salary; they imposed age requirements where the previous plans allowed full benefits after twenty to thirty years of service at any age. However, no individual was cut back; persons already employed when the systems were established were given a choice between the new provisions and the old, although no constitutional or judicial guarantee was then in effect to require such "grandfathering" of rights.

New York City Plans, 1920–1960

Benefit formulas were liberalized in the next thirty years, but on the basis of cost-sharing; that is, contribution rates were increased to

[6] *Report*, Part III, pp. 15–16.

pay for the more liberal plans. In fact, each member had a choice as to whether to accept the improved plan—and higher contributions— or remain under the old one. This pattern in New York was not unique; optional plans became fairly common in public employee systems. In fact, by 1959, the City's teachers had a four-way choice, with a different schedule of contribution rates for each.

Funded systems for the city's policemen and firemen were not created until 1940. They were made mandatory for new members of the force and optional for old members. Members were then given a choice between a twenty-year plan and a twenty-five-year plan, each plan paying, regardless of age, half of the highest five consecutive years' pay. Contributions varied in proportion to cost. The twenty-year plan has been the most popular by far. These plans started on the basis that the member-paid annuity would account for 45 percent of the retirement allowance and the city-paid pensions for the other 55 percent.

Liberalization—The Fifties and Sixties

The tempo of change quickened noticeably in 1949–50, concurrent with the massive increases in pension and welfare benefits in private industry in the 1950s and collective bargaining on fringe benefits. The surge of liberalization also coincided with an upgrading of salaries in public employment and the economic boom of that decade.

In 1951, the financing of the Police and Fire Department plans was shifted so that the city assumed 75 percent, instead of 55 percent, of the cost. The Firemen's plan was changed so that the entire retirement allowance (not just the pension part) was guaranteed at 50 percent of final average salary. Obviously, the rationale of the 1920 plans, the basic insistence on cost sharing, was coming apart.

In 1957, Social Security coverage was provided for all city employees, retroactive to March 15, 1956. This was a voluntary action by the city and state under provisions of the federal act that allowed members of state and local retirement systems to join. Current employees, but not future employees, had the option to stay out. The city added Social Security to its system benefits, with the proviso that employees could offset their own Social Security contributions against the otherwise required system contribution rates, thus reducing the annuities purchasable out of their own contributions.

In 1960, a "take-home-pay" provision was enacted—an important step in abandoning the cost sharing principle completely. The city relieved groups of employees of part of their required contributions to the retirement system; at first 2½ percentage points, later 4 and 5 percentage points, for some employees 8 percentage points. This increased "take-home" pay more than an equal percentage raise in salary, on which the employee would pay income taxes. The money is accumulated at interest in an account called "Reserve-for-Increased-Take-Home-Pay" and is used to provide a money-purchase pension on retirement or as a benefit in the event of death. However, the account is not paid out if the employee withdraws without retirement rights. That forfeiture reduces the cost to the city: if the increase is 5 percent, actual cost is 4.2–4.7 percent. In a few years, the effect was drastically to reduce employee contributions (making the plans noncontributory for many city employees) and to shatter any remaining concept of shared cost.

The 1961–64 Study

The rapid succession of changes in the 1950s inevitably raised questions in City Hall and in the press about where the retirement systems were going. City contributions had more than tripled in the period 1951–1961. Changes for some employee groups created demands from other employee groups. The principal basis for demands had become "inequity," not as against private industry or in terms of living standards, but as among different groups of City employees. The question was also raised whether the city's combined pension assets of more than $3 billion were not excessive, whether contributions could not be reduced. And administration of benefits by the Employees' System was badly bogged down; pension benefits were not paid until months after retirement.

The city authorized a broad review of the city's retirement systems, made in the period 1961–1963, by the consulting firm of Martin E. Segal and Company, under the direction of the author. The study report recommended that a new retirement system be established for all new City employees, that the paperwork of administration be centralized and computerized, that the actuarial foundations be drastically revised, and that the funding policy be changed.

The study found the City's plans to be relatively generous in comparison with the plans of the federal government and of other large states and cities. The City's plans were found to provide, for typical long-service (thirty-year) employees, benefits (including Social Security, which New York City provided but certain other systems did not) higher than any other system and more generous than benefits in private plans.

Even at that time the provisions of the City Employees' System could result in an award to a long-service employee equal to or exceeding 100 percent of final average pay, inclusive of Social Security. The City plans were found to be less generous than many other public plans in benefits for short-service employees, death benefits, survivor benefits, and in certain employee contribution rates. Moreover, a major characteristic of the City plans was the existence of differences among them that were "beyond rationalization."

The report recommended that: [7]

A new retirement system along modern lines should be established for all newly-hired employees. Present employees should be given the option of transferring into the new system.

The new retirement system should consist of four plans:

1. City employees generally;
2. Teachers;
3. Uniformed policemen and firemen; and
4. Employees in positions with unusual physical demands.

These plans would have different provisions only to the extent that the employment circumstances differ; they would otherwise be identical.

In comparison with the more liberal of the existing plans, the system would offer higher benefits in some respects and lower benefits in other respects. In terms of overall economic security for the employees, the new system would provide greater protection.

Whether the new system would involve, overall, a greater or lesser cost to the City is not known at present. . . .

The conclusion that a new system should be established, although reluctantly reached, is inescapable.

There are significant gaps in the present systems. They do not protect the employees adequately under certain circumstances, as, for example, against erosion from sustained inflation. Moreover, there are disturbing inequities among the systems and indefensible anomalies within them.

[7] Martin E. Segal Company, *The Retirement System of the City of New York,* Part V, (New York, 1964).

It is also clear that some features are unnecessarily costly. Some City employees have retired with City payments greater than their final salaries. In the past, a large part of such retirement income has been attributable to the employee's own contributions, but this will be less true in the future as present provisions reducing employee payments begin to be effective. Substantial numbers—15% to 20%— of the employees who retire at the typical age of 65 draw retirement income equal to at least 70% of their final five-year average salaries. Together with Social Security benefits, many of them draw total retirement income exceeding their full-time salaries, particularly if their wives are also drawing Social Security benefits.

Needlessly costly provisions cannot be eliminated from the present Systems. The State Constitution guarantees that "membership in any pension or retirement system of the state or of a civil division thereof shall be a contractual relationship, the benefits of which shall not be diminished or impaired." This has been held to mean that benefit provisions for present employees cannot be reduced, even for their future years of employment.

Consequently to rationalize the present systems by eliminating all inequities would mean adding the most expensive features of each to all of the systems, on top of the maintenance of provisions that already are needlessly expensive.

The most compelling reason for a new system is the fact that City employees are covered by Social Security, as well as by their retirement system. Social Security benefits have been increased vastly in the past 25 years. It would not be rational to assume that there will be no further changes in the next 25 years. Consequently, if the present systems were in no feature excessive and if their deficiencies were removed so that they were fully adequate today, they would inevitably become excessive as Social Security changes.

The report made specific recommendations spelling out a framework for the proposed new system.

It was anticipated that the municipal employee unions and associations would object to any provision that was in any respect less generous than an existing provision, even though the new provision would apply only to employees not yet hired. Even so, recommendation of a new package of benefits had certain practical possibilities. In some respects, it would increase benefits; for many of the incumbent employees, a voluntary switch to the new system might therefore be attractive. Moreover, it was obvious that many of the improved benefits suggested for the new system could be adopted for the incumbents who remained under the old systems. This had the makings, presumably, of a reasonable bargain—a new system for new employees tied in with increased benefits for present employees.

The bargaining process never got started. The City administration evinced no desire to pursue the idea of a new system. On the contrary, it approved piecemeal benefit increases even while the study was still in process. The unions and employee associations felt that they could get the benefit increases they were interested in without having to consider a new system, and their assessment of the situation was entirely correct. This was, incidentally, before the retirement plans became a subject of collective bargaining. The employee organizations had strong influence on pension legislation—at state as well as city levels—well before pensions became an item in contract negotiations.

1960–1969

What the Segal report called an "inescapable conclusion" was not perceived as inescapable by others. Instead, there was still more piecemeal change on a large scale. Many of the changes in the ensuing decade corresponded to the study recommendations; others were contrary.

Choice of plans by individual employees was restricted; for all practical purposes, eliminated.

Provisions among the systems were made more uniform, by extension of the more generous provisions of each system to the other systems.

On the other hand, separate benefit plans were created, with substantially higher benefits, as the result of collective bargaining with several unions: Transit Authority police, Housing Authority police, and uniformed correction officers; another for uniformed sanitationmen; and a third for Transit Authority (subway) operating personnel.

Each of the three special security groups managed to effect an enormous leap in one year—out of line with the general employees of the City to pension equality with the regular police force. Demand is common among the states for a variety of security personnel—park police, correction officers, probation officers, sheriffs, marshals, game wardens, etc.—to get benefits that equal or approach those of state troopers or municipal police. In New York City that change was swift and complete.

The uniformed sanitationmen were on precisely the same level as other city employees until 1964, when they won a separate plan and then, by a succession of negotiations and legislative acts, achieved by 1967 benefits only a little short of those of the police and firemen— half of final pay after twenty years, any age, plus something more for additional years. The position of these street cleaners and refuse collectors is unusual for a group that, in practically no other city, has won retirement benefits so markedly different from those of other municipal employees. New York City sanitationmen wear a uniform (they were once called "white-wings") and in recent years they have been referred to by mayors and the governor as part of the city's "uniformed forces."

The employees of the New York City Transit Authority (subway system) have also won a special niche for themselves—somewhat above the level of most city white-collar workers whose pension plan they once shared, but not quite equal to that of policemen, firemen, and sanitationmen.

Union bargaining had the effect of establishing separate plans for separate groups. Whether this would have happened if pensions had not been a subject of bargaining is open to speculation. The unions were effective in getting pension legislation, generally with the consent of the city, even before 1967, which was the year when the pensioners were first included in collective-bargaining agreements. It is fair to say, however, that the process of negotiation has added impetus for higher benefits and special plans for separate groups.

The "twenty years–half-pay" pension was brought dramatically to public attention in the early hours of 1968 with an agreement between the New York City Transit Authority and the Transport Workers Union and a number of smaller unions shortly before the deadline for a strike that would have shut the subways. The agreement was to seek legislation to provide half-pay (using pay of the last year) after twenty years of service, after age 50. Although the sanitationmen had earlier won outright half-pay after twenty years and provided the precedent, the transit situation dramatized the basic change. The prospect to every New Yorker of a possible subway and bus strike beginning on New Year's Day riveted attention on the fact that a large group of regular workers were going to get half-pay after twenty years, at an age when quitting for another job was still possible.

The transit workers' victory and earlier gains had other results. When other groups move up to the levels of the police and firemen, the latter feel that their traditionally special position has been lost; they then consider that they are entitled to something still better. The process—variously referred to as whipsawing, leapfrogging, me-tooism—is fairly common. It is the almost inevitable outcome when the various employee groups measure their positions principally in terms relative to other civil servants.

The 1962 Segal Report identified one of the weaknesses of the City plans as the continued use of the "pension-plus-annuity" formula, because the annuity part did not fulfill expectations in relation to final average pay. That was changed. Now all of the plans guarantee the retirement allowance as a percentage of final pay. However, the old pension-plus-annuity method remains applicable for years of service over 20 or 25 (depending on the plan). This shift—away from pension-plus-annuity to a fixed overall formula—has occurred over the past decade in a large number of systems throughout the country in response to continuing inflation.

As of 1972, the benefit formulas in New York City provided:

General City employees	55% at 55 after 25 years
City employees in physically-demanding jobs	55% at 50 after 20 years
Teachers	50% at 55 after 20 years
Transit employees	50% at 50 after 20 years
Uniformed groups	50% after 20 years, any age

In each case, additional benefits accrue for additional years of service, without maximum limit. These additional benefits are substantial. A general City employee accrues, for each year of service (after July 1, 1968) over 25, a pension of 1.7 percent of final year's salary, plus a money-purchase pension.

The statute uses the term "compensation," which the City's Corporation Counsel ruled many years ago includes overtime and penalty pay (such as for a night shift). This apparently meant very little when salary was averaged over the last five years, but when the shift was made to last year's salary, it became very important. One subway motorman doubled his pay in the last year over the average in the preceding four years and retired on an allowance higher than his regular pay. A bus driver increased his earnings 93 percent over the average of the preceding four years. These were, of course, extreme cases, not typical of most employees on the verge of retirement; nevertheless, actual and potential abuse of the provision under State as well as City plans led to limiting legislation. This legislation was subsequently nullified, however, under New York's constitutional guarantee that pension benefits may not be diminished.

One of the deficiencies of the City plans, pointed up in the 1961–64 study, was the lack of vesting and the comparatively high age / service threshold for pension eligibility. That has changed— vesting is provided with fifteen years of service, except for sanitationmen and a twenty-year requirement for transit employees.

Employee contributions have been cut. With 4–5 percent "take-home pay" credits, the remaining employee contribution is only a fraction of what it was before 1960. The Transit plan is entirely noncontributory and the Firemen's is practically that.

A variable annuity was established for teachers, allowing them to put 50 percent to 100 percent of their contribution accounts into a common stock fund which pays benefits based on its changing market value. This was an option for the teachers, not a cost to the city, except that the city had to give up recapture of any of the yield earned in excess of the rate of interest credited. Teachers also won the right to secure voluntary additional retirement benefits through their system in the form of tax-sheltered annuities; that is, teachers could agree to accept individual salary reductions in exchange for equivalent, non-taxed, employer payments to fully vested fixed-dollar or variable-dollar accounts in the system.

A cost-of-living adjustment was added for those who retired before 1968. It provided, for all pensioners 62 years old and older, and for disability pensioners, an adjustment (applicable only to the first $8,000 of retirement allowance) equal to the increase in the Consumer Price Index from the year of retirement to 1969. The enactment was temporary and although this adjustment was subsequently renewed, as of 1973 it had not been extended for cost-of-living changes after 1969. In this respect New York provides less assured real income security for retirees than most large states, which have enacted automatic postretirement adjustments.

There was also an entirely new development—additional retirement benefits outside the retirement system but paid for by city contributions. Policemen, firemen, housing and transit police, and sanitationmen won agreement for city contributions of $1 a day, for up to 261 days a year, to annuity trust funds under the aegis of the respective employee organizations. The money accumulates in individual employee accounts and provides supplementary retirement income. Police and fire officers get higher contributions, proportionate to their salaries. The teachers won agreement for $400 a year to be contributed to such a supplementary fund for each teacher who was at the maximum salary step. In the case of the teachers, the supplementary fund is handled by the retirement system, which treats the funds as equivalent to voluntary additional contributions. These annuity funds will be providing future retirees who have had a full career with an additional $500 to $1,500 of annual income. Also, in 1966, the transit workers won direct payments from the Transit Authority of $500 a year to retirees employed before 1966.

The Level of Benefits of New York City Employees

The benefits that the New York City plans will produce at 65 for an employee on a $14,000 salary who retired after thirty years of service are shown in Table 14.1. The methods used in these benefit illustrations have been explained in chapter 3. It has been assumed that the individual had 4 percent salary increases in every year of the past. The benefits are expressed as a percentage of the *final year's* salary. A quick summary is as follows:

The retirement allowance ranges from 64 to 72 percent of final salary. With primary Social Security at 65, the total amounts to roughly 87 to 95 percent. In terms of "take-home" pay, that is, after taxes and contributions, the benefits range from 75 to 86 percent, and with primary Social Security from 106 to 117 percent, and if the wife's Social Security is taken into account, from 118 to 129 percent.

How much of the New York City retirement benefits will the individual retiree have paid for? The answers range from zero to as much as 25 percent of the cost, depending on the particular plan and the member's age at entry. Generally speaking, the New York City employee who receives these pensions will have paid for less than 10 percent of the value of his benefit.

In every case, with retirement at 65 after thirty or more years of service, a male employee who is married will draw retirement in-

Table 14.1 ◆ Benefits Of Principal New York Retirement Plans In Relation To Final Year's Salary Of $14,000, Retirement At 65 With 30 Years Of Service, With And Without Social Security, As Of July 1, 1973 [a]

	Benefits as Percentage of Final Year's Salary ($14,000)					
	Benefit from system alone as percentage of salary		Benefit from system plus primary Social Security		Benefit from system plus primary and wife's Social Security	
Type of Employee	Gross	Net [b]	Gross	Net [b]	Gross	Net [c]
State Employees	57.7%	68.6%	80.5%	99.3%	91.9%	112.3%
State Teachers	57.7	68.6	80.5	99.3	91.9	112.3
State Police & Firemen (20-year plan)	64.2	75.5	87.0	106.2	98.4	119.1
N.Y.C. Employees (General)	65.5	78.4	88.3	109.6	99.7	122.6
N.Y.C. Transit	63.9	75.2	86.7	105.9	98.1	118.8
N.Y.C. Sanitation	69.5	81.9	92.3	112.9	103.7	125.9
N.Y.C. Police, Transit and Housing Police, and Correction Officers [d]	69.5	84.4	92.3	116.1	103.7	129.0
N.Y.C. Firemen [d]	64.1	75.4	86.9	106.1	98.3	119.0
N.Y.C. Teachers	72.2	85.7	95.0	116.5	106.4	129.0

[a] All figures are based on benefits calculated on current (July 1, 1973) rates of accrual; that is, they do not reflect lesser credits under certain of the plans for particular years of past service. The figures are intended to reflect what the plans will produce in the future by way of salary replacement. The date of July 1, 1973, is used for purposes of establishing Social Security amounts and income tax and Social Security contribution rates.

[b] Both final salary and benefits net after taxes and required contributions, assuming single person.

[c] Both final salary and benefits net after taxes and required contributions, for married person.

[d] Assumes retirement at 55 but figures as to net income and Social Security are those applicable at age 65.

come, net after taxes, inclusive of Social Security for himself and his wife, when she is 65, that will be greater than his after-tax income in his final year of work.

Clearly, the City of New York will be providing total retirement income to many full-career employees higher than their net income immediately before retirement.

It is questionable, however, that many New Yorkers were aware of that fact. Consequently, most of the public was startled in 1970 when the largest unit of city employees, represented by District Council 37 of the American Federation of State, County, and Municipal Employees, won agreement for 100 percent of final pay after forty years of service. That new agreement was for 100 percent, *before* taking account of Social Security.

The Negotiated Plan

The benefits to be provided by this "New Career Pension Plan" were as follows:

1. Retirement at age 55 (50 for physically taxing positions) with at least 20 years of service—a retirement allowance of 2.5 percent of final year's compensation for each year, that is,

20 years	50%
30 years	75%
40 or more years	100%

2. With less than 20 years of service, 2.1 percent per year of service.
3. Employee contributions—½ of 1 percent; 1 percent for physically taxing positions.

The union's newspaper termed it the "finest pension plan agreement in the country" and characterized it as follows: [8]

The new pension plan just negotiated by District Council 37 represents a major fulfillment of dreams and aspirations held by tens of thousands of workers for decades.

Not only did we achieve the goal of 50% of pay after 20 years of service, at age 55, but we also attained, for the first time, a guarantee of 100% for 40 years of service. All other Civil Service groups in New York City have the 50% concept, but no other group is guaranteed a rate of 2.5% for each year up to 40 years of service. The 100% guarantee has been "the Impossible Dream" for municipal workers for all these years. Now it is a reality.

[8] *Public Employees Press,* December 11, 1970, p. 4.

The terms of the "new Career Pension Plan" have by and large jumped us over the pension plans of all other Civil Service groups. The Uniformed Forces, traditionally the leaders in pension benefits, are now behind us.

The unions expected—quite understandably—that the negotiated pension agreements would be automatically enacted into law by the 1971 action of the legislature. That had been the established procedure for the preceding five years. A weekly for civil service employees reported that the necessary bill, a measure that "will contain some 150 pages of language that only a Philadelphia lawyer will understand" would soon be introduced, and "there is no indication that the bill will have anything but clear sailing, since it is the product of a collectively-bargained agreement, the sanctity of which always has been upheld by legislation and the Governor." [9] Instead the state legislature refused to enact the plan. As a result, on June 7, 1971, New York City was bogged down in one of the worst traffic jams in its history. *The New York Times* reported:

Hundreds of thousands of motorists were trapped in massive traffic jams on the hottest day of the year yesterday when municipal workers opened drawbridges in the city and abandoned trucks on major highways.

Angered by the failure of the State Legislature to approve a pension agreement negotiated last year with the city, the workers caught commuters by surprise in an unusual strike action that left 27 of the city's 29 movable bridges—many of them stripped by workers of critical parts—inaccessible to motorists throughout the day and into the night.

The legislative leaders responded by killing the pension bill. Then they went on to establish a permanent commission to review the state retirement system. What ensued will be described later.

Funding of the City Systems

New York City's retirement systems have since 1920 (1940 for policemen and firemen) been financed on a comparatively rapid schedule of funding. However, in recent years, that funding has run rapidly downhill.

The basis on which the City is to contribute to its retirement sys-

[9] *The Chief,* March 1971.

tems is specified in the law. Unchanged until 1967, that basis was in effect a form of aggregate funding. As explained earlier that involves comparatively high rates of contribution in the earlier years, the accrued liabilities being amortized over approximately the average prospective working lifetime of the incumbent employees.

Contribution requirements are determined by the City Actuary, who heads a full-time staff. Legally, he is engaged by the boards of trustees of each of the retirement systems, although his budget is subject to the City's budget director.

The Actuary's calculations are required to be made on the basis of officially authorized actuarial tables or assumptions. He is required to make a study of experience every five years and to recommend such new assumptions as he thinks warranted. However, an actuarial assumption can be made official only when it is adopted by the system's board of trustees. The boards include employer and employee representatives. (The board for the general City Employees' System was until recent years the Board of Estimate, a top legislative body.)

Actuarial Foundations

The New York City systems offer a classic case of actuarial assumptions that lost any relation to reality many years ago. The assumptions for the City Employees' System were elaborately constructed for the 1916–1920 Commission on Pensions from the City's records of experience in 1908–1914; data from the same period were used for the Teachers' System and subsequently, with only a little modification, for the actuarial-reserve Police and Firemen's Systems created in 1940. With the exception of two changes made in 1946—one on mortality after retirement and the other on interest credits—there have been no adjustments in actuarial assumptions since the systems were established (1917, 1920, and 1940). The result is a set of actuarial projections that can only mislead.

The quinquennial tests against actual experience made by the City Actuary have consistently revealed how obsolete the assumptions are. For the five-year period ended June 30, 1965, the number of deaths in active service under the City Employees' System came to only 37 percent (male) and 19 percent (female) of the number officially projected. Mortality after service (non-disability) retirement was only 70 percent of the number predicted. The salary scale (projection of salary increases) is patently unrealistic. A clerk entering service at age 20 is expected to get an increase of only 50 percent by 45. From age 45 to 60 a clerk is expected to get an increase of only 4 percent (not annually, but altogether). A laborer entering at 25 is assumed to retire at a final salary only 15 percent higher than his starting wage. If he enters at 40, the assumptions project a total salary increase of 1 percent by the time he retires.

The assumptions for the Teachers System predict almost three times as many deaths in active service as occurred in the five years ended June 30, 1967. Among women teachers age 28–32, the table predicted 65 deaths; there were 6. Among those age 38–42, the official prediction was 66 deaths; there were 16. Mortality after service retirement has been only 73 percent of the projected.

While the Policemen's and Firemen's Funds were set up as late as 1940, their actuarial assumptions are no less obsolete. Surprisingly, experience among policemen and firemen up to 1940 was not used; the City's Actuary at that time went back to the general 1908–1914 experience, with some modification. The experience study for the five years ended June 30, 1968, showed deaths among employees were about one-third of the projected, service-connected deaths were 28 percent of the expected, ordinary disability retirements were 7 percent of the expected, service retirements were 187 percent of the expected, deaths among service retirees were 32 percent of the expected.

In the 1950's the City Actuary noticed that experience differed from assumptions, that heavy actuarial losses were being incurred, and that contributions should be higher than the assumptions indicated. Consequently, for several years during the 1950s, the Actuary then in office "loaded" his budget request by increasing his elaborately calculated results by 60 to 70 percent. That practice was gradually eliminated by the time the valuation for 1962 was made.

As of 1972, the City Actuary acknowledged the inappropriateness of the individual assumptions but expressed the belief that taken together they were an adequate basis for calculating contributions. It is barely possible that by coincidence that was true at the time.

In recent years, funding has been made less adequate by stretching out the schedule and by a series of manoeuvers for avoiding or postponing contributions. In 1967, the unfunded accrued liabilities of the City Employees, Teachers, and Police Systems were put on a schedule of thirty-five-year amortization in place of the aggregate funding schedule, which had amounted to amortizing over roughly fifteen years and perhaps as little as ten years in the case of the Police Fund. The same technique was applied to the extra liabilities incurred because of various plan improvements in 1968. The shift in funding method reduced contributions by 22 percent for the Employees' System, 15 percent for the Teachers, and 9 percent for the Police. Because that stretch-out of funding was not accompanied by a shift to realistic assumptions, there has to be serious doubt about the long-range adequacy of the current rates of contribution.

Except for a relatively small contribution of $18 million a year, contributions to the Teachers' System were entirely omitted for the two fiscal years ending June 30, 1972, a period in which substantial improvement in the Teachers' System was enacted. The technique for that cut was a shift to the practice in the other City systems of a two-year gap between (a) the time as of when contributions are required and (b) the time when the contributions appear in the budget. (This is essentially analogous to paying nothing for two years if an individual or firm were to shift from paying bills currently to paying them two years late.)

Despite these changes, the rates of employer contributions to the system have remained substantial. For fiscal year 1971–72, the rates of contribution, as percentages of the 1969–70 payrolls were:

Employees' System	19.8%
Police Pension Fund	27.7
Firemen's Pension Fund	22.5
Board of Education	19.3

If it were not for the temporary deferral of contributions, the rate for the Teachers' System would have been on the order of 24–25 percent. The rate for the security group in the Employees' System (transit and housing police and correction officers) was 33.3 percent.

Funding Developments, 1951–1970

The growth and the funding position of the City's Employees' System in the last twenty years presents a classic case. Since 1951 payroll has gone up four times, but annual retirement benefits have gone up nine times. The number of beneficiaries has, since 1962, been 16 to

18 per 100 active members, close to the average for public systems. Assets, as of June 30, 1970, were $2.7 billion, 27 times the benefit payments. That is a respectable figure, higher than the corresponding median ratio for large state and local systems throughout the country. Assets are several times larger than the liability for lifetime payments to all current pensioners, for whom a figure of 8 times benefits would generally suffice, indicating a sizable accumulation for benefits accrued by active employees. This does represent, however, a backsliding in the funding of the systems. In 1957–58 system assets were 54 times benefits. That has been cut in half and is probably still on the way down. Some of the rapid downward movement is due to benefit increases, plan amendments, and higher salaries, but a good part is attributable to the slow-down in funding practices and the inadequacy of assumptions.

The Teachers' System, which began in 1917, shows stronger evidence of having reached a stabilized ratio of pensioners to active employees. There were 39 retirees per 100 active teachers in 1962 and 1963. Since then growth in employment has outpaced growth of pension rolls, but the 39 per 100 ratio will probably be restored in time. The Teachers' System was not as heavily funded as the City Employees System, but its asset-to-benefit ratios in the 1960s were 22–28, close to national norms.

The Policemen's and Firemen's Systems are relatively new, having supplanted nonactuarial systems in 1940. Consequently they have only 16–17 pensioners per active member. However, a picture of what fully developed pension rolls look like is developed by adding the pensioners and pensioned widows from the old non-actuarial plans that were closed to new employees in 1940. This shows 64 annuitants—44 retired men and 20 pensioned widows—for every 100 active policemen. For every 100 active firemen, there were 78 annuitants—57 retired men and 21 pensioned widows. These high ratios are not unusual for police and firemen's systems that provide half pay after twenty years, any age, and produce numerous retirements when the men are in their forties.

Combining all the City's actuarial systems as of 1970, City contributions were about 13 percent of total payroll, beneficiaries on the rolls were 23 per 100 employees, and assets were a little over $6 billion, about 26 times the annual retirement benefit payments of $230 million.

The shifting degree of funding can be examined more adequately by relating the assets of the systems to their calculated liabilities [10] (Table 14.2).

Table 14.2 ◆ **Percentage, Assets Of Present Value Of Benefits, Exclusive Of The Value Of Employee Contributions, N.Y.C. Retirement Systems, 1952–70**

			System		
Year	Employees	Teachers	Police	Fire	Board of Education
1950	51	52	8	13	49
1951	47	44	8	18	47
1954	57	50	11	19	49
1956	62	52	14	21	50
1958	67	53	18	23	54
1960	71	56	25	24	56
1962	61	47	25	24	47
1964	58	47	22	24	45
1966	50	48	26	28	45
1968 [a]	45 [b]	61	36	37	47
1970	40	39 [c]	35	36	41

Source: N.Y.C. Actuary
[a] Interest assumption changed from 3% to 4%.
[b] Transit Authority 20-Year Plan adopted.
[c] Teachers' 20-Year Plan adopted.

These funded ratios, adjusted to extract the value of employee contributions, have gone down, with the exception of the Police and Fire Systems, which are relatively new. The decline was particularly sharp for the largest, the Employees' System, which had assets equal to 71 percent of all projected benefits in 1960, but was down to 40 percent in 1970 as the result of successive benefit changes. The benefit and salary increases since 1960, together with a stretch-out of

[10] The ratio used compares assets to the present value of benefits. "Assets" means the book value of cash and securities. Present value of benefits is the computed value, discounted to each of the valuation dates, of all future benefit payments. A system should not be expected to have assets equal to the "present value of benefits"; if it did, it would presumably not need any more contributions, except for new members or for changes in its plan.

funding and outdated actuarial assumptions, has meant a decline in funded position.

Pricing Benefit Changes and Pension Policy

One of the major reasons for actuarial funding is to put a proper price tag on benefit changes by reflecting their ultimate cost consequences. But funding cannot answer the question adequately if the actuarial assumptions are wrong. The New York City experience shows how wrong the guidance of inadequate assumptions can be.

In 1967 the transit workers asked for half-pay after twenty years, any age. Negotiations wound up with half-pay after twenty years beginning at age 50. The City Actuary furnished cost estimates. The key question in determining projected cost was the extent to which employees would in fact retire after twenty years, twenty-one years, twenty-two years, etc. The transit workers had no previous experience with retirements after twenty years, any age. But the City Actuary's official tables, unchanged for forty-five years, had rates of withdrawal from City employment in the period 1908–1914. It was on that basis that the actuary's office predicted certain rates of retirements on half-pay at ages 40–55. The irrelevancy of those rates is so patent that it may seem to be beating a dead horse to remind the reader that in 1908–1914 the City had no subway and bus system and that the pension system then was one that retired employees only for disability after thirty years of service. Needless to say, the estimates of retirement ages resulted in severe understatement of the ultimate cost of the proposal. The City's table predicted that 6 to 10 percent of the eligible employees would retire at ages 52 to 60. In the first 15 months of the new schedule, it was 25 to 30 percent, and in 1970 when retirements had subsided from the first rush, it was still 15 to 20 percent.

The salary projections officially relied on by the City involve practically no change in salary over the last five years of service. Consequently, if the City Actuary is asked what extra contribution will be required if the final year's salary is substituted for the average of the last five, he is bound to say, "none," unless he sets his tables aside and explains that extra cost will emerge notwithstanding his "official" calculation of unchanged contribution requirements.

The third example is a peculiar estimate that played an important role in 1971 in shaping the conclusions reached by a three-man impartial fact-finding board set up to resolve a dispute between the city and the policemen, firemen, and sanitationmen. On the heels of the agreement that general city employees should get 50 percent of pay after twenty years and 100 percent of pay after forty years (the 1970 agreement that was rejected by the 1971 legislature), the policemen, firemen, and sanitationmen asked for a formula that would provide 100 percent of pay after something shorter than forty years and elimination of member contributions, in order to restore them to their superior pension position. The fact-finders considered the cost of giving each of the three groups a formula of 2.5 percent of final pay per year of service, up to 100 percent, while eliminating employee contributions. Each group already enjoyed 2.5 percent for the first twenty years. What the panel had before it was the question whether the years *over* twenty should also earn a guaranteed 2.5 percent. For each group that would represent an increase. Whatever the impact on the firemen, it was clear beyond question that the benefit increase would be greater for the sanitationmen than for the police. As for the contribution side, using a man coming in at age 25, the panel found the rates of employee contributions (net after the city's pick-up via the "take-home pay" contribution) to be as follows:

Sanitationmen	2.50%
Policemen	2.30
Firefighters	0.36

In short, elimination of contributions would be of greatest benefit to the sanitationmen, while the increase in benefits would be greater for sanitationmen than it would be for the police.

The panel then found that the twofold change would involve the following costs:

Sanitationmen	0.07%	or	$ 7.89 per man per year
Policemen	1.50%	or	$205.00 per man per year
Firefighters	2.06%	or	$278.00 per man per year

At first blush these cost estimates seem incredible; on close examination, they are. Astonishingly, they were based on honest calculations by the Actuary: they simply issued from statutory methods of calculation applied with meaningless but officially frozen assumptions. Obviously, the results bear no relation to the facts. However, based on these "actuarial" figures, the panel recommended a benefit of 2.5 percent for each group, but with contributions eliminated only for the sanitationmen, since for them "it cost so little."

The inappropriateness of the City's actuarial assumptions has been recognized by the City Actuary. Ever since 1960 the Actuary's reports of experience have ritually called attention to the discrepancies between the assumptions and experience. But the System trustees have not acted to change the assumptions, and progress is further hampered by inadequate staffing and resources.

The result is that New York City does not really know what retirement system changes will cost. It acts, and it asks the legislature to act, on the basis of price tags that bear little relation to the future obligations the City will have to assume.

How is it possible for the City of New York to get into such a position? There are several reasons, each equally instructive. The actuarial assumptions involve a complicated chain reaction. The assumptions adopted for determining contributions have also been the assumptions used in converting employee contributions into annuity amounts, for converting the "take-home pay" contributions into pension amounts, for fixing the amounts of "return-of-reserves" death benefits, for fixing the amounts of optional forms of retirement income, and in setting rates of employee contributions. Furthermore, some of these changes would have the effect of reducing benefits for future employees, in which event the new assumptions can be applied only to new employees since old employees are legally entitled to the advantages of the old assumptions (such as obsolete but advantageous annuity factors). Changing assumptions might create a complicated structure of two classes of members each time an assumption is changed: the old employees to which the change does not apply and the new employees. If any change is to be made, the Actuary must recommend it and it must be adopted by a bilateral board. And changes in assumptions may dictate higher contributions by the City, a consideration that no doubt generates some reluctance on the employer side.

Still another element is the fact that this state of affairs required no errors of commission; it developed entirely out of errors of omission. Fifty years of disregard and what was in its time an elegant actuarial foundation has been reduced to a misleading set of numbers. A final and very important element is that the City has not had a ranking official with the responsibility and effective authority to shape pension policy. No one is charged with controlling what happens to the retirement systems or with developing a retirement policy. New York City is probably not unique in that regard.

THE STATE SYSTEMS

Benefit developments on the state level have in the main paralleled those for New York City. Historically, the City was the first to move on pensions. Even though the City's retirement systems are determined by state legislation, changes in the state systems often reflected changes made first for New York City. This was particularly true at the beginning, less so now.

Development of the Systems

The example of the New York City study led to a New York State Commission on Pensions in 1918 and enactment in 1920 of laws establishing the New York State Teachers' Retirement System and the New York State Employees' Retirement System.

City and state had similar backgrounds—trouble with financing the old plans. The state had adopted a teachers' retirement law in 1911. All teachers not covered by local systems could join the state system by a two-thirds vote and all did (1912–1921) except for New York City. Typical of its time, the plan was financed on a basis totally unrelated to its obligations; teachers contributed 1 percent and could be retired after twenty-five years of service, whatever the age, on half of the last year's salary. No employer contributions were called for. Local systems that were in bad financial shape were glad to join the state system and shift their liabilities to it. It became obvious very quickly that the 1 percent teacher contribution could not support the benefit. To add to the problem, a school board would increase, in some cases double, an administrator's salary for the final year, an abuse that resulted in an act of 1914 that shifted the annuity base to salary in the last five years.[11] (This problem recurred fifty

[11] J. Albert Holbritter, "A History of the New York State Teachers Retirement System, 1921–1959" (doctoral dissertation, New York University, 1960), p. 13.

years later.) Two years later, the system's board raised the age and service requirements, in an attempt to stave off insolvency.

In 1920 the legislature created the New York State Teachers' Retirement System on the model of the 1917 law for New York City Teachers. The benefit was somewhat more generous than the City's. Eligibility for service (non-disability) retirement began at age 60 with twenty-five years of service, or any age with thirty-five years of service, or age 70 with any service. The retirement allowance was a combination of a pension per year of service of 1 percent of final salary (five-year average) plus a money-purchase annuity provided out of a teacher contribution of 4 percent. This did not come close to duplicating the previous half-pay after twenty-five years. The employer-paid pension was considerably higher than New York City had established, but the flat employee contribution was lower. This law was made mandatory in 1923 for school boards and teachers outside New York City.

A system was enacted for state employees in 1920 in response to the same needs the City commission had recognized: to replace a patchwork variety of inadequately financed plans. These state plans followed the pattern of half of final pay after twenty or twenty-five years of service—nothing less and nothing more. Age was not a requirement for pension eligibility.

Some of the local governments had pension plans under earlier enabling acts, mainly for teachers, policemen and firemen. There was, the commission noted, "no direct relationship between the cost of the benefits provided by the funds and their income." [12]

The new plan was subsequently expanded to cover all employees except those in New York City. At first the new system covered only the minority of state employees in agencies then not covered by a pension plan. Much like the City's plan, it aimed at half of final pay (five-year average) at age 60 after thirty-five years of service. The retirement allowance combined a pension of $^1/_{140}$th of final pay per year of service with an annuity purchasable from employee contributions. The combination was supposed to provide 50 percent of final average pay after thirty-five years. The system was, of course, to be actuarially funded.

[12] New York State Commission on Pension, *Report,* March 30, 1920 (Albany, N.Y., 1920), p. 11.

Consolidation at the state level continued; all of the old state employees' systems were frozen and new employees were mandated into the new system. The state system was also opened to local governments, which were subsequently forbidden to establish new plans (1922–1926). Otherwise, there was relative stability in the twenty-nine years after the system was established.[13]

A burst of expansion came in the 1950s, just as in the City, in other states, and in private industry. The question debated in many states—whether the state could, or should, supplement pensions of persons already retired—was fought out in 1951. It had been argued that supplementation was unconstitutional as a gift to a private person. To avoid that argument, it was at first voted as a welfare measure.

Social Security coverage was added in 1957 for both of the state systems as well as for New York City employees, with coverage effective back to 1956 and without modification of the systems.

Changes of the 60s

In the 1960s, benefit increases came in rapid succession. The State adopted the 5 percent "take-home pay" provision for state employees and empowered localities to do likewise. Also adopted were vesting after fifteen years, higher death benefits, "death-gamble" provisions, cost-of-living supplements for pensioners (by formula, but reenacted from year to year without automatic application to the future), new and more liberal plans for policemen and firemen, and increases in the pick-up of employee contributions ("take-home pay" contributions) from 5 percent to 8 percent.

Plans proliferated—special provisions for the Nassau County police, the State Police, the Westchester County Park Police Force, the state correction officers, etc. By 1956 the State Employees' System had 21 special plans, some limited to certain named groups, others optional for local governments. In 1966 the police and firemen's plans were put into a separate state system, to underscore the idea of separate benefits.

This proliferation resulted from the pressures of particular em-

[13] Harold Rubin, "New York State's Retirement Program: A Critical Analysis" (doctoral dissertation, Syracuse University, August 1963). An excellent history of the System to 1962.

ployee groups, but without benefit at that time of outright collective bargaining.

The Moore Committee, 1966-69

Given these many changes, study was needed, and in 1965 a broad and comprehensive review of the State Employees' System was launched by the governor, who defined its task as simplifying a complex system that had been made more complex, and insuring comprehensiveness, adequacy, and fairness.

The Moore Committee, which made this study, had a curious but significant fate. It started work in 1966 and handed the governor a report dated June 3, 1969. The report was never made public. It was not secret or confidential; it was just not circulated. The reason: in 1967, just a year after the Committee started to work, the state enacted its Taylor Law, giving public employees the right to collective bargaining. Pensions were understood to be one of the bargainable terms of employment. By the time the report was completed, the established state policy was for legislation to follow the results of collective bargaining; consequently there did not seem to be much point to a report that strongly recommended establishment of a new system, not negotiated, and an arrangement for permanent central review of pension legislation, regardless of what might be agreed upon in negotiations.

The Committee rendered its judgment in words all too familiar in the history of public systems:

What had started out in 1921 as a comprehensive, uniform plan had become a patchwork of provisions, no longer clearly understood by employees and based in large part on temporary legislation renewable from one year to the next. Furthermore, there were specific inadequacies and inequities. . . . The various changes through the years, both of a temporary and permanent character, had made a hodgepodge of the State Employees' Retirement System.[14]

It went on to state its conclusions, even after it recognized that its work had foundered on collective bargaining:

The committee reached the conclusion that the development of a simplified, uniform, equitable, noncontributory plan in accordance with the Governor's

[14] The Governor's Committee to Study the State Employees' Retirement System, *Report*, June 1969.

instruction would require the establishment of a new plan for future State employees. Such a plan would in one stroke eliminate the clutter and patchwork of the old system at least for future employees. Furthermore, if it could be made attractive enough, many, perhaps most, employees in the existing system might also come into the new program.

The Committee thought that the new system should have an independent formula set after taking account of Social Security, Workmen's Compensation, and federal and state income tax provisions, with safeguards against future duplication. The plan should, the Committee thought, also include protection of benefit levels against erosion from inflation.

There should also be enacted, the Committee concluded, constitutional provisions that all public employee pensions in the state be fully funded, that funding of all benefits begin in the first year of adoption, and that all changes in benefits in the State Employees' System be legislated as general law. In this respect, the report proved ultimately to be not entirely a dead letter. Legislation in 1971 established an advisory commission and required that all benefit improvements, to be effective, must be accompanied by a start in the funding of the change.

In the period 1966–1969, during which it was deliberating on what should be done with the State Employees' System, the legislature enacted changes that ran counter to the objectives the Committee was to declare desirable. In 1966, directly after the Commission started to work, State employees got a straight non-contributory plan which, if nothing else, dissipated a potential bargaining point for a new system. The same year, the teachers got an 8 percent "take-home-pay" allowance that effectively made their system non-contributory. Moreover, in 1968, the legislature voted itself a new retirement plan, broadened to include legislative employees. In 1969, just before the Moore Committee handed up its report, the legislature voted a new and liberal "Career Retirement Plan" for the State Employees' System which clearly exceeded what the Committee was to suggest.

Clearly, the Moore Committee was bucking a tide that was running in favor of greater benefits. Collective bargaining lent impetus to that trend, but was not solely responsible. Going back to 1950, long before collective bargaining entered the picture, employee organizations had repeatedly demonstrated their ability to win pension improvements. Moreover, after contract negotiations became the accepted practice, there were several employee organizations that pursued *both* routes—they negotiated and they also lobbied for legislation. For example, police and firemen won the computation of benefits on the basis of final year's pay through lobbying, not negotiation, at a time when collective bargaining had already been established as the practice. The New York City police and firemen got a cost-of-living adjustment in 1968, over the objections of the City Mayor, John Lindsay, but with Governor Rockefeller's help.

The State Teachers' System has not been affected by collective bargaining, but its benefits have been liberalized, broadly speaking, in step with the other systems. Also, elected teacher representatives have comprised three of the nine members of the system's board of trustees, which works out an influential legislative program. In fact, it was that board which developed the present Career Retirement Plan. However, in this process, there is no collective bargaining as such, since bargaining is at the level of the local school district, and the state has only one plan. The situation is somewhat different in the State Employees' and Policemen's and Firemen's Systems, each of which has a variety of plans established in response to demands from localities, often based on collective bargaining.

For state and local employees, leadership for benefit changes has been exercised by the employee organizations, by the State's comptroller, Arthur Levitt, a Democrat who has held his elective office since 1955 in what was until 1975 an entirely Republican administration (and as comptroller the sole administrator of the Employees' and Police and Fire Systems), by Nelson Rockefeller when he was governor, and by the board of the Teachers' Retirement System. However, among the forces for change, it is the strength of the employee organizations, able to reach legislators and to impress them with their power to influence substantial numbers of voters, that is fundamental.

Liberalization of pensions has, over the years, been voted without notable party division. (This observation applies to most states.) Governor Rockefeller was generally rated a moderate Republican and the comptroller is a Democrat. The votes in the legislature have not been partisan, with the sole exception of the 1971 action by which the legislative leaders (Republicans) killed in committee the liberalized pension plan that the City of New York had negotiated. Indeed, some bills to liberalize pensions have borne the name of Senator Marchi, who has been considered a conservative Republican.

It is worth noting that sometimes the pace for benefit increase has been set by the legislators, acting on their own behalf. In 1969, members of the legislative plan were given the right to get credit for up to three years of military service in World War II, if the member paid for it on the basis of the full normal rate of contributions. That rate was applied, however, to the World War II salary of a legislator ($2,500, as against $15,000 in 1972) or his entry salary, if then a non-legislator. Credit for military service seems fair enough, except that the service was creditable even if it had been served long before the member had entered government service. Also, the member's payment for it was entirely incommensurate with the benefit. That precedent was extended in 1970 to the State Employees. Some 7,000 employees availed themselves of the additional credit and put in contributions of about $8 million. It had been estimated in advance that the provision would cost the state $2–4 million; it will actually cost about $17 million.

What legislators do in respect to their own pension rights may ultimately affect what they do for others. True, in New York as in other states, special provisions can often be made for legislators and judges without ever being carried over for other employees. However, in opposing a bill in 1971 for a commission to review the retirement systems, Theodore C. Wenzl, President of the Civil Service Employees Association, was quoted as saying: [15]

It is inconceivable that legislators, who are also public employees, would set the pace in granting themselves liberalized retirement benefits and then criticize other public employee pension plans which are far less liberal.

Pension Benefits of State Employees

The State Employees' System provides a "Career Retirement Plan" for the great majority of state employees and for those units of local government that choose it for their employees in preference to the lower-benefit plans offered within the system. Altogether, the New

[15] *The New York Times,* April 10, 1971.

York State Employees' System has 16 different plans, with additional options or variations depending on employer choice with respect to (1) degree of employer assumption of contributions in the plans that are otherwise contributory, (2) whether unused sick leave may be applied as additional service credits, (3) whether World War II service may be purchased, and (4) whether additional death benefits are to be provided.

The "Career Retirement Plan" of the Teachers' Retirement System is its only plan, covering the 200,000 teachers and school administrators outside of New York City. The two plans have much in common, if we disregard credits for past service:

1. The normal retirement age is 55, that is, full benefits (no reduction on account of age) are payable for retirement after attainment of 55.

2. The benefit for someone with at least twenty years of service is 2 percent of final average salary for each year of service. That means 50 percent after twenty-five years and 60 percent after thirty years. A maximum is fixed at 75 percent.

3. The benefit for someone with less than twenty years of service is on a lower schedule. The service fraction is $1/60$th, which was the earlier benefit level, superseded by the 2 percent "career" formula.

4. Final average salary is defined as salary in the best three consecutive years.

5. The plans are entirely non-contributory. In that respect, they are at the time this is written distinctive among public employee retirement systems, which almost always require substantial employee contributions. The elimination of employee contributions from the New York State systems was accomplished over a period of ten years, from 1960 to 1970.

6. There are no early retirement provisions as such, that is, nothing is provided on a reduced basis before the normal retirement age; on the other hand, the *normal* age is 55, which is relatively low.

7. Vesting—the right to a deferred pension—is granted with ten years of service. It is in the full amount for the number of years credited and is payable at 55.

8. The disability pension is at the lower benefit level—$1/60$th—the same rate as is prescribed for employees with less than twenty years of service.

9. If the disability is attributable to the employment, the benefit provided by the State Employees' System is much higher—75 percent of final average salary.

10. A substantial death benefit is provided—three times salary up to a benefit of $20,000, except that employees hired after March, 1969 are limited to one month's salary for each year of service. If the member was eligible for retirement the value of a pension calculable on the ¹/₆₀th formula is paid to his beneficiary.

11. If death resulted from an occupational accident, the State Employees' System pays a greater benefit—an annuity of 50 percent of pay to the widow, children, or dependent parent.

12. There is a post-retirement cost-of-living adjustment, although it is not automatic for the future. It adjusted benefits to 1969 and requires further legislative action both for continuance of payment and for any further updating for subsequent cost-of-living changes.

The plans provided by the State Policemen's and Firemen's Systems are different, as pensions for policemen and firemen are almost invariably. The System offers a variety of 14 plans involving half-pay after twenty or twenty-five years of service. The one with the largest membership is the "non-contributory twenty-year plan," covering the state troopers and a number of local police departments.

It, too, is fairly simple in its basic provisions:

1. Normal retirement is possible after twenty years, regardless of age, or at age 55 with at least ten years of service.

2. The benefit formula is 2.5 percent of final average salary for each of the first twenty years plus 1.67 percent for each year in excess of twenty—to a maximum of 75 percent.

3. The final average salary is the average of the best three consecutive years—or, if the employer has chosen that alternative plan, salary for the final year, if better than the three-year average.

4. The employees make no contributions.

5. Vesting is provided after ten years of service, but the deferred benefit, which is payable at 55, is on a lower formula of 1.67 percent.

6. A disability pension is payable with a minimum of 33⅓ percent or 50 percent of final average salary, depending on the employment unit. If the disability is service-connected, the benefit is higher—up to 75 percent of final average for some groups.

7. There is a death benefit of three times annual salary, limited to $20,000 for some groups.

8. In the event of duty-connected death, an annuity of 50 percent of salary is paid to the widow, children, or dependent parent.

9. The same cost-of-living adjustment is in effect as for other employees, likewise subject to legislative extensions.

Benefit Results

For an employee retiring at 65 after thirty years of service from a final salary of $14,000 the major state plans provide 58 percent. With primary Social Security as of July 1, 1973, wage replacement is 69 percent; net after taxes, retirement income is 99 percent of preretirement take-home pay. If a wife's Social Security at 65 is considered, the replacement of net income is 112 percent.

Patterns of Retirement

When, in fact, do the members of the state systems retire?

In the State Employees' System, employees retire on age pensions at ages from 55 to 70 (the compulsory age). More retirements take place before 65 than after. In the year ended March 31, 1971, under the Career Retirement Plan, they peaked at: [16]

62–63, the ages when Social Security becomes available on a reduced basis (20 percent);

65–66, when full Social Security is available (19 percent); and

70, when retirement is compulsory (14 percent).

While the system provides unreduced benefits at 55, three-fourths wait until 62 or later. It is significant that a high percentage of the retirees—32 percent—had completed twenty-five or more years of service, but an even larger percentage—46 percent—had completed less than fifteen years of service. This means that almost half the retirees entered employment by the state or by some city or county after they were 40. As a matter of fact, hiring was even later—age 45 or 50—for most of them. At least 21 percent of the members of the State Employees' System were hired when they were 45 or older. Hiring in such large numbers after 45 or 50 is rare in private industry, but not at all uncommon in public employment.

[16] N.Y.S. Comptroller, 51st Annual Report: *State of the Systems* (Albany, N.Y., 1972).

Throughout the country, public employment gathers an unusual percentage of older workers. A middle-aged worker who is looking for a job will generally find it easier to find public employment than private employment. A result is that the public systems play a particularly significant role in providing security for the elderly. It also means that public employees have more than average interest in retirement provisions. The young tend to think of pensions as something unreal for an implausibly remote future. Moreover, hiring in the forties and fifties means that the plans are more expensive than equivalent plans in private industry.

Retiring teachers usually have long service. In the year ended June 30, 1971, teachers with twenty or more years of service comprised 82 percent of all retiring teachers. On the average, they qualified (before choice of option) for an allowance of $7,831, which represented 65 percent of final average salary.[17] With full Social Security, the combined income must have replaced 85 percent of final average salary. If a wife's Social Security is added, in the case of male retirees (18 percent of the total), the combination amounted to 95 percent.

Retiring teachers who had put in at least thirty-five years of service—and they comprised a full 36 percent of the total—averaged $9,612 (before choice of option), which amounted to 76 percent of their final average salary. With primary Social Security, the combination amounted to about 95 percent. Clearly, at these levels, after-tax income at 65 will exceed net preretirement income.

Among policemen and firemen, the pattern of retirement was to a large extent dependent on the plan—the twenty-years half-pay or the twenty-five-years half-pay plan. There is a distinct difference. Under the twenty-year plan, 60 percent of the retirees, in the year ended March 31, 1971, left before they were 50 and 86 percent left before they had worked twenty-five years. In short, the typical pattern was "twenty years and out," and that generally happened when the man was 45 to 49. The retirement allowance was 50 percent of final average salary. The minority that postponed retirement until after thirty years of service drew allowances of about 60 percent of final average salary.[18]

[17] N.Y.S. Teachers' Retirement System, *1971 Annual Report* (Albany, N.Y., 1971).
[18] N.Y.S. Comptroller, *51st Annual Report: State of the Systems* (Albany, N.Y., 1972).

With the twenty-five-year plan, retirement takes place much later. Two-thirds of those who retired in the year ended March 31, 1971, were from 55 to 64 years of age. The average retirement allowance was 56 percent of final average salary. For those who stayed on beyond twenty-nine years, the allowance averaged 60 percent of final average salary.

Funding of the State Systems

The state systems have followed a demanding schedule of funding. In the Employees' System, aggregate funding is used to determine the "normal rate" of contributions, but in addition, there is a "deficiency contribution rate" fixed individually for each participating employing unit when it first entered the system. The deficiency contribution was intended to make up the actuarial gap if any entering group was more expensive than the average. It has been calculated by a different method ("entry-age-normal") and, once fixed for a unit, it remains until it is discontinued.

The Employees' System has the problem of allocating cost among the state and the other 2,122 participating employees. The only differentiation is in terms of the original deficiency rate; and the normal rate is differentiated only as to benefit plan, that is, each plan of benefits carries its own normal rate and every participating unit within a given plan pays the same normal rate. This New York practice ultimately eliminates differences in cost characteristics among employee units (age, years of service, turnover rates, etc.). This uniformity of rate is bolstered by the fact that in New York local governments do not have any alternative; once they enter a state system, they must continue.

To the normal rate are added uniform rates for supplemental pensions (cost-of-living adjustments) and for administrative costs. The combined rates charged for several of the more significant plans (exclusive of deficiency rates charged local units) were as follows for the fiscal year ended March 31, 1971:

Career Retirement Plan	22.9%
Age 55–60 Year plans (old plan with few members)	9.5
25-year Correction Officers plan	28.8
20-year Legislators Plan	35.2
State Police	40.1
Regional State Park Police	23.6

Police and firemen's 25-year plans   11.0–18.3
Police and firemen's 20-year plans   20.1–26.5

Police and fire units are subject to additional rate charges if they have elected the option of basing pensions on last year's salary.

On March 31, 1970, the State Employees' System had on its rolls 13 annuitants for every 100 active employees, up from a ratio of 5 per 100 in 1931. That ratio is bound to grow. It is below the national average, not because of more restrictive eligibility rules or of higher-than-usual employee turnover, but because the membership of the State Employees' and the Policemen's and Firemen's Systems in 1970 was more than double that of 1960 and five times that of 1941.

The assets of the Employees' System—almost $3.5 billion on March 31, 1970—amounted to 32 times the then-current level of annual retirement benefits. That ratio represents a very substantial degree of funding, although not as high as it used to be:

Year ended in	Ratio, assets to annual retirement benefits
1970	31
1960	42
1951	46
1941	36
1931	31
1921	15

Measurement by the more adequate standard of the ratio of assets to the actuarially calculated present value of benefits reveals that while the state systems have maintained positions of substantial funding, their asset growth has been outpaced by benefit increases. Table 14.3 shows these ratios (value of employee contributions excluded). Over the past twelve years, the Teachers' System has virtually maintained its relative position, but the State Employees' System has been pushed back from 50 percent to 38 percent. The funding plan of each system should produce a gradual increase in this ratio, but setbacks occur from time to time because of salary changes or benefit liberalizations.[19]

[19] Table 14.3 for the State systems should not be compared with the corresponding ratios in Table 14.2 for the City systems because the actuarial bases for calculating liabilities are so vastly different. Simple comparison would make it seem that the City systems are more highly funded than the State systems. In the author's judgment that is not true; the apparent result is no doubt attributable to the questionable set of actuarial assumptions used by the City.

Table 14.3 ◆ Percentage, Assets Of Present Value Of Benefits, Exclusive Of The Value Of Employee Contributions, N.Y.S. Employees' Retirement System And N.Y.S. Teachers' Retirement System, 1959–71

Year Ended March 31 (State Employees) or June 30 (State Teachers) of:	Employees' System	Teachers' System
1959	50%	28%
1960	50	29
1961	44	31
1962	43	32
1963	43	34
1964	45	32
1965	42	33
1966	42	31
1967	38	32
1968	40	32
1969	43	26
1970	34	33
1971	38	30

Source: Actuaries of the systems.

Funding of the State Teachers' System

Like the other state systems, the State Teachers' System is funded on the basis of aggregate funding, with a modification made in 1970 so that the contribution rate could be held down in the face of adoption of the more costly Career Retirement Plan. The law was amended so that liabilities added by changes made after June 30, 1968, were to be amortized over a twenty-five-year period, a respectable period but longer than "aggregate funding" would have involved. Also, the interest assumption was increased to 4.5 percent for the next ten years and 4 percent thereafter, and employer cost resulting from employee purchase of prior service credits, which had previously involved full and immediate funding, was shifted to funding over the period of prospective service.

The rates of contribution to the Teachers' System are fixed by its board of trustees, which is composed of elected teacher representatives, appointees of the State Commissioner of Education, and appointees of the Governor. The rate decisions are based on the findings of the system's actuary. When the board started out in 1921 it fixed the rate at precisely what the actuary recommended. In 1923 it balked and for about twenty years set rates substantially below the actuarial findings. About 1946 the two came back into correspondence and they have remained so since. The rates charged have of course increased, as the plans have become more generous, from 5.1 percent in 1922 to 14.8 in 1962 and 18.8 in 1972.

Funded Position

In the year ended June 30, 1971, the Teachers' System had only 13 annuitants for each 100 active members. That fact is attributable to the phenomenal growth of its membership—a combination of the post-World War II baby boom, improved educational standards that have meant higher teacher-pupil ratios, and the disproportionate growth of New York City's suburbs, which come within the scope of the state plan. In the 1950s membership almost doubled; and it almost doubled again in the 60s. That rate of growth was far more rapid than before; earlier, it had taken twenty-seven years—from 1925 to 1951—for the membership to double. The recent growth has, however, not yet reached the retirement rolls.

At June 30, 1971, the Teachers' System had assets of $3.1 billion, 28 times annual expenditure for retirement benefits. Like the other New York systems, that represents substantial funding, and it is a standard that has been maintained.

Year ended in	Ratio, assets to annual retirement benefits
1971	28
1961	24
1951	31
1941	24
1931	22
1922	31

The System also has maintained its position in terms of how its assets relate to the value of prospective benefits. The percentage was 30 in the year ended June 30, 1971; and it was 28 in 1959 (Table 14.3).

THE CONSTITUTIONAL GUARANTEE

New York has had the longest history of any state with a constitutional provision that forbids the diminution of benefits for any member of a retirement system.

The New York State Constitution provides (Article 5, Section 7) that "membership in any pension or retirement system of the state or of a civil division thereof shall be a contractual relationship, the benefits of which shall not be diminished or impaired." The provision was adopted by the Constitutional Convention of 1938 because of concern during the depression that benefits might be cut as an economy measure. It has come to have far-reaching significance. It has been construed to mean that, for each individual employee, the benefits incorporated in a system's law at the time that he first becomes a member may not in any way be diminished, not only with regard to benefit accruals based on his past years of service, but also with respect to his future years of service. It means that a provision, once enacted, is guaranteed for as much as one hundred years, from the time a new employee starts to work to the time when he or his beneficiary-annuitant dies.

A key decision has applied this guarantee to the actuarial tables used to convert an accumulation of employee contributions into an annuity.[20] Employee contributions were accumulated at interest and converted at retirement into an annuity. The mathematical factors used to establish the amount of the annuity were based on actuarial tables involving mortality rates and interest. The law empowered the trustees of the system to adopt the necessary tables, based on the recommendations of their actuary. The actuary was required to make studies of experience every five years so as to develop the basis for suggesting any changes in assumption. About 1940, the actuary

---

[20] N.Y. Court of Appeals, *Matter of Ayman*, 19 Misc. 2nd 355, 193 N.Y.S., 2nd 2 (1959). This involved the New York City Retirement System.

found that life expectancy had improved over the preceding twenty-five years and he recommended a new table for the necessary annuity values, which the trustees adopted, to be effective June 1943. The new tables were applied and an employee went to court because his annuity was less than it would have been under the old tables. The highest court of the state held that he was entitled to use the old actuarial tables. New tables were subsequently adopted, but they were applied only to new employees.

The guarantee has the same effect as if the permanent provisions of the retirement plans were incorporated in the constitution itself. When an amendment to a retirement system plan is drafted, whether as a result of collective bargaining or of legislative agreement, it is the same as if an amendment to the constitution were being drafted; each phrase is no less permanent. To draft amendments to a complex statute—and frequently within sharp deadlines dictated by legislative schedules and collective bargaining negotiations—in language that will stand for one hundred years without error or unintentional by-products is probably beyond human capacity. The law on the State systems consists of more than 130,000 words; on the State Teachers, a comparatively brief document, 28,000 words. It is, in fact, a tribute to the ability of the draftsmen that the results have not been more capricious.

In many parts, the language, particularly of the city plans, has grown impenetrable. In this regard, the New York statutes are not unlike many of the state retirement laws old enough to have accumulated generations of clutter.

The guarantee provision obviously imposes an awesome burden in the drafting of amendments. One would suppose that this hazard of writing provisions, no jot or tittle of which can be altered, would inhibit change; apparently it has not—it has only meant an inability to correct those errors that favor claimants.

For example, in the New York City Teachers' Retirement System, a pensioner had chosen to reduce her own allowance in order to get the joint-and-survivor benefit. Then her husband died and she therefore wanted to change to a maximum "no option" allowance. However, one cannot change an option during retirement. So she went back to work for a couple of days, had her retirement allowance ended, and retired again—this time choosing the maximum allowance. This was obviously a complete circumvention of the intention of the option provisions, but the law was read to say that she was within her rights. It is understandable that a circumvention like that was not foreseen and adequately guarded against. The real question is whether the law can now be corrected, the loophole plugged. The answer is no, not for anyone already a member of the system. It could, theoretically, be changed for future members. But the plug in the loophole would have to read: "Good only for persons becoming members after _____ [date]." The thought of a statute that would gather a collection of corrective amendments each with its own generation of members to which it applied is, of course, dismaying. Consequently, as loopholes are found and exploited, they are with rare exception permitted to exist in perpetuity.

In certain respects, the legislature has been able to avoid the guarantee. It has, for example, provided supplementary pensions—that is, additional benefits for persons already retired—that are exempt from the guarantee. The law simply recites that "the supplemental retirement allowances provided pursuant to this article shall not constitute membership in a pension or retirement system nor shall the granting of such allowances create a contractual relationship between the city or a public authority and any city retired employee or between the city and any police or fire widow or dependent or between the city and any police or fire line-of-duty widow or dependent."[21] Of course these supplements are in an important sense distinguishable: they apply only to persons already retired.

As noted earlier, the constitutional guarantee has led to the growth of a practice that is its very opposite. With increasing frequency the legislature has voted benefit changes through temporary enactments. The change usually is intended to be permanent, but because of concern that it may have implications that cannot be entirely foreseen, the legislators have frequently voted a statute automatically due to expire after one year, or perhaps two. Perpetual reenactment becomes necessary. For example, for all of the systems, the cost-of-living adjustment is temporary legislation. The "take-home-pay" provisions, which substituted employer contributions for all or part of employee contributions, have been temporary enactments. The resort to temporary enactment has gone much further

[21] L1961 No. 2, D49-18.0, *Admin. Code of City of New York.*

for the state, than for the city, systems. In 1969 there were eight major acts necessary to renew temporary legislation for the State Employees' System, including vesting after ten years, the 33 percent minimum for disability pensions, and the entire Non-Contributory Age-55 Plan. The Teachers' System had accumulated at least ten provisions in the form of temporary enactments, including the entire "Career Retirement Plan." In short, the existence of the constitutional guarantee had resulted in making the entire pension plan subject to repeated reenactment. Its existence has, in this respect, led at times to greater, not less, uncertainty.

The resort to temporary enactment has not meant that benefits enacted have in fact been withdrawn later. On the contrary, they have consistently been continued with only a couple of exceptions and those only when the unit of employees involved agreed to the change.

Even before the constitutional guarantee was adopted, when New York changed plan provisions, reduction was avoided. That was true in the 1920s, when most of the actuarial systems were established, and in 1940, when new plans were enacted for New York City policemen and firemen.

Tax Exemption

The state constitution also provides [22] "that all salaries, wages and other compensation, *except pensions,* paid to officers and employees of the state and its subdivisions and agencies shall be subject to taxation." In addition, each statute explicitly recites the exemption of the benefits from state and city taxation. The provisions apparently stem from a time when state, city, and county employees were regarded as proper objects of charity, so underpaid that it was only fair to exempt their pensions from taxation.

THE CROSS-CURRENTS OF 1971–73

In 1971, the continuing movement in New York for expanded pensions of public employees ran into resistance. It was a year of almost universal fiscal crisis for state and local governments. Expendi-

[22] Art. XVI, Sec. 5.

tures had been growing. Economic recession had resulted in a short-fall of revenues. Resistance to increased taxation was high and the pressure for curtailing costs was unusually strong.

The state comptroller, who had over a long period of time iden-tified himself with the cause of adequate pensions, described the mood of the year: [23]

The wind is blowing hard up in Albany.

The fact is we are witnessing a counter-attack—a reaction to all the demands made by our State employees over the past few years. This is part of a larger revolution by taxpayers. And high on the list of targets is the growing cost of our public pension systems.

If we are going to achieve fiscal prudence in the future, we must balance pension benefits and the burden on taxpayers.

The press carried an unusual number of stories about public em-ployee pensions. Stories about a number of subway accidents in New York City included reference to the twenty-year half-pay pension agreement and the fact that it had drained away experienced em-ployees. The Transit plan had in fact had heavy impact. In early 1971, the Transit Authority reported that 40 percent of its hourly employees had less than two years' service and 55 percent of its supervisory personnel had been in their present classifications for less than two years.[24] It is, of course, difficult to say exactly why ac-cidents increased, but it is entirely possible that a sudden shortage of experienced personnel was a contributing factor.

Newspapers also reported that some motormen and bus drivers were able to push their earnings beyond $20,000, and retire on com-mensurately increased pensions. A large part of the public was made aware of the fact that the City had agreed to a pension of 100 per-cent of final year's pay, even though it involved 40 years of service. On May 4, 1971, the *Daily News* claimed that the pension agreement with the teachers would double in cost when the city really began to pay for it.

Samples of banner headlines in New York papers read:

[23] Arthur Levitt, *Developments in State and Municipal Pension Plans,* Fifth Annual Conference on Employee Benefits, May 14, 1971.
[24] Wilbur B. McLaren, Executive Officer for Labor Relations and Personnel, *N.Y. Daily News,* April 7, 1971.

"Rich Legislature Pension Plan Affords Death Benefit Bonanza" (source unavailable)

. . . .

"Legislative Pensions—Gold in Them Thar Hills" (Rochester *Times-Union*)

. . . .

"City Fiscal Officials Worried by Sharp Increases in Pension Costs" (*The New York Times*)

. . . .

"The Built-in Albany Bonanza—Millions of $ in Fringe Benefits" (*Buffalo Evening News*)

. . . .

"State Pensions: A Gravy Train" (*Schnectady Union-Star*)

. . . .

"Pensions Have Skyrocketed Under Law" (New York *Daily News*)

. . . .

"Retirement Costs of City and State Top Industry's (*The New York Times*)

Some of the stories used items like these:

A convicted official is entitled to collect his pension in prison.

Some lobbyists and members of large law firms have built up credit for years of service based on part-time jobs; they then got substantial pensions because of three years in positions with high salaries.

An official or employee with political influence, no longer in public employment, but close to retirement age, may get reemployment in some sort of position, in order to qualify for a pension.

The death benefit covering long-service officials runs into the hundreds of thousands of dollars.

A hard line formed in 1971. As we have noted, the legislature broke its previous precedents and voted down the pension agreement that the mayor of New York City had negotiated. It also voted to require all pension bills to be accompanied by fiscal notes and to forbid putting any pension liberalization into effect prior to the year in which its funding started. A limitation was enacted on the salary to be used in computing benefits: no lump-sums (such as accrued terminal leave or sick leave) were to be included and the salary used for the last year could not exceed that of the previous year by more than 20 percent (a limitation subsequently voided by the courts).

Moreover, it established a permanent commission on pension legislation, made up of 5 non-legislators, and charged it with the obligation of reporting on pension bills and of making recommendations for possible change of the existing plans.

The commission came to the 1973 legislature with a sweeping proposal to close all of the existing plans to new members and establish a new plan for all new employees. That new plan was to provide guaranteed retirement allowances, inclusive of primary Social Security, keyed to producing for thirty-year career employees full continuance of net income from age 65. To be more specific, the benefit formula would have provided for the employee retiring at 65 after thirty years of service 80 percent of his final average salary if it fell within the Social Security salary base. The 80 percent was figured to be the equivalent of 100 percent of disposable income, after taking account of taxes and Social Security contributions. Lesser benefits, with only partial inclusion of Social Security, would have been provided for employees with shorter service. The benefits would also have been tapered downward, as a percentage of salary, for employees earning more than the Social Security base. Special benefits, with earlier retirement, were to be provided for policemen and firemen.

The proposed plan was designed to guarantee retirement goals that would be completely inclusive of Social Security, a radical departure from past practices. Its presentation to the legislature and the public was sudden—no public preparation, no prior exposure or discussion with the unions, and no time for the cross-fires of criticism or the give-and-take of bargaining. Nothing was included to provide responsiveness to the cost-of-living. The proposal met with unanimous opposition from the employee organizations. It was turned aside when the governor reached agreement with the civil service association representing most state employees on a substitute plan for new employees. However, this was followed, several months later, by the enactment after all of new plans for all employees (including those of New York City) hired after June 30, 1973. Except for more generous death benefits (up to three times salary after three years service), the new plans provided benefits that are independent of Social Security but somewhat pared down from the older plans:

1. The normal retirement age is fixed at 62, instead of 55.
2. Retirement before 62 is subject to a reduction of 6 percent a year for age 60 and 61 and 3 percent a year down to 55. (Teachers will get full benefits at 55, if they have 30 years of service.)
3. A maximum is imposed equal to 60 percent of the first $12,000 of final average salary plus 50 percent of the remainder. Teachers retained their old plan limits: 75 percent in the state system; none in the City system. Police and firemen are to be subject only to a 30-year maximum on credit.
4. Final average salary is to be computed on the best three consecutive years, not the final year.
5. Final average salary is not to include lump-sums nor may any year's salary for pension computation exceed 120 percent of the average of the two preceding years.
6. Higher death benefits to three times salary after three years' service were added as an option, in place of the right to a return-of-reserve guarantee in the event of death.
7. Half pay was preserved for new policemen and firemen, except that it is to be computed on a three-year average.
8. New sanitationmen and correction officers may retire after 20 years, any age, but on no more than 2 percent per year of service, applied to a three-year average.
9. New transit workers in New York City will be able to draw their benefits from age 55, instead of 50.

To avoid its being frozen by the constitutional guarantee, the entire plan for new employees was made temporary—this time for a three-year period.

The cost-of-living adjustment was extended again, but with no correction of level beyond 1969.[25]

The state's Taylor Law on public employee collective bargaining was amended to eliminate pensions as an item of bargaining, but at the same time the Pension Commission was directed to report a plan for "coalition bargaining," an idea aimed to open the way for a new style of future negotiations intended to avoid fracturing of the retirement plans because of diverse union pressures.

At the same time, the employees were partially mollified by acts

[25] An increase unrelated to the cost of living was voted in 1974. It amounted to 4 percent for the most recent retirees up to 11 percent for those who retired many years earlier. The 4 percent compared to a 31 percent increase in the Consumer Price Index.

that transformed many of the temporary, renewable provisions into permanent benefits, constitutionally guaranteed.

It is too early, as this is written, to judge whether the legislation of 1973 will prove to be a significant turning point, a mere hesitation in the previous march of events, or part of a long-sustained deadlock. As this book goes to press, New York City and several state authorities are on the brink of bankruptcy. The prospect for years to come is for less open-handedness.

The issues are not easily resolved. The stakes are great for both the beneficiaries and for those who pay the bill. New York's state and local governments contribute about $2 billion a year for their employee retirement plans, including Social Security. These contributions amount to almost $300 a year for every working person in the state. The state's Budget Division reported in 1971 that pensions took 11 cents of every tax dollar. Assets totalled more than $13 billion. That amounted to about $11,000 for every state and local employee and pensioner.

The systems covered almost 1,200,000 persons, inclusive of those on the benefit rolls. One out of every seven employed persons in New York works for state or local government. This indicates both the importance of the institution and the many people it affects. They constitute a major political force. In terms of legislative effectiveness, they probably account for many more than one out of seven, because they are highly organized voters who have an unusually direct interest in state and local government, particularly when their pay and benefits are involved. It would not be surprising if employees of state and local government in New York comprise 20 percent or more of those who actually vote for state and local offices.

This may not be essentially different from the situation in other states and other municipalities. Under these circumstances, it will not be a simple task to cope with a future in which state legislation and federal legislation will somehow have to be made complementary in order to effectuate durable retirement policies that are fair to public employees and to the general public.

15 ❖ Massachusetts

For over twenty years, Massachusetts, unlike other states, has had a single pension law for all new employees. However, that law is applied and administered through 100 separate systems, covering 200,000 public employees. The statewide and most of the local systems are financed on a pay-as-you-go basis, and none of the employees is covered by Social Security.

Before 1945, when this uniformity was achieved, there was no effectively consistent pension policy. As in so many states, disparate laws had accumulated—many of which are still in effect for those whose employment predates repeal of the old statutes. The earlier plans are generally called "non-contributory" plans to distinguish them from the single contributory plan now in force.

For the most part, the uniform Massachusetts plan is clear and simple in design. It includes a single schedule of benefits, with uncomplicated variations for security personnel and others in hazardous occupations. Teachers, legislators, and constitutional officers are included with the mass of state and local employees.

The retirement benefit is 2.5 percent of final average salary per year of service to a maximum of 80 percent. Final average salary is defined as the average of the last three years. Normal retirement age for the general body of employees is 65, with compulsory retirement at 70. For retirement at 65 the benefit formula results in 50 percent of final average pay with twenty years of service and 75 percent with thirty years of service. However, as noted above, Social Security coverage is not provided.

Early retirement is permitted at any age with at least twenty years of service, or at age 55 with any service. Benefits are reduced for early retirement, but at the most significant ages the reduction is less than full actuarial equivalence would require—for each year the retiring employee is younger than 65, 0.1 percentage points is subtracted from the full 2.5 percent (2.4 percent at age 65; 2.0 percent at 60; 1.5 percent at 55).

For policemen and firemen, normal retirement age is 55; that is, the full 2.5 percent is effective at that age. Early retirement is possible at any age after twenty years of service—with the same 0.1 percent per year subtraction—but in this case for each year younger than 55. Other safety occupations are in a third category: park and public-works police, conservation officers, fire wardens, prison guards and any employees "whose regular and major duties require them to have the care, custody, instruction, or other supervision" of prisoners, parolees, mental patients, mental defectives, and "defective delinquents" or "wayward children." For these employees, 60 is the normal retirement age, and benefits are reduced by the 0.1 percentage point factor for retirement between 55 and 59. Officers of the state police are also in a special category, with normal retirement age at 50 or upon completion of twenty years of service.

The schedule produces the following benefits in terms of percentage of final average salary per year:

Age	General	Park police, mental health, fire wardens, etc.	Policemen and firemen
65 or over	2.5%	2.5%	2.5%
64	2.4	2.5	2.5
60	2.0	2.5	2.5
59	1.9	2.4	2.5
55	1.5	2.0	2.5
54	1.4	1.4 *	2.4
50	1.0	1.0	2.0
45	0.5	0.5	1.5
44	0.4	0.4	†
41	0.1	0.1	†

* The reduction changes abruptly at age 54.
† Whether the rate at age 44 is 1.4% or 0.4% was a legal issue at the time of writing; similarly, the rates at 41–43.

An unusual feature of the Massachusetts law is preference for veterans. They get an extra yearly benefit of $15 for each year of service, to a maximum of $300, the total allowance not exceeding 80 percent of final average pay. Pensions for veterans who were in covered employment before July 1, 1939, can go as high as 72 percent of highest pay plus $300 plus a refund of the employee's contributions. Veterans hired after 1939 do not receive as much as those hired earlier; veteran provisions are less generous than they once were.

The distinction between veterans and non-veterans also extends to ordinary disability pensions. The general rule is eligibility after fifteen years of service, with the full normal benefit payable as if the employee were 55. For veterans, the requirement is ten years and the benefit is 50 percent of the last year's salary plus the annuity from employee contributions.

Annuities are provided for survivors, as might be expected in a system without parallel Social Security coverage. When an employee dies while in active service, the spouse is entitled to receive "Option C benefits" (the survivor receives two-thirds of the adjusted benefit of the retired member). If the employee was younger than 55, it is calculated as if he had been 55. However, since this is of little use to the survivor of an employee with relatively short service, there is an alternative option: a widow can receive $100 a month; a child under 18, $50 a month; and each additional child another $35 a month. If death was attributable to the job, the spouse or other eligible beneficiary receives 72 percent of the last year's salary plus $312 a year for each child under 18; also, the employee's contributions are returned. Workmen's Compensation is offset, and total benefits cannot exceed final salary. The widow of a policeman or fireman killed in line of duty under specified circumstances receives the full maximum salary of the position, automatically adjusted by the percentage change in salary of the grade last held by the member.

Automatic "cost-of-living" adjustments for pensioners and survivor annuitants were made effective in 1967, providing annual increases in pensions and survivor annuities whenever the Consumer Price Index increases by at least 3 percent. The first annual adjustment was made in 1970. Patterned after the cost-of-living provisions of the federal civil service, the adjustment is distinctive among state and local plans in having no top limit. At first the increase was limited to pensions of less than $6,000, but in 1971 it was extended to the first $6,000 of any pension or survivor's annuity.

Since the state is covered by a single law, there is complete portability within the Massachusetts public service. The employee's accumulated contributions are transferred to the new system and the accretion of credited service continues without change; employers share the cost on the basis of years of service. All benefits, including employee contributions, are exempt from the state's income tax law, which would otherwise impose a rate of 5 percent on virtually all income over $2,000, or $2,600 for husband and wife.

For an employee retiring at age 65, who received during his career salary increases of 4 percent per year, benefits range from 48 percent of final salary with twenty years' service to 77 percent for thirty-five years' service. The employee's contributions would pay for 20–22 percent of the benefit. After income taxes, the net benefit of a married employee retiring at 65 equals 54 percent of net pre-retirement income (twenty years of service, final salary of $5,000) to 87 percent (thirty-five years of service, final salary of $14,000).

Although employees do not have Social Security coverage on their public employment, a retiree may receive Social Security benefits from employment before or after public employment, moonlighting, weekend and summer employment, or as the wife of a covered employee. How many Massachusetts public employees qualify for Social Security? No dependable statistics had yet been compiled at the time this was written; however, informed judgments place the figure high, well over half the employees.

Development of the Massachusetts System

The single pension law was achieved only after a long history of disparate, unfunded, non-contributory plans.

As in most other states, the policemen, firemen, and teachers of the largest city were the first to get pensions. Typical of the times, these were simple non-contributory plans, generally keyed to half of final pay. In 1878 the plan for Boston policemen was non-contributory, providing one-third of pay for retirement on account of disability or after fifteen years' service.[26] The police plan was changed in 1892 to half-pay at 65, or after twenty years, if disabled. In the same year, comparable provision was made for policemen outside Boston.[27]

[26] It was preceded by a "Charitable Fund" established for retired needy policemen.
[27] Massachusetts Commission on Pensions, *Report, House Doc. No. 2450* (Boston, 1916). Information on developments to 1913 was derived from this report.

Firemen were next; they were first covered in Boston in 1880 with a non-contributory plan providing half-pay at 55 with twenty-five years of service, after fifteen years' service if disabled or at two-thirds pay if the disability was duty-connected. Legislation in the 1880s covered firemen in cities and towns outside Boston—again, it was non-contributory and provided half-pay either when disabled or at 60, after twenty-five years.

Judges have received pensions since 1885, with retirement at 70 on three-quarters of final pay. Teachers were not covered until 1900, when an employee-financed plan was set up for Boston's teachers through a "Retirement Fund Association," familiarly known as the "180 Fund." (Several of the earliest teacher plans in the country involved no government contributions.) Teachers contributed $18 a year; they could retire, after thirty years or on disability, on a pension fixed by the Association's trustees. The amount was first fixed at $150 a year, then $180 from 1904 to 1914, and reduced later to $120. In 1908, this was supplemented by a "Permanent School Pension Fund" financed by the city, which at first matched the $180, then was increased to one-third of final salary. At the time, the combination happened to approximate half-pay.

The state authorized a pension plan for teachers outside of Boston in 1908. Non-contributory, it provided half-pay at 60 or upon disability, and after twenty-five years of service. Only a few communities adopted this plan.

The Landmark Report of 1910

In 1907 the state established a Commission on Old-Age Pensions, Annuities, and Insurance to study the various plans in effect. Its report, delivered in 1910, proved to be a landmark. The study stimulated establishment in the following ten to fifteen years of state and municipal plans in many parts of the country.[28] Although initially intended to consider proposals to eliminate destitution in old age through a general pension law covering all residents, the Commission recommended against any compulsory system for residents or wage-earners generally, but offered a basis and guidelines for state and local governments to provide pensions for their employees:

[28] Massachusetts, Special Commission on Old Age Pensions, Annuities, and Insurance, *Report, House Document No. 1400* (Boston, 1910).

The present practice of keeping on the municipal payroll superannuated workers who have lost their effectiveness means waste of the taxpayer's money and demoralization of the working force. Considerations of economy and efficiency, not to mention other motives, demand the establishment of municipal pension systems. These considerations are even more imperative in the case of the municipality than in that of the private corporation, for political influences come into play to prevent the discharge of city employees who have outlived their usefulness. . . .

The Commission recommended that employees contribute because non-contributory pensions are expensive and employees can afford to pay. Moreover, it feared that non-contributory pensions for government employees would encourage the demand for non-contributory state pensions for all aged persons:

Any non-contributory pension system must exert a depressing effect on wages, a demoralizing reaction on character, and a disintegrating influence on the family. A policy that threatens social consequences of so sweepingly harmful a character is not one that the State, the county, the city, or the town, as an employer of labor, can afford to sanction.

A non-contributory plan, the Commission argued, would depress wages since, taking account of its cost, the public employer would offer lower wages. It would be demoralizing because it would be a handout. It would have a disintegrating effect on the family, because children would no longer take care of their aged parents if the latter drew pensions from the state or under a compulsory state law.

But the government was not relieved of responsibility toward its employees. The Commission concluded that:

It is just and right that the State, county, or town should contribute something to the funds out of which pensions to superannuated employees are paid. Such contributions should be regarded as in the nature of extra compensation for long, faithful, and efficient service; that is, in addition to the payment of current wages, the public employer pays a special extra allowance to workers who remain in the service a certain period of years and reach a certain age.

Employees should share in the management of the retirement system, the Commission said. Benefits should be contractual, so that "payments cannot be withdrawn or discontinued by the employer at will, as in the cases of most non-contributory pension systems established by private corporations." The Commission considered it essential for the plan to be compulsory for all new employees.

The proposed plan was to be money-purchase, based on matching employer-employee contributions of up to 5 percent of pay. Eligibility was suggested at 60 after fifteen years of service, or after thirty-five years of service at any age, or upon permanent disability.

The Failure of Local Initiative

The Commission's report led to the creation in 1910 of a system which cities and towns could join. None did. A similar system for counties was adopted by only three. A local-option plan for city and town laborers met with somewhat greater, but by no means universal, success. Mandatory plans were enacted for state employees in 1911 and for all teachers outside Boston in 1913.

Except for a laborers' plan, all were money-purchase systems. Employees contributed a uniform percentage of pay translated into an annuity on an actuarial basis upon retirement. The employer provided a matching pension. The state employees' law authorized the system board to set up employee contribution rates at 1 to 5 percent. Starting with a minimum of 3 percent, it was soon increased to 5 percent. The state paid for past service. Retirement was compulsory at 70, voluntary after thirty-five years, or at the discretion of the department head at age 60 after fifteen years of service. The minimum allowance was $200 a year; the maximum, half of average pay for the last ten years. The teachers' system was similar, with a contribution rate of 5 percent from the beginning.

The 1910 report achieved national significance. It gave the country as a whole a sober and reasoned recommendation from a prestigious commission, based on detailed study of pension provisions for public employees throughout the United States and Europe. Reports done a few years later for New York City became authoritative on the essential actuarial data and plan design, but the Massachusetts report established the basic proposition that public employees needed definite pension plans, designed to last.

The Commission's report came at an opportune time. It was popular interest, of course, that had led to the Commission's appointment in the first place. The Commonwealth had enacted pension laws in 1908 and 1909, even while the Commission was conducting its studies. Other industrial states took similar steps during those same years. Much the same atmosphere continued into the early

1920s; the Commission's recommendations therefore found a ready public. The history of the Massachusetts law establishes rather clearly that sweeping reform is adopted when—and only when—the public is ready for it.

Mandating Local Plans

The early contributory laws were optional for local governments—and in that respect failed. Localities continued to set up their own very individual plans. A commission report in 1914 described the familiar pattern which we quoted at the very beginning of this book: [29]

The large number and variety of pension and retirement laws now on the statute books of Massachusetts, some of which have been repealed in part, while others are effective in full, are startling; their proper understanding by the beneficiaries or the public is possible only after exhaustive study.

. . . .

The pension legislation of Massachusetts has grown from the first pension law of twenty-five years ago, inspired by the humanitarian and just impulse to protect the firemen and policemen against the hazard of their calling, to nearly 100 laws which are contradictory, unsystematized, and pregnant with unknown cost.

. . . .

About 100 new bills have been introduced this year into the Legislature relative to pensions. No consideration of cost, no study of principle involved, enters into the minds of those who seek extension. If the solution is not furnished new pension legislation will complicate the situation year by year, making future effort for sound economic legislation well-nigh hopeless.

At this point the Commission declared unsuccessful the permissive non-contributory laws for localities and proposed a single mandatory law. The proposal was ignored. Subsequent Commission reports in 1921 and 1925 along similar lines were also in vain.[30]

The first real step toward uniformity was taken in 1936, during the Depression. Aimed as much toward assuring pensions for employees of local governments as toward blending the patchwork of

[29] Massachusetts Commission on Pensions, *Report, House Document No. 2450* (Boston, 1914), pp. 9, 22, 23.
[30] Massachusetts Joint Special Commission on Pensions, *Report, House Document No. 1203* (Boston, 1921), and Commission on Pensions, *Partial Report, House Document No. 340* (Boston, 1925).

plans, the 1936 law required every community with a population of more than 10,000 to submit the plan to a referendum. The plan was contributory, with a matching pension, financed on a actuarial reserve basis through local systems.

More comprehensive uniformity was achieved in 1945 with codification of the retirement law, the result of two years' work by another commission.[31] Creating uniformity coincided with liberalizing benefits and with codification into a single law. The money-purchase formula was ended. A new formula based the retirement allowance on total earnings. The annual retirement allowance was fixed at 3 percent of the first $15,000 of career earnings plus 2 percent over $15,000; the normal retirement age was 65, or 60 for safety occupations; early retirement was permissible five years before normal retirement age, with a reduction of 3 percent for each year; employees contributed 5 percent.

The law rationalizing the Commonwealth's pension plans was not in effect very long before the wage and pension upsurge of the 1950s brought sweeping changes. In 1949, a minimum based on final average salary was introduced. For anyone retiring at 65 with thirty or more years, the allowance was to be not less than 50 percent of the five-year final average salary plus an additional 1 percent for each year over thirty, to a maximum of 80 percent. A later amendment changed the five-year base to two years. The early retirement adjustment was radically reduced from 3 percent to 1 percent a year, and the basic allowance was increased to 3 percent of the first $40,000 of earnings (instead of $15,000), plus 2 percent of earnings above that amount. Survivor benefits were added for some classes of members.

In 1951 further drastic change was voted. A minimum allowance was enacted for anyone retiring after 65 with at least twenty, instead of thirty, years of service: 50 percent of final pay (two-year average) plus 2 percent for each year over twenty. This liberalization was limited, however, to the first $ 5,000 of salary. The same logic, forced by constantly rising price-and-salary levels, led finally to an entirely new formula, based wholly on final average salary.

[31] Massachusetts, Special Commission Established for the Purpose of Making a Further Investigation of the Retirement Systems of the Commonwealth and of the Political Subdivisions Thereof, *Report, House Document No. 1950* (Boston, 1945).

Focus on Employee Contributions

In discussions of Massachusetts retirement laws, uniformity and member contributions have been persistent themes. It appears almost as if "contributory" has been accepted virtually as shorthand for "systematic" or "equitable," while "non-contributory" has stood for "patchwork." Actuarial reserve funding was not overlooked, but as a means of creating a disciplined approach to retirement law, it was the idea of cost-sharing through a contributory system that took clear precedence. The 1925 Commission had this to say: [32]

One of the difficulties of the non-contributory plan is that its costs are concealed. At first the cost of a non-contributory plan is not large, but as more employees go on the pension roll the cost mounts rapidly from year to year. The non-contributory plan also means, as experience teaches, that additional demands for increased benefits will be made of the legislature, either to reduce the eligibility qualification or to extend the provisions of the law to those who retired before its passage, or to provide that pensions be continued to the widows and children of beneficiaries.

The non-contributory plan further provides no retirement benefits (or no benefits except in some cases where retirement is caused by disability) to those who resign or are dismissed from the service before fulfilling the requirements of age or service for the pensions.

A Retirement Law Commission

Recognizing the need for more information and more consistent policy, the legislature established in 1958 a permanent Retirement Law Commission. It was slow in getting started; for the first five years it had no significant appropriation with which to do its work. More recently, it has been active and influential in reviewing and proposing legislation in projecting the development of the system. The Commission is not required to review all pension legislation, nor does it attempt to; but matters may be referred for an opinion. It does engage in a continuing study of the major aspects of the system and it sponsors legislative proposals of its own.

Actuarial valuations for the Commission have established that if the systems were funded on the basis of normal cost plus the payment of interest only on the unfunded accrued liability, rather than

[32] *Ibid.*, p. 19.

pay-as-you-go, public contributions as percentage of payroll would be much greater than they are: [33]

	Actuarial funding requirement	*Actual (1970) government contributions*
State system	21.5%	6.3%
Teachers' system	23.3	7.4
Local policemen and firemen	23.7	8.0
Local retirement systems	21.4	8.0

These figures raise the obvious question of the public reaction when, as they must, the government contribution rate triples in response to growing pension disbursements.

Legislators' Pensions

From 1947 to 1952, Massachusetts had a relatively brief encounter with special benefits for legislators. It started in 1947 with a fairly modest plan for members of the General Court, constitutional officers and state officials. But it expanded rapidly. In 1948, the formula was made 4 percent of pay per year of service; one year later, it was changed to 25 percent of final year's pay for six years' service plus another 4 percent for each additional year. In 1952, the base was changed to the highest *single* year and a pension was voted to any former member of the legislature who had twenty-five years of government service. At this point, a public protest erupted, stirred by newspapers and by the Massachusetts Federation of Taxpayers Association.[34] In a special legislative session, the plan for legislators was repealed and they were left without coverage until 1955, when they were covered by the same formula as for other state employees.

Contractual Guarantee

Directly after repeal in 1952 of the special plan for legislators, Massachusetts added a guarantee against benefit reductions to its retirement law:

[33] Martin E. Segal Company, *Report to the Massachusetts Retirement Law Commission on Actuarial Valuations of All Systems Under Contributory Retirement Law* (Boston, November 1971).
[34] Elwyn E. Mariner, "Pension History" (unpublished manuscript, Arlington, Mass., 1969).

The provisions of sections one to twenty-eight, inclusive, and of corresponding provisions of earlier laws shall be deemed to establish and to have established membership in the retirement system as a contractual relationship under which members who are or may be retired for superannuation are entitled to contractual rights and benefits, and no amendments or alternation shall be made that will deprive any such members or any such group of such members of their pension rights or benefits provided for thereunder, if such member or members have paid the stipulated contributions specified in said sections or corresponding provisions of earlier laws.

This section has been held not to apply to disability pensioners.[35]

Although the state had in general observed the principle of respecting commitments made to current employees, repeal of the legislators' plan was sufficiently unsettling to prompt adoption of this guarantee.

Public Safety and Hazardous Occupations

The single or uniform plan has not, of course, meant the end of all pressure for increased benefits for particular groups of employees. There have been significant shifts out of Group 1 (for which 65 is the normal retirement age) into Groups 2 and 4 (normal retirement at 60 and 55). Earlier retirement is encouraged for policemen and firemen, for whom Group 4 was established in 1967, and more liberal benefits for retirement before 65 are extended to other employees in public-safety occupations or hazardous work.

Acceptable occupational grouping is a current problem in Massachusetts, as it is in many states. Changes have been almost annual. In every year from 1967 to 1971, some group was shifted from Group 1 to Group 2 or from Group 2 to Group 4. The broadened nature of Groups 2 and 4 is apparent from descriptions given earlier. This consistent movement into Groups 2 and 4 has resulted in strong pressure for proposals that *all* employees be given the advantage of age 55 or age 60 retirement on unreduced benefits.

Administration, Assets, and Investment

The law is implemented through 100 separate systems. Two are at the state level—the State Employees' and the Teachers'. The latter covers all of the teachers except for those in Boston. Then there are

[35] *Smolinski* v. *Boston Retirement Board,* 346 Mass. 210, 190 NE2d877.

39 city systems, 46 town systems, and 12 county systems. The Massachusetts Turnpike Authority makes it 100. Each is run by a three-man board; one is a named official, ex-officio; the second is an employee covered by the system; and a third is picked in some cases by the other two, and in other cases by the official(s) of the locality. The State Insurance Department performs extensive work in auditing the operations of the local systems.

In the fiscal years ending in 1969–1970, assets totaled one billion dollars. Reflective of their pay-as-you-go nature, government contributions were less than total benefit payments; the assets, which represented employee contributions for the most part, amounted to only seven times annual benefit payments.

Investments are limited to those legal for savings banks, which means that only certain types of stock can be held. Only a small percentage of funds is invested in equities. The fact that the assets represent employee money is no doubt related to the maintenance of this restrictive policy. Investment for the state systems is made by an investment committee, consisting of the State Treasurer (who holds custody), the Superintendent of Banks, and a third person chosen by those two.

Implementation through 100 systems has not generally been challenged, in deference apparently to the idea of local control, although at the expense of the fractured handling of investments, diversity of rules and interpretations of the law, and administration that is sometimes inadequate, considering the specialized nature of a retirement system.

As elsewhere, payments and contributions have been on a sharply upward curve. From 1954 to 1968, total disbursements increased threefold—from $44 million to $159 million and government contributions have gone up even more, by three-and-a-half times—from $26 million to $141 million.[36]

Summary

In the history of Massachusetts pension plans, there was a long succession of commission reports that repeatedly preached uniformity and joint financing. The pleas often went unheeded. Uniformity remained for a long time a stated but unfulfilled ideal. It was, how-

---

[36] Tabulations of the Massachusetts Taxpayers Foundation, Inc.

ever, ultimately achieved by way of two important steps, one in 1936 and the other in 1945. Both steps, it is worth noting, coincided with significant benefit increases.

From the beginning, government financing was on a cash-disbursements basis and it has remained so. The 1936 law for cities and towns provided for actuarial reserves, but in 1945 that was undone. One may speculate—but it can only be speculation—whether the state would have enacted a 2.5 percent formula if government contributions were on an actuarial-reserve basis under which contributions would be about three times their present pay-as-you-go level. At the same time, one must acknowledge that despite its pay-as-you-go financing, on the whole the state has an orderly and largely nondiscriminatory retirement act for all of its public employees and, at this point, a tradition and practice that subjects further change to informed debate. With what resolution the state will cope with the future tripling of pay-as-you-go costs is a question worth asking.

16 ❖ Illinois

Illinois's retirement plans have a stamp of their own: a high degree of uniformity, but with many significant differences that cannot be rationally defended. The relative uniformity is attributable to the fact that all plans in the state are established by state law and to the effective functioning since 1945 of a continuing commission on pension laws.

There is a multiplicity of pension systems: some divide Chicago from the rest of the state; others separate municipal workers from state employees, teachers from university personnel, policemen from firemen, judges from legislators, etc. As a result there are five state-financed systems including the State Employees' system, the State Teachers' system (all public-school teachers, except for Chicago), the State Universities, the system for the Illinois General Assembly, and the state judges' system. Chicago and Chicago area systems include those for teachers, police, firemen, laborers, other city employees, Cook County employees (with a separate system, for tax-levy purposes only, for employees of the Forest preserve), the Park District, and the Sanitary District.

Downstate (other than Chicago) systems are set up under a state pension law for downstate police, implemented through 251 locally administered funds; a state pension law for downstate firemen, implemented through 168 locally administered funds; and the Illinois Municipal Retirement Fund for employees of municipalities except for Chicago or for teachers, police, and firemen anywhere in the state.

The Early Years

Illinois's retirement provisions began in 1874 when localities were authorized to pay disability pensions to policemen and firemen. The provisions were subsequently made mandatory and benefits broadened. During World War I, Chicago policemen and firemen were covered by separate systems. This sequence is contrary to developments in most other large states, where plans for the largest city normally preceded statewide provisions.

The period from 1909 to 1920 was one of expansion—the laws were reviewed by a special commission in 1915–1917, about the time when Massachusetts, New York, and New Jersey were doing the same. In 1919 a number of systems were established as money-purchase plans, based on percentage-of-pay contributions from both employees and the government. The parallel to the New York and Massachusetts developments is striking.

The Chicago Teachers System, one of the oldest in the country, was established in 1895—long before provision was made for the downstate teachers. As was fairly typical of that time, the pension was half of final pay after twenty years (women) and twenty-five years (men), whatever the age. Contributions were totally unrelated to cost: 1 percent of pay from the teachers, nothing from the public. The limits thus imposed began to bind almost immediately, and in 1901 the benefit was cut to a maximum of $180 a year and participation was made optional. Starting in 1911, and until as late as 1955, teachers' contributions followed a schedule that increased with length of service. Public money was added on a systematic basis, generally in terms of the yield of a fixed property tax (millage rate). Benefits were set on the basis of fixed-dollar amounts for twenty-five or more years of service.

The national pension upsurge of the 1950s transformed the system. Widows' pensions were added in 1953. In 1955 benefits were shifted to 1.5 percent of final average salary per year of service, payable at age 60, with reduced benefits payable from age 55. Employee contributions were shifted to a percentage of salary, and the government contribution was freed from a millage rate. For the first time investments were broadened to include corporate issues.

In 1959, the formula was increased to 1.67 percent, the survivors' annuity was made a percentage of salary, and an automatic postretirement adjustment of 1.5 percent a year was added. Then, in 1971, higher rates of benefit accrual were established for employees with long service and the postretirement increase was raised to 2 percent a year.

Illinois Benefit Pattern

Illinois benefits, as of January 1, 1972, fall into this distinctive pattern:

Normal retirement age is 60, except for the downstate Municipal System, in which it is 55. Further exception is made for police and firemen, for whom unreduced benefits are payable at 55 (Chicago police), 53 (Chicago firemen), and 50 (downstate police and firemen). Judges and members of the legislature may draw full benefits from age 55. Otherwise, normal benefits are available earlier than 60 only when there has been a very long service; e.g., state employees and downstate teachers at age 55 with thirty-five years of service and state university employees after thirty-five years, any age.

Early retirement benefits are payable at 55, at a reduction of 6 percent for each year the employee is younger than 60 (½ of 1 percent per month), a fairly common formula based on approximate actuarial equivalence.

Illinois is one of the states that has remained relatively unreceptive to federal Social Security. Only two of its systems make Social Security coverage available—the Municipal System, for all its members, and the State Employees' System, under an arrangement that allows incumbents the right not to join. A majority of state employees are now covered.

In 1971, a step-rate formula was adopted, favoring long service and based on salary in the best four consecutive years:

Years of service	Members with Social Security	Members without Social Security
First 10	1.0%	1.67%
Next 10	1.1	1.90
Next 10	1.3	2.10
Thereafter	1.5	2.30
Maximum	75%, exclusive of Social Security	

This sort of step-rate schedule is a means of improving the benefits of career personnel without making benefits for shorter-term employees much more costly. At the end of 27 years, it produces 50 percent of salary for those covered by Social Security.

For the great bulk of employees, the combination of "coordinated benefits" and Social Security is greater than the "uncoordinated schedule" alone. The state's Municipal System takes account of Social Security in a different way—by offsetting part of the federal benefit. Its formula is 1.67 percent of final average salary, less 1.4 percent of the 1971 Social Security formula, per year of service. The effect, for someone with thirty years of service, is a benefit of 50 percent of final average salary less 42 percent of his Social Security under the 1971 law.

For most career public employees, Illinois provides benefits ranging from 33 to about 60 percent of final salary.

Benefit formulas for police, firemen, and legislators and judges are higher. Illinois's hierarchy of benefits for special groups is a little unusual. Downstate police and firemen and state-employed safety officers can retire at 50 percent of pay at an earlier age than Chicago policemen and firemen can. Legislators and judges have higher benefits than any safety officers.

Much of Illinois policy on pensions has been pegged to the idea that cost should be fully shared by the employee. In general, the Illinois systems involve substantial employee contributions, typically 6.5 percent, plus 0.5 percent for the post-retirement adjustment, plus 1.0 percent for male employees to help pay for survivors' annuities. However, from members covered by Social Security, the State Employees' System requires only 3 percent.

The Illinois systems provide automatic post-retirement increases: 2.0 percent per year without regard to indices, a method that has the advantage of being simple, predictable in cost, and —significant for Illinois's traditional policy—of permitting the sharing of cost by employees (a contribution of ½ of 1 percent). By contrast, an adjustment based on the Consumer Price Index is not entirely predictable and therefore not readily tied in with employee contributions.

Illinois systems also provide substantial survivors' annuities, which resemble widows' and children's benefits under Social Security— generally monthly benefits for children under 18 and for a widow who has either attained 50 or 55 or who has care of a minor child. Monthly benefits are related to the final salary or accrued benefit of the member and survivor annuities are financed in part by separate employee contributions, ranging from 0.5 percent to 1.5 percent, depending on the system. For those members of the State Employees' System covered by Social Security, the survivor's benefit is adjusted by subtracting half the Social Security benefit. The statewide Municipal System has no such accommodation.

An unusual feature of the Illinois laws is that, with some exceptions, the disability benefit is temporary. The State Employees' System pays 50 percent of final salary (less Social Security earned as a state employee) but only for a period of time equal to half the member's length of service. The combination of the two provisions means that if an employee in his fifties with ten years of service becomes permanently disabled, he will probably receive lifetime payments—a temporary disability benefit for five years, followed by a service pension.

Other Illinois plans follow almost the same pattern. For example, the Teachers' System pays a temporary benefit for one-fourth the service credit, but someone with ten years' credit is provided a lifetime pension. The University System pays disability benefits until the total equals half the employee's earnings. The idea, presumably, is to avoid a commitment for lifetime benefits to someone disabled when young or after relatively short service.

On the other hand, Chicago teachers, the downstate municipal employees, and the state judges and legislators are protected by permanent disability benefits. Moreover, if the disability is attributable to employment, the pension benefit is generally permanent.

Requirements for vesting range from twenty years (downstate police and firemen) to only five years of service.

The Illinois Retirement Systems' Reciprocal Act protects an employee who transfers from the jurisdiction of one public system to another. All systems except police and firemen have agreed to participate.

The Pension Laws Commission

The Illinois Public Employee Pension Law Commission has been a strong influence in shaping the state's pension laws. The situation that led to its creation and continuance was described by the Commission in one of its reports. It is worth quoting, not because it is unique, but precisely because it repeats what has been said before in other states: [1]

A necessary consequence of the existence of these many individual systems has been the efforts of each to secure advantageous amendments without regard to their effect upon other systems. Each has been in competition with the others. The result has been the absence of any general statewide pension policy. The chaotic conditions of most pension systems, due in large measure to unwarrantedly low retirement ages, inadequate and improper financing techniques, and non-uniform and discriminatory rates of contribution and benefits, are the result of this lack of policy. Until 1945, the legislature had been unable to cope satisfactorily with this problem since pension legislation necessarily involved complex technical problems which are not readily comprehended except by persons having more than a passing familiarity with them. Seemingly simple and innocuous amendments dressed up and presented in appealing terms, but in fact carrying profound hidden factors often costly and adverse to the principles of sound pension policy, readily secured legislative acceptance. The fault was not the legislature's, for in the absence of authoritative and informed advice, its members by and large could not reasonably be expected to analyze and dissect the true effect of such proposals. The matter, finally, reached a critical state during the 64th General Assembly in 1945. A flood of pension proposals, new and amendatory, most of which were violative of sound principle, affecting all levels of government, descended upon that legislature. Governor Dwight Green, alarmed by the potentially destructive effect of these proposals upon the financial stability of the systems, and further cognizant of the growing nature of the problem, issued a formal statement to the General Assembly suggesting that it defer action on all pending proposals. He recommended the creation of a Pension Commission which would not only define proper principles of pension legislation, but also examine and review existing pension laws and the deferred proposals to determine their conformance or nonconformance to sound principles. The legislature heeded this suggestion and approved a measure for the establishment of the Pension Commission. Each succeeding legislature has recreated the Commission in recognition of the value of its research studies and its advisory guidance on pension proposals.

The Commission, made permanent in 1959, has 15 members, 5 each from the House of Representatives, the Senate, and by appointment by the Governor. It is rare for a proposal to be enacted if the Commission opposes it, and most of its own proposals are enacted.

[1] Public Employees Pension Laws Commission, *Report,* 1953.

It is significant that the Commission includes influential legislators and laymen and that there is high continuity of membership. The effectiveness of the Illinois Commission is partly attributable to the personalitites involved, including particularly its actuary for many years, A. A. Weinberg, whose vigorous advocacy of policy positions has had major influence. Those favoring a particular bill are careful to present their case to the Commission. Policemen and firemen have had independent influence with legislators, but on basic issues affecting their plans, the Commission's viewpoint has been influential.

The influence of the Commission is far-reaching. Its biennial report highlights the major problems of the systems and strongly expresses positions on each of them. It reviews every bill, summarizes its effect and cost, and recommends adoption or rejection. During each legislative session, it maintains for each legislator a looseleaf notebook containing Commission summaries and recommendations. The Commission is represented at practically every legislative committee meeting when pension legislation is being considered.

Public pension funds are also subject to biennial audit by the state's Department of Insurance, which requires a standardized annual report by each system, somewhat like that required of private insurance companies. The department itself also issues an annual report. These procedures have added to an atmosphere of public accountability.

Also, the Commission was effective in persuading the legislature to establish standing committees of each house to consider all pension legislation, as a way of avoiding special legislation and of encouraging coherence and continuity of policy.

The Commission has consistently worked for consolidation, more adequate funding, cost-sharing by the employees, and uniformity of benefits where possible. It has sometimes yielded on its positions. It fought against increases to already retired persons as unconstitutional grants of public funds and as steps more suitable as social-welfare measures than as part of a retirement plan. For a period of several years it opposed, but later approved, expansion of investment authority beyond government bonds. Until 1963 it approved inclusion of tax-exempt bonds in system portfolios, as a concession to the fact that many of the systems were already heavily invested in these securities.

Funding

Adequate funding has been one of the major problems of Illinois systems—as in so many other states. The statutes all require reserve funding of one kind or another—each system is supposed to get appropriations in amounts determined by actuarial calculations—but this is not always observed in practice. The Chicago area plans are funded by specific real property tax levies, described as maximums in the statute. For some of the funds the tax levy is to be fixed at a rate sufficient to produce revenues equal to a multiple, such as 1.3 or 1.5, of the expected aggregate of employee contributions. Municipalitites participating in the Illinois Municipal System are required to impose a levy sufficient to meet the normal cost of the system and amortize the municipality's unfunded accrued liability over 40 years.

Except for some of the downstate police and firemen's funds, all Illinois systems are funded, but with wide variations. The Insurance Department reports their "funded ratios," that is, assets as a percentage of the calculated accrued liabilities, but these figures are not precise since the actuarial assumptions differ from one fund to another. Nevertheless, they indicate roughly the relative position of each system running from the exceptionally high figure of 90.7 percent for the Chicago Park Department to a low of 22.8 percent for downstate police plans.

The latter figure is an aggregate for some 235 separate funds. Some of them extend only slightly beyond pay-as-you-go financing; for example, the Cicero Police Pension Fund, as of the fiscal year ending in 1970, had assets of $551,000 toward accrued liabilities of $4,804,000. It disbursed more than it took in and its assets were less than three times its annual expenditures.[2]

Taken as a whole, the Illinois systems are modestly funded. Assets are only 13 times annual benefit payments, not a high figure for systems in which a large percentage of assets derives from employee contributions. This aspect of the situation improved from 1946 to 1962 but has since remained stationary. Another indication of a comparatively low asset position is the fact that only 19 percent of in-

[2] Illinois Department of Insurance, *1971 Report of Examination, Public Employee Pension Funds* (Springfield, Illinois, 1971).

come is derived from investments, a percentage well below the national average.

The Pension Laws Commission has preached the need for consistent actuarial funding, attacking both the practice of financing on the basis of a fixed or pegged tax rate unrelated to current actuarial requirements and the inadequacy of contributions to many of the small local police and firemen's funds. It has argued repeatedly for pension contributions to be appropriated, not as a separate lump-sum, but as part of the payroll of each department and agency, a practice followed by the State Employees System. This practice spells out the relations of pension cost to payroll and avoids making pension contributions a single large target for budget cuts.

That the device does not always work was manifest in 1971, a year of almost universal fiscal difficulty. The State Employees' System was supposed to get employer contributions of 5.4 percent, but the Budget Bureau cut it down to 4.8 percent by ordering each agency to set the difference aside as a reserve. However, the employees' association and union sued and won a court order restoring the 5.4 percent rate. In the same year, the Universities System asked for $68 million based on the statutory directive to meet normal cost and interest on the unfunded accrued liability. The legislature cut this to $21 million and the Governor cut it further to $15 million. Yet in the same year the benefits of both systems were liberalized.

In an effort to rectify the most serious deficiencies, the Pension Laws Commission has proposed, as a minimum standard, what it calls a "current liability approach," which requires the maintenance of a reserve equal to accumulated member contributions and the actuarial (lifetime) value of pensions and benefits in force. This objective was not being met by the State Employees System, nor by the Chicago and state-wide teacher systems.

Consolidation

The Commission and the Insurance Department have repeatedly argued for consolidation of the 251 downstate police funds and 168 downstate firemen's funds into the Illinois Municipal System. These are very small systems, averaging 35 participants. Since they simply apply the uniform provisions of two state laws, they cannot argue accommodation to local circumstances. Their assets are separately invested and, because they are small and handled locally, large percentages are held in cash and in savings accounts. Repeated efforts to consolidate have failed because of opposition from local police, firemen, and banks.

Although the Commission favors Social Security coverage, which it regards as inevitable, most of the systems remain outside. A survey of state university personnel in 1967 found that a large percentage of employees expected to be eligible for Social Security on the basis of other employment, some of the women because of their eligibility for wives' benefits. Consequently, they were unwilling to contribute to Social Security, which remains a debated issue.

Investments

The types of investment authorized for the retirement systems have been broadened in recent years, moving from concentration on government bonds to emphasis on corporate bonds and stocks. Still, investment scope and policies differ considerably among the several systems. As of 1971, of the total assets of the Illinois funds of $2.4 billion, 23 percent ($551 million) was invested in U.S. Government bonds and 5.6 percent ($136 million) in state and municipal bonds. As discussed earlier, the latter were obviously inappropriate for a tax-exempt pension fund. Some of the Chicago area funds are extreme examples of continued adherence to an outdated investment policy. The Cook County system invested 38 percent of its assets in state and local bonds, the rest in U.S. Government obligations. The Forest Preserve System's funds were invested in state and local securities (69 percent) with the remainder in government bonds. Inappropriately high percentages of government paper were also held by the funds of the Chicago policemen, firemen, laborers, and the Park District.

For the trustees of these funds to sell those low-yield investments and switch to securities with better yields would mean that sales would have to be made at a bookkeeping loss. The mistake in avoiding change for that reason is discussed in chapter 11. A reasonable estimate, based on the situation in 1971, indicates that the Illinois systems could have increased their aggregate earnings by at least $7 million a year by trading in their federal, state, and local bonds.

The Pension Laws Commission has sought to encourage just such conversion, arguing that the merit of the decisions can be adequately explained to the public. Nonetheless, the systems for the most part have decided to wait for these bonds to mature.

The Commission was also in large measure responsible for 1969 legislation that established a centralized investment agency, the Illinois State Board of Investment, which manages the investment portfolios of state employees, judges, and the General Assembly systems. Other systems have been given the right to convey their assets to management by the board. The board consists of nine members, including the State Treasurer, the chairman of each of the three state retirement systems, and four members appointed by the governor. The board, which may invest as much as one-third of the assets in common stocks, maintains a full-time investment staff, with the advice (as of 1971) of two trust companies and two investment advisory firms. For ready handling it has created a commingled Illinois Equity Fund.

Illinois runs the gamut from sophisticated, professional central-investment management, to sizable funds that have been unable to break away from unrewarding investment in federal, state, and local bonds, to many tiny funds too small for efficient asset management.

Constitutional Guarantee

The 1970 Constitution of Illinois includes a provision that:

> Membership in any pension or retirement system of the State, any unit of local government or school district, or any agency or instrumentality thereof, shall be an enforceable contractual relationship, the benefits of which shall not be diminished or impaired.

This provision, written by a constitutional convention, was copied almost verbatim from New York's constitution of 1938. Supported by organized labor and other employee groups and by some system trustees and administrators, the clause was opposed by the Pension Laws Commission, which argued that it was too rigid, would inhibit change, and would preclude correction of errors or equitable adjustments in rates of contribution, eligibility conditions, and the like. There was one major argument in favor of the clause: the failure of the state and its municipalities to fund the systems adequately. The danger of benefit cuts because of fiscal pressure seemed a real possibility at the time.

The Commission speculated in its next report on the effects of this new development: [3]

It may be necessary for the General Assembly to resort to a policy of limiting liberalizing changes in the pension laws to periods of short duration, say one or two years, with a reexamination of the renewal thereof at the end of the prescribed period. This may prove to be a hardship to the employees or the prospective beneficiaries but it might be the only logical course of action for the General Assembly in the circumstances.

Illinois permits collective bargaining by public employees, but pensions have not become a matter for contract negotiation. This is still a subject for legislation, and the unions and associations put their efforts into lobbying.

Illinois has had one of the most effective pension commissions—a permanent body combining leading legislators with laymen. The Commission has not yet reformed Illinois pension practices to the extent it has intended, but it has been generally effective. Whether the situation is stabilized remains to be seen, particularly since Illinois public employees will undoubtedly seek to match the benefits of other large states.

[3] *Report of the Commission*, p. 69.

17 ✤ Summary of Conclusions

The most significant policy question for the public systems is how they are to be coordinated with Social Security. The question is unavoidable. If a state does not somehow coordinate its system with Social Security it will have no control over its employee retirement benefits.

Approximately 70 percent of state and local government employees are now covered by both Social Security and a staff plan. It is the combination that comprises their retirement program, yet the two are determined independently. The staff plan is fixed by state or local legislation. Its terms, virtually permanent, at least for those already employed, are with few exceptions independent of Social Security. The latter is separately shaped by Congress in answer to the needs of a different constituency—almost all of the nation's workers. How can a state or local government fulfill a chosen objective for retirement income if its pension laws are fixed independently of Social Security and Social Security is in a state of perpetual change beyond the control of the state? That question has now been crystallized, as never before, by the permanent escalation of Social Security benefits enacted in 1972.

The same question arises for the more advanced plans in private industry, but not as immediately nor as critically because the plans are less generous and somewhat more adaptable to changing circumstances.

Comparison with Private Industry

The benefit levels of the public plans are, as of January 1, 1972, approximately double those prevailing in private industry. Many of the public employees do not, however, have the dual coverage of

Social Security. When that is taken into account, the combined benefits provided to the employees of state and local government are approximately one-third higher than are provided by the plans in private industry. However, a good deal, though not all, of this advantage is balanced by the greater employee contributions which the public plans generally require. The public plans, with few exceptions, require substantial employee contributions, while 80 percent of private plans are entirely non-contributory.

Pensions in private industry are sometimes the basis for judging the merits of provisions for public employees. The comparison is relevant but far from dispositive. The public is generally prepared to provide employees with benefits it considers fair even if they exceed the prevailing levels of private industry. For example, the public readily sets aside the fact that half the workers in private industry are not covered by plans at all. Even voters who have no pension coverage themselves are willing to approve plans they consider fair for public employees. Furthermore, the public plans are older; their maturity accounts, to an extent, for their fuller benefit levels.

Continuance of Net Income

The critical issue is not a comparison between public and private plans but the prospect that many career public employees will be provided a combination of pensions and Social Security that will afford them more net income after retirement than while working.

As of January 1, 1972, one-quarter of state and local employees were covered by plans which will provide the $10,000-a-year employee retiring at 65 after thirty years of service with a pension which, combined with primary Social Security, will amount to at least 80 percent of his final year's salary. That 80 percent level is of special significance, because at that point the average retired employee of 65 is receiving at least as much net income as he took home during his last year of employment. Whether employees should receive more net income after retirement than before is bound to raise the question of public reaction.

There is no absolute standard by which retired workers can be expected to meet some specific portion of their retirement needs out of personal savings. It is therefore not out of the question, assuming the ability to pay, for a staff plan and Social Security together to provide full-career employees who are in modest income brackets with continuance of net income. But to do more is to invite public repudiation. Moving benefits from 50 to 70 percent of net income—a shift of 20 points—is a quantitative change; shifting 20 points from 90 to 110 percent is a qualitative change that is hard to justify.

An "outside limit" equal to continuance of net income may need further definition. We have, in our analysis, associated it with the employee who is 65 years of age, because that is still the most common age for retirement, and who has completed thirty years of service because in a typical work-life of forty or more years, that seems to be a fair representation of a full career. Using these figures does not imply that pensions beginning before 65 must necessarily be reduced on a fully actuarial basis nor that pensions for twenty-five years of service need necessarily be reduced in strict proportion from the thirty-year target.

It must also be recognized that a fixed-dollar benefit that continues preretirement net income for the life of the pensioner does not necessarily provide full economic security. Inflation can rob fixed dollars of their purchasing power. When a person retires from the labor market he gives up his economic bargaining power. The active employee can negotiate or resell his labor and manage sooner or later to bring his income somewhat into the line with prices. The retiree cannot. If the cost-of-living increased by 5 percent a year, a retiree of 65 is worse off on a fixed pension equal to 100 percent of net income than he would be on a pension equal to only 60 percent of that income, if the latter were fully adjusted to the cost of living. Moreover, a surviving spouse, who may have been wholly dependent on the employee, needs lifetime income too.

On the other hand, these considerations do not adequately justify pensions which, with Social Security, provide more disposable income immediately after, than before, retirement. Benefits at that sort of level will tend to induce pre-65 retirements that may be premature from the standpoint of efficient public service and a fully productive labor force. They may also overreach the goals of employee security; for example, for the unmarried employee or if the cost-of-living remains stable. Moreover, pensions providing net income greater than 100 percent reach levels where clear standards of equitable income distribution disappear. What is the proper cut-off point? If career employees in public service retire on more net income than when they last worked, the majority of the public is apt to be deeply resentful. Considering the competing claims on government, as well as protection of the pensioner against inflation and provisions for the dependent spouse, more net income for not working than for working is not a policy that can endure for long.

Future Combined Benefit Levels

There has been little public recognition as yet of the benefit levels which many of the large public systems will produce in combination with Social Security, partly because these high benefits have been reached only recently. Moreover, benefits for many of the current retirees are diminished under many of the plans by lower benefits for past service. It is the future retirees who will draw the fullest pensions.

The average person tends mentally to separate pensions and Social Security. That mind-set is bound to disappear as the total results become increasingly apparent.

The most compelling reason for coordination between staff plans and Social Security is the uncertainty of future Social Security benefits. Historically, the primary Social Security benefit for a worker earning the maximum taxable wage has replaced about 30 to 33 percent of his final wage. What the wage-replacement ratio will be in the future, under the benefit escalation formula, depends on the rate of change in real wages and, to a lesser extent, on the absolute magnitude of the changes in average wages and consumers' prices. Under the formula in effect in 1973, if wages increase 5 percent and the cost of living by 3 percent, by the year 2015 Social Security will replace 36 percent of the final wage for the worker whose earnings are at the taxable maximum, 48 percent for the worker with median earnings, and 71 percent for the low-wage worker. However, if the cost of living goes up by 4 percent, instead of 3, while wages rise by 5 percent, primary Social Security will in 2015 replace final wages by 50 percent for the employee at the top of the taxable wage, 70 percent for the median earner, and 106 percent for the low-wage worker.

On those assumptions (5 percent wage and 4 percent cost increases), when a wife's benefit is added, Social Security will by itself provide approximately 100 percent continuance of net income for the worker at the top of the wage base; the median wage-earner will receive net income 30 percent higher than before retirement; and the low-wage worker will be drawing almost double his last take-home pay.

The year 2015 sounds impossibly far off, but it is the year for which present public employee retirement laws are now irrevocably promising benefits for someone who is hired in 1975 and who retires forty years later. If these were not solemn commitments—as they are and should be—there would be nothing to be concerned about. But the benefits are now being pledged and the impact on the cost and efficiency of public service will inevitably be felt. People not yet born are now being obligated to pay the cost. Those are the facts—the problems they foretell will become more vividly visible as the 70s move into the 80s and the 80s into the 90s.

Congress can of course intervene to call a halt. Presumably it would if escalation threatened to make Social Security excessive. But at what point? Half the nation's workers are not covered by any private or staff plan and the slow movement of coverage for the past decade gives no ground for confidence that they will ever be covered by plans, at least in the absence of government mandate. That half of the country—and it is the poorest half—has only Social Security to rely on. Congress has to be responsive to that need. Adequate Social Security for those who have nothing else means Social Security that requires coordination on the part of a staff plan if it is to avoid paying, at public expense, more net income after than before retirement.

These conclusions flow from the escalation of Social Security. There is also the possibility that Social Security will be expanded in the future (as it has in the past) in ways other than simple increases in the benefit amounts—ways such as the age when full benefits are paid, the adjustment for early retirement, the benefit rights of the spouse of the employed worker, the extent of increase for postponed retirement, and in ways not yet anticipated. All these possibilities make coordination imperative.

As solutions, the broad alternatives are (1) noncoverage of public employees by Social Security, (2) accommodation of Social Security provisions to the state and local plans, or (3) accommodation of the state and local plans to Social Security.

The Merits of Social Security Coverage

Although participation in Social Security has been optional for units of state and local government, about 70 percent of the employees are now covered. Contrary to the initial misgivings of some opponents of coverage, combining Social Security and staff benefits has heightened—not diminished—the protection of state and local employees.

Whether to enter Social Security is still debated in some sections of the country. The employees that are most reluctant are teachers, policemen, and firemen. Many married women do not consider it worthwhile to contribute to Social Security if all they earn by it is the possible difference between their primary Social Security and their Social Security as wives of covered workers. Many of the male teachers and policemen and firemen count on becoming eligible for Social Security through moonlighting, summer work, or covered work before or after their non-covered employment.

Social Security has proven to be a very rewarding program, particularly when it is judged not simply by its provisions at any one time but in terms of what it has produced, through successive changes, for each generation of retirees. It provides complete continuity of coverage for those who change jobs. Part of the Social Security contribution is a payment to achieve a social purpose—a flow of income for the aged to help eliminate poverty. Moreover, it may be headed toward universal protection against catastrophic lifetime illnesses or national health insurance.

No public employees should have the privilege of exemption from the required taxation for this social program, with added burdens on others. Moreover, many, probably most, of the public employees whose jobs are not covered by Social Security expect to receive Social Security anyhow on the basis of other employment—benefits computed on the relatively liberal basis that is built into the law for those with low average covered wages.

The Social Security law should therefore be amended to include all public employees hired in the future. That change should be set for a date—such as two or three years after enactment—that would allow the time necessary for the staff pension plans to be adjusted. Such a mandatory extension should coincide with changes in the

Social Security Act giving greater incentive for participation by women workers. This legislation should also contain provisions to eliminate gaps between retirement plans and Social Security for employees not now covered by Social Security, along lines that have been recommended for federal employees.

An appropriate unit of public employees may elect to withdraw from Social Security, and some have done so. If the employee was covered for at least ten years, he continues to be insured, although he stops contributing. How a unit of employees is to evaluate such a proposal is a complex question since it involves evaluating the dynamics of change in Social Security benefits. In this connection, escalation has no doubt seriously damaged the case for withdrawal.

Nevertheless it is possible for a particular group of long-service incumbent employees to see some immediate advantages from termination, at the expense of the Social Security system and of all other workers. On the other hand, new employees are imperiled because the employment unit may not subsequently reenter the Social Security system. Moreover, if general revenues are eventually used as a major part of Social Security financing, employees who are not covered may find themselves paying for part of it anyhow.

The provision in the Social Security law permitting withdrawal ought to be revised. Employees who elect to terminate should not be eligible for future increases in benefits, such as cost-of-living adjustments. It is anomalous for benefit improvements to be automatically extended to a unit of employees who have chosen not to pay for them, after saddling the Social Security system with the expensive obligations flowing from their ten years of previous participation. A further possibility might be the imposition of a benefit decrement for each year of non-participation attributable to a decision to terminate.

Accommodation by Social Security

One possibility, bearing on coordination, would be for the federal government to mandate a minimum pension on all employers, public and private, analogous to a universal minimum wage. If the existing plan were not equal to the minimum, the employer would have to make it up either through contributions to a government fund (Social Security or other) or through a separate staff plan.

This proposal has been advanced as a way of providing more adequate old-age income for that half of the work force not covered by pensions, without adding to the benefits of those who have adequate coverage. While proposed with a view to its effects on the private sector, the idea may be relevant to the ·public staff plans as a means of avoiding excessive combined benefits.

This answer may, however, be too late for the public plans. The benefit levels they have already established, in combination with escalating Social Security, represent an existing problem. The future will only make evident what is already contained in the present statutes. It has not been suggested that any part of present Social Security be split off as the mandatory layer, leaving the remainder at a lower level than the federal law now provides; and it is highly questionable that such a reduction would be desirable or feasible.

It does not appear, then, that the problem of establishing control over the totality of benefits can be achieved by accommodation on the part of the Social Security system. In fact, it seems inappropriate, on general principles, for the larger system—Social Security—to accommodate to the peculiarities of the many federal, state and local staff plans. Coordination is the task of the states.

Accommodating a Staff Plan to Social Security

One of the traditional ways of coordinating with Social Security is an "integration" formula—one rate of benefit accrual on the part of salary subject to Social Security and a higher rate on the excess portion of salary. The ordinary form of such integration, already undermined by the successive increases voted by Congress in the wage base, has now been complicated by the automatic escalation of that base.

Another possibility is to design a staff retirement plan so that the wage base, and perhaps the formula as well, will follow every change in Social Security. Although possibly complicated, such a plan might serve to coordinate the benefit levels. A problem is that this design might not cope with other Social Security changes, such as the retirement age for full benefits, adjustments for early retirement, the amount or basis for spouse benefits, etc. It is the combined benefit, the total outcome, that must be brought under control.

Theoretically, an alternative is for state legislation to be so flexible that it can be adjusted as Social Security changes, but that would introduce too much uncertainty into future benefits to be desirable or acceptable.

A third alternative is a staff plan that would provide an all-inclusive benefit, that is, it would guarantee fulfillment of specified goals, inclusive of Social Security. For example, a staff plan could guarantee to an employee, at the completion of a full career, retirement income which, with his primary Social Security, would continue full net income. This could of course be defined to include cost-of-living adjustments and life income for a surviving spouse. The staff plan would pay whatever was necessary, after Social Security benefits, to fulfill these goals. A schedule could be included for earlier retirement benefits and for whatever scaling-down was considered appropriate for above-average salary brackets or for shorter service than twenty-five or thirty years, with commensurate paring-down of the portion of Social Security taken into account in determining the system's payments.

A plan of this kind would be radically different from prevailing practice and would no doubt involve many problems. It would certainly require a change from currently prevailing attitudes, which generally regard an employee's system benefits and his Social Security as entirely independent. Yet it has the merits of proceeding most directly toward accomplishing the intended goal of recognizing that an employee's retirement income consists both of Social Security and system benefits and that Social Security is subject to change.

More common have been plans that offset half or some other percentage of Social Security. This is more readily acceptable to employees (and to the Internal Revenue Service) because it does not offset any part of the Social Security benefit attributable to the employee's contributions. On the other hand, it is less reliable than the full offset arrangement for accomplishing the desired goal. If Social Security turns out to be different from what is assumed, a 50 percent offset plan would miss the goal—by half the difference between actual and expected Social Security. How successful that would be depends on the future variability of Social Security.

These proposals would of course be "offset" plans. Partial offsets among plans in private industry were tried in the early 1950s, then discarded, and are now being revived. However, in the 1950s the offset plan served entirely different purposes—to make a low benefit sound more generous, to justify proportionately higher benefits for the higher-paid, and to effect employer savings with each step-up in Social Security. Such an offset was relatively easy to discard in the 1950s, when to do so increased combined benefits from the equivalent of 40 percent of final net earnings to perhaps 50 or 60 percent. Now the question is 100 percent—which is an entirely different situation.

Still another variation would be a plan with a formula independent of Social Security, but subject to an overriding limitation to avoid an excessive combination.

This much is clear: when well-defined retirement objectives have to be fulfilled or specific limits observed, the features of staff plans will inevitably be pressed, one way or another, no matter what the technique or form, into a pattern complementary to the Social Security system. Current state and local plans are not at all in that mold. Their reshaping in that direction is inevitable. Considering the long-range nature of pension commitments, it will be better for the appropriate action to come sooner rather than later.

Funding

Public employee retirement systems should be funded on an actuarial basis. Pay-as-you-go arrangements encourage irresponsibility—the grant of benefits without recognition of the cost—and expose employees to the hazards of disappointment if the jurisdiction financing the system loses its ability to pay or if the taxpayers revolt against the ultimately high costs. Under pay-as-you-go plans, costs are not allocated properly for the current employment on which the benefit claims will be based.

On the other hand, public systems do not generally have to observe the same kind of funding that is desirable for private industry. With some exceptions, public plans do not have to accumulate assets against the possibility of termination. The larger the system, and the broader its jurisdiction and economic base, the more assured is its perpetual life and the less necessary is "full funding" of the sort toward which private plans are generally directed. But not every governmental unit can validly assume perpetual ability to pay. The smaller the political and economic base of the system, the less assured is its future against diminution of benefits and the more reason there is for the accrual of greater reserves.

The current funding of a public employee system should fully and honestly reflect all of its long-term costs. A fairly wide choice of funding schedules is available. Funding policy should be chosen to fulfill a desired goal or policy, not be accepted on the assumption that a single actuarial formula is inevitably correct in all cases. The formula should be one that lends itself readily to defense in legislative forums. Contribution requirements should reflect all long-term costs, and the funding basis should apply both to determination of contributions and to the realistic pricing of every proposed change. Once adopted, the funding plan should be consistently observed.

Not only funding formulas, but actuarial assumptions as well, should reflect all long-term costs. They should both apply to determination of contributions and to the pricing of proposed changes. Insofar as possible, actuarial assumptions should be explicable and defensible in legislative forums.

Some of the more important actuarial assumptions involve policy decisions. To what extent should present contributions anticipate future general salary increases? Does the answer rest on projections of future inflationary trends? If so, should these trends also be reflected in the assumed investment yield? If the answer is "no," do cost calculations based on future general salary increases mean that "hard dollars" paid in now will finance "soft-dollar" benefits to be paid out in the future?

The author's conclusions are that all future expectations should be reflected in costs, including at least minimum projections of annual changes in salary and price levels. Contributions that are a level percentage of payroll represent a fair sharing of the burden between this generation and those of the future, a judicious allocation of cost between today's "hard dollars" and tomorrow's "soft dollars."

Actuaries should more often advise those responsible for the systems and for the legislative decisions as to the variability or range of cost flowing from alternative assumptions. Policy decisions should be based on the spread of possibilities as much as on a single and therefore somewhat arbitrary projection.

Portability

From the standpoint of the employee and those employers who hope to hire a public employee away from another jurisdiction, transferability of pension credits is obviously desirable. This can be accomplished, at least in part, by liberal vesting. Vesting is particularly desirable for those in age and service brackets at which loss of accrued pension rights is a real obstacle to employment mobility. But vesting does not make the employee whole as to his pension because part of his benefit will be based on outdated salary levels, nor does vesting help the transferring employee meet the requirements for full pension eligibility in his new job.

Vesting might well be conditioned on nonwithdrawal of employee contributions. This might act as a selective device—those who value deferred benefits can hold them as vested rights; those who don't, won't.

Universal Social Security coverage, with its all-encompassing scope, would add to portability.

For transfers within a state, a statewide system provides a simple and full answer. In its absence, states should enact reciprocity laws so that each system in the state would recognize total years of public service in the state and each plan would pay a pro rata share of the total pension. If such an arrangement based the entire benefit on the employee's last final average salary, it would indeed make him whole.

Where transfers occur among federal and state agencies—whether because of joint projects or transfers of employment units from one level of government to another—full protection of pension rights should certainly be accorded.

Policemen and Firemen

Pensions for police and firemen are distinct from those for other public employees. They generally provide half of final average pay at 50 or 55 after twenty or twenty-five years of service. Some provide half pay after twenty or twenty-five years at any age. These plans are much more expensive than others. Most of these employees are not covered by Social Security—at least not on their public jobs.

In some systems, the disability provisions are overutilized, particularly for disabilities attributed to the job. In some cases, the figures are so high as to suggest that disability attributed to the job is the standard way to retire. Service-connected disability pensions are usually higher than ordinary service pensions, require a lower threshold of eligibility, and may qualify for substantial income-tax exemption.

Transferability of credits in the interest of developing a national cadre of professional public safety officers is another problem to which greater attention ought to be given.

Some of the police and firemen's plans are designed to let the men retire when they are comparatively young. Whether the plans are universally effective in that respect is questionable. Certainly, men are readier to retire in their 40s than in their 50s because earlier retirement opens the way to adequate second careers. But there is practically no distinction in these systems, as there should be, between benefits that help to effect or support a change to a second career and benefits paid for complete retirement from the labor market.

There has been a regrettable lack of attention to the particular pattern of retirement that would best serve the efficiency of a police and fire force and to what pension benefits would develop that pattern. Much could be done to bring retirement policies for police and fire departments into line with the public need for optimum efficiency in the public safety services.

Investments

Investment results play a large role in the cost of funded systems; small changes in yield have enormous leverage. Great progress has been made in the past two decades in improving investment policies and procedures, particularly by the larger systems and by agencies created for centralized investment management. Still, most of the public systems lag behind modern policies and procedures.

Many systems have been unwilling to trade bonds—even to trade in their tax-exempt and federal bonds for corporate obligations—because they have not wanted to show bookkeeping losses. That unwillingness means the actual loss of tens of millions of dollars of annual income. Sometimes the problem is lack of understanding by the trustees; in other situations, it is simply fear (not without foundation) of attack by the uninformed or politically opportunistic. System trustees should be made to understand the losses they are responsible for if they succumb to that fear. They should act as the real interests of the system require and rely on adequate defense of their actions from their investment, accounting, and actuarial advisors.

Too often, system trustees reserve buy-and-sell decisions for themselves, when they have neither the expertise to judge nor the time to react quickly enough. Their law may require them not to delegate this function. However, they should not be saddled with that responsibility if they do not have the full capacity to discharge it adequately. State laws should therefore be changed to give boards of trustees responsibility to fix overall investment policies and to see to the arrangements necessary for good management and review. That would leave them with the responsibility for choosing the professionals, whether in-house or on contract, and setting up all of the checks, balances, and reviews necessary to monitor every aspect of investment management.

Without flexible, quick-reacting investment policies and procedures public systems are in potentially dangerous positions. With a changing economy, dynamic markets, and shifting investment styles, those who lag behind are apt to lose out. The challenge, then, to the public systems is not only to catch up but also to stay abreast of the professionals in their handling of investments—a challenge which, considering the political pressures to which they are subject, is extremely difficult to meet.

Social policy issues may in the future affect the investment programs of the public systems. There have already been cases in which institutions, and sometimes pension funds, have bought or sold stock or voted proxies in line with views on corporate social policy on such matters as pollution, minorities, and military supplies. Intervention of this kind may have a good deal of political appeal—what is now an occasional incident may become a common problem.

Consolidation

Consolidating systems at a state level is worth careful consideration, particularly if it would pull together many small systems. It can serve to provide equitable though not necessarily uniform benefits, while minimizing for the future benefit competition among the various jurisdictions or employing units. Also it can provide more efficient administration and investment policies.

Uniformity versus Diversity

Uniformity of benefits within a state is desirable, but not at the expense of overlooking differences between jobs and perhaps localities that may truly justify differences in retirement policy and benefits. The ideal is a rationalized structure, rather than one that is uniform in every respect.

Collective bargaining

In the great majority of states, public pensions are not in fact collectively bargained, partly because they are legislated and partly because the retirement plan has much wider scope of coverage than the bargaining unit. Bargaining is still in the early stages of development. Where there is bargaining, a complex situation may develop. If pensions are subject to state legislation and the legislator refuses to accept automatically what an employing unit and a union have negotiated, then the collective bargain becomes no more than a collective recommendation.

Collective bargaining is one among several instruments of employee pressure for more benefits. New York's laws in the late 1960s developed, to a large extent, out of collective bargaining; California's did not. Yet, except for its substantial rate of employee contributions, California has a more liberal state employees' retirement system than does New York.

Postretirement Adjustments

Few economic situations are more frightening than being retired on a fixed income in an inflationary period, without bargaining power—collective or individual—to secure an increase.

Most public employees are covered by plans which give them automatic postretirement adjustments. (Adjustment to inflation *before* retirement is accomplished to a large extent by basing benefits on some version of final average salary.) These are certainly valuable additions to the security of the employee, an advantage that almost no employees in private industry enjoy in any comparable way.

Pensions as Contractual Guarantees

Pensions are promises which should be fulfilled; an employee counting on a pension of certain dimensions should not find at retirement that something substantially different has been substituted. That principle has been observed in the public systems, whether by law or by practice.

In some states, the principle has been embodied in a rigid rule, by constitutional provision or judicial decision, that the terms of the retirement law are a contract with each employee that may not be diminished, whether for future service or past service. A rule of that kind is difficult to live with, for it means that every word of the retirement statute is in effect written into the state's constitution. These laws are complex and unforeseen consequences are inevitable. Total inability to change, except for new employees, means that mistakes, small or large, general or specific, are made permanent.

In New York State the result has been the adoption of many amendments in the form of temporary enactments, which avoid the constitutional guarantee by requiring annual renewal. In this case, the guarantee has created its opposite. General fulfillment of commitments, without total inflexibility for the correction of errors, is preferable.

The Process of Change

The history of the public systems shows a repeated pattern. The phrases "complex patchwork" and "escalating cost" can be found in documents half a century old as easily as in yesterday's newspaper.

Plans were established at first for cohesive groups able to exert political pressure (such as police, firemen, and teachers) and then for other public employees. In time the benefits were increased; differences or inequitites became glaring. The cost impact began to be visible. These facts created at some point a wave of reform—after which new, more uniform plans were established. Then the patchwork began to accumulate once more. The cycle repeats itself.

One is tempted to compare it to the movement of a pendulum, but swings are not equal in length or timing. There is constant pressure for change from the employees, acting as large groups, small groups, or as individuals. They represent an intense and incessant interest, while the public reaction is necessarily diffuse. Only after a long accumulation of diverse changes, the emergence of heavy cost, or a strong general impression of inequity or abuse, does a demand for rationalization of the laws become effective. The rhythm of change has therefore never been uniform—the process of piecemeal change stretches over long periods of time; the process of integrating a consistent whole is relatively rare and occasional.

Nor does the pendulum of change return to some earlier status quo. Just after World War I, new systems were established for new employees. In some respects the benefits they offered were lower, but in many other respects they were more generous. And the new systems offered greater security—contributions to the earlier plans bore no relation to their costs, but the new systems were actuarially funded.

Subsequent waves of reform often substituted for patchwork a more uniform design that represented an advance for some or all of the employees. If an existing benefit was reduced, the lesser benefit provision applied only to new employees. In essence, reform has generally cured inequities and unsound financing without undoing a trend toward more adequate benefits.

Sixty years ago a professor at New York's City College could retire on half of his final pay after twenty years of service, regardless of age. He cannot do that now, even though he is covered by one of the most liberal pension plans in the country. Yet there are no proposals that the original half-pay provisions ought to be restored; there is general recognition that the overall provisions for employee security are better today than they were then.

In short, advances have not been made at the expense of earlier advances. On the whole, over the decades, there has been progress toward more adequate benefits and sounder financing.

One of the disturbing aspects of the process of change is the evidence that public employees have often had a disproportionate influence over their own retirement laws. Simple illustrations are the exemptions in many states of state and local employees from state income taxes and the favorable provisions which some state legislators have voted for themselves.

Of course, this is not the only area in which a particular interest group has had more-than-proportionate influence over legislation.

Our political life is replete with concessions to powerful industries, groups, and individuals In fact, a great deal of it is more flagrant and favors groups that are wealthier than the public employees. Still, the evidence of self-serving influence is disturbing. The author believes that the role of government is bound to expand, that public services are increasingly important, and that government intervention is a necessary counterweight to economic inequality. The larger the role of the public sector, the more important it becomes that public employment should be neither substandard nor privileged.

Rationalizing Pension Legislation

Many ideas have been tried or proposed to encourage responsibility and rational structure in pension legislation—funding, employee cost-sharing, fiscal notes for pension legislation, tax limits on unfunded liabilities, and popular referenda on pension proposals. Some have had a measure of success; others have not.

Special pension commissions—some temporary, some permanent—have often been created and with varying degrees of success. Certainly there is value in a central source of continuing analysis of pension legislation. It is the first step toward acting on principle rather than on special interest. A special pension commission can serve a major role in the creation and observance of a fair pension policy. Inclusion of legislators or high-ranking executives or their nominees may be able to win essential support. Inclusion of laymen of independent stature can help shift focus from political expediency to matters of principle. If the commission can include, or establish communication with, representatives of employees and taxpayer groups, it can profit from the stimulus of a cross-section of views.

But there is no magic formula for success. Inevitably essential is the statesman's art of combining, with judgment and integrity, the ideal with the possible. Capable individuals, rather than organizational charts, may account for those commissions which have been effective.

The history of commissions and of changes in the systems also reveals the importance of timing. Some times are ready for change; other times are not. The lesson, perhaps, is that what is perceived as necessary or desirable may also have to be judged for its timeliness.

This book has centered on major policy questions, and is therefore oriented to what the laws, as they now stand, will produce in the future. Problems have been identified, with the conclusion that public systems need new policies for the future.

Very little has been said about state and local systems that are seriously substandard. Obviously, employees in such systems have a case for improvement of their position.

Public systems have provided a reasonable measure of security in old age and disability to millions of men and women who needed it. Career public employees who have retired in recent years and who are retiring today were for many years of their lives underpaid. The same may not be true for the future, but it is nevertheless a fact of life for most of those who are pensionable now.

Moreover, public employment engages a heavily disproportionate share of older workers. Many are hired in their 40s, 50s, and even 60s. Government is in fact often the "employer of last resort." Since private pension plans began to spread on a mass basis only after 1950 and provided vesting only in the 1960s, the present generation of employees who were hired into public employment when they were middle-aged do not have multiple pension sources. They have Social Security and one public pension based, not on a career of twenty-five or thirty years but on five to twenty years of service. Still another consideration is that many of the plans provide somewhat lower benefits for "past service" (service preceding the plan or some major change). The pensions of those retiring now are therefore not quite as good as those who will be retiring in the future.

On the whole, the benefits paid by the public systems have been a major contribution to the security of several generations of men and women. New circumstances, rising levels of real wages and benefits, and a new Social Security system confront public employee pension plans with the need for redefinition of purpose and for new approaches to the accomplishment of their goals. Realization of that fact is essential and in fact inevitable. Hopefully, that recognition will occur in time to avoid present commitments to future crises of retirement policy or costs.

Index

Actuarial assumptions, 6, 19, 91, 142, 143, 148, 156, 160, 166, 171, 173, 174–91, 250, 281–83, 288, 334; conservative, 175, 183, 190–91; of mortality rate, 175–76, 282, 304–5; of new employees, 180; optimistic, 185–87; of retirement age, 177; of retirement rates, 177–78; of survivors' benefits, 180; of turnover, 176–77; wrong, 286; of zero population growth, 189; *see also* Contributions, Funding, Investment yield, Reserves

Actuarial equivalence, 35, 314, 329

Actuarial experience, 160, 175, 178, 187, 281, 282, 304

Actuarial formulas, 10, 68, 163, 167, 319, 349; disability benefits, 178

Actuarial gains, 159, 161, 165, 175, 188, 250

Actuarial increases, 13

Actuarial liabilities, 203

Actuarial losses, 149, 153, 157, 158, 159, 161, 165, 166, 175, 183, 188, 190, 282

Actuarial projections, 281; fixed-period, 159–60

Actuarial reductions, 42, 242, 288

Actuarial Society of America, 265

"Actuarial soundness," 165, 166, 255

Actuarial valuations, 188

Age discrimination, 86

Alaska: S.S. coverage in, 100

American Federation of State,

County, and Municipal Employees, 279

Annuities, variable, 43–45, 250, 276

Arizona: benefit formula in, 13; post-retirement adjustments in, 250

Assets, *see* Reserves

Bankers Trust Company Survey, 18, 27, 32, 43, 49

Benefit accrual rates, 12, 124, 143, 147, 148, 149, 177, 178, 193, 194, 266, 304, 346; longevity step-rate, 22, 26; money-purchase annuity, 25, 31, 266; pension-plus-annuity, 22; percentage-of-pay, 22; single-rate, 24, 26, 29, 30; step-rate, 22, 24, 29, 30; years of service, 25, 29, 31, 195

Benefit and withdrawal payments, 171, 172

Benefit changes, pricing, 155–56, 160, 161–62, 163, 167–68, 181, 190, 257, 286–89

Benefit disbursements, 133, 140, 141, 142, 143, 153, 154, 166; annual, 168, 169, 171; *see also* Contributions, ratio to disbursements; Reserves, ratio to disbursements; Revenues, ratio to disbursements

Benefit formulas, 7, 9, 10, 12, 13, 50, 75, 93, 102, 155, 199, 200, 240, 249, 263, 275, 330; career-average, 7, 19, 20–21, 22, 28, 29, 124, 242, 249, 296; current service, 52, 53, 68,

Benefit formulas (*Continued*)
168; final average salary, 18–19, 20, 21, 22, 23–27, 28, 30–31, 32, 50, 101, 102, 103, 124, 126, 127, 177, 182, 195, 198, 199–200, 201, 242, 246, 266, 267, 268, 271, 275, 286, 290, 296, 297, 298, 299, 300, 310, 311, 312, 314, 315, 321, 328, 330, 350, 353; final-salary, 18, 22, 51, 127, 178, 241, 246, 249, 262, 268, 274, 275, 276, 278, 286, 287, 289, 290, 294, 308, 315, 316, 317, 323, 331, 355; fixed, 123, 249, 267, 275, 328; fixed-dollar, 21, 82, 341; fixed-percentage, 48; flat-dollar, 19, 249; for early retirement, 35; integration, 26, 124–30, 248–49; money-purchase, 7, 19, 20, 21, 25, 34, 68, 196, 266, 267, 270, 275, 290, 319, 321, 328; past service, 52, 68, 112; pension-plus-annuity, 19, 20, 27, 45, 48, 275; percentage-of-pay, 21, 62–63, 64, 65, 66, 67, 71, 127, 180, 189, 264n, 279, 286, 310, 329; single-rate, 22, 23; step-rate, 23–26, 45, 101, 103, 124, 129, 329–30

Benefit levels, 7, 9–50, 62–63, 67, 76, 78, 80, 128, 132, 133, 160, 179, 245, 277–79, 293, 325, 339, 340, 341, 342–43, 346, 357

Benefit liability, 160, 169, 267, 299; accrued, 149, 150, 151–52, 154, 155, 156, 157, 161, 165, 281, 334; "commuted value," 142; current service, 157, 161; "discounted value," 142; frozen initial, 159; future service, 160, 216, 253, 255, 267; normal cost, 150, 151, 152, 153, 154, 155, 159, 161, 322, 334, 335; past service, 149, 150, 151, 157, 161, 165, 253; past service amortized, 163; "present value," 142, 147–48, 149, 151, 152, 157, 158, 159, 285, 301, 302; prior ser-

vice, 161, 302; supplemental, 149, 150, 151, 152, 159, 161, 162, 165, 261, 277; unamortized frozen, 162; unfunded accrued, 3, 137, 151, 152, 153, 155, 156, 160, 162, 165–66, 167, 190, 257, 282, 316, 322, 334, 335, 356; unfunded present value, 158, 160–63, 167

Benefit liberalization, 7, 23, 103, 133, 134, 154, 157, 158, 166, 171, 178, 194, 268, 269–70, 272–73, 284, 285, 291, 294–95, 301, 309, 321, 322, 324, 328, 335, 338

Benefit payments, *see* Benefit disbursements

Benefits, 142, 159, 172, 201, 257; adjusted to S.S., 11, 12, 13, 23–27, 40, 126; and increasing salaries, 20, 43, 44, 154, 157, 240, 241, 251, 315; as percent of payroll, 139; average, 53–69; current service, 11, 86; death, 10, 40, 41, 42–43, 176, 228–31, 268, 270, 271, 281, 282, 288, 291, 296, 297, 298, 310, 311; death, after retirement, 11, 40, 41–42, 175, 199, 281, 282; deferred, 36, 38, 193, 195, 196, 201, 296, 350; disability, 10, 37, 38–39, 80, 102, 103, 179, 199, 223, 228–31, 235–36, 237, 238–39, 254, 262, 263, 264, 268, 276, 286, 296, 297, 307, 315, 316, 319, 322, 324, 328, 331, 350–51, 357; disability, job-connected, 10, 39–40, 179, 223, 228, 235–36, 238–39, 297, 315, 317; early retirement, 13, 32–36, 37, 103, 129, 226, 279, 296, 310, 313, 314, 321, 328, 329, 346, 347; eligibility for, 14, 15, 16, 34, 38, 41, 179, 195, 199, 224, 240, 276, 290, 301, 315, 319, 322, 337, 346, 350; full, 67, 85, 86, 177, 178, 242, 268, 296, 298, 324, 339, 346; future service, 11, 21, 160, 255–56, 304, 354; high, 60–61, 342; joint-and-survivor, 10–11, 41, 42, 242, 305; low, 60–61; lump-sum, 11, 40, 42, 193, 196, 247, 262, 309, 311; medium, 103, 104, 345; normal retirement, 10, 12, 37, 39, 179, 224, 315; past service, 20, 52, 86, 149, 152, 159, 319, 354, 357; postponed-retirement, 13, 20, 177, 274; post-retirement adjustments, 7, 11, 43–45, 50, 126, 127, 133, 154, 184, 231–32, 249–51, 276, 297, 299, 329, 330, 333, 353; purchasing power of, 82; self-interest in determining, 2–3, 5, 242, 355–56; survivors', 40–42, 82, 83, 84, 103, 126, 127, 129, 180, 223, 228, 231, 237, 271, 297, 315, 321, 328–29, 330–31, 341, 342, 347; uniform, 244, 245, 273, 313, 320, 321, 322, 324, 325–26, 327, 333, 352, 353; vested, 10, 36–38, 50, 85, 101, 103, 123, 160, 161–62, 176, 193, 194–96, 200, 201, 202, 225–27, 242, 243, 247, 276, 291, 296, 297, 307, 331, 350, 357; without S.S., 28–32, 51, 52, 53, 55, 62, 119, 278, 315, 329, 339–40; with S.S., 23–28, 29, 50, 51, 52, 53, 55, 60, 61, 63, 64, 65, 66, 67, 68, 76, 84, 88, 103, 123, 127, 223, 240, 242–43, 277, 278, 279, 298, 299, 329, 330, 339, 341, 342–43, 357; *see also* Cost of living, benefit adjustments to; Retirement income; Wage-replacement ratios

Board of Education Retirement system (N.Y.C.), 261, 283, 285

Board of Estimate (N.Y.C.), 281

"Buck Plan," 265

California, 257; collective bargaining in, 253, 353; contractual rights in, 254; funding in, 131; investment policy in, 218, 219; legislators' pensions in, 243; police-firemen in, 79, 237, 254, 257; S.S. coverage in, 100, 111; water and power employees in, 35

Career Retirement Plan (N.Y.S.), 293, 294, 295–96, 300, 302, 307

Cash and security holdings, 171, 172, 336

Civil Service Employees Association, 295

Civil service system, 176

"Coalition bargaining," 311

Collective bargaining, 3, 39, 56, 82, 178, 246, 247, 251–53, 256, 259, 269, 273, 274, 279–80, 292–94, 305, 310, 311, 338, 353

College Retirement Equity Fund, 196; investment policy of, 218, 219

Colorado: S.S. coverage in, 100

Commission on Old-Age Pensions, Annuities, and Insurance (Landmark Report), 317–19

Commission on Payments (N.Y.), 135–36

Commission on Pensions (N.Y.C.), 262, 263–64

Commission on Pensions (N.Y.S.), 289, 311

"Compensation," 275

Congress, 8, 45, 88, 89, 93, 105, 108, 119, 121, 122, 154, 248, 255, 339, 343, 346

Connecticut: funding in, 131; S.S. coverage in, 100

Consumer Price Index, 11, 43, 44, 45, 88, 89, 92, 184, 231, 250, 276, 315, 330

Contribution level, 152, 153, 158, 160, 161, 164, 166, 174, 203, 268, 325

Contribution liability: "present value," 142–43

Contribution rate schedule, 45–48, 127, 132, 137, 138, 139, 140, 141, 142, 143, 148, 149, 151, 152, 153, 158, 160, 161, 164, 167, 171, 182, 184, 191, 255, 266, 267, 268–69,

Contribution rate schedule (*Cont.*) 271, 281, 283, 286, 288, 295, 300, 302, 303, 328, 332, 337, 349

Contributions, 187, 335; accumulated, 142, 266, 316; actuarial assumptions and, 184, 190–91, 282, 283, 288, 349, 355; as percent of benefit, 277, 316; as percent of pay, 11, 45, 135, 141, 150, 158, 162, 164, 167, 181, 190, 238, 245, 264, 266, 268, 270, 276, 279, 284, 319, 323, 328, 330, 335, 349; current service, 147, 148; employee, 7, 11, 19, 20, 40, 45–48, 50, 60, 64, 65, 66, 67, 71, 76, 115, 119, 120, 126, 132, 133, 135, 142, 145, 147, 150, 152–53, 155, 157, 159, 161, 168, 170, 172, 193, 196, 197, 200, 215, 223, 232–33, 241, 242, 253, 261, 262, 263, 264, 266, 267, 268, 269, 270, 272, 276, 285, 287, 289, 290, 295, 296, 297, 301, 306, 315, 316–17, 318, 321, 322, 325, 328, 330, 333, 334, 335, 340, 347; erratic, 143; future, 133, 134, 135, 161, 175; government-employer, 7, 8, 20, 57–60, 127, 152–53, 159, 161, 163, 168, 169, 170, 172, 182, 191, 197, 215, 247, 261, 266, 270, 283, 284, 288, 290, 296, 306, 312, 316, 317, 323, 326, 328, 335, 345; insufficient, 161, 335; matching, 319, 322, 325; past service, 147, 148–50, 245; postponed, 282, 283; ratio of government to employee, 170, 172; ratio to disbursements, 169, 172, 325; reduced, 157, 190, 203, 270, 283; step-rate, 48; systematic, 136; "take-home-pay," 287, 288, 291, 293, 306; tax-exempt, 248; total, 8, 156, 161; uniform, 245; withdrawal of, 10, 38, 193, 195–96, 201, 350

Corporation Counsel (N.Y.C.), 275

Cost of living, 7, 43, 82, 83, 90, 93, 94, 126, 250, 297, 310, 341, 342; benefit adjustments to, 43, 44, 45, 79, 82, 182, 276, 294, 297, 298, 300, 306, 311, 315, 341; *see also* Social Security, automatic cost-of-living escalation

Delaware: funding in, 131

Demogrant, 115

Disability, definition of, 179; *see also* Benefits, disability

Disability insurance, 39

District of Columbia: police-firemen, 179, 239

Education Association (Wash.), 136

Employee Benefit Security Act of 1974, 165

Employees, 136, 194; active, 132, 138, 151, 153, 154, 155, 157, 160, 168, 180, 189, 269, 271, 272, 281, 284, 324, 339, 341, 357; career, 51, 119, 121, 125, 128, 279, 299, 310, 330, 341, 342, 345, 347, 357; federal, 8, 45, 100, 118, 119–21, 193, 345; future, 121, 269, 272, 288, 344; middle-aged, 86, 180, 193, 236, 299, 357; new, 114, 119, 120, 121, 137, 152, 162, 180, 197, 269, 270, 271, 284, 288, 290, 304, 305, 310, 313, 318, 345, 354, 355; older, 121, 151, 152, 179, 180, 189, 193, 269, 288, 298–99, 350, 357; ratio of retired to active, 154, 169, 236, 283–84, 301, 303; retired, 82, 142, 151, 153, 154, 155, 162, 168, 170, 341, 342, 353; second-career, 177–78, 233, 274, 316, 336, 344, 351; short-service, 118, 119, 120, 179, 271, 310, 315, 330, 331, 347; women, 192, 328, 336, 344, 345; young, 85, 151, 189, 193, 299, 331; *see also* Contributions, employee; Turnover

Employees' Retirement System

(N.Y.C.), 246, 261, 271, 281, 283, 284, 285

Employees' Retirement System (N.Y.S.), 7, 133, 214, 246, 260–61, 289, 291, 292, 293, 294, 295–97, 300, 301, 302, 307

Employees' System (Ill.), 327, 330, 331, 335

Employer of last resort, 86, 180, 189, 298, 357

Executives, 241–42, 356

Federal Civil Service Retirement System, 100, 110, 119, 153, 154, 156, 195, 315

Federal Employee Retirement Income Security Act of 1974, 50, 201–2

Federal Employees' Health Benefits, 120, 121

Federation of Taxpayers Association (Mass.), 323

Financial rations, 168–73

Financing, *see* Funding

Fire Department Pension Fund (N.Y.C.), 261, 269, 281, 284, 285

Firemen, *see* Police-firemen

Florida: contractual guarantee in, 254; investment restrictions in, 204

Funded position, 286, 303–4

"Funded ration," 334

Funding, 131–73, 176, 257, 259, 267, 269, 293, 309, 333, 334–35, 337, 348–50, 356; actuarial, 131, 132, 136, 141–63, 180, 190–91, 284, 286, 290, 322, 323, 334, 335, 348, 355; additional, 164–65; advance, 132; aggregate, 145, 147, 157–58, 159, 190, 281, 283, 300, 302, 334; amortized, 144, 145, 146, 147, 149, 150, 151, 152, 153, 154, 155, 156, 157, 158, 165, 171, 190, 281, 283, 302, 334; attained-age-normal, 145, 147, 157, 159; by deferring to future, 1, 2, 3, 6, 52, 131, 134, 135,
136, 137, 181, 256–57, 343, 349; by earmarking special taxes, 131, 135, 263, 328, 334; cash-disbursement, basis for, 326; court action requiring, 166; "deferred annuity," 150; enforcing responsibility in, 134–35, 168, 256–57, 348; entry-age-normal, 144–45, 146–47, 150–51, 152, 153, 156, 157, 158, 159, 161, 167, 277, 300; fixed-period amortized, 156, 158, 159; full, 164–68, 190–91, 202, 303, 348; inadequate, 136, 222, 264, 282, 289, 290, 332; individual level premium, 157, 158, 159; interest-only, 144, 146, 150, 153–56, 167, 322; level percentage of pay, 167; long-term, 132, 143, 349; pay-as-you-go, 3, 6, 131, 132–41, 143, 144, 146, 171, 172, 173, 202, 237–38, 313, 323, 325, 326, 334, 348; perpetually amortized, 156–57, 159, 162; perpetually level, 161; shortcomings of interest only, 153–56, 161–62; short-term, 132; "single premium," 150; stepped-up, 154; terminal, 142–48, 159; unamortized, 155; unit credit, 144, 145, 146, 147–48, 149, 150, 152, 159

Funding developments, 283–86

Funding formulas, 142, 160–63, 171, 190, 191, 349

Funding goals, 141, 142, 152, 153, 160, 161, 162, 163, 166, 171, 190, 349

Funding methods, 163–68, 174, 180, 283; slow-down in, 284; traditional, 163–64, 167

Funding policy, 141, 142, 155, 156, 158, 163, 164, 166–68, 172, 174, 270, 349; long-term, 164, 167, 168, 349

Funding requirements, 202

Funding schedule, 133, 141, 144–45, 148, 152, 154, 156, 163, 165, 167,

Funding schedule (*Continued*)
172, 190, 237, 280, 283, 285, 300, 349
Funding standards, 165

General Assembly System (Ill.), 327
Grady Law, 262, 263

Hawaii: investment policy in, 216–17, 220
Health insurance, 105, 108; *see also* Social Security
"Home rule," 7, 251, 261

Illinois, 327–38; benefit accrual rate in, 22–23, 195; benefit pattern in, 329–31; consolidation of plans in, 245, 333, 335–36; contractual guarantee in, 254, 337–38; development of pension system, 328–29; funding in, 334–35, 337; investment management in, 213, 336–37; judges in, 329, 330, 331; legislators in, 329, 330, 331; pension commissions in, 258, 259, 327, 328, 331–33, 335; pension portability in, 199, 331; pension uniformity in, 327; police-firemen in, 245, 259, 327, 329, 330, 331, 334, 335; post-retirement adjustments in, 45; S.S. coverage in, 100, 329, 336; teachers in, 327, 328, 329, 331
Indiana: employee contributions in, 48
Inflation, 20, 32, 77, 82, 141, 178, 181, 183, 184, 190, 249, 251, 271, 275, 293, 341, 342, 349, 353; cost effects of, 183
Intergovernmental Relations, Advisory Commission on, 200–1
Internal Revenue Code, 127, 247–49
Internal Revenue Service, 163, 247, 248, 347
Investment committees, 211–12, 214, 325

Investment counsel, 212, 214
Investment decisions, 212, 213, 215, 220, 221, 250, 337, 352
Investment earnings, 188–90, 196; *see also* Investment yield
Investment management, 203, 204, 220, 337, 351; corruption in, 217; evaluation of, 213, 215, 217, 220, 221, 351; inactive, 210–11, 221; nonprofessional, 211–13; professional, 213–15, 220, 221, 337
Investment policy, 203–21, 325, 336, 351, 352, 353; and social policy, 217–19, 352; conservative, 210; flexible, 213, 352; improvement of, 220; local pressures on, 216–17; speculative, 204, 210
Investment procedures, 203–21, 351, 352
Investments, 257, 324–25, 351–52; "approved list" of, 212, 214, 215; bond-swapping, 206–10, 212, 221, 351; changes in, 204, 336–37; concentration of, 213; disclosure of, 213, 217; due diligence in, 215; fixed-income, 187, 203, 209, 215, 216, 220; in bonds, 43, 141, 186, 204, 205, 206–10, 214, 215–16, 336; in equities, 187–88, 196, 203–4, 214, 215–16, 220, 325, 328, 336, 337; in mortgages, 205, 210, 214, 215, 216–17; in tax-exempt bonds, 204, 205–6, 214, 333, 336, 351; performance analysis of, 215–16; portfolio turnover of, 204, 211; restrictions on, 203, 204, 219–20, 221, 325, 337
Investment staff, 214
Investment trustees, 216, 217, 336, 351–52; authority of, 211, 352; boundaries of, 220; function of, 220; responsibility of, 209–10, 211, 213, 221, 352
Investment yield, 137, 139–40, 142, 148, 159, 167, 168, 170, 172, 174,

183, 184–89, 203, 205–6, 215, 247, 250, 335, 336, 349, 351; actuarial assumptions of, 183–89, 216, 302, 304

Iowa: investment policy in, 218

Judges: pensions for, 3, 7, 12, 68, 240, 241, 248, 295, 317, 329, 330
Judges' System (Ill.), 327

Kentucky: pension portability in, 199; S.S. coverage in, 100

Labor, N.Y.S. Dept. of, 32, 45, 52, 53, 55, 56, 60
Labor Statistics, U.S. Bureau of, 17, 22, 52, 68, 79
Landmark Report, *see* Commission on Old-Age Pensions, Annuities, and Insurance
"Leapfrogging," 3, 252, 275
Legislators: pension portability of, 198; pensions for, 2, 5, 7, 12, 68, 240, 242–43, 295, 312, 323, 329, 330, 355, 356; staff members of, 2–3
Louisiana: S.S. coverage in, 100

Maine: S.S. coverage in, 100
Massachusetts, 313–26; benefit formulas in, 35; consolidation of plans in, 7, 245; contractual guarantee in, 254, 323–24; development of system, 316–19; employee contributions, 322; funding in, 6, 131; general workers in, 324–25; investment policy in, 218, 325; investment restrictions in, 325; judges' pensions in, 317; legislators' pensions in, 243, 313, 323; pension commissions in, 1, 258, 259, 317–19, 320, 322–23, 328; pension portability in, 199; pension reserves, 325; police-firemen in, 314, 315, 316–17, 320, 323, 324; S.S.

coverage in, 100; teachers in, 313, 317, 319, 323, 324; veterans in, 314–15
Michigan: pension portability in, 199; S.S. coverage in, 102–3
Military service, 255; age of employees, 189, 222; credit for, 295, 296, 314–15; disability pensions, 179; pension portability, 197
Minimum wage, 115, 122, 345
Minnesota: automatic postretirement adjustments in, 43, 250; contribution rates in, 48; pension commissions in, 258; police-firemen in, 237; teachers in, 21
Mississippi: investment restrictions in, 204; postretirement adjustments in, 250
Missouri: contribution rate in, 48; S.S. coverage in, 23, 100
"Mobile Teachers Bill," 200
Modified cash refund, 42
Moore Committee, 292–95
Municipal Employees' Fund (Chicago), 206, 329, 330
Municipal Manpower Commission, 192–93
Municipal Retirement System (Ill.), 327, 331, 334, 335

National Council on Teacher Retirement, 200
National Education Association, 200
National Health and Welfare Retirement Fund, 196
Negative income tax, 115, 116
Nevada: S.S. coverage in, 100
New Jersey, 138; funding in, 6; investment management in, 213; pension commissions in, 328; postretirement adjustments in, 250
New Mexico: investment management in, 213
New York City, 7, 42, 49, 89, 134, 138, 261–89; actuarial foundation of

New York City (*Continued*)
plans, 281–83; benefit levels in, 277–79; collective bargaining in, 251–52, 279–80; development of plans, 261–69; funding in, 267–68, 280–81, 283–86; health workers in, 262, 263; investment policy in, 218; pension policy in, 286–89; police-firemen in, 237, 262, 264, 265, 269, 271, 273, 274, 276, 277, 278, 287, 294, 307; sanitation men in, 49, 262, 263, 264, 273–74, 277, 278, 287, 288, 311; teachers in, 262, 264, 265, 269, 271, 276, 277, 278, 289, 308; transit workers in, 274–76, 278, 286, 308, 311

New York City Actuary, 281, 282, 286, 287, 288

New York State, 174, 289–312; benefit accrual rate in, 195; collective bargaining in, 253, 292–94, 353; contractual guarantee in, 254, 256, 304–7, 312, 337, 354; development of plans, 289–92; funding, 6, 134, 300–4; investments in, 214; legislators' pensions in, 243, 295, 300; pension benefits in, 35, 36, 43, 56, 295–98; pension commissions in, 258, 259, 289, 292–95, 310, 319, 328; pension portability in, 194, 198; police-firemen in, 237, 278, 290, 294, 299–300, 301, 310, 311; retirement patterns in, 298–300; tax-exempt pensions in, 244, 307; teachers in, 278, 289, 299, 311

Ohio: pension commissions in, 258; S.S. coverage in, 100

Oregon: investment management in, 213; postretirement adjustments in, 250

Patronage system, 176

Pennsylvania: benefits in, 23, 42; collective bargaining in, 252; consolidation of plans in, 245; funding in, 168; legislators' pensions in, 242; turnover rate in, 176

Pension commissions, 1, 135, 192–93, 200, 219, 257–59, 262, 280, 289, 292–95, 310, 317–19, 320, 322–23, 327, 328, 331–33, 335, 338, 356

Pension forfeiture, 193

Pension legislation, 1, 2, 3, 7, 8, 88, 201, 256, 258, 261, 273, 274, 276, 280, 289, 290, 292, 293, 297, 298, 305, 309, 312, 316, 317, 319, 320, 322, 331, 332, 339, 343, 353, 356

Pension management, 142, 257, 300, 324–25, 353; evaluation of, 325; locally administered, 5, 6, 14, 15, 16, 169, 170–71, 172, 205, 222, 317, 323, 327; of personnel, 80–81, 179, 193–94, 234–35, 239, 308, 318, 341, 351; state-administered, 5, 6, 7, 14, 15, 16, 169, 170–71, 172, 205, 222, 238, 244, 317, 323

Pension policy, 1–8, 67, 76, 78, 125, 141, 142, 189, 234–37, 241–59, 286–89, 292, 313, 330, 332, 333, 342, 349, 351, 356, 357

Pension portability, 192–202, 238, 350, 351; federal intervention in, 200, 344; fund transfers, 198–99; interstate, 198, 200, 350; intrastate, 197–98, 200, 315–16, 331, 350; reciprocity, 198–200, 201, 350; recommendations, 200–2; unilateral credits, 197

Pension reform, 263–65, 270–73, 321, 354–56; difficulty of, 2, 4, 81

Pension Reform Act of 1974, 38

Pensions, private, 5, 9, 53, 56, 57, 77, 121, 248, 270, 291, 357; actuarial assumptions for, 184; benefit formulas for, 21–22, 27–28, 49, 50, 60, 75, 266, 348; benefit levels for, 67, 78, 129, 269, 271, 339, 348; cost of, 4, 299; death benefits in, 43; deferred benefits in, 17; disability benefits in, 39; early retirement for, 35–36; employee contributions for, 27, 48–49, 50, 57, 67, 340; employer contributions to, 27, 60, 215; federal legislation, 122; final base pay, 32; for high-salaried employees, 76, 348; for low-salaried employees, 75–76; funding for, 122, 123, 132, 137, 138, 163, 165, 348; funding goals of, 165; funding policy of, 163, 164; integrated plans to S.S., 100, 122–23, 128, 129; investments of, 208, 210, 215, 217, 221; mandatory minimum funding of, 165; portability of, 192, 197; postretirement adjustments of, 249, 353; reserves, 168; retirement age in, 17–18, 32; vesting of benefits in, 17, 38, 50, 86, 122, 123, 194; wage-replacement ratio in, 61; with S.S., 75, 122–23, 339, 347–48; workers covered, 49, 56–57, 78–79, 86, 94, 122, 340, 343, 346

Pensions, public, 56, 152, 163, 166; accountability to public, 333; actuarial assumptions for, 184; actuarial reserves for, 264, 265–68; and low salaries, 79–80; and taxpayers, 2, 3, 4, 82, 136, 137, 257, 356; and voters, 2, 4, 5, 78, 79, 252, 312, 340; "closed systems," 12, 263; consolidation of, 8, 194, 200, 201, 244–47, 270, 291, 333, 335–36, 352–53; contractual guarantee of, 3–4, 7, 119, 136, 137–38, 253–56, 268, 272, 304–7, 312, 318, 323–24, 337–38, 354; coordinated plans to S.S., 100, 102, 103, 330, 338, 342, 343, 344, 345, 346–48; cost accounting, 139–40, 320, 330; court action affecting, 254–55; current expenditures, 132, 159; development of, 5–7, 85, 260–69, 289–91, 316–17, 325; immature plans, 154;

insurance contract underwriting of, 157, 159; integrated with S.S., 118–19, 122–30, 346; mandatory coverage, 7, 319, 320–21, 328, 345; mature systems, 132, 138, 139, 153–54, 161, 169; membership of, 6, 8, 303; noncontributory, 316–18, 320, 322; number of plans, 3, 5, 6; occupational groups in, 5, 6, 7, 8, 196–97, 198, 247, 261, 266, 270, 274, 275, 294, 324, 330, 333, 354; offset plans to S.S., 100, 102, 103, 119, 127, 128, 129, 249, 269, 330, 347; "over-mature" systems, 154, 161; "patchwork," 1, 259, 290, 292, 320, 322, 354, 355; pressures on, 3, 8, 82, 129, 163, 164, 171, 216–17, 240, 247, 253, 257, 259, 262, 273, 291–92, 311, 324, 333, 337, 353, 354; proliferation of, 8, 246–47, 291–92; supplementary plans to S.S., 100, 101; tax-exempt, 244, 307, 316, 336, 351; voluntary coverage, 7, 116, 328; workers covered, 49, 222; young systems, 169

Pensions, universal, 85, 115

"Permanent School Pension Fund" (Boston), 317

Police-firemen, 6, 8, 43, 169–70, 244, 246, 247, 307, 316, 329, 330, 333, 334, 335, 354; collective bargaining, 253; compulsory retirement, 227, 235; death benefits, 228–31; death benefits, job-connected, 228; disability benefit eligibility, 230; disability benefits, 223, 228–31, 235–36, 237, 238–39, 316, 350–51; disability benefits, job-connected, 179, 223, 228, 235–36, 238–39, 317, 351; early retirement, 236, 237, 314, 321, 324; early retirement benefit eligibility, 226; early retirement benefits, 225–27, 310; employee contributions, 223,

Police-firemen (*Continued*)
232–33, 264, 269, 316–17, 335;
moonlighting, 108, 233, 234, 316,
344; normal retirement benefit
eligibility, 224; normal retirement
benefit formulas, 223, 225, 226,
235, 239; normal retirement
benefits, 223–25, 236, 238, 239,
275, 311; pension cost, 237–38;
pension plans for, 7, 12, 68, 108,
222–40, 269, 290, 291, 320,
350–51; pension portability, 197,
198, 200, 238, 351; postretirement
increases, 231–32; ratio of retired
to active employees, 169, 236, 284;
retirement age of, 80, 84, 170, 224,
228, 235, 263, 314, 351; retirement
patterns of, 299–300, 351; retirement policy of, 234–37; second-
careers, 233, 234, 236–37, 239,
240, 265, 351; S.S. coverage of, 97,
108, 223, 228, 233–34, 344, 350;
survivors' benefits, 223, 228, 231,
237, 315; vesting, 225–27, 331;
vesting eligibility, 227; wage-
replacement ratio, 228
Policemen's and Firemen's Fund
(N.Y.S.), 214, 246, 260, 294, 297,
301
Police Pension Fund (N.Y.C.), 261,
269, 281, 283, 284, 285
"Prudent-man rule," 204
Public Employee Pension Law Commission (Ill.), 331–33, 335, 336–37,
338
Public Employee Relations Act, 252
Public Employees' Retirement System
(Calif.), 12–13, 40, 185, 213–14
Public Employees' Retirement System
(Ohio), 13*n*
Public Employees' Retirement System
(S.Dak.), 49
Public opinion, 4, 78, 164
Puerto Rico, 11; benefit accrual rate
in, 195; investment policy in,

216–17; police-firemen in, 233;
S.S. coverage in, 97, 100

Reserve funding, 132–33, 136, 334
Reserve position, 155, 163, 334
Reserves, 134, 136, 151, 153, 154,
158, 159, 160, 167, 312, 324–25,
335–36; accumulated, 164, 166,
168, 191, 349; actuarial, 131, 326;
as percent of disbursements, 154,
302, 334; contingency, 132, 138;
modest, 143; ratio to disbursements, 168–69, 171, 172, 284, 285,
301, 303, 334
Retirement age, 51–52, 157, 177, 255,
263, 264, 268, 286, 290; compulsory, 10, 32, 80, 177, 227, 235, 298,
313, 319; early, 10, 38, 50, 51, 80,
81, 125, 176, 178, 179, 311, 313,
321, 328, 332; normal, 9, 12–16,
20, 38, 45, 49–50, 51, 80, 84, 85,
125, 157, 170, 177, 179, 224, 228,
235, 263, 267, 279, 296, 297, 311,
313, 314, 321, 324, 329, 341, 351;
postponed, 84, 117, 125; trends in,
16, 34–35; voluntary, 319
Retirement Fund (Wis.), 21
Retirement income, 85, 86, 125, 133,
256, 269, 283; and work-related
expenses, 74; as percent of final
income, 70–74, 75, 76, 78, 81, 83,
84–85, 86, 93, 125, 243, 265–66,
269, 272, 279, 298, 299, 300, 310,
316, 321, 340, 341, 347; from personal savings, 75, 76–78, 79, 340;
from S.S., 75, 77, 78, 85, 279, 310,
340, 342–43, 347; goals, 74, 78, 81,
93, 94, 126, 127, 132, 266, 310, 339,
341, 347, 357; limits, 74, 81–83,
182, 311, 341; more-than-net-pay,
83, 93, 242, 272, 277–79, 340, 341,
342; sources, 88, 272; total, 126,
267, 272, 279, 298, 339, 347
Retirement Law Commission (Mass.),
322–23

Retirement security, 5, 76–78, 82, 105, 113, 126, 135–37, 138, 158, 161, 166, 168, 170, 173, 268, 276, 307, 341, 344, 355, 357
Retirement System (Maine), 43
Retirement System (S.C.), 194
Retirement Systems' Reciprocal Act (Ill.), 331
Return of reserve, 42, 288, 311
Rhode Island: benefit accrual rate in, 195; legislators' pensions in, 243

Safety officers, *see* Police-firemen
Salary: final average, 68, 125; increasing, 269, 342, 357; terminal, 68
Salary levels: actuarial assumptions of, 183–84, 190, 349; high, 51, 55, 61, 62–63, 65, 71, 75, 91–93, 127, 128, 249, 278, 342, 343, 347; low, 26n, 51, 55, 60, 61, 62–63, 66, 67, 71, 75, 91, 92, 105, 109, 110, 114–15, 118, 127, 128, 249, 342, 343; medium, 51, 62–63, 64, 67, 70, 71, 90–91, 92, 109, 341, 342, 343
Salary projections, 174, 180–82, 183, 286
Sick leave, 296, 309
Social Security (S.S.), 21, 23, 39, 51, 57, 69, 194; accommodation by, 345–46; administrative costs of, 105; and public employees, 7, 94–95, 96–100, 101, 269, 271, 272, 291, 293, 313, 316, 336, 339, 343, 344; as insurance, 105, 106, 114, 115; as welfare, 100, 105, 106, 114, 115, 118; automatic cost-of-living escalation, 88, 89, 90, 91, 93, 94, 105, 107, 110, 117, 123, 124, 125, 339, 342, 343, 345, 346; benefit formula, 70, 88, 94, 103, 109, 112, 114, 330, 342; benefit schedule, 89, 105, 106, 116, 139; cash-benefit program, 120; contribution schedule, 139; deferred benefits, 111, 113, 124; disability insurance, 106, 108, 113, 119, 139, 179; eligibility for, 106, 110–11, 112, 113, 114, 116, 118, 125; employee contributions, 87, 88, 91, 97, 102, 106, 107, 109, 113, 115, 116, 118, 119–20, 125, 139, 330, 345; employer contributions, 106, 109, 116, 128, 139, 232, 310, 312; full benefits, 9, 18, 107, 343; funding of, 114, 116, 118, 121, 138–39, 345; future projections of, 89–94; goals, 105; health insurance, 112, 113, 117, 344; history, 77, integration with federal plans, 119, 120; liberalization, 107, 108, 117, 128, 178, 272; mandatory coverage, 116–19, 121, 122, 123, 344–45; Medicare, 107, 108, 114n, 120; merits, 96–121, 344–45; minimum benefits, 120, 121; normal retirement age, 84, 343; payroll tax, 114, 115; portability of benefits, 118, 120, 121, 197, 201, 344; reduced benefits, 9, 85; reform of, 88–95, 114–15; second-career coverage, 108–9, 110, 111, 120, 228, 231, 233, 237, 315, 316, 336, 344; self-employed workers in, 106; spouses' benefits, 61, 67, 70, 71–74, 83, 90, 91–92, 105–6, 109, 111, 299, 336, 342–43; survivors' benefits, 107–8, 112, 113, 117, 125, 139, 330–31; tax exempt, 70; universal coverage, 117, 118–19, 121, 201, 350; vesting of, 118, 124; wage base, 26, 48, 88, 89, 94, 103, 124, 125, 139, 242, 310, 346; wage-replacement ratio of, 90–91, 92, 93, 94, 126, 342; withdrawal from, 111–17, 121, 345
Social Security, Advisory Council on, 93–94, 121
Social Security Act, 69, 93, 95, 233, 345; 1955 amendments, 97; 1956 amendments, 97; 1961 amendments, 17; 1972 amendments;

Social Security Act (*Continued*)
52–53, 88, 89, 91, 105, 107, 110, 124, 338
Social Security Administration, 45, 120
South Carolina; benefit accrual rate in, 22; investment restrictions in, 204

Taxation, power of, 137–38, 164
Taylor Law (N.Y.S.), 292, 311
Teachers, 178, 192, 214, 244, 246, 263, 264, 265, 269, 316, 335, 354; benefits for, 55, 275; contributions of, 46–47, 289, 293, 317, 328; pension portability for, 196, 197, 198; pensions for, 4, 6, 7, 11, 14, 15, 16, 34, 64, 65, 108, 200, 299, 308, 311, 319; S.S. coverage for, 100, 108, 109–10, 344; university, 76, 110
Teachers Insurance and Annuity Association, 196–97, 218, 219
Teachers' Retirement System (Calif.), 214
Teachers' Retirement System, (N.Y.C.), 214–15, 250, 261, 264, 266, 281, 282, 283, 284, 285, 290, 305
Teachers' Retirement System (N.Y.S.), 168, 260, 289, 294, 296, 301, 302, 303, 305, 307
Teachers' Retirement System (Wash.), 136
Teachers' System (Ill.), 327, 328, 331
Terminal leave, 309
Texas: S.S. coverage in, 111
Transit Authority (N.Y.C.), 274, 277

Turnover, 85, 176–77, 193
Turnover rates, 176, 300, 301

Unionization, 176
Universities' System (Ill.), 212, 327, 331, 335

Vesting, *see* Benefits, vested
Virginia: benefit accrual rate in, 103; funding in, 156

Wage replacement: during disability, 84
Wage-replacement ratios, 51–69, 90–91, 92, 93, 94, 105, 126, 128, 129, 228, 298, 342; career-average formulas, 52; current service formula, 53; final-pay formulas, 52, 55; flat-dollar formulas, 52, 60; money-purchase formulas, 52
Washington: contractual rights in, 255; pension commissions in, 258
Wisconsin: investment management in, 213; pension commissions in, 258; postretirement adjustments in, 250
Workers, general, 6, 265, 266–67; pensions for, 14, 15, 64, 65, 244, 271, 273, 275, 278, 287, 319
Workers, health: collective bargaining and, 4; pension portability and, 196
Workmen's Compensation, 40, 119, 239, 293, 315
Wyoming: investment restrictions in, 204